The Swiss Reformation

MANCHESTER
UNIVERSITY PRESS

NEW FRONTIERS IN HISTORY

series editors

Mark Greengrass
Department of History, Sheffield University

John Stevenson
Worcester College, Oxford

This important series reflects the substantial expansion that has occurred in the scope of history syllabuses. As new subject areas have emerged and syllabuses have come to focus more upon methods of historical enquiry and knowledge of source materials, a growing need has arisen for correspondingly broad ranging textbooks.

New Frontiers in History provides up-to-date overviews of key topics in British, European and world history. Authors focus on subjects where revisionist work is being undertaken, providing a fresh viewpoint, welcomed by students and sixth formers. The series also explores established topics which have attracted much conflicting analysis and require a synthesis of the state of debate.

Published titles

David Andress French society in revolution 1789–1799

Jeremy Black The politics of Britain, 1688–1800

Paul Bookbinder The Weimar Republic

Michael Braddick The nerves of state: taxation and the financing of the English state, 1558–1714

Michael Broers Europe after Napoleon

David Brooks The age of upheaval: Edwardian politics, 1899–1914

Carl Chinn Poverty amidst prosperity: the urban poor in England, 1834–1914

Conan Fischer The rise of the Nazis (2nd edition)

T. A. Jenkins Parliament, party and politics in Victorian Britain

Neville Kirk Change, continuity and class: Labour in British society, 1850–1920

Keith Laybourn The General Strike of 1926

Frank McDonough Neville Chamberlain, appeasement and the British road to war

Alan Marshall The age of faction

Evan Mawdsley The Stalin years, 1929–1953

Alan O'Day Irish Home Rule 1867–1921

Panitos Panayi Immigration, ethnicity and racism in Britain 1815–1945

Daniel Szechi The Jacobites

David Taylor The New Police

John Whittam Fascist Italy

The Swiss Reformation

Bruce Gordon

Manchester University Press

Manchester and New York

Distributed exclusively in the USA by Palgrave

Published by Manchester University Press
Oxford Road, Manchester M13 9NR, UK
and Room 400, 175 Fifth Avenue, New York, NY 10010, USA
http://www.manchesteruniversitypress.co.uk

Distributed exclusively in the USA by
Palgrave, 175 Fifth Avenue, New York, NY 10010, USA

Distributed exclusively in Canada by
UBC Press, University of British Columbia, 2029 West Mall,
Vancouver, BC, Canada V6T 1Z2

British Library Cataloguing-in-Publication Data
A catalogue record for this book is available from the British Library

Library of Congress Cataloging-in-Publication Data applied for

ISBN 0 7190 5117 7 *hardback*
0 7190 5118 5 *paperback*

First published 2002

10 09 08 07 06 05 04 03 02 10 9 8 7 6 5 4 3 2 1

Typeset in Palatino
by Koinonia, Manchester
Printed in Great Britain
by Bookcraft (Bath) Ltd, Midsomer Norton

For James K. Cameron

Tratto t'ho qui con ingegno e con arte
(Dante, *Purgatorio*, Canto XXVII)

Contents

List of maps

Acknowledgements

This book began many years ago when I showed up at the Institut für Schweizerische Reformationsgeschichte in Zurich to start my research on Heinrich Bullinger and the clergy. Over the past dozen years the members of the Institute have been more than generous with their advice, assistance, hospitality, and good humour. Professor Fritz Büsser encouraged and challenged me, and I owe him a debt of gratitude. Likewise Heinzpeter Stucki, who taught me how to read Alemannic texts. The editors of Bullinger's correspondence, Hans Ulrich Bächtold, Rainer Henrich, and Kurt Jakob Rüetschi, have allowed me to camp in their office, ask lots of questions, and drink their tea. I am grateful to them for all they have done, but most of all for lunch at the Bauschätzli. For theological advice and learned pastoral care I am indebted to my friend Daniel Bolliger. In Basle I have enjoyed the hospitality of Frau Greti Guggisberg, widow of Hans Guggisberg, whose numerous kindnesses I can never repay. My stays in Berne were made very enjoyable by Heinrich Richard and Gabi Schmidt.

Others have given of their time and expertise and it is a pleasure to thank them. Euan Cameron offered trenchant advice and kindly shared references. Peter Marshall read the manuscript and suggested numerous improvements, as did Mark Greengrass and Mark Taplin. Diarmaid MacCulloch made some very helpful suggestions. In St Andrews, Andrew Pettegree, Michael Brown, Max von Habsburg, and Matthew McLean read the text much to its benefit.

I am grateful to the AHRB for a leave award which allowed me to concentrate on the book. Likewise the University of St Andrews afforded me sabbatical leave. The research committee of the School of History has been generous in its financial support of my work in Switzerland. Duncan Stewart of Reprographic Services expertly prepared the maps. Alison Whittle of Manchester University Press made the final stages of this book a pleasure rather than a labour.

My wife, Rona, has endured the writing of this book with good, if at times slightly ironic, humour. More than that, she has read the text and made many corrections. Our two-year-old daughter, Charlotte, asked the question which everyone else resisted out of politeness, 'What is Daddy doing?'

In thinking of the many people who have shared their learning and offered encouragement I remember those no longer with us. In particular, Gottfried Locher and Hans Guggisberg; men of learning who embodied the humanity and civility of true scholarship. The final stages of this book were written in the months following the death of my mother and a beloved uncle. Those who have lost parents will know what this means.

Finally it is with the greatest pleasure that I dedicate this book to my teacher and mentor James K. Cameron.

Abbreviations

ARG	*Archiv für Reformationsgechichte*
BHR	*Bibliothèque d'Humanisme et Renaissance*
BM	*Bündner Monatsblatt*
EA	*Amptliche Sammlung der Ältern Eidgenössischen Abschiede, 1245–1798*, ed. A.P. von Stgesser and J. Strickler. 8 vols (Lucerne and Berne, 1839–78)
HBBW	*Heinrich Bullinger, Werke*, ed. Fritz Büsser et al. Letters (Zurich, 1973–)
HBLS	*Historisch-biographisches Lexikon der Schweiz*. 7 vols (Neuchâtel, 1921–34)
S	Huldreich Zwinglis Werke, ed. Melchior Schuler and J. Schulhess. 8 vols (Zurich, 1828–42)
SCJ	*Sixteenth Century Journal*
Z	*Huldreich Zwinglis sämtliche Werke*, ed. W. Köhler *et al.* (Leipzig, 1905–)
ZKG	*Zeitschrift für Kirchengeschichte*
ZSKG	*Zeitschrift für Schweizerische Kirchengeschichte*

Principal figures

Amerbach, Bonifacius (1495–1562). Basle jurist and humanist. Member of distinguished family and close friend of Erasmus. Originally refused to accept the Reformation but eventually adopted a moderate Reformed position. Important figure for university in Basle.

Anselm, Valerius (1475–1547). Born in Rottweil. Became city physician in Berne. Early supporter, along with Berchtold Haller, of evangelical movement. He was part of the failed Reformation movement in his native Rottweil. Wrote several historical works.

Asper, Hans (1499–1571). Painter in Zurich. Painted a series of portraits of Swiss reformers. Became most important artist in the city after the Reformation. His work was largely with frescoes and portraits. Highly honoured in his native city.

Beza, Theodor (1519–1605). Born in Burgundy. Rector of the Genevan Academy from 1559. Successor to Calvin in 1564.

Biandrata, Georgio (1516–1588). Born in Piedmont. Influential member of the Italian community in Geneva. Fell out with Calvin over the nature of Christ. Left Geneva in 1558 for Zurich, where Bullinger tried to reconcile him with Calvin. Biandrata's views made it impossible for him to remain in Zurich. He went east to Poland and Transylvania.

Bibliander, Theodor (*c.*1505/6–64). Professor of Old Testament in Zurich and distinguished linguist. Wrote a Hebrew grammar in 1542. Opposed Calvin's views on predestination. Eventually forced to resign with the appointment of Peter Martyr Vermigli in Zurich.

Blarer, Ambrosius (1492–1564). South German reformer, born in Constance. Key figure in Constance Reformation. Also preached extensively through the southern German cities. Involved in reforming Württemberg from 1534. Stressed pastoral care over doctrine. A highly talented poet and hymn writer. Forced from Constance in 1548 and became minister in Biel. Died in Winterthur, near Zurich.

Blaurock, Georg (Cajakob) (*c*.1492–1529). Anabaptist in Zurich from 1523. Expelled from city in 1527. Active in Berne and the Tyrol before being burnt at the stake.

Bolsec, Jérome (*c*.1524–84). Physician from Paris. Objected to Calvin's doctrine of predestination in 1551. Disagreed with burning of Servetus. Eventually returned to Catholicism.

Bucer, Martin (1491–1551). Reformer in Strasbourg. Submitted *Tetrapolitan Confession* to Diet of Augsburg in 1530. Opposed 1548 Interim in Strasbourg and had to leave the city. 1549 went to England, where he died.

Bullinger, Heinrich (1504–75). Born in Bremgarten. Studied in Cologne. Zwingli's successor from 1531. Head of the Zurich church 1532–75.

Capito, Wolfgang (1478–1541). Educated at Freiburg. Worked in Strasbourg during 1520s with Martin Bucer. Played key role at Berne Synod of 1532. Tried to negotiate between Zwinglians and Lutherans.

Castellio, Sebastian (1515–63). Savoyard humanist and biblical scholar. Left Geneva after quarrel with Calvin and settled in Basle in 1545. Completed one translation of Bible in Latin (1551) and one into French (1555). Advocate of religious toleration. Wrote his *Concerning Heretics* in 1554. Centre of circle in Basle which opposed the execution of Servetus and Calvin's teaching on predestination.

Collin, Rudolf (1499–1578). Studied in Vienna under Vadianus. Friend of Myconius and early supporter of Zwingli. Professor of Greek in Zurich. Highly talented linguist, so occasionally sent on diplomatic missions for his city. Important figure in the development of higher education in Zurich.

Comander, Johannes [Dorfmann] (1482–1557). Reformer in Graubünden. Studied with Vadianus in St Gall. Served in churches in Zurich and Lucerne before returning to his native land. From 1526 he supported the evangelical cause and took part in the Ilanz Disputation. He was instrumental in developing the church in the Graubünden, writing the synodal ordinances in 1537, a catechism, and the church ordinances of 1552–53. Also worked on the *Rhaetian Confession*. Close friend of both Bullinger and Vadianus.

Curione, Celio Secundo (1503–69). Born in Ciriè, near Turin. Had contacts with evangelicals in Italy and fled north in 1542. Settled first in Lausanne to teach at the Academy and then in Basle, where he received a chair at the university. He was close friends with Bonifacius Amerbach and supported the Italian exiles in Basle. His views were treated with suspicion by the reformers, but he was never censored.

Eck, Johannes (1486–1536). Greatest Catholic theologian at the time of the Reformation. Professor of theology at Ingolstadt. Took leading role at Baden Disputation in 1526.

Fabri, Johannes (1478–1541). Vicar-general of diocese of Constance. Humanist and one-time friend of Vadianus and Zwingli. Took part in

First Zurich Disputation (1523) and the Baden Disputation (1526). Forceful and effective opponent of the Reformation. From 1531 bishop of Vienna.

Farel, Guillaume (1489–1565). Key reformer of French-speaking lands conquered by Berne in 1536. Educated in Paris, he came to Basle where he met Erasmus. Close collaborator with Calvin in Geneva.

Froben, Hieronymous (*c*.1460–1527). Humanist printer in Basle and friend of Erasmus. Set new standards for the printed book. A considerable number of Swiss reformers began their careers working in his printing house.

Froschauer, Christoph (d. 1564). Printer. Arrived in Zurich in 1519 and became a follower of Zwingli. Printed the works of most of the leading Zurich reformers. 1524–64 printed twenty-seven editions of complete Bible. Also wrote prefaces to some of the works.

Gallicius, Philipp (1504–66). From Ardez. Reformer in Graubünden. Took part in Ilanz Disputation in 1526. Served in various parishes introducing the Reformation. From 1542 until his death he was in Chur. As teacher and preacher he was responsible for the successful spread of the Reformation in the Engadine, as well as in the Italian-speaking parts of the Graubünden. Corresponded extensively with Bullinger.

Gesner, Konrad (1516–65). Humanist in Zurich. Born in Zurich and studied in France. Taught at Lausanne Academy from 1537. Published his *Bibliotheca Universalis* in 1545. Made professor of theology in Zurich. Wrote extensively on bibliography, zoology, linguistics, and medicine. Died of plague.

Glareanus, Heinricus (1488–1563). Leading Swiss humanist. From Glarus. Wrote numerous works on geography and music, including his *Helvetiae Descriptio* in 1515. Refused to accept the Reformation, but his work was highly influential on all the Swiss humanists.

Grebel, Konrad (*c*.1497–1526). Friend of Zwingli. Humanist and member of prominent Zurich family. His father was executed for corruption. Led the opposition to Zwingli among the 'radicals' from 1523. Expelled from Zurich.

Grynaeus, Simon (1493–1541). Professor of Greek and leader of the Basle church. From Swabia. Came to Basle in 1529. Friend of Erasmus, Grynaeus was central to the rebuilding of the university in Basle after the Reformation. Involved in dispute over academic degrees at the university. He was the leading scholar in the Confederation. Visited England and opened lines of contact to men such as Thomas Cranmer.

Gwalther, Rudolf (1519–86). Native of Zurich. Studied in England in 1537. Married Zwingli's daughter. Served as minister in St Peter's church in Zurich. Prolific writer. He had close connections with reformers throughout Europe, especially England. Succeeded Bullinger as head of Zurich church in 1575.

Haller, Berchtold (1492–1536). Reformer in Berne. Friend of Zwingli and energetic reformer. Played key role at Berne Disputation of 1528, but not a strong leader. Suffered from illness during 1530s and was unable to resolve disputes in the city. Campaigned hard against Anabaptists.

Haller, Johannes (1523–75). Preacher in Augsburg and then head of the church in Berne. In Augsburg 1545–47. Forced out by the Interim of 1548. Went to Berne, where it was hoped that he would improve relations with Calvin. Haller had to restore order in the Bernese church after the long-running disputes between the Lutherans and Zwinglians. He corresponded extensively with Bullinger, on whom he depended heavily.

Hochrütiner, Lorenz (dates unknown). Weaver from from St Gall. Attended disputations in Zurich. Involved in key iconoclastic events in the city. Promoted Anabaptist ideas in Basle, Berne, and his native St Gall.

Hofmeister, Sebastian (1476–1532). Native of Schaffhausen. Became friend of Zwingli in Zurich. Briefly in Lucerne before returning to Schaffhausen. Close to Balthasar Hubmaier and Erasmus Ritter. Attended Berne Disputation with Zwingli. Became minister in Zofingen and in Berne, and took part in numerous disputations with Anabaptists. A learned and effective preacher.

Hohenlandenberg, Hugo, bishop of Constance (1460–1532). Was born near Winterthur (Zurich) and studied in Basle and Zurich. Bishop of Constance from 1496 until his resignation in 1529. He enjoyed contact with humanists, though he was not himself well educated. He had shown enthusiasm for reform, so that Zwingli had high expectations. Was powerless in face of the Reformation. His diocese was largely run by his vicar-general, Johannes Fabri.

Holbein, Hans the Younger (1497/98–1543). Painter From Augsburg. Worked in Basle. Taken on by Erasmus, of whom Holbein painted several portraits. 1526 Holbein went to England. Returned to Basle in 1528, where he remained until 1532, when he once again travelled to England.

Hubmaier, Balthasar (*c*.1485–1528). Anabaptist leader born near Augsburg. Brilliant career after studying under Eck. Came to Zurich in 1523 and then to Waldshut. Sympathetic to Zwingli's theology, but ultimately arrived at his own positions. Fled to Zurich after Peasants' War and then to Moravia. Executed by Austrians.

Joris, David (*c*.1500–56). Apocalyptic radical thinker. Born in Delft. Driven from the Low Countries, he came to Basle, where he came in contact with Sebastian Castellio. Lived under a pseudonym, but was posthumously burnt as a heretic.

Jud, Leo (1482–1542). From Alsace. Reformer in Zurich and Zwingli's closest friend and collaborator. Played central role in development of the *Ehegericht* in Zurich. Jud was a talented linguist and translator. He produced vernacular editions of works by Erasmus, Augustine, and Thomas à Kempis. Also a Latin Bible (1542).

Karlstadt, Andreas (1480–1541). Born in Bodenstein. Luther's colleague at the university of Wittenberg. Exiled from Saxony in 1524. Came to Zurich with Zwingli's help in 1529. He then moved to Basle, where he was professor of biblical theology. He was the most powerful theological influence in Basle during the 1530s. Quarrelled openly with Oswald Myconius.

Kessler, Johannes (1502–74). Reformer in St Gall. Worked as craftsman and schoolteacher. Close friend of Vadianus. His great work was the *Sabbata*, a chronicle full of documents.

Kilchmeyer, Jodocus (d. 1552). Reformer in eastern Swiss Confederation and Berne. Born in Lucerne. Student of Vadianus in Vienna. Supported Zwingli's petition to allow priests to marry. Forced out of Lucerne. Held several posts in the eastern part of the Confederation. Returned to Zurich before becoming dean of the Münster in Berne in 1547.

Kolb, Franz (1465–1535). Reformer in Berne. Born in Lörrach. Studied in Basle. Served as field preacher to Swiss troops during Swabian War. Opponent of mercenary service. Was preacher in Nuremberg before returning to Berne in 1527. Became a friend of Zwingli and an advocate of his theology. He took part in the Berne Disputation (1528) and worked with Kaspar Megander and Berchtold Haller in reforming the Bernese church.

Kunz, Peter (1480–1544). Priest in Interlaken. He was an early supporter of the Reformation. Came to Berne in 1535. Along with Kaspar Megander he led the Lausanne Disputation of 1537. His theology was Lutheran and he supported Martin Bucer's work in Berne. Kunz became one of Calvin's arch-enemies in Berne.

Lasco, Johann à (1499–1560). Polish noble, sympathetic to Swiss theology. Became head of the Stranger Church in London from 1550. Close to John Hooper. Both men tried to implement Swiss-style reforms in England.

Lavater, Hans Rudolf (1492–1557). Soldier and politician in Zurich. Member of prominent Zurich family. As *Landvogt* he had pacified the peasants during the troubles of 1525. During the First and Second Kappel Wars he took to the field commanding troops. His conduct in the Second Kappel War was investigated. He played a central role in the political life of Zurich, serving as Bürgermeister from 1544. A close friend and ally of Heinrich Bullinger.

Lavater, Ludwig (1527–86). Reformer in Zurich. Son of Bürgermeister Hans Rudolf and Bullinger's son-in-law. Prolific author who wrote description of church order in Zurich. Served as head of Zurich church for seven months from 1585.

Mantz, Felix (*c.*1500–27). Zurich Anabaptist. Came into contact with Thomas Müntzer and Andreas Karlstadt. Objected to infant baptism and was expelled from Zurich in 1525. Spent time in Basle. Captured by Zurich authorities in December 1526 and executed for conducting rebaptisms.

Manuel, Niklaus (1484–1530). Politician, artist, and reformer in Berne. Prominent painter, poet, and dramatist who served as bailiff in a Bernese rural district from 1522 to 1528. 1528 elected to small council of Berne. Negotiated First Peace of Kappel in 1529. Enthusiastic supporter of the Reformation but rejected the necessity of religious war to bring about reform.

Megander, Kaspar (1484–1545). Reformer in Zurich and Berne. Native of Zurich, Megander belonged to Zwingli's close circle of friends. Worked closely with Zwingli in Zurich during 1520s. Attended Berne Disputation in 1528. Called to serve as minister in Berne, where he remained until 1537. Controversial preacher who was suspended by Bernese council. Resisted attempts by Bucer and Capito to move Bernese church towards Lutheranism. Eventually relieved of his post in 1538.

Meyer, Sebastian (1467?–1545). From Neuenburg on the Rhine. From 1521 in Berne, where he worked alongside Berchtold Haller. Attended First Zurich Disputation in 1523. He was forced to leave Berne for his evangelical sympathies. Preached in Schaffhausen. Travelled through southern Germany. Recalled to Berne to succeed Haller in 1536. 1541 returned to Strasbourg.

Montfaçon, Sébastien de (1489–1560). Bishop of Lausanne. Studied in Basle. Not very religious, but was highly cultivated. In 1517 he succeeded his uncle as bishop of Lausanne. Was constantly in dispute with the city of Lausanne. When Berne took control of the city in 1536 Sébastian was not present. He simply withdrew to his native Savoy.

Münster, Sebastian (1480–1553). Hebrew scholar and reformer in Basle. Born in Ingelheim. Professor of Hebrew at Heidelberg until 1528, then held the chair of Hebrew at the university of Basle. Wrote Hebrew lexica and grammars and was among the leading scholars of his age. His *Cosmographia* was a sixteenth-century bestseller.

Musculus, Wolfgang (1497–1563). Reformer in Augsburg and Berne. Born in Euze, Lorraine. From 1531 to 1548 minister in Augsburg, where he generally followed a Zwinglian line. With the Interim he fled to Swiss Confederation, going first to Zurich and then, from 1549, to Berne. Leading theologian and churchman, his most important work was his *Loci Communes* of 1560.

Myconius, Oswald (1488–1552). Native of Lucerne. Schoolteacher in Zurich and early supporter of Zwingli, whose invitation to the Grossmünster he actively supported. Close collaborator with Zwingli. From 1532 he was head of the church in Basle. More of a pastor than a theologian, he found himself caught in the crossfire of theological disputes.

Ochino, Bernardino (1487–1564). Born in Siena. Vicar-general of Capuchins from 1538. Regarded as greatest preacher in Italy. Part of evangelical circle in Naples around Juan de Valdes. Fled Italy in 1542. Arrived in Zurich in 1555, but was forced to leave in 1563 on account of his theology. Died in Moravia.

Oecolampadius, Johannes (1482–1531). Reformer in Basle. From Swabia. Studied in Italy and Heidelberg. Was appointed city preacher in Basle and worked for Froben. Very close to Zwingli, but with his own theological emphasis. Led the evangelical party at the Baden Disputation. His works were widely read throughout Europe.

Oporinus, Johannes (1507–68). Scholar and printer in Basle. Trained in the classics, Oporinus held a chair of Latin and Greeek in the university of Basle before giving it up to devote himself to printing. His sympathies were with those Italian figures in Basle who opposed Calvin's theology. He printed works by Curione, Castellio, and Bibliander, as well as many others.

Paracelsus (1493–1541). Born in Einsiedeln in Schwyz. Studied in Vienna and Italy. Called to Basle in 1547 as physician. Taught at the university. Forced out of the university for controversial views. Had sympathies with radical religious thinkers, but did not leave the Catholic faith.

Pellikan, Konrad (1478–1556). Humanist from Alsace. Hebrew scholar in Zurich. Taught Hebrew by Johannes Reuchlin. From 1526 until his death professor of Old Testament in Zurich. Wrote the only complete Latin commentary of the Bible.

Phillip of Hesse (1504–67). Landgrave. Supported Luther from 1524. In contact with Zwingli to form Protestant alliance. Worked hard to resolve theological differences between Zwingli and Luther. Force behind Colloquy of Marburg in 1529.

Platter, Thomas (1499–1582). A native of the Wallis. Studied in Zurich under Myconius, and then in Basle, where he also worked as a corrector. He worked on the first edition of Calvin's *Institutes* in 1536. Rector of the Latin School in Basle. Wrote an autobiography.

Reublin, Wilhelm (*c.*1484–1559). Anabaptist from Rottenburg in Germany who was active in Zurich. Effective preacher and opponent of both the tithe and infant baptism. Expelled from Zurich in 1525.

Ritter, Erasmus (d. 1546) From Bavaria. Was called to Schaffhausen to refute Sebastian Hofmeister, but after contact with Hofmeister and the First Zurich Disputation he converted to the evangelical cause. After a bitter dispute with Benedikt Burgauer in Schaffhausen both men were dismissed. Ritter went to Berne, where he became minister in the Münster. A Zwinglian, he fought the Lutheran influences in the city, but remained after Megander's departure.

Sam, Konrad (1483–1533). Early reformer in Ulm. He had studied in Freiburg and Tübingen and was a supporter of Zwinglianism. Served as preacher in a variety of communities before being appointed to Ulm in 1524.

Sattler, Michael (*c.*1490–1527). Anabaptist leader from Freiburg. Benedictine monk who came to Zurich and married. Joined the early Anabaptists. Expelled from Zurich in 1525. Presided over meeting which determined *Schleitheim Articles* in 1527. Executed in Rottenburg along with his wife.

Schlegel, Theodul (1485–1529). Born in Chur. Abbot of the Praemonstratanian house in Chur from 1515. Defended the Catholic faith against the reformers in Chur. Took part in the Ilanz Disputation (1526) against Comander. He was suspected of conspiring to restore Bishop Ziegler in Chur and was arrested, tortured, and in January 1529 executed.

Schwenckfeld, Kaspar von (1489–1561). Silesian nobleman. Read and had some sympathies with Zwingli's theology. Also influenced by Karlstadt. Resident in Strasbourg during the 1520s. His spiritualist ideas influenced many in the Swiss Confederation. Zwingli and Oecolampadius at one point claimed him as one of their own. Bullinger wrote extensively against Schwenckfeld, who had influenced Leo Jud.

Servetus, Michel (*c.*1509–53). Born in northern Spain. Spent time in Basle before settling in Lyon. Antitrinitarian. Tried and executed in Geneva. His death became central to the anti-Calvin alliance which formed in Basle. The execution led to a bitter exchange between Calvin and Sebastian Castellio.

Sozzini, Fausto (1539–1604). Antitrinitarian. Nephew of Lelio Sozzini. Native of Siena. Came to Zurich in 1562 to collect his uncle's papers. During his time in the Swiss Confederation he wrote a number of important antitrinitarian works.

Sozzini, Lelio (1525–62). From Padua. Antitrinitarian who spent many years in Zurich and Basle. In 1554 travelled to Basle, Geneva, and Zurich. After travels to Poland and Bohemia he returned to Zurich, where he remained until his death. Whilst in Zurich he wrote his crucial work on the nature of Christ. He had enjoyed the support of Bullinger and others, but they soon grew suspicious of his ideas.

Stumpf, Johann (1500–78). Former head of Knights of St John house in Bubikon. Close friend of Zwingli. One of the most important Swiss chroniclers of the sixteenth century.

Sulzer, Simon (1508–85). Reformer in Berne and Basle. From Berne. Visited Luther in Wittenberg. Attempted to move Bernese church towards Lutheranism. Was forced to leave Berne in 1548. In 1552 he became professor in Basle and in 1553 he succeeded Oswald Myconius as head of the Basle church. He opposed Calvin's theology and refused to sign the *Second Helvetic Confession*. He retained his Lutheran sympathies.

Tschudi, Aegidius (1505–72). Politician, historian and opponent of the Reformation. Born in Glarus. He had been a student of Zwingli. Devoted himself to the defence of the Catholic Church in Glarus. In Sargans and Baden he had overseen the restoration of the old faith after the Kappel War. He was an ardent supporter of the French and received a handsome pension for his efforts on behalf of France. He was greatly admired for his political, legal, and administrative activities. He also wrote a series of historical works. His attempt to oust the Reformed from Glarus (1559–64) was known as the Tschudi War.

Utenheim, Christoph von (1450–1527). Bishop of Basle. From an Alsatian noble family. Well educated, and in 1473 became rector of the new university in Basle. He had strong humanist and reformist sympathies. He protected Erasmus during his stay in Basle. He was forced from the city in 1527 and took up residence in Pruntrut.

Vadianus (Joachim von Watt) (1484–1551). Humanist and reformer in St Gall. Studied in Vienna. From 1518 city physician in St Gall and then in 1526 Bürgermeister. Had known Zwingli since 1511. He was moderator of the Berne Disputation of 1528 and brought about reform of St Gall abbey in 1529. Wrote numerous historical and theological works, though he remained a layman. Worked closely with Bullinger.

Vermigli, Peter Martyr (1499–1562). Native of Florence. Fled Italy on account of his evangelical views in 1542. Stopped briefly in Zurich and Basle before going to Strasbourg. In 1548 he arrived in Oxford. He left in 1553 and in 1556 was appointed professor of theology in Zurich. From Zurich Vermigli prepared his work for publication. He had extensive contacts throughout Europe and his presence in Zurich greatly enhanced its status in the Protestant world. His *Loci Communes*, prepared after his death, was widely read.

Viret, Pierre (1511–71). From Orbe in the Pays de Vaud. Closely connected to Guillaume Farel. Energetic and controversial preacher who played an important role in the reformations of Neuchâtel and Lausanne. Colleague of Calvin. From early 1560s heavily involved with Huguenot churches in southern France.

Wick, Johann Jakob (1522–88). Minister in Zurich and collector of wondrous stories. His vast collection of stories, known as the *Wickiana*, was produced between 1560 and 1587.

Wittenbach, Thomas (1472–1526). From Biel. From 1505 professor in Basle, where he taught Zwingli and Leo Jud. Returned to Biel in 1520 to preach the Gospel. He had become a supporter of his former pupil. Played key role in the establishment of the Reformation in Biel.

Ziegler, Paul (d. 1541). Bishop of Chur. From southern Germany and a member of the Habsburg family. Became bishop in 1505. Found himself in an impossible position between Habsburg and Swiss lands. Unable to prevent the spread of the Reformation in the Graubünden. In 1526 he withdrew from Chur to Vintschgau, where he remained until his death. After his resignation he enjoyed good relations with the evangelicals.

Zurkinden, Niklaus (1506–88). Bernese statesman and friend of John Calvin. Took an active interest in the theological disputes of the 1550s. He opposed Calvin's teaching on double predestination. He advocated a form of religious toleration and became patron to many of the radical thinkers who found refuge in the Confederation.

Zwingli, Huldrych (1484–1531). Born in Wildhaus in Toggenburg. Studied in Vienna and Basle. Came to Zurich in 1519. With the adoption of the new church order in 1525 Zwingli assumed role as head of the Zurich church until his death at the battle of Kappel on 11 October 1531.

Chronology

1484	Zwingli born in Wildhaus in Toggenburg (1 January).
1509	Jetzer affair in Berne.
1516	Treaty of Fribourg: perpetual treaty with French monarchy to provide mercenaries.
1519	Zwingli elected stipendiary priest in Grossmünster (1 January).
1521	Zurich's rejection of military alliance with France. Treaty with French monarchy (7 May) regulating numbers of mercenaries.
1521–29	Erasmus in Basle.
1522	Sausage-eating incident in Froschauer house (9 March). Disputation in Zurich with delegation from Bishop of Constance (16 April). Battle of Bicocca (16 May).
1523	First disputation in Zurich (23 January). Edict on scriptural preaching in Berne (15 June). Reform of the Grossmünster chapter (29 September). Second disputation in Zurich (26-28 October).
1524	*First Ilanz Articles* (Graubünden) (4 April). Federal diet at Lucerne (8 April) considers proposals to exclude Zurich from Confederation. Council order to remove images from churches in Zurich (8–15 June). Sack of Carthusian house at Ittingen (18 July).
1525	Zurich disputation with radicals (17 January). First rebaptisms in Zurich (21 January). Hubmaier promotes Anabaptism in Waldshut.

	Brötli appointed minister in Hallau, protected against Schaffhausen troops by inhabitants. First evangelical communion service (Easter, April). Founding of *Ehegericht* (marriage court) in Zurich (10 May). Beginning of '*Prophezei*' in Grossmünster (19 June). Second disputation in Zurich against opponents of infant baptism (6–8 November).
1526	First Zurich council mandate against Anabaptists (March) Disputation at Baden (19 May–9 June). Disputation in St Gall between Zwinglian preachers and Anabaptists. Images removed from churches in St Gall (5 December). Grebel dies of plague in Graubünden.
1527	Execution of Felix Mantz by drowning in the Limmat in Zurich (5 January). Ilanz Disputation (7–9 January). Expulsion of Anabaptists from Zurich. First evangelical celebration of Lord's Supper in St Gall (Easter). *Second Ilanz Articles* (25 June). *Schleitheim Confession* (24 February). Michael Sattler burned at Rottenburg.
1528	Disputation in Berne (6–26 January). Reformation in Berne (7 February). First Reformed Synod in Zurich (21 April).
1529	Banning of mercenary service in Berne. Introduction of Reformation at Basle (1 April). Formation in April of Catholic 'Christian Alliance' (Lucerne, Uri, Schwyz, Unterwalden, and Zug) (26 June). First evangelical service in abbey of St Gall (7 December). Colloquy of Marburg (1–3 October). Formation of Christian Civic Union (Zurich, Berne, Basle, St Gallen, Biel, Strasbourg, Mühlhausen, and Schaffhausen) in February. Introduction of Reformation in Basle (1 April). First Kappel War (June). First Peace of Kappel (26 June). Dissolution of 'Christian Alliance'. Colloquy of Marburg (Luther and Zwingli) (October). Debate between Anabaptists and Zwinglian preachers in Appenzell.
1530	Diet of Augsburg (July). Zwingli presents his *Fidei Ratio* to the Diet. First execution of Anabaptist in Basle. Zurich's alliance with Hesse.
1531	Second Kappel War. Defeat of Zurich (11 October) and of

	Berne and at Gubel (24 October). Second Peace of Kappel (20 November). Death of Oecolampadius in Basle (22 November). Bernese council decides to remain with Reformation. Election of Heinrich Bullinger as Zwingli's successor in Zurich (9 December).
1532	Synod of Berne (10–13 January). Zurich council mandate confirming adherence to Reformation (19 May). Synodal Ordinance in Zurich (22 October). Debate between Anabaptists and Bernese preachers at Zofingen.
1534	*First Basle Confession.* John Calvin in Basle.
1536	Conquest of Pays de Vaud (January). *First Helvetic Confession* (signed 4 February). Wittenberg Concord. Disputation at Lausanne (1–8 October). Reformation edict in Pays du Vaud (24 December).
1537	First evangelical synod in Graubünden (14 January). Founding of Lausanne Academy (January).
1538	Kaspar Megander dismissed from post in Berne.
1547	Rudolf Gwalther's work on the Antichrist printed in Zurich.
1547–48	Jacob Stumpf publishes his great chronicle of Swiss and Reformation history. Opening of Landolfi printing house in Poschiavo.
1548	Simon Sulzer leaves Berne (April). Catholic troops enter Constance (14 October).
1549	*Consensus Tigurinus* (November). Wolfgang Musculus appointed minister in Berne.
1550	Bolsec affair in Geneva (18-23 December). Joachim Westphal publishes his *Farrago* against the Swiss 'sacramentarians'.
1553	Burning of Michael Servetus in Geneva (27 October). *Rhaetian Confession.*
1554	Evangelicals expelled from Locarno (3 March). Religious Colloquy at Worms (27 August).
1558	Agreement between Catholics and Reformed in St Gall.
1559	Controversy over church discipline in Pays du Vaud. Musculus's *Loci Communes* published.
1559–60	Glarner Handel.

1562 Bullinger publishes his *History of the Reformation*.

1563 *Heidelberg Catechism*.

1564 Peace which ended Glarner Handel or 'Tschudi War' begun in 1559.

1566 *Second Helvetic Confession* printed (21 February).

1575 Heinrich Bullinger dies (17 September).

Introduction

The Swiss Reformation is a peculiar subject. The name itself is easily deconstructed with the recognition that the Swiss Confederation was not a state but a collection of semi-autonomous lands bound together by alliances, language, culture, and history. Indeed, the very term 'Swiss' implies an artificial unity. At every turn the Confederation defies generalisations, and the historian of religious change in the sixteenth century must consider each region individually. My intention in this book is to present a view of the Swiss Reformation in English which is attentive both to the historical developments which shaped the Confederation and to the localities in that union. At the same time there is a central narrative constructed around the pivotal roles played by Huldrych Zwingli and Heinrich Bullinger. This is an account of the Reformed Reformation; the Catholic Reformation in the Swiss Confederation is a fascinating and complex subject which requires its own full-length study. Indeed, this examination of the Protestant Reformation has been delineated; I have chosen to end the story in 1566 with the appearance of the *Second Helvetic Confession*, the fullest statement of Swiss Reformed thought.

The Swiss Reformation has occupied a curious place in the historiography of the European Reformation. By and large it has been treated as the story of Huldrych Zwingli, although there has been considerable interest in Anabaptism. English historians are increasingly sensitive to the importance of the churches of Zurich and Basle to the development of Protestantism, especially under Edward VI, but also under Elizabeth I. However, linguistic barriers, as well as the dearth of scholarship on important aspects of the Swiss Reformation, have continued to obscure many points of contact. In Germany and the United States the continuing fascination with Luther has kept the

Swiss Reformation on the periphery. Zwingli generally makes an appearance in the role of Luther's theological foil, especially regarding the Lord's Supper. The bitter divide between Luther and Zwingli has continued to cast its shadow on Reformation scholarship. There have been some notable exceptions, and the work of these scholars is to be found in the bibliographical essay.

The prominence of Zwingli owes a great deal to a decision made by the Zwingli Verein in Zurich at the end of the nineteenth century to commit itself to producing an edition of the works of Zwingli, and not Bullinger. During the hundred years it took for the critical edition of Zwingli's principal theological works to be completed, Bullinger virtually disappeared from Reformation scholarship. Sporadic efforts have been made to produce critical editions of some of his writings, but these remained largely individual initiatives. The Institute for Swiss Reformation History in Zurich is seeking to make more of Bullinger's writings available, but a full critical edition does not appear in sight. Yet, while most of Bullinger's theological and historical works remain inaccessible, his correspondence is being edited and published by the excellent team of Hans Ulrich Bächtold, Rainer Henrich, and Kurt Rüetschi. The task is daunting but the results are remarkable, revealing the breadth and depth of Bullinger's European connections. The gradual appearance of these letters continue to throw light on the darkened landscape of the post-1531 Swiss Reformation.

The situation of the other Swiss reformers is even less encouraging. The work of Vadianus, reformer in St Gall, has been edited, but for most of the reformers of Basle, Berne, Schaffhausen, and even Zurich, there is little available. In the early part of the twentieth century, fired by the enthusiasm generated by the four hundredth anniversaries of the Swiss Reformation, scholars such as Emil Egli, Rudolf Steck, Gustav Tobler, and Ernst Staehelin produced volumes of edited documents, but in almost every case they stopped in 1532. These editions have proved invaluable repositories for scholars, but they also perpetuated the idea that the Swiss Reformation lasted from 1519 to 1532. The subject does not have a mature histiorography, and much of the type of work now being done, as well as the work which desperately needs to be done, was covered many years ago for other parts of Europe. If this book helps to direct scholars towards new research in the field, it will have achieved one of its primary goals.

This book takes a long view of the Swiss Reformation. The first chapter examines the historical development of the Confederation. Although a sketch, the chapter attempts to convey the uneven development of the Confederation, to outline crucial events, and to discuss its culture. The second chapter deals with Zwingli and the Reformation in Zurich. The emphasis on Zurich reflects a central contention of this book that Zwingli was the key to the Swiss Reformation.

The third chapter looks at the expansion of the reform movement beyond Zurich, though the role of Zurich continues to be emphasised. Prominent themes which emerge include the importance of networks, the common background of the reformers (in particular the university of Basle), preaching, and relations with the ruling authorities. This book argues for the power of personalities in reform movements by examining how certain individuals were able to marry a persuasive articulation of evangelical views with local aspirations and resentments. The evangelical movement was always in a minority position; it never became a mass movement, but that was not necessary. As Zwingli demonstrated in Zurich, reform could be brought about without the active participation of the majority of people.

Chapter 4 deals with the crucial years 1529–36, following the highpoint of the Zwinglian Reformation, the Disputation at Berne, through to the disaster of the Second Kappel War and its resolution. The collapse demonstrated both the fragility and success of the Reformation. The catastrophe was precipitated when Zwingli, desperate for a breakthrough and too reliant on the alliances he had sought, reached too far. He had established the Reformation in Zurich on the basis of his prophetic authority. This was underpinned by personal relations between Zwingli and leaders in Zurich such as the Bürgermeisters Röist and Lavater, on the one hand, and his sodality of friends, men like Leo Jud and Kaspar Megander, on the other. This web of relations, while able to bring about reform, was not strong enough to pull against the traditions of the Confederation. And when Zurich attempted to cajole the rural areas and then its reluctant allies into a war against the Catholic Confederates, disaster ensued.

Chapter 5 looks at the recovery from Kappel and the rebuilding of the Swiss Reformed churches. The fraught issue of relations with German Lutherans is central to the discussion. The chapter also examines the last expansion of the Reformed churches, into the French-speaking lands of the Pays de Vaud. This naturally raises the question of the role of Calvin and Geneva. This book does not attempt to cover Geneva except as the city related to the developments in the Confederation. There are a couple of reasons for this decision. First, the literature available on Calvin and Geneva in English is so extensive that no purpose would be served by yet another brief overview. Second, Geneva was not officially part of the Swiss Confederation, though not for want of trying.

Chapter 5 marks the end of the chronological study of the Swiss Reformation. I have decided to end the story with the *Second Helvetic Confession* in 1566. Not only was the Confession the fullest expression of Swiss Reformed theology, but it also marked a turning point.

Although Bullinger would live for another nine years, the theological and religious climate was changing. The principal reformers of the Swiss Reformation who had known Zwingli or emerged in the period after Kappel had died, and the new generation increasingly looked to Geneva and the so-called Calvinist orthodoxy. The Swiss churches became part of an international Reformed community, but not as leaders.

Having concluded the historical narrative, the book turns to examine the development of radicalism. This concerns not only the rise of Anabaptism, but also the powerful strand of spiritualism which emerged out of the Swiss Reformation. The book argues that Zwingli's attack on what he saw to be the materialistic nature of late medieval religion, and his profound attachment to a Pauline view of the primacy of the spirit, attracted a wide range of figures who, drawing on late medieval mysticism and the spirituality of the *Devotio Moderna*, looked to an immediate relationship with God. Zwingilian theology had at its core a radical message which was variously appropriated.

Chapter 7 attempts to provide a sense of church life in the Reformation by looking at parish structures, the role of the minister, church discipline, and worship, while chapter 8 looks at a range of contemporary sources to illustrate Swiss society in the sixteenth century, briefly considering issues such as weather, economic conditions, the place of women, and death. Both of these chapters are necessarily impressionistic in order to convey something of what the Reformed churches looked like and the mental and physical world in which the Reformation took place.

The last two chapters of the book open up the subject and consider its international implications. Chapter 9 looks at the role of the Swiss churches in the wider European Reformation, both as a powerful influence and as a refuge. The survey highlights southern Germany, England, and Eastern Europe. The Confederation had no political or military influence (apart from mercenaries); its Reformation was spread by personal contacts and the printed word. Swiss influence was never exclusive; it formed one strand in the complex evolution of local reform movements, but the breadth of its dissemination and the density of contacts illustrate the central place occupied by the Swiss reformers.

This theme is taken up in a final chapter on the enduring significance of the Swiss Reformation which argues that the legacy resides in the remarkable intellectual achievements of the period. The powerful conjunction of Erasmian humanism with evangelical thought brought about a cultural and intellectual explosion in the half-century following the introduction of the Reformation. During this time a remarkable collection of figures, many of whom were foreigners, lived, worked, and wrote in the Confederation. They defined the profile of Reformed theology and expanded their range of intellectual enquiry to printing, natural science, bibliography, geography, history, and medicine. In order to give an impression of the vast array of achievements and the richness of this intellectual world, the book offers a series of portraits of the some of the leading figures.

From this complex story there are certain key themes which the reader should bear in mind:

- The Swiss Confederation was a curious development of the late Middle Ages, an association of upland communities and city states governed by the need for mutual protection and resolute self-interest. It is hard to speak of a Swiss identity, but there was a recognition that a dissolution of the Confederation would disadvantage all the members.
- The strength and weakness of the Reformation was Zwingli's close association with Zurich. It both made the events of the 1520s possible and precluded the fulfilment of Zwingli's dream of refashioning the Swiss Confederation as a religious league of reformed states. This vision failed because of the old enmities towards Zurich and the unwillingness of Berne, in particular, to resign its own strategic priorities.
- The key figure after Zwingli was Heinrich Bullinger, who used his unique authority in Zurich to propagate a moderate Zwinglian reformism, a coherent and balanced theological vision of a confederation of Reformed states which were often in conflict and lacked a collective sense of purpose.
- The intellectual energy of the Swiss Reformation, born of Erasmian humanism and evangelical thought, brought the Confederation into the forefront of Renaissance culture in the middle of the sixteenth century. For a period of time the Swiss cities stood alongside the leading cultural centres of Europe. By the time of Bullinger's death, however, this golden period was coming to an end.

Finally, something needs to be said about the terminology adopted in this book. I have favoured the name 'Swiss Confederation' over the anachronistic 'Switzerland' (which emerged in the nineteenth century). I have also preferred 'state' or 'confederate' to 'canton' (again a post-Napoleonic creation) as a translation for '*Ort*'. Religious labels are notoriously misleading, but I have chosen 'evangelical' over 'Protestant', and I use 'radical' for those who found Zwingli's reforms and theology too tepid. From the 1528 Berne Disputation, where the Swiss theology took shape, I use 'Reformed', although I also use 'Zwinglian' to stress the centrality of Zurich in theological formulations. I am aware that all of these terms are open to multiple interpretations, but I have tried to maintain consistency.

1

Peasants, priests, and soldiers: the Swiss Confederation in the late Middle Ages

Growth of the Confederation

The Swiss Confederation was a creation of late medieval Europe. The *Sweicz,* which as an appellation is first found in documents from 1320, derived from the name of one of the founding states, Schwyz. The name Switzerland, as we now use it, was a much later creation, adopted in 1803. From the middle of the fifteenth century, the formative age of the Confederation, the term 'Swiss' found currency, but what it meant is harder to say. With their spectacular victories over the Burgundians this collection of mountain and valley peoples emerged on the mental map of Europe, acknowledged by others with respect and contempt in equal measure. Most Europeans, forced to consider these people for the first time, conceived of the Swiss as ruddy, war-like peasants whose ferocity in battle was not only to be feared, but was also for hire. Sufficient money, it was widely believed, was all that was required to hold the loyalty of the renowned peasant armies which had humiliated and slaughtered (famously, the Swiss did not take prisoners) the noble troops of Austria and Burgundy. The stereotype of the typical Confederate as rustic, bellicose, and avaricious, however, conveyed a false sense of homogeneity. While most Swiss were peasants, there was considerable social diversification; the lesser nobility, the urban patriciate, the rising burgher class, as well as the peasantry, formed rungs on the traditional social hierarchy as they did elsewhere in late medieval Europe. The social and economic changes which swept Europe in the fifteenth century did not bypass the Swiss. Within the cities the guilds struggled to dislodge the patrician families, whilst in the countryside the hand of urban control was increasingly felt. Rural society was hardly homogeneous, employment was not regular for most, and the majority worked as labourers hired by the day for agriculture, which made them itinerant and difficult to control. The Swiss lands had witnessed considerable rural unrest in the late medieval period.[1] Apart from the political rulers, power resided with those with land and livestock who were able to establish themselves as local elites; and the communal networks of family and work framed daily life for most Swiss. Fifteenth-century Swiss humanists may have dreamt of a republic of letters rooted in antique virtues struggling against tyranny, but these were the Latinate aspirations of the few. The Swiss readily acknowledged their fellow Confederates as *Eidgenossen*, and by the middle of the fifteenth century there was palpable sense of a common destiny, but that did not diminish the jealous regard of each Confederate for the particular privileges which ensured its autonomy.[2]

The origins of the Confederation lay in the mists of the thirteenth century when the peoples of Uri, Schwyz, and Unterwalden concluded a permanent pact in August 1291 following the death of Emperor Rudolf I. The departure of the powerful emperor created uncertainty in the empire and regional forces began to assert themselves, and the communes of mountainous regions around the Vierwaldstätter See felt threatened. The agreement had several purposes: mutual defence, the peaceful settlement of internal disputes, and the replacement of private feuds with the rule of law.

The absence of contemporary historical documents such as chronicles has frustrated the efforts of historians to discern exactly what the peoples of Uri, Schwyz, and Unterwalden were attempting to achieve. As a more overtly 'Swiss' historical consciousness appeared in the fifteenth century a creation myth began to take shape, and writ large in this tale was the figure of William Tell. The earliest extant chronicle account of Swiss origins is the *White Book of Sarnens*, written in the 1470s, almost two centuries after the events it describes.[3] The avaricious counts of Tyrol, according to the Tell story, gained control over the Swiss after the death of Rudolf Habsburg, leading the three states of Uri, Schwyz, and Unterwalden together on the Rütli, on the shore of the Vierwaldstätter See, in an endeavour to free themselves from their evil overlords. One of these, a man named Gessler, a bailiff in Uri, sought to humiliate his Swiss subjects by setting his hat on a staff at Altdorf and requiring all to make obeisance. William Tell refused to bow before this idol, and, as a result, was compelled to shoot an apple from the head of his son. Marvellously, Tell split the apple with an arrow, but as a reward he was immediately taken prisoner, escaping only when Gessler was later killed in an ambush. The news of Gessler's death stirred the Swiss to revolt and the three states renewed their alliance. Randolf Head has recently studied the fifteenth- and sixteenth-century accounts of the Tell myth and has argued that they

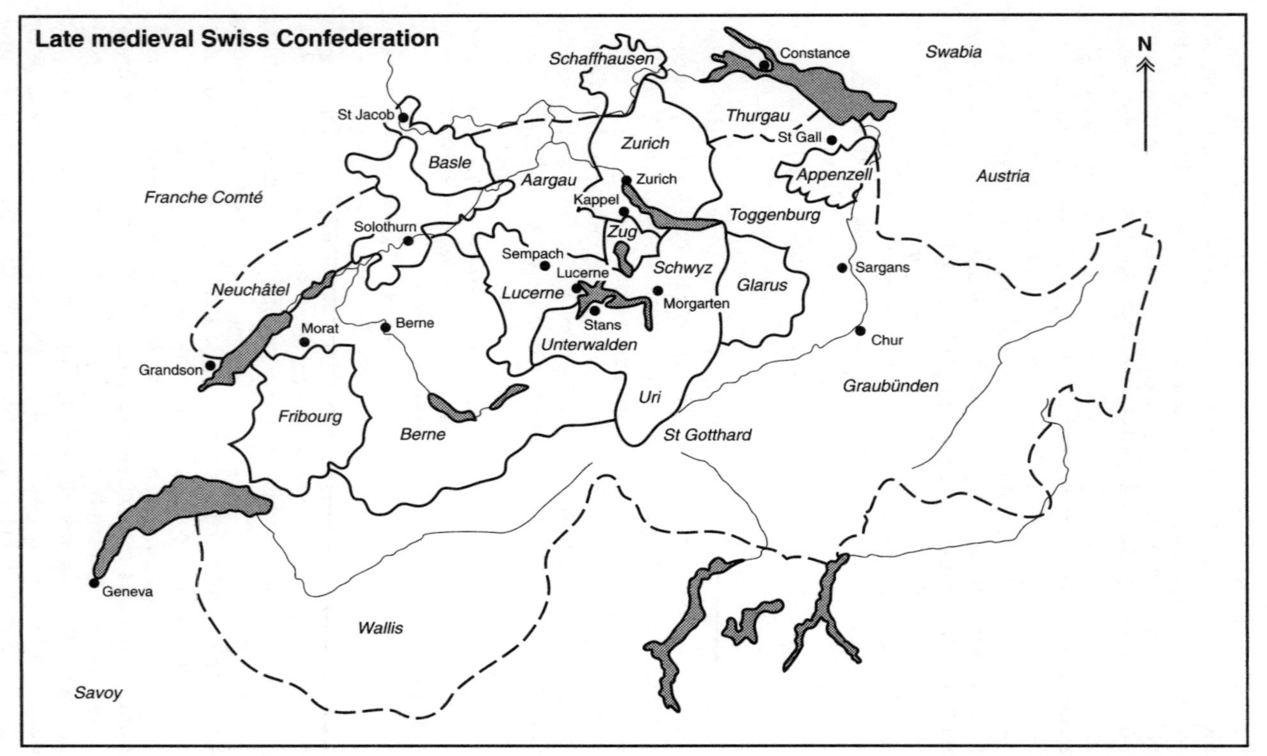
Late medieval Swiss Confederation
N
Schaffhausen
Constance
Swabia
St Jacob
Thurgau
Zurich
St Gall
Basle
Aargau
Zurich
Appenzell
Austria
Franche Comté
Kappel
Toggenburg
Solothurn
Zug
Sempach
Lucerne
Schwyz
Sargans
Neuchâtel
Lucerne
Glarus
Morgarten
Stans
Berne
Morat
Unterwalden
Chur
Grandson
Graubünden
Uri
Fribourg
Berne
St Gotthard
Geneva
Wallis
Savoy

reflect the concepts of 'freedom' and 'oath' as central to Swiss political thought.[4]

It is important to remind ourselves that it was the Habsburg dynasty, and not the Holy Roman Empire, which the Swiss saw as their great enemy. The leading German dynasties, eager to keep the imperial crown away from the Austrian Habsburgs, rather enjoyed the sight of their rivals humbled by mountain peasants. The three original states of Uri, Schwyz, and Unterwalden won a degree of recognition from the German emperors, but this meant little in the face of Habsburg domination of southern Germany and the Swiss lands; the Habsburgs were not prepared to surrender their lands south of the Rhine, and conflict loomed. The first of a famous string of victories for the Swiss came at Morgarten on 15 November 1315 when the footmen of Uri and Schwyz massacred the mounted knights of Duke Leopold of Austria, who were ambushed whilst passing between a rock wall and a marsh. Before the Austrians were able to deploy in battle positions they were cut down in a bloody slaughter. This humiliating victory of a peasant army over a noble army was a terrible shock, but it was only the beginning of a series of triumphs which would last until the early sixteenth century. The surprise rout at Morgarten forced the Swiss to reflect on the purpose of their confederation; what was required was greater clarity of intention and a new treaty was drawn up on 9 December 1315 in which the essential foundations of the Swiss Confederation, as they were to remain until the end of the *Ancien Régime*, were put in writing. The Confederates had a pragmatic sense of the benefits of their union: it would bring internal peace and rule of law, as well as a degree of security in the proscription of foreign alliances which did not have unanimous consent.

Through the fourteenth and fifteenth centuries the disputes between the Swiss and the Habsburgs rumbled on, largely unresolved. The Habsburgs stood by their claims to territories within the Confederation, whilst the Swiss countered that they were free communes directly subject to the Holy Roman Emperor. Such bold assertions, as the Confederates learned to their cost, rang hollow unless backed by the force of arms; the goodwill of distant emperors in the fifteenth century was ephemeral. No monarch was prepared to put an army in the field to defend the rights of peasant communes, and although the houses of Luxembourg and Wittelsbach sought to keep the imperial crown out of Habsburg hands, they were little troubled by the regional territorial interests of their rival. Internally there were also complications. Many among the Confederate elites, particularly in the cities, were reliant upon Habsburg patronage. The guilds and merchants were particularly well aware of the fact that the Habsburgs controlled many of the major trade routes through the Confederation.

Anti-Habsburg sentiments among the Swiss were less well defined than contemporary authors sought to portray.

The aggressive expansion pursued by the Swiss at the beginning in the fourteenth century was, essentially, forced upon them as a matter of survival. The valleys that formed the nucleus of the alliance held, perhaps, thirty to forty thousand souls, most of whom barely eked a living from the infertile mountain soil.[5] The land may not have been arable, but what the valleys offered were natural fortifications, virtually impregnable to assault by larger armies. As the Confederation expanded to survive, its topographical character was transformed by the addition of new, non-mountainous members, such as Lucerne in 1332. The decision of the towns to join the Confederation was entirely pragmatic; in Lucerne the well-to-do merchants, despite some benefits, generally felt stifled by the agrarian nature of Habsburg rule, and they came to believe that their economic prosperity would be better served by an alliance with the dynasty's enemies.

Zurich was a different case. It was a powerful city with two royal abbeys and a considerable amount of territory. It had become an imperial city in the thirteenth century when in 1245 it had sided with the emperor against the pope. The result of this judicious alliance was the expulsion of a large portion of the clergy from the city and the acquisition by the council of toll, coinage, and market rights which had belonged to the church. By the fourteenth century, the emerging guilds in Zurich sought to displace the patrician families, but they needed leverage from outside the city. There were two options, the Austrians or the other Confederates. The knight Rudolf Brun (c. 1324–60) brought about a revolution in the city through an effective alliance of the nobility with the craft guilds.[6] Brun chose the Confederates as allies over the Austrians, despite their close connections with the Zurich patrician families, and the city entered into the Confederation in 1351.

With the addition of Lucerne and Zurich the Confederation moved out of the central valleys and into the rolling hills of the lower lands. This brought advantages as well as dangers. With Lucerne as an ally, for example, the Confederation surrounded the Lake of Lucerne, an important waterway leading to the St Gotthard Pass. At the same time the fledgling alliance, no longer entirely walled in by mountains, was exposed to the military might of its enemies, who were eager to meet on an open battlefield. The entry of new states (*Orte*) also changed the structure of the Confederation: the terms by which these new Confederates joined were not identical. Zurich, crucially, retained the right to make separate alliances with other powers, though the Confederation was promised first place in its affections. Glarus and Zug were admitted in 1352 when the Confederates liberated the Glareans from their overlord, the monastery at Säckingen on the Rhine, a Habsburg foundation. Subsequent wars meant that these two Confederates were briefly lost, before returning again at the end of the century. Glarus became a full member in 1388 following the battle of Näfels. These two additions added another aspect to the Confederation; they were admitted as subordinate members, required to follow the instructions of the more senior Confederates.

The addition of Zurich in 1351 was balanced in the west by the admission of Berne two years later. Berne and Zurich had much in common: both had emerged from the feudal rule of the Zähringer dynasty and were approximately the same size, with about five or six thousand inhabitants. Berne, however, did not lie on the great trade routes between the Rhine and Italy, and, therefore, became a centre of government, plying the trade of war. The city had been established in the twelfth century as a military outpost to guard against the French, and mentally it faced west. The Bernese were aggressive and expansionist, and by the middle of the fourteenth century they had moved beyond the city walls to seize control of many of the failing feudal territories in the surrounding countryside. It was a desire to secure these territorial gains which had brought the Bernese into the Confederation; they were not much interested in the anti-Habsburg politics which had forged the initial alliance. Indeed, the Bernese made peace treaties with the Habsburgs in 1358, 1363, and 1370 in order to pursue their acquisition of lands with impunity. Bernese interests were closely entangled with the dynasty, and only one year (1357) after joining the Confederation Berne took part in the Habsburg siege of Zurich, a fellow Confederate. If the Bernese saw themselves as the natural rivals of Zurich, and if they saw the Habsburgs as convenient allies rather than reviled foes, they clearly felt nothing for the communal interests of the peasants, so much at the heart of the states of Uri, Schwyz, and Unterwalden. From the perspective of Berne, the Confederation was a useful bulwark against foreign predators and little more. Berne played a canny game within the alliance, choosing to enter into military conflicts only when it saw the opportunity to prise land from others. At the key battles of Sempach (1386) and Näfels (1388), where peasant armies once again laid low the Austrian forces, the Bernese were not present, though they moved quickly in the wake of these victories to secure the spoils.

Looking at the final years of the fourteenth century, it is impossible to speak of the Swiss Confederation as anything other than a jumble of alliances. As one historian has written, 'the confederacy ... possessed no constitution, no regular representative assembly, no executive organs, no capital, no treasury, no chancery, no depository for documents, not even a seal of its own'.[7] It was a rudimentary federal system composed of members who were neither equal nor similar and, as the events of the fourteenth and fifteenth centuries amply demonstrated, the Confederates had rather elastic interpretations of their obligations. Some, such as Glarus and Zug, continued to pay money to the Habsburgs, although they were no longer under the political authority of that dynasty. More importantly, the urban and rural members of the Confederation had two very different, and rather antagonistic, cultures: the original three states (Uri, Schwyz, and Unterwalden) were carved from mountain valleys, a world apart from the changing urban worlds of late medieval Zurich and Berne, where the newer craft guilds were wresting control of civic affairs from the patrician families.

In one respect the urban and rural states stood in particular contrast. In places such as Uri, Schwyz and Unterwalden the *Landsgemeinde*, a popular assembly, was sovereign. These assemblies would delegate particular business to elected officials, and, indeed, local families began to assert themselves in particular regions. As we shall see, this was replicated in the local *Gemeinden* (communities) where each village had its elected officials who acted on behalf of the body. Against this form of popular government in the rural areas, the urban centres of Zurich and Berne were dominated by oligarchies. In Lucerne and Berne the towns were governed by patrician merchants in part descended from the old noble families. Zurich alone in the fourteenth century had succeeded in imposing a guild structure.

The end of the fourteenth century, however, brought significant changes to the Confederation in the form of two important documents. In 1370 the *Priests' Ordinance* (*Pfaffenbrief*), agreed by all the Confederates except Berne and Glarus, established that all residents of the Confederation, lay and clerical alike, who were bound by oath to the duke of Austria had to take another oath to the Confederation which took precedence. Further, no appeal was to be made to any court, lay or ecclesiastical, outside the Confederation, and provision was taken against private warfare and for the maintenance of peace on the principal roads. The second text was the *Sempach Covenant* (*Sempachbrief*) of 1393 in which common actions for the enforcement of laws and conduct of warfare were agreed. Particular attention was given to the vexations of plundering (especially of religious houses and churches) and violence against women.

The fifteenth century has been described as a 'golden age' for the Swiss. Without doubt the hundred years before the Reformation saw a dramatic expansion of the Confederation and, perhaps more importantly, a prominent role for the Swiss on the larger stage of European affairs. It was the Swiss mercenary who became the currency of this newly minted importance.[8] The poor soil of the mountain valleys could not sustain the relatively modest population, forcing young men to move off the land and find new paymasters. The endless wars of the fourteenth and fifteenth centuries made mercenary service a lucrative employment, although a recent study has suggested that mercenaries gained little social advancement through their prowess on the battlefield and that the traditional elites retained control of the military.[9] The Swiss had emerged as mercenaries in the thirteenth century; the rugged, well-conditioned mountain men wielded the halberd, an eight-foot shaft with an axe at one end and a hook or spear at the other. This remained the standard weapon of the Swiss mercenaries until the fifteenth century when they took up the pike, which had been imported from Italy. The fame of the Swiss on the battlefield owed much to their acumen in combat and their undoubted courage – they were referred to by the Austrians as the *montani bestiales*. The Swiss were shrewd fighters who chose their positions well, and their reputation was based on their ability to defeat armies of much greater size.

The military success of the Swiss was above all due to two factors: efficient organisation and good discipline.[10] Each of the eight states was responsible for providing, equipping, and training its own forces, and this was facilitated by the introduction of conscription in the middle of the fifteenth century. This meant that the Swiss could quickly field an army of around 55,000. The main bulk of these armies consisted of unmarried men between the ages of eighteen and thirty, but there were also contingents of older men who were prepared to participate in campaigns. Behind these armies was a large militia, made up by the rest of the male population, which was prepared to fight in an emergency. Each village and city had a detailed account of the number of men to be recruited and what weapons they should use. The responsibilities of each Confederate, and of each community within the Confederation, were set out precisely. All of this was underpinned by the *Sempach Covenant* of 1393, which laid down both the conditions of military co-operation between the states and a strict code of conduct for the contingents to control discipline. Officers were elected by the elders of the community when the troops were summoned, and campaigns were conducted by councils of war at which the military leaders of each state gathered to make decisions collectively.[11] Generally only the supreme commander of a state's contingent was chosen by the rulers. The military system reflected the democratic communal traditions of the Swiss; indeed, at some battles, such as Morat, there was no supreme commander and the units acted fairly independently. Thus, despite being the great age of military success, the fifteenth century produced no memorable Swiss military heroes. However, what this tightly defined web of communal responsibilities did create was a society highly capable for war, able to demolish the chivalric army of Burgundy.

The first Confederate conquest of the fifteenth century was the acquisition of the Aargau in 1415. A piece of verdant land south of the Rhine between Zurich and Berne, the Argau was the homeland of the Habsburgs, and Berne persuaded the other Confederates to join in an invasion. A combined force quickly overran the territory and the land was efficiently divided with Berne seizing the lion's share from its former Habsburg ally. The remaining portion of the Aargau was to be administered jointly by the other Confederates (except Berne and Uri). This was the first example of what was to become the common practice of Mandated Territories (*Gemeinen Herrschaften*), an arrangement which would play a crucial role in the Reformation. In the Aargau this jointly governed territory, known as the Freiamt, was managed by bailiffs (*Vögte*) appointed in turn by each of the controlling Confederates, who ruled in the name of the whole Confederation. These mandated territories were included in the Confederation not as full members, but as occupied lands.

While most of the Confederates viewed Habsburg Austria as the Behemoth to be slain, this sentiment, we have noted, was not shared by Berne and Uri, whose territorial aspirations, despite their involvement in the Aargau, lay elsewhere. The Bernese had undertaken the accession of noble lands in the south-east castle by castle, a campaign which drew them towards an inevitable conflict with the House of Savoy. For Uri, the natural realm of expansion was into the lands of the duke of Milan south of the Alps. The rulers of Uri were especially concerned with the transalpine passes and the relevant commercial privileges. After some thoroughly indecisive military actions and subsequent financial transactions – the destitute nobleman Sax zu Misox sold his control over Bellinzona to Uri in 1419 – a peace was mediated by Berne and Basle in 1426, giving some of the Italian lands to be jointly ruled by the Confederates. This messy arrangement left unresolved the territorial claims of Milan and the Swiss, driving home the point that in matters other than defence the Swiss had little sense of mutual co-operation.

The acquisition of land by the Confederates took place through a variety of means: war, purchase, mortgage, and inheritance. The military campaigns resulted in considerable expansion, but more commonly, and mundanely, it was money that secured the deal. The lower nobility and religious houses faced financial ruin on account of the spiralling costs of food and wages, and Zurich and Berne, with pockets full of money loaned by the wealthy Baslers, appropriated the right of protection (*Schirmverpflichtung*) over territories through either outright purchase or by the extension of loans which the owners could not ever repay.[12]

The territorial aspirations of the states, it must be remembered, had much more to do with particular interests than with any common agenda for enlarging the Confederation, and conflicts were inevitable and frequent. A particularly nasty example was the rivalry between Zurich and Schwyz, who jostled for control of the trade routes in the east through mountainous Toggenburg, whose childless duke lay dying. Frederick VII was the last of the great feudal lords in the region, and he had carefully cultivated a web of trade agreements with the various Confederates. His death in 1436 unleashed a bitter struggle for his vast compilation of lands. What became known as the Old Zurich War (1439–50) very nearly brought the fragile Confederation crashing down and its consequences were to be felt seventy-five years later when Zurich used the Reformation to reopen its expansionist dreams.[13]

Under the leadership of Bürgermeister Stüssi, Zurich pressed its case for Toggenburg by closing its markets to the other Confederates – a cruel measure against the rural peasants – and by concluding a pact with Austria on 17 June 1442. It will be remembered that Zurich was entitled under the terms of her entry into the Confederation to make foreign alliances, but an alliance with Austria was unforgivable act of mendacity. Zurich, it was very apparent, had no qualms about using her position as an imperial free city to damage the Confederation when circumstances required, while the Austrians saw in the territorial aspirations of Zurich their best hope of bringing the Swiss to heel. The other Confederates rushed to arms. The resolution was brutal and bloody. It was a remarkable battle between 30,000 Armagnac troops, given to the Austrians by Charles VII of France, and 1,200 –1,500 Confederate troops at the leper house of St Jakob on the Birs on 26 August 1444. The battlefield was visible from the walls of Basle, where a council of the church was meeting, and the Confederates, desperately outnumbered, were cut to pieces. The massacre of Confederate soldiers was not in vain, however, as the losses they inflicted upon the opposition were so enormous that the victors were forced to sue for peace, thus confirming the place of the martyred Swiss in the developing mythology of the Confederation. At the peace of Ensisheim in October 1444 the French recognised for the first time that there was a new political entity on their eastern frontier. For the Swiss, their victory in defeat was bitter-sweet. It had been the first civil war in the Confederation and it had revealed the shallowness of Zurich's commitment to the principles of union. When push came to shove, territorial expansion and economic hegemony ran as deeply as any sense of fraternity. The battle also put paid to Austrian hopes of bringing the Swiss lands back under their control. The Austrians had tired of the Swiss, who had humiliated them once again, and who had now established an international reputation as ferocious fighters. The kings of France themselves began to ponder the usefulness of these peasants. The cities of Fribourg, St Gall, Schaffhausen, the abbeys of St Gall and Reichenau, and Appenzell, sensed the changing winds, and exchanged Austrian patronage for alliances with Swiss Confederates. What the Old Zurich War demonstrated, however, was that despite their differences the Swiss Confederates could not easily disentangle themselves; they were bound together in a system in which security was preserved by checks and balances in which any single member could be silenced by the collective weight of the others.[14]

The second half of the fifteenth century saw the continued growth of the Confederation and a central role in European politics. In 1452 the 'Confederates of the Old League of Upper Germany', as the Swiss styled themselves, concluded their first treaty with the French. It was at this time that the Confederation began to gather the *Zugewandte Orte*, or associated districts, which were closely linked to the Confederation without having the status of full membership (*Orte*). Among these associates, three, the abbot (1451) and town of St Gall (1454) and the town of Biel were given seats at the Swiss diet. Those connected to the Swiss as *confoederati* – not so closely bound – included the Wallis (1416–17), Schaffhausen (1454), Rottweil (1463), Mülhausen (1466), Neuchâtel, the Graubünden, and Appenzell (1452). These associated states were bound by the ancient practice of commendation, that is, they were required to follow orders in matters of military campaigns and peace treaties.

The Swiss relieved the Habsburgs of the last of their lands south of the Rhine when they seized the Thurgau in 1460 and then purchased Winterthur in 1467. The Thurgau was to be governed as a Mandated Territory. In 1468 the Bernese laid siege to the Rhenish towns of Rheinfelden, Säckingen, Laufenburg, and Waldshut, which, for the most part, were not inclined to exchange the languid administration of the Austrians for the more aggressive Bernese. Sigismund, archduke of Austria, offered to buy off the Swiss with 10,000 gulden on the condition that if he did not pay up the towns would pass to the control of the Confederates. Inevitably, Sigismund was unable to pay and turned instead to Charles the Bold of Burgundy to bail him out. The Swiss drove a hard bargain, but more importantly their success along the Rhine brought them into conflict with the Burgundians.

It was the Bernese who were primarily interested in defeating the Burgundians, whom they saw as a threat to their plans in the west against Savoy. During the 1470s alliances began to shift. The major players were Charles of Burgundy, Louis XI of France, the hapless Sigismund, and the Swiss. Charles and Louis were in open rivalry, but the thinly veiled ambitions of Charles, combined with the brutal treatment of the Alsatians by his lieutenant Peter von Hagenbach, lost the Burgundians the support of both Sigismund and the Swiss. Charles believed he had to destroy this new rival on his south-eastern frontier.

In January 1476 Charles crossed the border into the Jura, and successfully laid siege to the castle at Grandson. Of the 412 occupants of the castle, 410 were slaughtered; the two men spared had been forced to act as executioners. Some days later, a Swiss army of 18,000 men met the Burgundians on the shores of Lake Neuchâtel. A failure of communications among the Burgundians led to panic when the Swiss appeared to have outflanked them. The terrifying sounds of the Swiss war horns, along with their reputation for dispatching captives, unnerved the Burgundian soldiers, who fled the field. The battle of Grandson was a classic encounter of Swiss pikemen and halberdiers against heavy war-horses. The victory was total. The booty brought great wealth to the Swiss: 400 canon, 800 arquebuses, 10,000 horses, jewels, silver, and tapestries worth three million florins.

Charles retreated to Lausanne to lick his wounds and regroup his army. He was determined to take on Berne directly, and he moved against the city, laying siege to Morat, where, on 22 June, the decisive battle took place. Once again the Swiss outflanked the Burgundians, and this time, in driving rain, they crashed through Charles's palisaded camp, resulting in an utter rout. The losses were staggering: 10,000 Burgundians lay dead against a mere 410 Swiss. As the Burgundians had feared, no prisoners were taken and no ransoms demanded; Charles's soldiers were driven into the lake by the Swiss, where they either drowned or had their throats cut.

The final battle came at Nancy in January 1477, when Charles attempted to retake the city, which had fallen to an army from Lorraine the previous October. Charles was determined to lay siege to the city, and upon hearing that a Confederate army was advancing to relieve the city, he decided to attack. In snow and freezing weather the Swiss troops effectively carried out a pincer movement against the Burgundians, whose horse and artillery proved disastrously useless against flexible infantry formations. Swiss pikes crashed through the Burgundian central position and panic broke out; the slaughter, even by the standards of earlier battles, was horrendous and Charles's mutilated body was found several days later.

The Burgundian war brought a sea-change to the Confederation. As a consequence of the victory, Fribourg and Solothurn joined as the ninth and tenth members. This was especially significant, as Fribourg was the first French-speaking land to become a full member of what had previously been a purely German-speaking league. The destruction of the Burgundian army, first at Grandson and Morat, and then finally under the walls of Nancy placed the Swiss on the map; not only were they admired for their military prowess, but they were now treated as something more than rebellious peasants.

An impressive monument to the victory was the *Great Burgundian Chronicle* written by Diebold Schilling the Elder (d. 1486). Born into a distinguished family in Solothurn, Schilling the Elder entered the services of the chancellery of Berne in 1460 after long years of service in Lucerne.[15] In Berne, Schilling the Elder became familiar with both the administration and jurisdiction of the city as well as Berne's complex external affairs. From 1468 he was a member of the large council in Berne and was also a judge. He was entrusted with several delicate missions and also participated personally in the Burgundian Wars. As a citizen of Bern, he also got to know Bendicht Tschachtlan, the then leading chronicler of the city. In 1474 Schilling was commissioned by the council of Bern to write a chronicle of the city, from its beginnings to contemporary times, and the result was a three-volume work which he produced between 1474 and 1483. The extraordinarily detailed account of the Burgundian wars, also known as the 'Zurich Schilling', was written around 1480. Schilling's chronicle owed nothing to humanist learning – the work is not poetic - rather it is a vast repository of news, stories, and piquant scenes from daily life. Schilling was a servant of the Berne council and he saw it as his duty to defend the policies and actions of his masters: Berne is portrayed as the stabilising force in the Confederation, drawn into war only by the mendacity of her neighbours.[16] The text is richly illustrated with over six hundred pictures, making the chronicles an object of great beauty, though it is not known whether Schilling himself was responsible for the drawings. For a man who barely lived past the age of fifty, Schilling's accomplishment was astounding, a remarkable piece of history-writing by a man with a busy public life. His words and pictures gave shape to the Swiss historical imagination of the fifteenth century and his chronicles crowned a century of distinguished historical writing in Berne.

The triumph over the Burgundians, however, also revealed more ominous portents for the Confederation. Even in the eyes of contemporary writers there was a striking contrast between the ability of the Confederates to act as one against a common foe and their inability to speak with one voice at the negotiating table. Despite having destroyed the most powerful army in Europe, the Swiss showed little sense of how to take advantage of their victory. They had slaughtered the Burgundian soldiers, including many of their nobility, and secured an enormous booty of armour and jewels which greatly enhanced the wealth of the Confederation. There was, however, no attempt to make any territorial demands or press any political advantage. Some historians have regarded the Burgundian wars as the lost opportunity for the Swiss to establish themselves as a major European power, but such an interpretation neglects the very nature of the Confederation. It was a collection of territories knitted together by overlapping, principally defensive interests. Unless threatened, each member was content to be left alone to pursue matters of internal political consolidation and the development of wealth through trade or the mercenary service. The Confederates were simultaneously allies and rivals, intensely jealous of any advantage gained by a neighbour.

The absence of any coherent strategy against their neighbours also reflected the preoccupation of the many of the Confederates with a series of internal problems. Most immediate was the escalating level of rural violence, which was directly connected with the mercenary service. Roving bands of armed men ravaged the countryside in search of money, drink, and sex, spreading syphilis as well as a host of other diseases carried home from Italy. Villagers and farmers were virtually defenceless against these gangs, who were distinguished by their torn trousers, considered a badge of honour by those who had served as soldiers in foreign lands. Other problems went to the very heart of the Confederation. The division of the Burgundian spoils and the question of whether to admit the cities of Fribourg and Solothurn threatened to pull apart a union which depended upon goodwill and co-operation. The admission of Fribourg and Solothurn deprived the rural Confederates of their ability to outvote the urban states in the diet; this was their one advantage over the cities, which outstripped them in wealth and influence. The wages of success on the battlefield for the Swiss looked to be civil war, a disaster averted only by the timely intervention of the holy hermit Nicholas von Flüe (or Bruder Klaus 1417–87), who negotiated in December 1481 an agreement which became the third great ordinance of the Confederation, the *Compact of Stans*.[17] At the age of fifty this former farmer and soldier had left his wife and ten children to take up the life of a pilgrim. Canonised in the seventeenth century, his reputation for sanctity grew from stories that he neither ate nor drank but lived on the eucharist alone.[18] The principles of the earlier *Pfaffenbrief* and *Sempachbrief* were confirmed in the *Compact*, but recent events required a modification to the manner in which the Confederates treated one another. Consequently, they swore not only to defend one another, but also to desist from supporting unrest in any of the other Confederates. Solothurn and Fribourg were admitted, but on restricted terms – they were forbidden from making foreign alliances without the permission of the other Confederates. On the vexed question of the Burgundian spoils, it was decided that treasures and movables were to be divided among all the combatants, while the newly acquired territories and towns would only be given to the full Confederates. Consistent with the character of the Swiss union, the *Compact of Stans* spoke in two languages: it was a confirmation of the federal nature of the Confederation as well as a statement of autonomy for its constituent members, perpetuating a paradox which, on the whole, remained hidden until it was rudely exposed by the religious furore of the 1520s.

It is tempting to think of the evolution of the Swiss Confederation as an emancipation from the Holy Roman Empire, but this is not a helpful perspective.[19] We have already noted that Swiss conflict with the empire only arose once a Habsburg was elected emperor in 1448, thus putting a regional struggle into a different context. The Swiss ferociously resisted attempts by the Habsburgs to regain control over their inherited lands, and it was only out of this struggle that they sought to free themselves from the empire. In most other respects, however, the empire played a fundamental role in the life of the Confederation through the fifteenth and sixteenth centuries. For many Swiss, most prominently politicians, patricians, and merchants, the empire was the framework within which the Confederation existed. The exercise of power within the Confederation at all levels, whether in the privileges of the imperial cities, the rights granted to religious houses or the feudal authority of the nobles, operated within the legal framework of the empire. From the Gotthard Pass to Basle on the Rhine the Swiss were closely integrated into the trading systems of the empire. Linguistically they were closely related to their southern German cousins, they knew the same legends, venerated many of the same saints, shared the same jokes. We must be careful not to imagine an independent Swiss identity struggling manfully against the imperial hegemonic force; in most respects the Swiss saw themselves as part of that inchoate, amorphous body of German-speaking lands which constituted the late medieval empire.

The greater tension was internal. The diversity of interests within the Confederation was graphically illustrated by the rise of Hans Waldmann and the reassertion of Zurich's territorial interests after the civil war of 1439–50. This remarkable man had led the Zurich contingent at the battle of Morat (1476) and Nancy (1477), and was among the most prominent of the Swiss leaders in the struggle against Charles the Bold of Burgundy. From humble origins he became extraordinarily wealthy and by 1479 was among the richest men in the Confederation. In 1483 he became Bürgermeister of Zurich and began to strip the patrician families of their authority within the city. His power base was among the guilds and his influence grew from his wealth, which was so impressive that many of the rulers of Europe courted his favour. It was brilliant diplomatic skills which enabled Waldmann to weave his way through the tangled politics of late fifteenth-century Europe – often working against a dynasty on one front whilst supporting it on another. Waldmann's power and affluence flourished as he lined his pockets with money for mercenaries.

Waldmann's aspirations for himself and his city lay in the triumph of Zurich over both the rural and urban Confederates. The traditional antagonism towards the inner states as well as the rivalry with Berne were to be resolved in Zurich's favour, and, further, in the establishment of Waldmann as the leader of the Swiss. This was the last serious attempt at centralising the Confederation before the Reformation. Waldmann's wealth, sumptuous lifestyle, and dictatorial intentions fertilised the traditional fears and resentments of both the rural communities and the urban patrician families. His attempts to form alliances which would protect Swiss interests along the Rhine following the collapse of Burgundy came to nothing in the face of ill-tempered opposition. When he returned to Zurich he encountered a series of local disputes, said to have concerned the shooting of some savage dogs. These troubles were used as a pretext by Waldmann's enemies to have him arrested, tortured, and eventually executed in 1489. His rapid fall from power brought to an end Zurich's plans for domination of the rural areas. It also graphically illustrated the Swiss phobia of powerful leaders. Zurich was plunged into chaos by Waldmann's precipitous fall, and the resulting instability was compounded by Berne's refusal to become involved in events in the eastern part of the Confederation. As G.R. Potter wrote, 'the Confederation was a ship without rudder or captain'.[20]

It was in this period of uncertainty that the Swiss began to drift towards France as a natural ally. French money, in the form of pensions, was readily received by mercenary soldiers and patrician families. In 1495 the close relationship between the Swiss and the French crown was renewed in the full expectation that the Swiss would provide the kings of France with military support.[21] At the same time, the Habsburg emperor Maximilian I was developing his plans to re-establish imperial claims in Italy. In order to wage war on the Italian peninsula, however, Maximilian had to undertake an ambitious programme of imperial reform north of the Alps. The Swiss rejected the reforms of the imperial diet held at Worms in 1495, refusing both to recognise the authority of the *Reichskammergericht*, which was established to resolve disputes between members of the empire, and to pay the taxes which Maximilian sought to impose. These acts of defiance against Maximilian's assertion of imperial authority only served to compound problems which had begun with the Swiss refusal to join the Swabian League (1488) which had been formed by the lords and cities of southern Germany to preserve public peace. The Swabian League had originally been directed against Wittelsbach Bavaria, but by the end of the 1490s the perceived enemy was the Swiss, whose *de facto* independence within the empire was resented by many southern Germans.

The renewed threat of Habsburg hegemony led many of the eastern Swiss states to align themselves with the three leagues of the Graubünden. The Graubünden, therefore, had the status of an 'associate' member of the Confederation, and when in early 1499 the Tyrolese seized Münsterthal – a part of the Gotteshausbund – the Swiss were drawn into a savage military conflict with the emperor. The hostilities were so bitter that the nomenclature of the conflict remains a point of dispute: the Swiss call it the 'Swabian War', while the Germans refer to it as the 'Swiss War'. Whatever its name, it lasted less than a year, but it stretched from the Rhine to the mountainous regions in the east. Almost all of the Confederates were involved, while Maximilian had the support of the Swabian League. The war was short but vicious, marked by a deep enmity between the Germans and Swiss, who were despised by their neighbours as rebellious peasants who needed to be taught a lesson. In each of the principal battles the Confederates emerged victorious: Triesen, Hard on Lake Constance, Bruderholz (Basle), Frastanz on the Ill (near Feldkirch).[22] The most important victory, however, was achieved at Dornach on 22 July, when the complete failure of the imperial offensive against the Swiss was underscored. By September 1499 a negotiated settlement was reached in Basle by which Maximilian essentially recognised Swiss independence and abandoned his plans to impose the reforms of 1495 upon the Confederation. Although the Swiss formally remained within the empire, no longer were they expected to comply with imperial decisions. The situation was left unresolved, and that seemed to suit both sides.

Following the conclusion of the peace of Basle, the Confederation sought to secure its northern Rhenish frontier by the admission of the imperial cities of Basle (June 1501) and Schaffhausen (August 1501) as full members. For the Swiss, Basle was a crucial bridge to southern Germany as well as the breadbasket and wine cellars of Alsace. Although the city had never had any formal relationship with the Confederation, its wealth had financed a good deal of Swiss territorial expansion (especially by the Bernese). Further, Basle alone had craftsmen, traders, and printers of international reputation, thus opening up the world of Renaissance Europe to the Swiss. This was enhanced by the presence of a university, founded in 1454 during the Council of Basle. The university was a modest foundation, offering the traditional scholastic curriculum, but together with the burgeoning printing industry it made Basle a centre of intellectual activity in the southern German region. Paradoxically, it was precisely Basle's cosmopolitan character, and its wealthy guilds, that aroused suspicion among the original, rural Confederates. Like Zurich and Berne, the Baslers had little in common with the rustic culture of the inner Swiss Confederates. Nevertheless, Basle proved a willing and able Confederate, placing its resources at the disposal of the Confederation and entering upon its first military campaign in 1503, when it assisted the Swiss of the inner states in taking Bellizona, an Italian territory essential to transalpine trade.

The unique character of Basle was enshrined in the conditions of its entry to the Confederation (*Bundesbrief*). As befitted a city of guilds and traders, men who depended upon peace and stability to ply their trade, Basle's official role in the Confederation was that of a mediator. Unlike the other urban members (Zurich and Berne), Basel did not have separate treaties with individual members; it stood apart from all and was to adjudicate disputes (territorial, financial, and jurisdictional) between fellow Confederates. This role provided the Baslers their own form of independence in the Confederation and it served their commercial interests by creating the stability essential for good business.

Schaffhausen, situated at the head of the Rhine, had had a longer association with the Confederation. The city which had grown up around the Benedictine monastery of All Saints had become an imperial free city in the thirteenth century. It had been mortgaged to Austria from 1330 until 1415 but had bought its freedom in 1418 to become an 'associate' of the Confederation in 1454. The entry of this small city into the Confederation in 1501 was seen as a necessary defensive measure, but there was little enthusiasm among the older Confederates for another urban member, whose admission tipped the city/rural balance in favour of the former. As a measure of compensation, the sparsely populated, poor land of Appenzell was promoted in 1511 from associate member, a status which it had received in 1452, to full Confederate. Thus, slightly more than a decade before the outbreak of the Reformation, the Swiss Confederation had become an alliance of thirteen members: the rural states of Uri, Schwyz, Unterwalden, Zug, Glarus, Appenzell; and the urban members Lucerne, Zurich, Berne, Fribourg, Solothurn, Basle, and Schaffhausen.

Each of the Confederates had entered the union as a result of specific historical circumstances, and those circumstances were reflected in the terms set out in the treaties of alliance. Conditions were demanded or imposed, depending upon the relative strength of the new member; the urban members vouchsafed guarantees to their rural partners, but there could be no masking the rivalries that existed between Confederates, all of whom vigorously guarded their rights to act in their own best interest when the situation demanded. At the beginning of the sixteenth century the Confederation was a tangled web of local arrangements among partners whose attitudes towards one another ranged across the spectrum: fraternal love, lofty disinterest, insecure envy, bitter rivalry, and patrician condescension. The rest of Europe had begun to marvel at the achievements of the Swiss peasants, who had brought down noble armies, humiliated emperors, and traversed the Alps. Yet despite the widespread image of the Swiss as peasants who stood for the ethics of communalism, Swiss society was deeply divided by struggles between the old nobility, the urban patrician families, the powerful craft guilds, and those who worked the land. The political strength and wealth brought by the fifteenth century had created a variegated political structure and a society which remained extremely hierarchical.

The only federal institution in the Confederation was the diet (*Tagsatzung*);[23] the name meant to set a day to meet. The diet had no authority to pass laws, and its authority was limited to negotiations that concerned the whole Confederation: declarations of war, peace negotiations, the sending and reception of ambassadors, the maintenance of internal peace and the preservation of the rule of law. Only the diet spoke for the Confederation, but, as ever, nothing was quite as it seemed, for the decisions of the diet, although reached collectively, were not binding on any of the constituent members. In addition to the general meeting of the federal diet, there were other diets in which some or all of the Confederates met with foreign representatives to discuss issues relevant to a particular region: in Brugg, Königsfelden, and Rheinfelden the Swiss met with the Austrians; in Basle there were meetings with the Austrians and representatives of the Alsatian cities; in Constance they met with representatives of the southern German cities; and in Solothurn it was customary to meet the ambassadors of the French king. Another form of diet took place when certain members of the Confederation came together to discuss matters of mutual interest, such as the administration of the Mandated Territories (ie. the Thurgau or the Freiamt).[24]

During the fourteenth and early fifteenth centuries the general diets of the Confederation were most often held in Lucerne, but from 1426 the favoured location became Baden, on account of its central position. Each of the full members sent two delegates, while the associate members sent one. Each delegation could only speak with one voice, and representatives were strictly required to express only the views of their political masters, not their own. Points of protocol were scrupulously adhered to and there was a clear sense of hierarchy within the session: most prominently seated were the representatives of the eight original Confederates (called the *Vororte*), who were ranked above the five later additions. One of the representatives of the original states served as leader of the diet; from the end of the fifteenth century until 1798 this role was always held by one of the delegates from Zurich. With the split between the Catholics and evangelicals in the 1520s Lucerne became the leader of the Catholic states, who held their own diets in that city. Zurich remained head of the diets of the Reformed states, which met in Aarau, as well as retaining the chair for the general diets of the Confederation. The emulous nature of federal politics remained until 1815, when it was decided that the presidency of the diet should rotate every two years among Zurich, Berne, and Lucerne.

The Swiss Confederation emerged into the sixteenth century as something of a political curiosity. It had strong communal, anti-feudal traditions which shaped its identity, and the Swiss were known for their achievements on the battlefield, yet this renown for wielding the halberd masked darker tensions. The mercenary service, in so many ways a lifeline for the inner Confederates, was destroying the social and moral fabric of Swiss communities. The ambiguity of this situation has recently been demonstrated for Lucerne, where Anne-Marie Dubler has shown that the willingness of the young men of Lucerne to serve as mercenaries caused a shortage of skilled workers. This brought artisans to the city from other lands, thus profoundly affecting the social make-up of the city.[25] The Confederation had two faces: the rural states, where the communal traditions were strong, and the cities, where the developing world of capitalism and trade was creating a new ethos which brought these urban centres into close contact with the cities of Alsace and southern Germany. As a collection of small states bound together by defensive oaths its origins mirrored events throughout the medieval Germanic world, but that it should have survived as such can only be explained by a constellation of factors. The geography of the Confederation was extremely uninviting for any potential invader, whilst the Swiss prowess for military activity was intimidating. As long as the transalpine trade routes remained accessible and the Swiss were prepared to sell their youth as soldiers no European power was prepared to take them on.

Religious life

Religious life in Swiss lands was shaped by many of the same exigencies found throughout fifteenth-century Europe. The situation in the Confederation was neither remarkable nor especially dire. In many ways the story was familiar: secular lords and civic magistrates sought to appropriate the rights and privileges of the church. The religious houses had suffered with the decline of feudalism in the Confederation; there was tremendous resentment of their privileges by the communities. There was no distinctively Swiss church; the lands of the Confederation fell, for the most part, within the enormous diocese of Constance, with the rest divided between the bishops of Basle, Sitten, Chur, and Lausanne. Nevertheless, while we cannot speak of any 'national church' we do find that the Confederation overflowed with vibrant local religious cultures, shaped by saints' cults, places of pilgrimage, and distinctive patterns of devotion which gave the people their own spiritual narrative.

The two great councils of the fifteenth century, Constance and Basle, had taken place on the very borders of Swiss lands, and many of the distinguished churchmen and scholars had made their way along Swiss roads to these meetings, and the learning which they brought in the form of ideas and books played a crucial part in the translation of Renaissance culture north of the Alps. Without this religious and cultural stimulus the Swiss Reformation of the following century would have been unthinkable. Basle remained closely associated with ideas of church reform, and its university, a product of the Council, a haven for reform-minded churchmen.

The flowering of devotional art and writings, great enthusiasm for saints and pilgrimages, and a vigorous mixture of popular and official beliefs is what gave the Swiss churches their identity, and it was highly variegated. The real problems lay in the structures of the church and its lines of authority. The Swiss bishops of the fifteenth century were for the most part scions of leading families, undistinguished and virtually powerless to exert any authority over the communities of their diocese which had sought to control their churches. Periodically, in the wake of the Council of Basle, they attempted to hold synods and issue reforming decrees, but to little applause. The diocese of Constance provides a useful example. A series of bishops applied themselves with zeal to reforming the most common abuses among the clergy: concubinage, card-playing, drinking in taverns, blasphemy and cursing and the keeping of undesirable company.[26] In addition, the priests of the diocese were regularly admonished not to neglect worship and the visiting of the sick and dying.[27] Remarkably, Hugo von Hohenlandenburg, bishop from 1497 until the Reformation, climbed into the pulpit and preached before the gathered clergy in Constance, encouraging them to do likewise in their parishes. There was no shortage of people prepared to talk about the abuses in the church and how reform was essential, but there was no effective means of implementing change. Across the dioceses of the Confederation the situation was depressingly familiar: powerful forces, such as cathedral chapters, religious houses, and secular rulers arrayed themselves against the bishops, reducing all reforming efforts to pious pronouncements. As ever, the ugly head of mercenary service was visible. A string of popes, desperate for Swiss soldiers, were prepared to pay handsomely and to bargain away ecclesiastical rights and privileges in return for men on the battlefield. Pope Julius II (1503–13) had an effective agent in the bishop of Sitten, Matthäu Schiner (1470–1522), a humanist, friend of patriotic young Swiss such as Huldrych Zwingli, and arch-opponent of French interests. Schiner travelled through the Confederation raising men for the cause of Rome, a city where he hoped one day to be pope.

The failure of the bishops to effect any change was largely due to their inability either to control the clergy in their dioceses or to defend their institutions against the encroachments of civic councils and local communes. There were several reasons for this. Firstly, the borders of the Swiss dioceses did not coincide with any political boundaries and the resulting mish-mash of jurisdictions rendered effective ecclesiastical governance virtually impossible. Secondly, a major development of the fifteenth century was the emergence of rural deans as the most important ecclesiastical figures. These men were agents of the bishop in the regions of the diocese, standing between the bishop and the priests to ensure that the diocesan statutes were implemented. Above all, this meant the collection of money and the implementation of discipline. For the most part the rural deans acted as semi-independent officials, stamping their own authority in their chapters, and often ignoring their bishop. The diocesan clergy rarely had any contact with their bishop, and most refused to undertake the arduous and often dangerous journey to the episcopal city to visit synods. The dean was the face of church authority throughout the Confederation, and with the collapse of episcopal authority they became *de facto* bishops in their own patch of the diocese. In Constance the rural deans would meet regularly in Lucerne in the guildhouse 'Zu Schneidern' to discuss affairs.[28] The strength of their position in the pre-Reformation church is witnessed by the fact that the rural deans became a foundation of the Reformed polities of Zurich and Berne, and especially in Basle.

The parish was the basic unit of religious life. At the local level the church was made up of a collection of officials, clerical and lay, who were responsible for its spiritual and material affairs and who were the face of the church to the faithful. The priest (*Leutpriester*) was to celebrate the Sunday mass and preach; he baptised children, administered last rites, and buried the dead. The standard of clergy varied, as one might expect. In the cities of Berne, Basle, and Zurich, for example, humanist influences had begun to make themselves felt by the middle of the fifteenth century, but in the rural areas few priests possessed more than a rudimentary education, though they were often the only literate people in the village. Religious houses increasingly provided young men with an education during the fifteenth century, and those intending to enter the priesthood could gain some elementary Latin and education in church practices. Those who showed promise might be sent to the larger urban centres to attend Latin schools. This was the way forward for ambitious young men eager to make something of themselves. Many of the Swiss parish clergy followed their fathers into the parish living, and it is common to find certain family names associated with the office of the priest for many decades before the Reformation. Being born the son of a priest did not preclude a life in the church, in fact it seems to have encouraged it. Those who travelled to Constance, for instance, could receive absolution from the bishop for any impediment (such as being illegitimate) which might bar one from either ordination or further education. Late medieval clerical education was highly practical in nature, providing priests with a rudimentary knowledge of liturgy and church law. According to the Council of Vienne (1311), a man could be ordained subdeacon at eighteen, a deacon at twenty and a priest at twenty-five, but there is little evidence in the Swiss lands that this stricture was upheld.

The average Swiss parish priest would have made do with a couple of books. Most possessed a breviary, a homiletic collection of miracle stories, and perhaps a handbook on pastoral care. Confessional manuals, such as the *Summa confessorum* of Raymond of Peñaforte were widespread in Swiss lands, as was the *Pastorale novellum* of Rudolf von Liebegg (1323), which was based on the *Regula pastoralis* of Gregory the Great, and was a collection of material for priests written in verse form.[29] The essence of the work was the familiar late medieval emphasis on the cataloguing of sins and the subjects of sin and penance.

From 1460 Basle offered the opportunity to study theology at the university. The curriculum was a typical late medieval hybrid of scholastic trends with perhaps a slight tilt towards Scotism. This remained intact until the Reformation, and it was only in the late 1520s that humanism began to make its mark in the university. The university was new, but it was not a purely Swiss institution; between 1460 and 1529 5,340 students entered its halls, of whom only 1,163 were from the Confederation.[30] There were distinguished teachers from across the empire in Basle, but few stars. Two exceptions were Johannes von Wesel and Johann Ulrich Surgant. Wesel was famous on account of his lectures on logic. Surgant, who taught Zwingli, had a doctorate in canon law and was a long time rector of the university. He was not a brilliant scholar, but was an outstanding teacher and pastor.

He was deeply committed to church reform, having participated in the Council of Basle, and in his writings he emphasised pastoral care. Theologically he was a scholastic, but his most important work, the *Manuale Curatorum*, was an instructional book on preaching and the pastoral duties of the priest.[31] His vision of a church, committed to the practical care of the people, had a profound influence upon the generation which would initiate the Reformation in the Confederation. Alongside Erasmus, Surgant was the spiritual father of the Swiss Reformation, even if he would never have countenanced its theology.

As we have already mentioned, the clerical family was well established in Swiss lands long before the Reformation. The women who acted as wives, kept the household, bore and raised the children were known as concubines, and they had no legal status. Yet the situation was hardly the scandal that we might imagine it to have been, for the well-ordered parish household seems to have met with widespread approval. The evidence for popular concern about the priest keeping a 'wife' surfaced only in connection with other complaints of indolence or negligence. Many of the leading reformers, including Leo Jud and Heinrich Bullinger, were the sons of clergy, and in the case of Bullinger the affection with which he recalled his mother gives some sense of the stability of the home and relationship. When Zwingli petitioned the bishop of Constance to permit married priests he was not seeking a radical alteration to clerical life but rather the removal of official condemnation of what already existed.

Despite the combined opposition of reform-minded preachers and fifteenth-century synods of the Swiss dioceses to concubinage, clerical families were well established in the parishes by the middle of the fifteenth century and had been given a quasi-legal status by the early sixteenth century by a regularised taxation system. In short, bishops and priests shared a highly pragmatic view of the living arrangements of the clergy, who clearly preferred to live with families. This perspective was reflected in the manner in which the fines for concubinage came to be viewed not so much as a penalty, but rather as a tax.[32] The benevolence of the bishops reflected several different points. First, there was little that the bishops could do to prevent these relationships as they had little direct control over dioceses which took in numerous political authorities. Second, the income generated from concubinage – in particular the set rate for having the children legitimised, the so-called 'cradle tax' – was crucial for episcopal finances, which had been severely eroded by the growth of communalism and the urban authorities. Finally, although for the reformers, and Zwingli in particular, the issues of clerical celibacy and marriage were absolutely central, there is little evidence that the presence of clerical families in the parishes before the Reformation stirred anticlerical sentiments among the laity. Lascivious priests, so often the target of early Reformation propaganda, were not associated in the popular imagination with those clergy who sought to maintain an ordered household.

The tension between custom and law brought about by concubinage did have evident social consequences in the parishes which arose from questions concerning legitimacy and inheritance. In most of the Swiss dioceses the bishops possessed the right of inheritance (*Spolienrecht*) to many parishes. This meant on a priest's death his income and goods reverted back to the bishop, and not to his 'wife' or children.[33] The bishop might make some provision for the priest's family, as might the community, but the result was the undermining of the stability of the clerical family. Destitute widows and children of clerics became a serious social concern for many communities, as did the attitude of many priests that, as their goods would simply pass to the bishop on their deaths, these worldly things ought to be enjoyed in the here and now. Drinking, gambling, and absenteeism were often associated with a desire to make hay while the sun still shone. Zwingli had first-hand experience of the trials and tribulations of priestly celibacy, and the regularising of marital and sexual relations was central to his vision of general moral reform. But the role of the clerical family ran deeper in the Swiss Reformation. Many of the leading Swiss reformers were the offspring of priests and 'concubines' (Heinrich Bullinger and Leo Jud, for example), and the centrality of the family to Christian reform owed much to their own experiences of strong familial bonds tinged with uncertainty over social and legal status.

Each parish had a group of men who assisted the priest. In rural areas the priest worked alongside a *Kirchmeier*, a lay official elected by the community who was charged with the collection of tithes and other monies relating to the church. The other official was the sacristan (*Sigrist*), who was also elected by the community, who looked after the church building and sacristy. The church building was the centre of the community; it was where the people met, where they worshipped, and where the mandates of distant rulers were read out. In most communities meetings were held twice a year to elect a local council, swear the oath of obedience, and conduct other business. It was in the church building that the secular local tribunal (*Kanzelgericht*) met. The bailiff (*Kirchherr*) plus another official from the community would hear disciplinary cases concerning matters of conduct or tithes.

The communal structures of the Swiss Confederation played a key role in the religious life of the people. Given the weakness of the ecclesiastical structures, the rural communes increasingly sought to control church life. The work of Peter Blickle has been especially important in drawing our attention to the extent of this late medieval development in which the leaders of the community (*Gemeinde*) saw themselves as responsible for the provision of pastoral care.[34] Randolph C. Head, in his recent study of the communalism in the Graubünden, has identified the following general principles of late medieval Germanic village life:

> It consisted of a finite and concrete membership who collectively benefited from the resources held in common, and who collectively shouldered the burdens of maintaining and defending those resources.
>
> The most important productive resources, especially cropland, were privately controlled, and individual peasants controlled the disposition of their labour. But the use of these resources was strictly regulated by collective institutions. The commune strove for maximum legal and political autonomy. The commune's decisions were ratified at assemblies of the entire membership, where an oath of membership in and obedience to the collective were taken. The commune displayed characteristics of both a voluntary association created by an oath among equals, and of a 'natural' hierarchically constituted community created by an oath to a lord.[35]

Peter Blickle has identified how the demands of the communes focused on particular issues of jurisdiction: control over the goods of their church, the authority of the morals tribunal, and the right to select their own priest. This movement was fuelled by the desire for local autonomy as well as by the failings of the church; by extending their control over the goods and clergy the villagers were attempting to rid themselves of feudal bonds of allegiance as well as ensuring that they received the spiritual care they demanded.

The rhythm of the church life was measured out in holy days and festivals. These varied throughout the Swiss lands: in Zug, for example, there were twenty-four such days in the year, while twenty-three of the fifty-two Sundays were taken up by special services.[36] On all of these days work was to cease and markets close. While these holy days were clearly of great importance to the people, and were often marked by extensive festivities, they had to compete against the demands placed on rural communities by the weather. Late medieval records are full of accounts of farmers staying away from church services, or working on festival days, to tend to their crops or animals.

The world was full of evil spirits, demons and ghosts, many of which were naturalistic forces. During the winter months the demonic companies of the *Wüetisheer* and the *Dürstegjeg* flew howling through the air. In the nights before Christmas the *Bürgelnherren*, natural spirits, appeared as ghosts, while in the Zurich Oberland there was a widespread belief that if you peered through the key-hole of the parish-church door on New Year's Eve you would see gathered around the altar the visages of those who were to die in the coming year. Particularly in winter and mid-summer there were hosts of malevolent spirits which snatched children, killed livestock, cursed men and women. They blew with the wind in the night. The defence of the people lay in a mixture of church rituals and long-established customs which made use of incantations and amulets. Wednesday was thought a cursed day on which nothing important should be done. Marriages were never held on a Wednesday.

Many of the customs were unique to parts of the Confederation, but the mentality reflected late medieval agrarian culture.[37] The number three was thought to have magical powers and virtually everything was done in threes. Some people carried a stone in the pocket as a defence against toothache, while on Christmas Eve a dish of milk was to be left out for the Christ Child and the angels. The Word of God was fully incorporated into these rituals: certain passages of the Bible, the psalms in particular, were thought to have especial qualities. Psalms 23 and 42 were thought to be helpful when digging for water, while the repetition of Psalm 52 was believed to aid the soul of a departed one through purgatory. Lightning and thunder were greatly feared, and in 1518 the Bernese council declared that in order to drive away thunder the bells of the city should be rung and the people fall to their knees to recite five Paternosters and Ave Marias.[38]

The most notorious case associated with supernatural activity was the Jetzer affair in Berne in 1506. A tailor named Hans Jetzer arrived in the city from Zurzach and entered the Dominican house. He was in Berne on business and the Dominicans took him in without much thought. Soon rumours abounded of Jetzer's behaviour in Lucerne, where he had staged some spurious religious apparitions. In Berne he once against claimed to have had visions, this time of the Virgin Mary, who had revealed that she had spent three hours in the state of original sin. This revelation thus confirmed the Dominican view of Mary over that of the Franciscans, who argued for her immaculate conception. A letter was then found in the choir of the Dominican church with five drops of blood on it. This was quickly interpreted as the blood of the martyr called Mary – although in fact there had been seven such martyrs. It was thought that the Virgin could be seen in Jetzer's cell through a peephole, and Jetzer himself was believed to have received the stigmata. He was venerated as a holy man and brought the Dominican house instant notoriety, making it a prime attraction for the faithful. People flowed into the city from the countryside to see Jetzer, who was reputed to have spoken directly to

Christ's mother.[39] Jetzer made the most of it, and intoxicated with his new-found celebrity he attempted to stage an apparition of the Virgin Mary, but the monks identified him in the costume and he was exposed as a prankster and a fraud.

The case was a disaster for the Dominicans, who had connived in Jetzer's circus act in their eagerness to humiliate their Franciscan rivals. Four friars were sentenced to death, while Jetzer, who claimed to have been put up to his stunts by the Dominican leadership, was banished from the land.[40] The four Dominicans were burnt at the stake on 31 May 1509. The whole affair brought great shame on the city, and no one emerged with clean hands. The long-term effect was a legacy of anticlericalism among the Bernese, who saw this sad affair as clerical charlatanism, a cruel play upon their profound attachment to the Mother of God. The political authorities determined never again to be duped by the church, and while the Jetzer affair does not alone explain why the Bernese magistrates ruled the church with an iron fist after the Reformation, it remained a vivid memory and a sobering reminder of the danger of clerical independence.

Like all Catholics after the Lateran Council of 1215 the Swiss were expected to confess and receive communion once a year, generally at Easter. Those who refused were technically to be sent to episcopal courts, but, as with marriage, the authority of the bishops in these areas had been severely curtailed in the fifteenth century by the encroachments of urban and rural communities on the jurisdiction of distant church courts. Nevertheless, there is evidence that many lay people took the matter very seriously. Bishop Rudolf von Montfort was typical of late medieval bishops in decreeing, following the disciplinary decree *Omnis utriusque sexus* of the Fourth Lateran Council (1215), that those who did not comply with the requirement for confession and communion were not to be buried in church ground.[41] From the fourteenth century the sale of indulgences in the Swiss lands became extremely popular, and the church attempted to ensure that the people communicated by declaring indulgences only to be of benefit to those who had first confessed and communicated. The development of the sacrament of confession in the late medieval church described by David Myers for Bavaria had echoes among the Swiss.[42] The Franciscans were especially active among the Swiss, working as confessors and often in place of the parish clergy, who often resented the intrusions of the mendicants. Nevertheless, the power of confession was without doubt. At Einsiedeln in 1466 at the festival of *Engelweih* four hundred confessors stood ready. In the diocese of Constance, those who had lived in open sin were required to go to the cathedral in Constance for two weeks of penance before receiving absolution on Maundy Thursday. We know that in 1427 almost thirteen hundred people performed this act of contrition, and between 1450 and 1460 the numbers swelled considerably.

The dead formed an important part of the late medieval church. The place of war in the evolution of the Confederation and the centrality of the mercenary service to the daily lives of the Swiss made the memories of those who died on the foreign battlefields central to communal expressions of piety. Confraternities sprung up across the Confederation to pray for those who had died in battle without the benefit of the last rites. The intense relationship between the living and the dead took different forms of expression. Most famous were the 'Dance of the Dead' paintings which appeared in on the walls of public buildings in Berne and Basle. In Basle the plagues of 1438–39 provided the deadly background for Konrad Witz's mural in the Dominican church in which leading citizens of the city were caught up in the dance of the dead. Witz produced a visual allegory of corruption and moral depravity in Basle. Each of the guilds was shown to be defrauding the people, and no one in the picture pays any attention to the preacher calling on the city to repent. Death is the great seducer and the plague is represented as God's punishment on a city which has abandoned all holiness. It was a devastating social satire in which Witz held a mirror up to Basle society.[43]

More common were the charnel houses in every village, where the bones of the dead would be collected after the flesh had rotted away. Many of these charnel houses were adorned with wall paintings depicting a range of important images: the Grim Reaper, St Christopher, who was believed to protect the faithful from sudden death, a mass being said for the salvation of the Wretched Souls, and the Archangel Michael as the weigher of souls.[44] Cemeteries, where the people believed the living and dead coexisted, were often cast in a pallid light by funerary lamps, giving rise to many ghostly tales. In the central Swiss lands the cult of the Wretched Souls was deeply rooted in popular belief. These souls of the dead were believed to wander among the communities until the people had performed sufficient intercessory prayers and masses were said to relieve them from the torments of purgatory. In moments of particular distress it was thought that dead came from their graves to stand by the living.[45] Such a lively intercourse between the dead and the living found expression throughout the Confederation.

The religious life of the people was interwoven with their environment. In Appenzell festivities surrounded the departure of the herdsmen and their cattle for the mountain pastures in the spring and their return in the autumn. For such people religion was inextricably part of the forces of nature, something which they both feared and understood as forming the essential rhythm of their lives. Change, particularly in matters of religion, made little sense where the church and its rituals explained the world and kept one in touch with one's ancestors. Life was harsh, but not necessarily short. The evidence from cemeteries suggests that there were more elderly people in the fifteenth century than was once thought the case. The mercenary service exacted a terrible toll on young men, women frequently did not survive pregnancy, and plagues made no distinction of gender or age. Many did, however, survive beyond the age of forty, though their bones tell us much about the afflictions which came with age. Gout, arthritis, and the enduring effects of wounds or injuries sustained during a life of labour were all commonplace. In Alpine regions goitres were an especial problem, while cavities ensured that most people in old age had no teeth. As in other parts of Europe, tuberculosis was a major killer.

One of the principal difficulties in mountainous areas was how to bury the dead. Where there was sufficient soil, most bodies were wrapped in a cloth, placed in a shallow grave, and then covered with a layer of chalk to speed putrefaction. In mountain communities the bodies were placed in small stone coffins; only the better-off families began in the fifteenth century to use wooden coffins. The dead of the parish were buried outside the church in an area marked off by a stone wall, erected to keep out the animals. Once the bodies had sufficiently decomposed they were exhumed and the bones were placed in charnel houses. Unbaptised babies were traditionally buried under the eaves of the parish church in a place marked by a simple wooden cross. Popular belief was that the rainwater washing off the roof of the church would provide some relief for those lost souls.

Swiss lands were rich in pilgrimage sites and those most significant were devoted to Mary, the Mother of Christ. The most important place of pilgrimage within the Confederation was the church of Our Lady at Einsiedeln. For the great celebration of *Engelweih* in the jubilee year of 1466 130,000 pilgrims made their way to Einsiedeln to receive a general indulgence. Indulgences offering relief from time in purgatory were especially sought after, and between the thirteenth and sixteenth centuries more than 120 letters offering indulgences to the faithful were sent to inner Swiss states alone. Zurich had a close relationship with Einsiedeln; from the middle of the fifteenth century the magistrates regulated the yearly pilgrimages from the city to the abbey on the Monday and Tuesday following Pentecost. The degree of organisation was remarkable. The officials of the city would gather outside the walls to take a record of who was making the pilgrimage, and twenty-four clergy from the three parish churches (Grossmünster, Fraumünster, and St Peters) were responsible for leading the faithful along the left side of Lake Zurich as they made the thirty-five-mile journey to the Benedictine house. By the early sixteenth century, the number of pilgrims ranged from 1,500 to 1,800 (from a population of 5,000), and according to a civic ordinance men and women were to travel separately.[46] The pilgrims would spend the night at Einsiedeln after having presented their offerings, heard a sermon, and completed their devotions. The city provided gifts (often a candle) for the pilgrims to take with them, and the close bond between Zurich and Einsiedeln became visible with the construction of a devotional chapel built from the largesse of the faithful. The following day the pilgrims would begin the return journey, no longer divided by gender, arriving by ships in Zurich, where they were joyously greeted by the rest of the city with banners, songs, and crosses.

On the Wednesday following the pilgrimage to Einsiedeln another procession was held in Zurich, this time led by one of the abbesses, to honour the civic patron saints, Felix and Regula. The gold and silver chalices, monstrances, and reliquaries from all the churches of the city were carried in procession along with sixty golden candles provided by the guilds. Along the route the city erected four marquees in which the Augustinians, Dominicans, and Franciscans celebrated mass, one after another. In the fourth marquee was wonderful music as a high mass was celebrated at which a representative of one of the mendicant orders would preach. Afterwards there was an enormous celebration in honour of Felix and Regula at which the citizens, clergy, and members of the religious orders would feast on bread, wine, and fish.[47]

Marian devotion was widespread across the Confederation; in Oberbüren in Bernese territory, an image of the Virgin was believed to be able to bring dead children back to life. Mothers would place their dead babies before the image between a burning coal and a candle. They would then place a feather in the mouth of the infant. Should the warm air cause the feather to move upwards, the child was then baptised. It was believed that the image had brought the child back to life, if only briefly, to be baptised. The child was then freed from the stain of original sin and the parents comforted. So popular was the shrine at Oberbüren that it brought in an income of over 25,000 pounds. The location was developed and in 1512 it received its own letter of indulgence.

Other important places of pilgrimage were the hermit's hole of St Beatus (at the Lake of Thun), the sanctuaries of St Lucius in Chur, St Placidus in Disentis, the Verena church in Zurzach and the shrine of the Theban legion in St Moritz, near Lake Geneva.[48] The cult of the Theban legion was very strong in the Confederation. In 290 when the Emperor Maximian ordered a legion of Christian soldiers to worship pagan gods the legion refused. It withdrew to what is now St Moritz in the Wallis, named after the commander, where every tenth man was condemned to be executed. The legion refused to obey until all were executed, including Maurice. In medieval art Maurice assumed the shape of a Christian knight wearing a martyr's crown.

During the fifteenth century the cell of the saintly Niklaus von Flüe became one of the most beloved places of pilgrimage. Each area of the Confederation had its own patron saints and local places of pilgrimage. In Bernese lands the people travelled to Würzbrunnen to honour St Wolfgang, to Einigen for the Archangel Michael, and to Reutigen for Our Lady.

Religious life in the Confederation in the late medieval period was characterised by a number of traits. In both the cities and rural areas the institutional church faced serious challenges to its authority. For much of the fifteenth century the urban magistrates had sought to roll back clerical privileges, to usurp church courts, and to claim ecclesiastical property within the walls of the city. In the rural areas, as Peter Blickle and others have demonstrated, there was a powerful trend towards communal control of the church in order to ensure the provision of spiritual care. The hierarchical church was virtually powerless to counter either of these movements. Nevertheless, beyond the institutional stasis the rural and urban communities were characterised by vibrant local traditions in which popular devotion thrived. The wealthy families and guilds decorated the churches with their largesse, large numbers of churches were built, and people of all social levels flooded into services, venerated relics, prayed to saints, and went on pilgrimages. At the same time they had little difficulty detesting indolent and rapacious clergy or responding in outrage when they felt defrauded.

The Swiss Reformation did not emerge from a religious world in decline. The Confederation was a patchwork of vibrant religious cultures replete with their traditions of pilgrimage, veneration of local saints, and worship. The clergy were integrated into the communities in which they lived; for the most part they raised children alongside the other families in the village. There is no evidence that the people complained about the mass or confession; their consciences were not unduly burdened by the demands of the church that they be absolved of their sins. The people participated in a myriad of festivities, increasingly made wills, and bequeathed much of their worldly goods to the parish churches. Churches were being built across the Confederation as the Swiss participated in the ecclesiastical building boom of the late Middle Ages.

It was hardly an Elysian world, but historians are confronted with the conundrum that the late medieval church does not offer an easy explanation for the Reformation. The people were naturally critical of the clergy, who were part of the declining feudal system; they resented the payments that they had to make to monastic and ecclesiastical landlords. But what they most objected to was supporting a local priest who did not perform his duties, who did not baptise their babies (or demanded payment for the sacrament), attend to the sick, or bury their dead. The huge appetite for religion demanded pastoral care. Anticlericalism was largely specifically directed against those who abused their office – it did not exist as an abstract idea. The Swiss would have remained Catholic had not a small group of men succeeded in persuading them that the old religion was wrong, that their zealous observances were in vain because they were contrary to the Word of God. It was an argument which had a tremendous impact on account of its conjunction with a range of other issues: the result was a religious and emotional explosion which succeeded, in some areas, in overturning the church. The reformers succeeded in redirecting religious energy and devotion away from Catholic worship and rituals to their understanding of the Word of God. It was a harsh and often brutal process, and the primary weapon was preaching, requiring remarkable men who could communicate and negotiate. In the end, it was a minority movement which converted only a minority of the population, but that was enough, for if the right people were persuaded, that was all that mattered. The vast majority of people made certain demands of their religion: namely, that it provide pastoral care and ensure their salvation. Ritual, ecclesiology, and doctrine were not enough, except at certain moments, to cause most people to oppose the established religion. The reformers may have been disappointed by the half-hearted manner in which the people adopted their ideas, but they also recognised that the people were not resisting them.

Humanists

Although men imbued with the spirit of humanism could be found in religious houses and cities across the Confederation the centre of humanist learning was Basle. The reasons for this are several and have already been indicated. Basle, perched on the Rhine, looked northward to Germany. It was a wealthy city of craftsmen and families able to act as patrons. Its university, although by no means a leading institution, brought scholars and students to the city from across Europe. No other Swiss city could boast of Basle's international status. Further, Basle was a centre of printing. Paper had been manufactured in the city since 1435 and there were enough craftsmen in the city who could do type-cutting and book-binding.[49] Basle, as a centre of trade, had important links to the major cities of Europe, and ready capital. Thus by the end of the fifteenth century it was a printing centre. Between 1475 and 1490 three men who would be central to the development of Basle printing settled in the city: Johannes Amerbach, Johannes Petri, and Johannes Froben – known as the 'three Hanses'. By 1501 there were seventy book-printers in Basle and the industry remained guild-free because printing was regarded as an art in the service of learning.[50]

Most of the humanist scholars in Basle came from elsewhere, and the number of Swiss scholars was few. Hans Guggisberg has noted that until 1510 most of the leading humanists in the city were closely connected with the university and were advocates of pedagogical and religious reform.[51] The major flowering of Basle humanism came in the period following 1510 and centred around such figures as Beatus Rhenanus and Heinrich Loriti Glareanus from Glarus. Later others made their way down the Rhine to the city: from Swabia came Johannes Oecolampadius, from Rouffach Konrad Pellikan, and from Hagenau Wolfgang Capito. At the centre of the city was the humanist-minded bishop of Basle, Christoph von Utenheim. In 1516 Erasmus wrote of the Basle scholars in a letter to the Schlettstadt schoolteacher Johannes Sapidus:

> They all know Latin, they all know Greek, most of them know Hebrew too; one is an expert historian, another an experienced theologian; one is skilled in the mathematics, one is a keen antiquary, another a jurist ... I have certainly never before had the luck to live in such a gifted company. And to say nothing of that, how open-hearted they are, how happy, how well they get on together! You would say they had only one soul.[52]

Erasmus arrived in Basle in August 1514 and stayed largely because of the Froben printing house, which he believed to have the most beautiful Greek type that he had seen.[53] Thus he decided to have his Greek New Testament, and his edition of the works of Jerome, printed in Basle. Erasmus was at the centre of group of scholars in the city who worked on his editions; the atmosphere was relaxed and Erasmus enjoyed Europe-wide fame. He relished working with Froben, and was godfather to one of the printer's sons, while at the same time he moulded a generation of young scholars with his ideas of textual scholarship and the 'philosophy of Christ'. The enduring influence of Erasmus on the Swiss Reformation was set during the years 1514 to 1525, although he was away in England and the Netherlands between 1516 and 1521. When Erasmus returned to Basle in 1521 things had begun to change; he was locked in a battle with Luther, whose works were now being printed in large numbers in Basle. Luther's message deeply divided the Basle circle of humanists and things became bitter, particularly when Zwingli and then Oecolampadius fell out with their erstwhile mentor.[54]

The humanist movement in Basle was limited to a small number of learned figures, some of whom taught at the university or served as jurists, but who for the most part lived away from the principal commercial activities of the city. Erasmus, for example, lived in dread of the filth and stench of the streets, and when he had to go outside he did so with a handkerchief over his mouth and nose. Nevertheless, printing and Erasmus's arrival in Basle shaped the intellectual and spiritual dimensions of the Swiss Reformation. Not only did Erasmus give rise to the humanist Christian culture central to the thought of Zwingli and the other Swiss reformers, but his sodality of scholars with himself at the centre provided the model for the Zurich Reformation. The circle of like-minded scholars, churchmen, politicians, and printers which Zwingli developed in Zurich at the beginning of the 1520s was fashioned after Erasmus's example in Basle.

Soldiers

The period from 1475 until 1515 marked the zenith of Swiss military achievements. The Burgundian army was destroyed and the Swiss held the upper hand in the affairs of the upper Rhine, where French and Habsburg interests were concentrated. Their reputation greatly enhanced by famous victories, the Swiss were courted by all the major powers, who were desperate for infantrymen. Formerly, foreign governments seeking Swiss soldiers had to apply to the diet. If permission was granted negotiations were carried out and the levy was shared among the member states. As John McCormack has written, however, this procedure was ignored by both foreign states and the Confederates; when a request was denied foreign powers would simply send recruiters into the villages of the rural areas, where there was no shortage of volunteers.[55] The unauthorized recruitment of Swiss soldiers peaked with the French invasion of Italy in 1494, where strict prohibitions on the participation of the Swiss was blatantly flaunted by the presence of 8,000 Confederate troops in Lyon. There was never any shortage of young men willing to enlist as the recruiters made their way through the villages. Politics played a very small role, these recruits were quite prepared to enter the service of anyone with pockets deep enough to pay their wages. Like modern-day sports stars, well-known mercenaries would attract a considerable following among the youth of their region, and foreign powers were shrewd in their employment of such celebrities. The whole system was fuelled by bribery; the large families in the cities received huge amounts of money for their co-operation. In Zurich in 1526 one of the most affluent men, Jakob Grebel, was in the pay of Pope Clement VII to the tune of 4,000 crowns, a huge sum, though he apparently wanted more. Grebel's son was Konrad, founder of the Anabaptist movement in the city. It was not just the soldiers and patricians who were benefiting; officials, from the smallest villages to the greater urban centres, could be easily persuaded with some cash to avert their eyes when the recruiters arrived. Recruitment during the fifteenth century was largely unchecked. It was not until the early sixteenth century that legislation was passed punishing with imprisonment or confiscation of property those who violated agreements on troop numbers. The effect was minimal. The porous borders of the Confederation did nothing to stop the flow of young men from one state into another when opportunity beckoned. The extent of the problem is brought into relief when we consider that during the Italian wars at the end of the fifteenth century about 20 per cent of the Swiss adult male population crossed the Alps in the service of the French Army.[56] By the end of the fifteenth century the Swiss states recognised that it was impossible to regulate the hiring of mercenaries, and soon a distinction was made between regular military contingents of the states, which swore to obey the Confederate military ordinances and were paid by the states, and the free bands of mercenaries which organised themselves.[57] In any case, the results were disastrous. The Confederation was stripped of labour and the social disruption was enormous; a problem compounded by the return of mercenaries riddled with disease.

There was little loyalty among the Swiss to any one side in the Italian wars of the early sixteenth century, and the Swiss continually exasperated the French with their contentiousness. During the ten-year agreement between the French and the Swiss which ran from 1499 to 1509 cracks began to appear in the plaster. Opponents were developing effective tactics against the squares of Swiss pikemen which had previously carried all before them. The development of arquebusiers made these formations increasingly vulnerable. More importantly, the French proved unreliable paymasters. Anti-French sentiments spread as soldiers and officials alike clamoured for what they were owed. The French had shown only contempt for the laws of the Confederation, and this had been possible as long as they could continue to bribe, but when the money ran out the Swiss grew angry. The Swiss had a reputation among contemporaries as the most cynical of soldiers, loyal only to those who could afford their services.

The growing anti-French feelings which blew across the Confederation in 1510 were managed by Cardinal Mathäu Schiner, the papal delegate to the Confederation. Schiner succeeded in negotiating an alliance between the Confederation and the Holy See in 1510; this was followed a year later by the entrance of the Swiss into the Holy League against France. The Swiss were to achieve one more great victory at Novara, but the message on the wall was not encouraging. French artillery had taken a terrible toll and the German *Landsknechte* of the French army had proved themselves a match for the Swiss. Effective use of cavalry was now starting to undermine the usefulness of pikemen. All in all, the Swiss had not really adapted to the changing forms of warfare, and their effortless domination of the battlefield was at an end.

The price for these endless wars proved too much for the Confederation. The social disruption and disorder caused by the mercenary service was pulling the Swiss apart. Despite their costly wars against the French in Italy, French recruiters continued to make their way through Swiss villages. The Swiss nightmare that their sons would find themselves on opposing sides of the battlefield was soon realised. The Confederation was riven by the question of what to do about France. In 1513 the Swiss joined the Holy League in an invasion of France, but they were soon bought off by the Treaty of Dijon, which involved the payment of huge war indemnities to the Swiss. France may have been the enemy, but at the crucial moment the Swiss had shown themselves more interested in money than principle. Later in 1515 Francis I was able to persuade the Swiss to abandon Milan and their lands south of the Alps in return for money. This led to outrage at home as many believed that the Swiss leaders had sold out to the French king, and Cardinal Schiner set about raising an army. In September 1515 the Swiss and French armies clashed at Marignano.

Marignano was a spectacular defeat for the Swiss. About six thousand Confederates lay dead, despite their amazing bravery and daring. The Swiss infantry had been defeated by an integrated use of infantry, artillery, and cavalry. It was the last battle fought by a Swiss army on foreign soil. All Swiss plans for territorial expansion evaporated and the policy of neutrality became the only way forward.

The effects of Marignano upon the Swiss have been frequently discussed. Decades of foreign wars had exhausted the Confederation, stripped it of manpower and thoroughly corrupted its political systems. Foreign powers continued to need Swiss infantry, but the myth of the invincible Swiss soldier had vanished into the mist, replaced by a reputation for unbridled venality. The Swiss were bitter and divided. The growth of the Confederation in the fourteenth and fifteenth centuries had been made possible by the weakness of its neighbours. Now that Europe was firmly ruled by the rival Habsburg and Valois dynasties, there was no place for Swiss expansion. There are powerful arguments that the Swiss did not make the most of their opportunities in the fifteenth century, but such opportunities were now gone. From 1515 the Swiss had to come to terms with the havoc wreaked by foreign wars and their social, political, and religious consequences.

Notes

1 Andreas Suter, 'Regionale politische Kulturen von Protest und Widerstand im Spätmittelalter und in der frühen Neuzeit: Die Schweizerische Eidgenossenschaft als Beispiel', *Geschichte und Gesellschaft*, 21 (1995), pp. 161–194.

2 See the essay of Carlo Moos, 'Freiheit für sich, Herrschaft über die Andern: Die Schweiz in der Frühen Neuzeit', *Wiener Beiträge zur Geschichte der Neuzeit*, 21 (1994), pp. 142–162.

3 Richard Feller and Edgar Bonjour, *Geschchichtsschreibung der Schweiz*, 2 vols (Basle and Stuttgart, 1962), I, pp. 100–101.

4 Randolf C. Head, 'William Tell and his Comrades: Association and Fraternity in the Propaganda of Fifteenth- and Sixteenth-Century Switzerland', *The Journal of Modern History*, 67 (1995), pp. 527–557.

5 L.R. Poos, 'The Historical Demography of Renaissance Europe: Recent Research and Current Issues', *Renaissance Quarterly*, 42 (1989), pp. 794–811.

6 A. Largiadèr, *Bürgermeister Rudolf Brun und die Zürcher Revolution von 1336* (Zurich, 1936); on the Brun revolution, see K. Dändliker, *Geschichte der Stadt und des Kantons Zurich* (Zurich, 1908), I, pp. 126–145.

7 Quoted in E. Bonjour, H.S. Offler, and G.R. Potter, *A Short History of Switzerland* (Oxford, 1952), p. 101.

8 John Casparis, 'The Swiss Mercenary System: Labor Emigration from the Semiperiphery', *Review (Fernand Braudel Center)* 5 (1982), pp. 593–642.

9 Bruno Koch, 'Kronenfresser und Deutsche Franzosen: Zur Sozial Geschichte der Reisläuferei aus Bern, Solothurn und Biel zur Zeit der Mailänderkriege', *Schweizerische Zeitschrift für Geschichte*, 46 (1996), pp. 151–184.

10 See the fascinating article, Dennis E. Showalter, 'Caste, Skill, and Training: The Evolution of Cohesion in European Armies from the Middle Ages to the Sixteenth Century', *The Journal of Military History*, 57 (1993), pp. 407–430, esp. pp. 423–426.

11 Douglas Miller and G.A. Embleton, *The Swiss at War 1300–1500* (London, 1979), pp. 3–6.

12 Werner Meyer, *Hirsebrei und Hellebarde. Auf dem Spuren des mittelalterischen Lebens in der Schweiz* (rpt. Freiburg-im-Breisgau, 1986), pp. 118–120.

13 Hans Berger, *Der Alte Zürichkrieg im Rahmen der europäischen Politik. Ein Beitrag zur 'Aussenpolitik' Zürichs in der ersten Hälfte des 15. Jahrhunderts* (Zurich, 1978), pp. 105–197.

14 Peter Moraw, 'Reich, König und Eidgenossen im späten Mittelalter', *Zeitschrift für Historische Forschung*, 6 (1979), pp. 390.

15 Feller and Bonjour, *Geschichtsschreibung*, I, 39–45.

16 Ibid., p. 42.

17 See Emil Walder, 'Zur Enstehungsgeschichte des Stanser Verkommnisses und des Bundes der VII Orte mit Freiburg und Solothurn von 1481', *Schweizerische Zeitschrift für Geschichte*, 32 (1982), pp. 263–292.

18 Pirmin Meier, *Ich Bruder Klaus von Flüe. Eine Geschichte aus der inneren Schweiz. Ein biographischer Diskurs* (Zurich, 1997); also, Peter Ochsenbein, 'Frömmigkeit eines Laien: Zur Gebetspraxis des Nikolaus von Flüe', *Historisches Jahrbuch*, 104 (1984), pp. 289–308.

19 A very helpful article on this point is Claudius Sieber-Lehmann, '"Teutsche Nation" und Eidgesnossenschaft. Der Zusammenhang zwischen Türken- und Burgunderkriegen', *Historische Zeitschrift*, 253 (1991), pp. 561–602.

20 Bonjour, Offler and Potter, *Switzerland*, p. 137.

21 Sabine de Ziegler, ' L'Alliance perpétuelle entre les Confédérés Suisses et le Roi de France–1', *Revue des Deux Mondes*, 6 (1984), pp. 553–561, part 2, 7 (1984), pp. 80–84.

22 Albert Winkler, 'The Swabian War of 1499: 500 Years since Switzerland's Last War of Independence', *Swiss American Historical Society Review*, 35 (1999) pp. 3–25.

23 Niklaus Bütikofer, 'Konfliktregulierung auf den Eidgenössischen Tagsatzungen des 15. und 16. Jahrhunderts', *Parliaments, Estates & Representation*, 11 (1991), pp. 103–115.

24 The most important work on the Mandated Territories is Randolph C. Head, 'Shared Lordship, Authority and Administration: The Exercise of Dominion in the *Gemeine Herrschaften* of the Swiss Confederation, 1417–1600', *Central European History*, 30 (1997), pp. 489–512.

25 Anne-Marie Duber, 'Zur "Reiselust" der Handwerksgesellen in Luzern/Schweiz: Wandel im Selbstverständnis einer Durchgangsposition vom 15. zum 18. Jahrhundert', *Jahrbuch für Regionalgeschichte und Landeskunde*, 18 (1991–92), pp. 65–76.

26 Oskar Vasella, *Reform und Reformation in der Schweiz* (Münster, 1958), pp. 26ff.

27 Bruce Gordon, *Clerical Discipline and the Rural Reformation* (Berne, 1992), pp. 28–29.

28 Carl Pfaff, 'Pfarrei und Pfarreileben. Ein Beitrag zur spätmittelalterlichen Kirchengeschichte', in Hansjakob Achermann, Josef Brülisauer, and Peter Hoppe (eds), *Innerschweiz und frühe Eidgenossenschaft*, 2 vols (Lucerne, 1991), I, p. 239.

29 Ibid., p. 242.

30 E. Bonjour, *Die Universität Basel* (Basle, 1960), p. 78.

31 Dorothea Roth, *Die mittelalterliche Predigttheorie und das Manuale Curatorum des Johann Ulrich Surgant* (Basel and Stuttgart, 1956).

32 Vasella, *Reform und Reformation*, pp. 30–31.

33 Ibid., pp. 32–34.

34 See especially Peter Blickle, *Communal Reformation: The Quest for Salvation in Sixteenth-century Germany*, trans. Thomas Dunlap (New Jersey and London , 1992).

35 Randolf C. Head, *Early Modern Democracy in the Grisons* (Cambridge, 1995), p. 24.

36 Achermann et al., *Innerschweiz*, p. 257.

37 On this see the fine article of Francis B. Brevart, 'The German Volkskalender of the Fifteenth Century', *Speculum*, 63 (1988), pp. 312–342.

Brevart makes use of a 1454 calendar held in the Zentralbibliothek in Zurich.

38 K. Guggisberg, *Bernische Kirchengeschichte* (Berne, 1958), p. 43.

39 Kathrin Tremp-Utz, 'Welche Sprache spricht die Jungfrau Maria? Sprachgrenzen und Sprachkenntnisse im bernischen Jetzerhandel (1507–1509)', *Schweizerische Zeitschrift für Geschichte*, 38(3) (1988), pp. 221–249.

40 Ibid., p. 40.

41 H.J. Schroeder (ed.), *Diciplinary Decrees of the General Councils* (Rockford, IL, 1937), pp. 259–260.

42 W. David Myers, *'Poor Sinning Folk' Confession and Conscience in Counter-Reformation Germany* (Ithaca, NY, 1996), pp. 27–60.

43 Hellmut Rosenfeld, *Der mittelalterliche Totentanz. Enstehung – Entwicklung – Bedeutung* (Cologne and Vienna, 1974), pp. 103–117.

44 Peter Felder, 'Memento Mori. Art and the Cult of the Dead in Central Switzerland', in Heinz Horat (ed.), *1000 Years of Swiss Art* (New York, 1992), pp. 130–134.

45 Ibid., p. 130.

46 Magdalen Bless-Grabher, 'Veränderungen im kirchlichen Bereich 1350–1520', in Niklaus Flüeler and Marianne Flüeler-Grauwiler (eds), *Geschichte des Kantons Zürich. Frühzeit bis Spätmittelalter* (Zurich, 1995), pp. 445–446.

47 Ibid., p. 441.

48 Meyer, *Hirsebrei und Hellebarde*, pp. 242–243.

49 Hans R. Guggisberg, *Basel in the Sixteenth Century* (St Louis, 1982), p. 8.

50 Ibid., p. 10.

51 Ibid., p. 13.

52 *The Collected Works of Erasmus* (Toronto, 1976), vol. 3, p. 244. Quoted from Guggisberg, *Basel*, p. 14.

53 On Erasmus's arrival in Basle, see James D. Tracy, 'Erasmus Becomes a German', *Renaissance Quarterly*, 21 (1968), pp. 281–288.

54 Kurt Maeder, *Die Via Media in der Schweizerischen Reformation* (Zurich, 1970), pp. 68–71.

55 John McCormack, *One Million Mercenaries. Swiss Soldiers in the Armies of the World* (London, 1993), p. 39.

56 Ibid., pp. 41–42.

57 Miller and Embleton, *The Swiss at War*, p. 31.

2
Zwingli and Zurich

Zurich

The defeat at Marignano brought a sea-change within Zurich, and with the return of the straggling soldiers the disparate voices calling for the abolition of the mercenary service swelled to an angry chorus. On 15 December 1515 a band of inhabitants from Zurich's rural territories marched on the city during a visit by the bishop of Constance. The bishop and Bürgermeister were besieged by the angry mob which refused to release them until a guarantee was given that those responsible for recruiting soldiers would be punished. Further, the crowd demanded financial compensation for losses suffered on account of Swiss participation in the Italian wars. The mood in the countryside was ugly, blackened by resentment against the urban elites and their exploitation of the rural communities.

The humiliation and fury caused by the defeat at Marignano dominated Swiss politics from 1515, yet behind the outrage and vexation lay at least some self-awareness that the Confederates had connived in their own downfall: a recognition of the unpleasant truth that with the military triumphs of the fifteenth century the members of the Confederation at all levels were implicated in the squalid business of selling young men to foreign paymasters. Money for soldiers had corrupted every office, and it was only the shame of a catastrophic defeat that had galvanised opinion against an evil likened by many to prostitution. Zurich in particular witnessed the growth of a strong isolationist movement which culminated in the 1521 refusal to renew the mercenary contract with the king of France. Opposition to mercenary service ran especially deep in the rural areas, a worry for the foreign recruiters and the patrician families as around 90 per cent of the hired soldiers came from the countryside. A survey

(*Volksanfrage*) of the rural subjects in Zurich in 1521 revealed that there was deep-seated opposition to involvement in foreign wars.[1] For the rural dwellers, mercenaries were part of a much broader problem; the economic situation was miserable and many young men were without work and living in poverty. Social unrest, violence in the villages, and drinking were all closely connected, as one sees in the mandates concerning mercenaries and poor relief issued by the council in the early 1520s.[2]

The delicate relations between the city and its rural subjects were rooted in the manner in which Zurich had developed during the fifteenth century. Once most of the rural territories along the lake had been acquired by purchase, the city began from 1470 to assert its authority by prohibiting artisan work in the country and by privileging manufactured goods from Zurich. The craft-dominated city sought to regulate rural agriculture and industry by insisting that all goods and animals be offered for sale either in Zurich or in a place under its jurisdiction which enjoyed a market charter. Fields and forests were strictly regulated and farmers were forbidden from turning unused land into pasture, as the city wished to retain a supply of cheap grain.[3] The results of this policy were to keep grain prices artificially low and to depress both the farm economy and rural industry.

Zurich with its subject lands held a population of about 55,000 souls, of whom about 5,000 lived within the city walls.[4] Following the upheavals of the fifteenth century it had become a guild city with a large and small council dominated by the twelve guilds.[5] The large council was more influential, for it exercised the rights to levy taxes, conduct wars, choose the Bürgermeister, and select the heads of the rural districts.[6] The proportion of clergy to laity was not especially striking for a middling city; of the five hundred clergy in Zurich just over half lived in the city, with the rest serving as parish priests or attached to one of the religious houses. Dominant among the ecclesiastical institutions in Zurich was the chapter of the Grossmünster. With twenty-four canons, thirty-two chaplains and a stipendiary priest (*Leutpriester*), the chapter was the wealthiest church body in the diocese of Constance, possessing the rights of patronage to many benefices in the rural areas. Its canons exercised considerable influence within the city, where their prebends (the stipends) and houses were supported by the tithes paid by rural parishes.

During the fifteenth century about three-quarters of the canons had been natives of Zurich, generally the scions of patrician families. Content with good living and influence, the canons expressed little interest in either church reform or the development of humanism. Zurich was without a university, and the intellectual and religious movements that had influenced Basle during the conciliar period

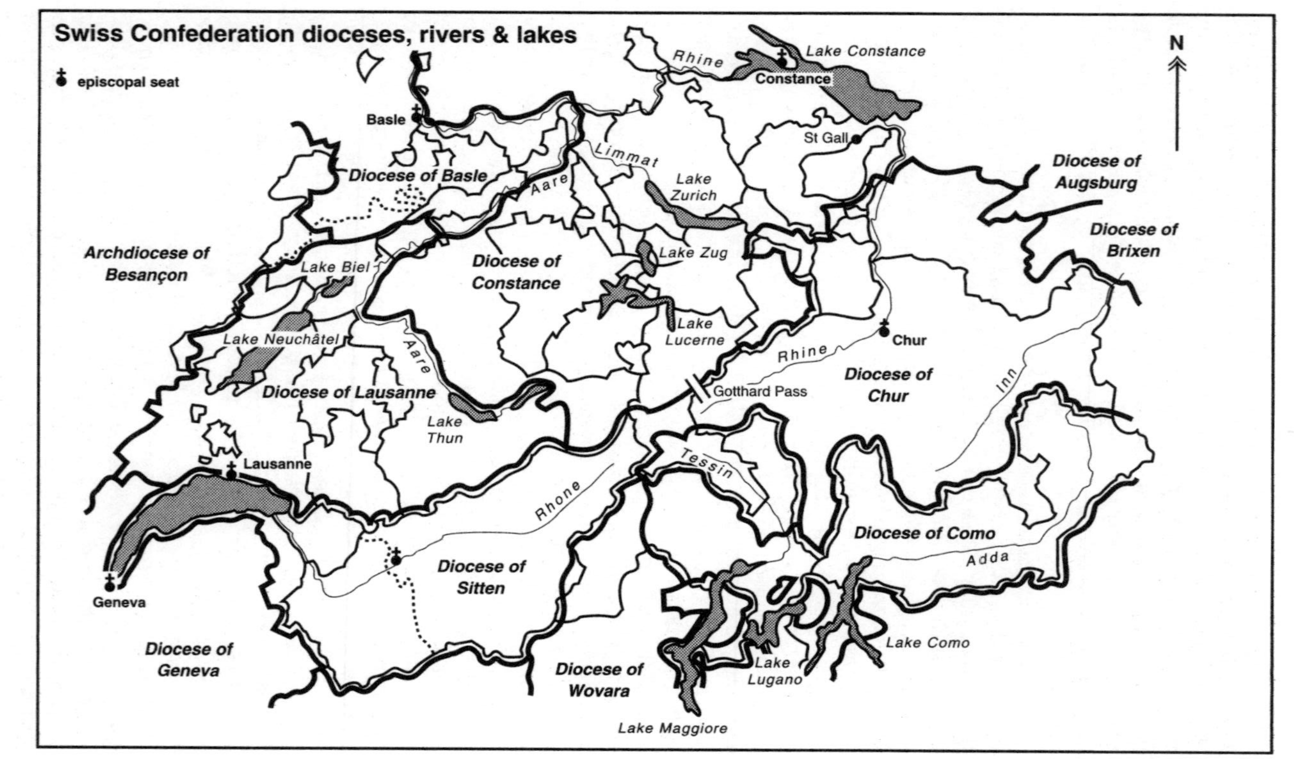
Swiss Confederation dioceses, rivers & lakes
episcopal seat
N
Basle
Constance
Lake Constance
Rhine
St Gall
Limmat
Aare
Lake Zurich
Lake Zug
Lake Lucerne
Diocese of Basle
Diocese of Augsburg
Diocese of Brixen
Archdiocese of Besançon
Diocese of Constance
Lake Biel
Lake Neuchâtel
Aare
Diocese of Lausanne
Lake Thun
Chur
Rhine
Diocese of Chur
Inn
Gotthard Pass
Tessin
Lausanne
Rhone
Diocese of Sitten
Diocese of Como
Adda
Geneva
Diocese of Geneva
Diocese of Wovara
Lake Lugano
Lake Como
Lake Maggiore

found no purchase in a city concerned primarily with the consolidation of land and power. The winds of change did, however, began to blow from the early years of the sixteenth century, when more non-Zurichers were elected as canons, such as the two humanists Conrad Hofmann (elected 1502 *Leutpriester* and canon) of Bremgarten and Erhard Battmann (elected *Leutpriester* 1511) who helped prepare the way for Zwingli's appointment in December 1518.[7]

Zwingli

It is impossible to explain the development of the Zurich Reformation without Huldrych Zwingli. Nothing about Zurich, its urban or rural conditions made it more or less propitious for a reformation than any other middling city of the empire. Indeed, the city's close relationship with Rome suggests that the aggressive political leaders of Zurich had little to gain by a religious revolution. The decisive element was the personality and preaching of Zwingli. Baptised 'Ulrich', Zwingli adopted the name 'Huldrych' ('rich in grace') as a sign of his prophetic confidence. A charismatic figure who possessed the ability to draw others to him and to shape public opinion, Zwingli was a humanist who embraced many of the skills cultivated by his mentor Erasmus: knowledge of ancient languages, familiarity with the classics, a commitment to learning and a burning zeal to reform religion.[8] He was an indefatigable worker whose energy for study was rewarded with an impressive knowledge of the Church Fathers and the medieval scholastics.[9] Quick-witted and a lover of word-play, there was a poet in Zwingli, and he loved music. One need only look to his 1525 liturgy for the Lord's Supper to sense his understanding of the power of language and drama. He was also, crucially, a shrewd politician, a key to both his rise and fall. Above all he was a powerful preacher who could reach and move the people in their own language. Yet, if such personal qualities enabled Zwingli to emerge as a religious leader, they also masked the most serious weakness of the Zurich Reformation: its utter dependence upon the character and thought of one man. Zwingli constructed a new Reformed order held together by his ability to keep magistrates, laity and clergy on side. When he erred, as he did disastrously in the months before the Second Kappel War of 1531, it was catastrophic.

Zwingli was already well known in Zurich as a preacher at the great Benedictine house at Einsiedeln, where he had been since 1516.[10] Einsiedeln was the most important place of pilgrimage for the Zurichers, and it was during the patronal festival of *Engelweih*, which commemorated the consecration of a church at Einsiedeln by an angel, that many, including influential politicians and businessmen, heard

Zwingli's preaching for the first time.[11] What made Zwingli especially appealing to the political masters of Zurich were his positions on crucial matters of the day: he articulated unequivocal opposition to both the French alliance and to pensions and mercenary service. Not all, however, within the city shared these opinions, and there were influential men who sought to block his appointment as *Leutpriester*.[12] The problem of pensions and gift-giving has recently been examined by Valentin Groeber in a groundbreaking study of the effects of the culture of pensions and gifts in early sixteenth-century Basle.[13] He contrasts the case of Hans Waldmann of Zurich, whose fall from power was precipitated by accusations of corruption and of receiving bribes from the Austrians, with the willingness of the elite in Basle to receive gifts and money from interested parties. The distinction between gifts and bribes was invisible, and the ready exchange of money was integral to Swiss social and economic life by the early sixteenth century. Zwingli is famous for his opposition to the pension system in the Confederation, but it was not a clearcut issue, as Groebner demonstrates. Money and gifts were part of the political discourse, and the line between legitimate practice and bribery was hotly debated. Thus for many Zwingli's preaching seemed extreme and intemperate.

There appeared to be sufficient grounds to achieve this end.[14] A rumour circulated in Zurich that Zwingli had had a relationship with a prostitute. The accusation was damaging, but not fatal, as the sexual proclivities of a priest did not raise many eyebrows, especially in a diocese where the bishop had a concubine. Zwingli, however, was deeply penitent, and in rather tortuous language he essentially admitted to the affair, avowing great shame and an overwhelming sense of guilt. The matter, however, went nowhere and Zwingli was elected to the position of stipendiary priest (*Leutpriester*) in the Grossmünster on 11 December 1518. The position required him to preach and carry out pastoral duties.

The years of study at Einsiedeln had prepared Zwingli for his position at the Grossmünster. The great folio volumes of St Augustine, as well as the works of Jerome, Ambrose, and Origen (a favourite of Erasmus) came with him from Einsiedeln, as did the works of Luther, recently printed in Basle. Zwingli's marginal notes and annotations bespeak countless hours of careful study based, largely, on critical methods developed by Erasmus.[15] It was also to Erasmus that Zwingli owed the inspiration for his intense interest in Paul; it was this study of Pauline anthropology, as well as his growing familiarity with Augustine's doctrine of predestination, that seems to have shaped Zwingli's early evangelical thought. Historians have sought, largely in vain, for a decisive 'breakthrough', a moment when Zwingli embraced the Reformation. Yet for Zwingli there was no 'tower experience', or, if there was, he has chosen not to let us know about it. Rather, Zwingli's road to evangelical thought was paved with a different type of stone.[16] Like most churchmen of his day Zwingli had received a scholastic education and was well versed in the writings of the medieval theologians, and he would continue to draw from their thought when necessary. As a young priest in Basle he had come under the influence of the pastorally minded reformer Johann Ulrich Surgant, who taught Zwingli a good deal about liturgy, prayer, and the spiritual needs of the people.[17] Erasmus had taught Zwingli to read scripture and the Fathers, and from long hours in his study Zwingli came to certain conclusions about the nature of God's relationship to humanity. To this we must reckon the impact of Luther's early writings, with their lucid articulation of justification by faith alone.[18] Finally, Zwingli's own experiences of the hideousness of war, the moral turpitude brought on by the mercenary service, and the venality of the church were fundamental in shaping his view of God and true religion.[19] In short, attempts to label Zwingli as a humanist, a rationalist, or anything else are facile. Like most men of his age, Zwingli drew water from many different wells. He came to advocate the principle of *sola scriptura*, but the lens through which he read the Bible was ground from a mixture of humanism and scholasticism, of politics and personal experience.

Beginnings of the movement

In the two years after his appointment in 1519 Zwingli's growing religious consciousness was displayed from the pulpit, where his hard-hitting sermons decried all manner of moral and spiritual failure. Famously, he declared shortly after arriving in Zurich that he would no longer preach from the pericope, the lectionary of biblical readings, but would begin with the first chapter of Matthew's Gospel and work through the whole text, genealogies and all. The text was to be treated as a whole, not only in selected parts, for every word of scripture, Zwingli held, issued from the mouth of God. Zwingli's inspiration for this approach to the exposition of the Bible, known as *lectio continua*, came from the fourth-century Church Father John Chrysostom, but the influence of Erasmus was considerable. The evidence for Zwingli's early sermons is sketchy, and for the most part historians are dependent on second-hand accounts recorded by Leo Jud and Kaspar Megander. What we do know, however, is that the core of his message was repentance and correction of life.[20]

There was, however, another side to Zwingli's preaching which was more incendiary. From the pulpit he took on the 'enemies of the

Gospel' and named them. They were priests, monks and even bishops, whose adherence to the material rewards of the church blinded them to the spiritual nature of God. Those who fell most frequently under the lash were the mendicants – Dominicans and Franciscans. Zwingli preached a faith wholly centred on Christ, and he employed biblical texts to remind his audience of the prophecies of the Old Testament and of their fulfilment in Christ.

In the autumn of 1520 the papal legate Antonio Pucci, attending a Confederate diet in Baden, demanded of the Swiss that they make public the papal ban on Martin Luther and forbid the publication and circulation of his books among the clergy. This placed the cities of Zurich, Berne, and Basle in a difficult situation, as the papacy wanted to know how they would respond to this decree. Zurich was, for the moment, able to get off the hook. Her pro-papal, anti-French tradition meant that Rome had come to rely upon the city's largesse. The response from Zurich in November 1520 declared the magistrates' desire to permit preaching from scripture without 'Lutheran' teachings. As in many other cities caught up in the swell of evangelical preaching, the magistrates in Zurich and Berne had little understanding of the theological issues involved and were extremely reticent about allowing themselves to become entangled in matters they regarded as belonging to the theologians. The preaching mandates of the early 1520s did not signal the willingness of the magistrates to accept the Reformation; they were rather naïve attempts to separate Gospel preaching from the heretical 'Lutheran' doctrines. The theologically illiterate magistrates were caught between the evangelical preachers and their supporters in the guilds, on the one hand, and influential opponents of the Reformation, both internal and external, on the other.[21]

Unsurprisingly, the mercenary service and war loomed large in Zwingli's sermons of 1520–21, and he compared the French and papal agents who recruited in the villages to the devil beguiling Eve in the Garden of Eden. In contrast to these corrupt servants of worldly princes, he opined, stood the virtuous Swiss youth, descended from their heroic forefathers who had fought to free the Confederation from feudal lords. In taking on the mercenary system Zwingli was directing his words against the establishment: the wealth brought in by the mercenary service was staggering; in 1497, for example, 3,104 crowns were paid to Zurich for mercenaries, from which 2,000 went directly to the treasury of the city while the rest was divided among the council members.[22] Nevertheless the effect of Zwingli's campaign was seen in the clear opposition of the rural areas to the French alliance in 1521, with only a handful of villages expressing themselves in favour. Most of the people stated that they wished to 'live in peace and quiet'. Such popular revulsion against foreign wars was bad news for Cardinal Mathäu Schiner, who sought to raise 6,000 troops from Zurich on behalf of Pope Leo X. He was granted only 2,700, and Zwingli had opposed that as well. Despite Zwingli's denunciations, however, the council had agreed to help the pope, but at the disastrous battle of Piacenza the Swiss troops endured another humiliating defeat; the residual anti-French sentiment in the city was now matched by resentment against the papacy, who proved to be an unreliable paymaster. The council was shamed by its venality and Zwingli's moral standing was greatly enhanced. The magistrates found themselves in an awkward position; the flow of pensions into the city, and into their pockets, was making the rural population restive, and this made the civic rulers jittery.

The preaching mandate in Zurich raised the curtain on a series of reforms that indicated the direction of religious thought within the city. Already in 1520 the Grossmünster chapter declared the Ave Maria, the great song of praise to the Mother of God, to be not binding, and that the breviary was to be simplified. Further, measures were passed by the city council to tackle immoral or violent behaviour in the city. Finally, in September 1520 the magistrates passed a reform of poor relief; the city was to take a more direct role in caring for the poor and homeless, taking the matter out of church hands.[23] The proposals were modest, but significant, representing a tepid mixture of reforms proposed by the late medieval diocesan synods in Constance and the new ideas inspired by the 'evangelical' preaching. No one, however, thought of these changes as other than properly Catholic.

Controversies

The mandate of 1520 could not disguise for long the fact that Zwingli's thought and sermons had passed far beyond the bounds of mere Bible-centred preaching. In his sermons he asked men and women to contrast the Christian Church in their own time with the teachings of the Gospel. The comparison was not favourable. He spoke of Christian freedom and his message fell on fertile soil; a clash between the hierarchical church and evangelical principles, which were interpreted by many as the rejection of feudal authority and a call for local autonomy. The form of the scandal, however, was rather unusual. For some time Zwingli had been meeting in private with sympathetic lay and clerical friends to discuss passages from scripture. On 9 March 1522, during Lent, sausages were cooked in the house of the printer Froschauer and served to this circle of men at table. Zwingli, who had actively encouraged the breaking of the

Lenten abstinence on meat, did not partake, though his friend Leo Jud, also a priest, did. Zwingli, aware that his preaching had already made him powerful enemies in the city, wished to preserve himself against disciplinary charges which might arise from breaking the rules of the church. When the matter became known, however, he took to the pulpit to declare his position. On 23 March he preached on the issue of a Christian's freedom in matters of food, and a month later Froschauer printed in pamphlet form the text of the sermon. Zwingli had clearly drawn from Luther's own position on eating and the individual conscience.

The essence of Zwingli's argument was that food does not make Christians acceptable before God, only faith can make a person holy. It was wrong, according to Zwingli, to think that the matter hung on the nature of the food consumed; the issue was whether a person believed in Christ or not. Christ had triumphed over the law, and Christians were no longer slaves to outward forms of observance, although this was not to be understood as a licence to sin. The freedom of the Christian, and here Zwingli clearly echoed Luther, is found in Christian love, not merely in the liberation from regulations. The contrast between inner and outer piety, between spirit and flesh, which was to become the hallmark of Zwingli's thought, found lucid articulation in this early pamphlet.[24] The argument also had a social dimension that must have had many heads nodding in agreement. The regulations concerning fasting were relatively recent in the Swiss Confederation, having been introduced in the fifteenth century. There is some suggestion that the breaking of the Lenten fast was hardly radical. Lent, the period before Easter when men and women were to abstain from meat, was a busy time for both farmers and artisans, and to be denied a proper meal after a hard day's work was not popular. The printer Christoph Froschauer stated: 'I have to work day and night, holidays and normal days in order to be ready for the Frankfurt book fair.'

There have been many jokes about how the Swiss Reformation began with an empty stomach, and indeed a similar incident took place in Basle. We should remember that Erasmus himself had lampooned such ecclesiastical practices. The event was, however, significant: first, it marked a clear stage in the development of Zwingli's thought, and, second, it brought the city and the bishop of Constance into jurisdictional conflict. The city fined the complainants who had taken the matter of fast-breaking to the episcopal court, and the magistrates attempted to thwart all efforts by the bishop to discipline the clergy involved in the matter. Thus a key to Zwingli's early success was the degree to which he was protected by the city's determination not to tolerate any encroachments upon its control of the church. The city's response to the incident, delivered on 9 April, was to condemn the breaking of the fast, but also to ask the bishop of Constance to consider whether fasting was consonant with scripture.

This was the first of many storms in 1522. A friend of Zwingli, the commander of the Order of St John at Küsnacht, preached an excoriating sermon against the pope in Lucerne, where the Swiss diet had been meeting. This did not go unnoticed by the other Confederate states, who were beginning to realise that Zwingli had been the cause of more than one disturbance. Indeed the Zurich reformer had friends throughout the Confederation, in Basle, Lucerne, Glarus, Einsiedeln, as well as in the rural areas. The new pope, Hadrian IV, was sufficiently concerned about the unrest among the Swiss to send a message of peace to his 'beloved sons, the thirteen Swiss Confederates'.

The other Confederates had no love for Zurich, and their belief that the magistrates in the city on the Limmat were harbouring a notorious 'Lutheran' (a generic term used by Catholics for evangelicals), who was fostering heterodox beliefs in their own lands, led to protests in the diet. Their suspicions were confirmed in the summer of 1522 when Zwingli fronted a petition to the bishop of Constance concerning clerical celibacy. The petition was in Latin – Leo Jud translated it into German – and it requested that the bishop unburden the consciences of those clergy unable to keep themselves chaste. The denial of marriage was driving priests into illicit acts that left them with an overwhelming sense of guilt and shame. Again, the principal argument was that celibacy had no foundation in scripture. The petition went off like a bomb in the Confederation.

Equally sensational was the rumour that Zwingli had written this petition as a married man. At some unknown point in 1522 Zwingli had secretly married Anna Reinhart, a widow, and adopted her son Gerold, a humorous young lad studying in Basle.[25] The reason for concealing the marriage was the scandal it would provoke, though it was known to a close circle of friends. The gossip around Zurich, however, soon grew to such a crescendo that the marriage was the worst-kept secret in the city. Three months before the birth of their first child, Anna left the home of her dead first husband to live openly with Zwingli.

Zwingli's preaching and his challenge to both Lenten fasting and clerical celibacy shaped the agenda of the crucial year 1522. Although the bishop of Constance seemed unable, in the face of support for Zwingli among the Zurich magistrates, to exercise any influence on the situation, opposition was mounting across the Confederation. In reply to his critics, Zwingli wrote his first statement of faith in August of 1522, the *Apologeticus Archeteles*. Bishop Hugo von Hohenlandenburg of Constance, under pressure to enforce the Edict of Worms, sought to exert some authority over the situation in Zurich. His letter to the magistrates contained the now standard Catholic repost to Luther's teachings of *sola scriptura*, that it rendered the interpretation of scripture wholly subjective, undermining any authority to rein in false readings of the text. Only the church, as the body of Christ, was able, by the Holy Spirit, to plumb the depths of God's Word.

Zwingli ventilated his views on this point in a sermon before the Dominicans at Oetenbach which was printed in September with the title *The Clarity and Certainty of the Bible*. The force of Zwingli's argument lay in the belief, soon to be abandoned by the Protestant reformers in practice (though not in theory), that the Word of God is crystal clear, certain, and unequivocal. The Word, flowing from God himself, would overcome all human and material obstacles, and the truth, released from the accretions of human traditions, would be self evident to all, and be accepted. The key to this was the preaching of Word; this was the human agency through which God worked.

This robust defence of evangelical preaching and biblical interpretation led to a further outrage when applied to one of the most cherished aspects of late medieval Christian belief, the Virgin Mary. Zwingli had been under some pressure in Zurich to state his views on Mary, and there were rumours that he wished to abandon the traditional Marian feast of the Assumption. It has been said, however, that Zwingli preserved the figure of Mary for Reformed spirituality, and there is something in this argument. In his sermon *On the Eternal, Pure Virgin Mary*, Zwingli deprived the Mother of God of any intercessory role, yet he gladly retained for her a place of honour as first among Christians.[26] 'The highest honour', he wrote, 'which one can give Mary is rightly to acknowledge and honour the goodness of her son revealed to us poor sinners and to run to him in all mercy.' Mary, in her humility, faith, and obedience, is the role model for Christians. For Zwingli, she was an edificatory, not an intercessory figure.[27]

After this sermon Zwingli made his break with the Roman Catholic Church. On 10 October 1522 the Zurich council released him from his priestly duties by creating a preaching office.[28] This was not the introduction of the Reformation, that was still over two years away, and the breaking of the Lenten fast and public criticism of saints and images in the churches remained contrary to the will of the magistrates, but it marked Zwingli's definitive break with the Catholic priesthood. The creation of a preaching office, styled after those which had long been in place in the German imperial cities, was a remarkable statement of the council's spiritual authority, and it marked the advent of Zwingli's prophetic office in the city. In this he was now supported by his close friend Leo Jud, who had been appointed preacher in the church of St Peter in June 1522, though he did not take up the post until February of 1523. This friendship formed the nucleus of the Zurich reform movement.[29]

Winning over the magistrates

Christmas 1522 in Zurich was celebrated with the traditional festive mass. For Zwingli it was clear that reform was to come from neither Rome nor Constance, and he began looking to the wider evangelical cause. His efforts to involve Zurich in German affairs through a missive to the imperial diet at Nuremberg had been ignored. Zwingli admired Martin Luther as 'undeniably devout and learned', and he warned the Germans that an alliance of the emperor with the king of France would result in the suppression of the evangelical cause. Within the Swiss Confederation, the reform movement was still limited to a few friends in other cities, and Zwingli saw the necessity of linking Zurich with events in Germany, where Luther's movement was taking shape.

By the end of 1522 there were too many unresolved questions in Zurich. 'Evangelical' preaching, understood as Gospel-based sermons, was permitted by the council, although the idea that such preaching could be separated from the theological ideas of *sola scriptura* and *sola fide* was a fiction which would soon be exploded. The older rites, honoured in the breech, remained, nevertheless, the formal worship of the church. Zurich's political orientation was still towards the papacy, although the city had little need of Rome and was not inclined to send troops to Italy. The magistrates in Zurich, in particular the large council, supported Zwingli, or at least what they believed Zwingli stood for, without really comprehending the drift of events. In the years leading to Zwingli's appointment as preacher in the Grossmünster in 1522, the politicians had demonstrated their resolve to keep the religious debate under their control, but the moment was fast approaching when the magistrates would be forced to make decisions about the content of religion. The desire of many urban rulers in German and Swiss lands to appropriate the jurisdiction of bishops proved to have consequences far beyond the legal and financial; it meant taking responsibility for the theological direction of the church under their control.

The moment of truth for the magistrates came in January 1523. Zwingli had been denounced as a heretic and traitor, and Zurich stood accused at the Confederate Diet at Baden of breaking ranks by tolerating his pernicious sermons. Within the city, the prosperous merchants, craftsmen and landowners, as well as the common people, wanted to know what the issues really were, so they could make a decision. They were proud of Zwingli, though he was a 'foreigner' (from Toggenburg), yet they did not really understand where he was taking them.

The council decided that a public disputation should take place at the end of January. It was not to be an academic disputation; Zurich had no university, there were no doctors of the church to sit in judgement, and the discussions were to take place in the vernacular.[30] Zwingli was to state his views, whilst the bishop and representatives of the diocese were invited to put the counter case in order that the 'people' might decide on the basis of what they heard. Invitations were issued and the response from other Swiss cities was striking: Basle, Berne, and Schaffhausen all sent representatives. Bishop Hugo von Hohenlandenberg, however, did not deign to attend; bishops of the fifteenth and sixteenth centuries seldom possessed the learning to take on academics. The bishop was in a difficult position. If he ignored the invitation, Hugo realised that he would have to abandon any hope of playing a leading role in the reform movement. Although the meeting was mocked as a 'tinkers' convention', the matter was taken seriously enough in Constance for the vicar-general of the diocese, Johannes Fabri, to be sent 'not to dispute, but to listen, advise and mediate'.[31] The council in Zurich also summoned the clergy from all its parishes to attend.

About six hundred people gathered in the Rathaus in Zurich for the debate. Zwingli sat at his own table with copies of the Bible in Latin, Greek, and Hebrew in front of him. Fabri had also brought his Greek and Hebrew Bibles, though he was not there to argue with Zwingli. Bürgermeister Markus Röist welcomed the participants, and in particular the delegation from Constance. Zwingli then introduced himself as the preacher who had started the quarrels, to which Fabri replied that Zwingli should abide by the decision taken at the Nuremberg diet that a general council of the church should be summoned to resolve these questions. Although a wide range of issues was discussed, it was the authority of the disputation itself that proved most vexing.[32] The refusal of the Catholics to acknowledge the right of this meeting in Zurich to make lawful decisions about the church pushed Zwingli towards a position that ultimately made the Swiss Reformation possible. According to Zwingli, the six hundred people in the Rathaus were the true church and could, therefore, make decisions based on scripture. This meeting of Christians was no less a gathering of the church than anywhere else, for what gave it legitimacy was not hierarchy or custom but its submission to the Holy Spirit, who empowered the meeting to grasp the Word of God as set out in scripture in Hebrew, Greek, and Latin.[33]

The verdict of the Zurich council was to exonerate Zwingli of all charges of error: yet the partialness of this decision must be stressed.

The Zurich council enjoined preachers to preach from scripture. This fell some way short of *sola scriptura* and should not be understood as marking the decisive break with Rome. The magistrates had taken some, highly tentative, steps in that direction by rejecting the arguments of the Constance delegation that stressed the authority of the hierarchical church, but Zwingli was not in control of events. The small council, under the leadership of Zwingli's backer Markus Röist, had protected Zwingli as well as its own aspirations to control the church in its lands. The large council was still unmoved. During 1523 Zwingli was not a dominant political figure in Zurich; his support was patchy and uncertain. The council's reasons for acting as it did must be seen in terms of the uncertainty of these early years, when a sincere desire for religious renewal, anticlericalism, local pride, and territorial politics brought together, if only briefly, a wide range of people into a loose alliance centred on Huldrych Zwingli. Many different people found in his words what they wanted to hear, and the evangelical movement in Zurich retained broad popular support until late 1524, when Zwingli and his circle began to speak in specifics about theology and politics.

The agenda of the disputation was set out in Zwingli's *Sixty-Seven Articles*, which were made available to the session but not printed until five months later, when Zwingli added a gloss which answered many of the objections raised by the Catholics. The text was designed to serve as a blueprint for the construction of an urban, magisterial church.[34] Zwingli's *Sixty-Seven Articles* declared the freedom of Christians from all necessity to make oneself holy before God. Christ's death and resurrection had removed all impediments to salvation; the Christian was only to believe.

Zwingli's theses represented the evangelical view that a reform of the whole society was possible and that the agent of change was the governing magistrates. Zwingli adopted the Augustinian dualism of the two cities (of God and the devil) and Christians, he acknowledged, would remain a minority within the community of unbelievers. From this perspective, however, it was impossible to know who truly belonged to the church of the elect, thus all ought to be treated as if they were believing Christians. Zwingli's conception of the reform of society never meant that all would be saved: Christ would be honoured by Christians following him in faith and non-believers would be kept from offences against the faith by Christian magistrates. The laws of the state were to be drawn from scripture and applied without distinction to all, for it was not the place of the magistrates to judge in matters of faith; that was for God alone. Zwingli's views on the subject found full expression in his sermon, *Divine and Human Righteousness*, preached in January 1523 and printed in July. Human righteousness is outward action in the world, behaviour which must be tempered by obedience to scripture and the ordinances of worldly magistrates. Divine righteousness is inward, essentially it is faith. In belief the Christian's will conforms with the will of God, but this is a matter of the heart, beyond the apprehension of other humans. Christian magistrates deal with human righteousness in the hope of facilitating divine righteousness, but ultimately the latter was a matter of belief between God and the individual.[35]

To grasp this we must consider briefly the theological underpinnings of Zwingli's understanding of law, faith, and Christian freedom. Zwingli was at one with Luther in speaking of a grace that comes to the Christian from outside. It is the gift of God which has nothing to do with any inner reality of a man or woman. Because it is something totally alien it frees humans from the need to be virtuous or moral in order to achieve salvation. The Word of God alone liberates, it brings forgiveness and absolution through the biblical word. The righteousness of the Christian, which allows one to stand before the judgement of God, is the righteousness of Christ, who intercedes for the elect. This righteousness has nothing to do with human nature; it is that which enables the Christian life in this world. Such a life, led under the guidance of the Spirit, is only a dim reflection of the perfection of Christ in the eyes of God. There can be no moral perfection in this world, for the Christian lives with the reality of sin. Men and women are freed from the law by Christ's perfect obedience, but the law is not made redundant. It is no longer a standard which impugns the Christian, but rather is a guide to the Christian life in a fallen world. Freed from worry about one's salvation, each Christian, according to Zwingli, can 'freely and cheerfully' obey God's law, and therein lies the essence of Christian freedom.[36]

It is impossible here to offer a full discussion of Zwingli's complex relations with the ruling families of Zurich, but these relations were crucial to the success of his reform movement. Of greatest consequence was his closeness to the Röist family in Zurich, who in many ways were his chief patrons. Markus Röist (1454–1524) was a much-respected soldier, who had been captain of the papal guard in 1518, and then Bürgermeister during the crucial years 1520–23. Röist had joined with Oswald Myconius in seeking to bring Zwingli to Zurich from Einsiedeln. At the disputation in January Röist's authority in the chair emboldened Zwingli to state his case. He knew he had an ally in the Bürgermeister.[37]

The centre of opposition to Zwingli was found among the Constaffel, a guild-like body which dated back to age of noble families in Zurich. Until the reforms under Rudolf Brun in the fourteenth century, which had advanced the cause of the guilds, the Constaffel had wielded considerable authority in the city, based on the social precedence of the knights and their military experience. With Brun's reforms their role was more ceremonial, they always carried the city's banners, but they had not been stripped of all political authority. They still held a number of seats on the small council and it was from there that they worked their opposition to Zwingli. After 1525 this last vestige of noble power in Zurich was dissolved, only to be restored after his death in 1531.

Reform

The events of 1523 showed Zwingli to be very much in control. Following the disputation of January he turned his sights to the religious orders, who had always figured in his sermons as agents of corruption and lethargy. Clerical celibacy as a wholly unnatural bind imposed by the church, formed a central part of Zwingli's view of Christian freedom. During the summer of 1523 the attack on monasticism was starting to take effect: the Dominican nuns at Oetenbach, following a sermon by Leo Jud, expressed their desire to be released from their vows. This followed the first open marriage of a priest, Wilhelm Reublin, in the parish church of Witikon, near Zurich.

The collapse of relations between Zurich and Constance also emerged in relief in the summer of 1523. Another attempt by the bishop to have Zurich enforce the Edict of Worms against Luther and his followers was brushed aside with the comment that in the city only Gospel-based preaching was allowed. In truth, serious doctrinal issues were being discussed as the preaching led more and more people to question such issues as the role of saints, images in the church, and the efficacy of the mass. The council wished, once again, to be guided in those matters that were animating the people, and a second disputation was planned for September. This time the Catholics had virtually no representation and Zwingli dominated, although dissent emerged among his followers, as men such as Konrad Grebel, Balthasar Hubmaier, and Johannes Stumpf clamoured for more drastic action.[38] About nine hundred people attended, of whom three hundred were clergy, providing Zwingli with a huge audience for his views on images and the mass.[39] Further, Zwingli wrote his *Short Christian Introduction* as a set of instructions for the Christian minister. In this text Zwingli addressed the practical difficulties of the parish priest who found himself in the confusing position of still being a Catholic priest while also a preacher of the Gospel. At the same time, Zwingli responded unequivocally to those who felt the pace of reform to be lacklustre. It was a text specific to that moment in the reform movement when many found themselves in a confusing and untenable position, caught in a no man's land between Catholicism and the evangelical preaching. All crucial decisions concerning religion, Zwingli argued, were in the hands of the magistrates, and it was the duty of Christians to obey. This remark proved prescient as Zwingli's position as a reformer would over the next two years be defined by his refusal to countenance popular reform. He was prepared to stir the people to pressure the council into accepting his position, but he would not accept any notion of reform from below.

In September 1523 Zwingli spoke to the council on behalf of the Grossmünster chapter, declaring the readiness of the majority of canons and chaplains to accept reform of their institution. This marked a turning point in the Zurich Reformation as the chapter was the largest financial institution in the city, the centre of a vast web of feudal obligations which stretched across the rural territories. Its reform would set the tone for the remainder of ecclesiastical change in the state. The first question in reforming the chapter was what should become of the large amounts of money which had been donated to the chapter for specific religious purposes which no longer formed part of the worship of the community. In particular this included the endowment of mortuary masses to speed souls through purgatory. According to the council mandate of 29 September, the money accrued for these purposes was to be redirected to the support of the clergy.

The agreement between the chapter and the council stated that the money should be redeployed to the benefit of the community. Some was hived off by the council to strengthen the defences of the city; a necessary precaution given the growing animosity of the other Confederates towards Zurich. The principal beneficiaries, however, were to be the poor, the rural clergy and schoolmasters. The rural parishes belonging to the chapter were to receive money to give the priest a decent living, and to repair the material fabric of the church.

Perhaps most significant for the development of Zurich was the use of the Grossmünster resources to secure provision for education within the city. Zwingli, as an Erasmian humanist, had long-cherished educational ideals, and once he was appointed principal (*Schulherr*) by the council he set about reforming both the institutions and the curricula. There were two schools in the city, attached to the Grossmünster and Fraumünster. Zwingli used the resources from the Grossmünster to create a school with four masters; it was a grammar school to teach boys Latin and some Greek as well as the traditional *trivium* and *quadrivium*.[40] The example of the school in Zurich was used in reforming the former religious houses at Kappel, Rüti, Winterthur, and Stein-am-Rhein.

Unrest and disenchantment

At the same time as education was being reformed the first signs of public unrest became manifest. It was between September and November 1523 that most acts of iconoclasm in Zurich took place, and the direct cause of this violence was thought, by most, to be the inflammatory preaching of Zwingli, Leo Jud, Ludwig Hätzer, Johannes Stumpf, and Konrad Schmid.[41] On 19 September, one week after Leo Jud had preached in his church of St Peter's against religious images, the frame enclosing the decorative panels over the altar as well as other church ornaments were found damaged. Similar incidents occurred: Lorentz Hochrütiner, a weaver from St Gall who had been present in the house of Froschauer for the sausage-eating incident, was reported to have entered the chapel of St Nicholas (Fraumünster) with two others and to have knocked over lamps in front of the altar and thrown holy water about. Hochrütiner was later involved in a much more public and scandalous act of iconoclasm, the taking down of a large wooden crucifix at the crossroads in Stadelhofen just outside the walls of the city. The leader of this incident was Claus Hottinger, a strong and vociferous supporter of Zwingli.[42] He too had been present in the Froschauer house and he had made numerous verbal attacks on the mass. He was from Zollikon, the birthplace of the radical movement, and scholars have linked him with Anabaptist views.

The attack on the crucifix at Stadelhofen was undertaken by a shoemaker, a weaver, and a tailor, and their intention, according to Hottinger, was to make as public a demonstration as possible. Hottinger's words that he wished to sell the wood and give the money to the poor may have been his personal response to what Zwingli was undertaking within the Grossmünster chapter: the tearing down of the old fabric of the church and the redirection of money to the poor. Hottinger was banned from the city for two years.

It was in response to these incidents of iconoclasm that the second disputation discussed above was held in Zurich on 26–28 October 1523. On the issue of images the evangelical preachers did not speak with one voice. Leo Jud, who had preached against images in St Peter's, took the hard line, arguing for the complete cleansing of the churches, a position also favoured by Zwingli. Others, however, counselled caution, and some intervened to argue for the continued use of images in the churches. The council was not impressed by the discord among the preachers. The position taken by the magistrates on 27 October was that those who had donated images to churches could, if they wished, remove them, but images donated by the congregation or funded by parish monies were not to be touched.[43]

The issue of images in the churches rumbled on until summer 1524. The council was extremely hesitant about making any theological decisions despite severe pressure from all sides. Iconoclasm spread to the rural areas as preachers declared material objects – altars, retables, banners, shrines, lamps, and images of Christ and the saints – to be idols. Lee Wandel has shown that in the rural parishes the iconoclasm was carried out by members of the community who were linked by profession and/or kinship.[44] Incidents took place in the villages of Höngg, Eglisau, Altstetten, and Zollikon, all of which lay close to the city of Zurich. The iconoclasm ranged from simple destruction to more elaborate displays of protest, such as in Zollikon, where a wooden donkey (*Palmesel*) with the image of Christ was dragged from the church and thrown into Lake Zurich.

The pressure proved so great that in early June 1524 the council set out a five-point position on images in which it forbade men and women from taking matters into their own hands. Donors were given five days to remove their gifts, but otherwise the material fabric in the churches was not to be touched. Nor, however, was the art in churches to be treated with veneration. The council declared that scriptural evidence inveiged against images and that the crucifix was not a sign of divinity. The council's first wish was to restore order, but by July 1524 a more clearly defined position was required. A commission was formed to remove the images from the Zurich churches, and for ten days seventeen members of the different guilds moved from church to church behind closed doors to remove the art, whitewash the walls, and dismantle the altars. The images were either burnt or melted down to make money to be distributed among the poor. The relics of the civic patrons, Felix and Regula, were removed from the Grossmünster and discreetly buried. The matter was more or less brought to an end, but Zurich had been changed by the whole series of events which had run from the autumn of 1523 through to the summer of 1524.[45]

One consequence of the iconoclasm in Zurich was the strain it placed upon the Swiss Confederation. Lucerne, Schwyz, Uri, Unterwalden, Zug, and Fribourg refused to meet with the representatives of Zurich in the diet. In cities where evangelical preaching was permitted, such as Basle, Berne, and Solothurn, there was at least tacit support for Zurich, whilst Schaffhausen, Appenzell, St Gall, and the Thurgau declared themselves openly on Zurich's side. Religion was beginning to pull the Confederation apart. With Zurich very much in the role of chief agitator, powerful Berne emerged as the only force which could halt the slide to chaos, and during 1524 the Five Inner States actively courted the Bernese. The magistrates in Berne based their calculations on a range of factors, of which the interests of the Inner States was only one. Berne had no desire to support Zurich's hegemonic interests, whilst at the same time its growing territorial interests in the east had to be balanced with a restive rural population with little appetite for religious change and strong evangelical support in the city.

Tithes and rebellion

The reform of the Grossmünster was part of a wider reorganisation that included the suppression of religious and monastic houses.[46] This marked the completion of a long process of bringing the church, its wealth and privileges under the control of the council. Many of the religious houses were wound up by leaders who had embraced the Reformation. In Embrach the chapter was closed on 19 September by Heinrich Brennwald, who alongside other heads of religious houses at Kappel and Stein-am-Rhein declared that he could no longer celebrate the mass, as it was against scripture. The abbess of the Fraumünster, Katharina von Zimmern (1478–1547) was likewise persuaded by the evangelical cause and closed her nunnery.

The outpouring of men and women from the cloisters culminated in the council mandate of 5 December 1524, which dissolved the religious houses.[47] The mandate recommended that the former monks, friars, and nuns should take up a craft or education, with the provision that those for whom this was impossible were to be offered a pension. The suppression of these houses meant that their rights of patronage passed into the hands of the council, which promised that monastic goods would be used for poor relief. On 15 January 1525 the council issued an extensive mandate laying out its response to poor relief. The structures of relief within the city and rural areas were reorganised, with the Dominican house in Zurich, for example, being converted into a hospital. Alongside the institutional changes the mandate described in detail the social ills besetting the city: drunkenness, beggary, and violence.

The magistrates' concern with social unrest in the city and rural areas reflected the uneasy atmosphere of 1524. Many who had heard Zwingli and his colleauges preach had interpreted the evangelical message as a validation of their aspirations for local autonomy. The hopes included the cessation of payment of tithes to overlords and the election of ministers to serve in the community. These were not just vague ideals, as the first election by a community of its own minister took place in the village of Witikon in 1523. The confluence of the desire for control over communal affairs with the teaching of the evangelical faith benefited both, but there was no automatic connection between the two ideals. Even in the Zurich territories there were communities which embraced one whilst rejecting the other.

In the parish of Mettmenstetten in 1525, for example, the evangelical minister was chased out of town by villagers throwing stones after hearing his first sermon. In April 1524 the parishioners of Meilern stormed the house of their priest following news of his plans to marry.

The Peasants' Revolt of 1525 that tore across Germany did not leave the lands of Zurich untouched, though the damage was minor. In April peasants stormed the Praemonstratensian abbey in Rüti and then the houses of the Knights of St John at Bubikon and the Dominicans in Töss. Although the mediation of magistrates and peasant leaders averted loss of life, a flood of peasant complaints appeared in print.[48] These pamphlets made use of evangelical language in framing demands for the abolition of tithes, or at least their redirection to poor relief, control over the parishes, and the reform of hunting and fishing rights. The peasants were disappointed by the council's response in May, which indicated that there was some sympathy, but no commitment to change.[49] The magistrates made it clear that they did not accept the Bible as the basis for worldly authority, and that in their eyes the tithe was a legal issue. This was confirmed in their mandate of 22 June in which a few minor concessions were made to the peasants, though not at the cost of the tithe.

This whole matter put Zwingli on the back foot. The magistrates held the preachers responsible for stirring up the rural communities. Zwingli, who had always made much of his own peasant background, had idealised the simple rural folk in contrast to the rapacious clergy, and he continued to urge the magistrates to treat the peasants with moderation. However, he was not about to advocate the abolition of the hated tithe. Zwingli argued that there was little in the Bible that offered Christians guidance on economic matters, and that the tithe was essentially an extra-biblical issue. The possession of property and goods should not be disturbed, he argued. What was required was a greater commitment on the part of the magistrates and laity to the church and the care of the poor. Farmers, in return, should demonstrate their obedience to the state by paying their due tithes. Zwingli's proposals subordinated radical change to the preservation of law and order. He had staked the Reformation cause on gaining and holding the support of the leading figures in Zurich and he was not about to abandon this course of action. The *status quo* was affirmed, but with the proviso that people should not seek to exploit others. It was at this point that Zwingli lost many of his supporters.

A new order

On 11 April 1525 Zwingli, Leo Jud, Kaspar Megander, Heinrich Engelhard, and Oswald Myconius appeared before the Zurich council with a petition for the abolition of the mass. Since summer 1524 there had been no more pilgrimages to Einsiedeln, the images had been removed from the churches and the processions of the relics of the city's martyrs had ceased, but the mass remained. Within the evangelical camp there had been a painful split. Konrad Grebel and his circle had parted company with Zwingli after the adult baptisms in January 1525, but a central reason for the rift was the radicals' impatience with Zwingli's slowness in introducing a new service of the Lord's Supper.[50] Zwingli was under no illusions concerning the depth of opposition to such reform; the abolition of the mass and the introduction of the new form of worship was only brought about by a slim majority of councillors in a poorly attended session held deep in the night. It was not an auspicious start. Nevertheless, the mass formally ceased to be celebrated in Zurich on Wednesday of Holy Week and on the following day, Maundy Thursday, the first Reformed celebration of the Lord's Supper was performed.

Zwingli's *Action or Practice of the Lord's Supper*, the liturgical text which he prepared for the sacrament owed much not only to the structure of the mass which it was replacing but also to the preaching services common in the late medieval church.[51] Although the Lord's Supper was to recreate the drama of the Last Supper, it remained for Zwingli controlled by the clergy. Only the minister could perform the ritual, for he represented Christ, though the people were drawn into the drama as the disciples gathered around the table. The receiving of the bread and wine was an act of faith which linked together the external world of the congregation with their inner belief in the saving power of Christ. Zwingli's liturgical drama was far more powerful than a mere act of memory; it was a profound and largely traditional expression of the command to imitate Christ. Zwingli designed the new liturgy for the Grossmünster in Zurich, and his conception was that people should sit to receive the body of Christ. In the churches of the rural areas, however, the people stood. Pews as we would recognise them only began to appear later in the sixteenth century.

The reform of the Lord's Supper was followed in May by a new service for baptism. In 1523 Leo Jud had drawn up the first baptismal order in German, but the advent of Anabaptism in Zurich required a more detailed outline of the rite. Whereas Jud had retained various Catholic elements in his service, Zwingli's reforms of 1525 were more extensive: the service was to take place in the parish church (not privately) and the parents or godparents were no longer to be asked the traditional questions about their faith. Zwingli did not regard baptism as a cleansing of the soul from original sin, but rather as a mark of faith – an outward rite by which the parents pledged to bring the child up in the faith of the church.[52] As we shall see later, Zwingli developed his baptismal theology in the direction of ideas of the covenant. A mandate from May 1526 required the ministers of every parish to keep detailed records of who was baptised as well as the names of the child's parents and godparents. This was a measure directed against the Anabaptists.

During the remarkable year 1525 Zwingli led the reform of poor relief in January, the Lord's Supper in April, and baptism and marriage in May. In each case the pace was set by the council, and Zwingli was careful never to push matters too hard. This, as we shall discuss later when we turn to the radicals, was a dangerous tactic, held together by little more than Zwingli's personal relations with the leading Zurich magistrates. Zwingli, however, did not labour alone. Men such as Leo Jud, Kaspar Megander, and Heinrich Uttinger employed their diverse talents in a vast array of tasks. Jud was a skilled translator and liturgist, and the Lord's Supper of 1525 owed much to his talents,[53] while Uttinger was a jurist, and the marriage laws and marriage court developed from his expertise in the law. Without doubt, Zwingli was the driving force and the man with the political acumen, but he was not acting alone. These crucial theological, liturgical, and political changes were implemented in the spring and summer of 1525 by magistrates deeply worried about the continued unrest in the rural areas. The Peasants' War and the rise of religious radicalism kept Zwingli's reforms in the balance. The expectations of the people, who had been stirred by the preaching, had to be set against a realistic understanding of how far the council, whose support of religious changes was essential, could be moved.

The reforms of 1525 placed Zurich outside the Catholic Church: the sacraments had been denied and the authority of the pope spurned. From his bastion in Zurich Zwingli was able to print works which were being distributed and read across the Confederation and the empire, and his ideas were winning followers. Within Zurich there was considerable support for the old religion, but no one capable of taking on Zwingli. A worthy opponent would emerge only from beyond the Swiss border. Dr Johannes Eck of Ingolstadt, the man who had debated with Luther at Leipzig in 1519 arrived in 1525 to take on Zwingli. Eck was vain and querulous, but also brilliant, the best Catholic mind in the German-speaking lands. He had become familiar with the writings of Zwingli and Oecolampadius whilst residing in Basle and he shrewdly noted that they were not saying the same thing as Luther. His eyes alighted on important differences in the matter of the Lord's Supper, and Eck was determined to exploit this division.

The events up to 1525 had put before the Swiss Confederation an unfamiliar problem. For all its regional diversity and local identities, the Confederates had been bound by one religion. It was perhaps the one thing which united them, and now one of the most powerful of the Confederates had fallen into heresy. No early modern political community could withstand religious schism. The problem was complex. Many agreed that a general council of the church was required to heal the breach, but the traditional language of reform was no longer adequate. Zwingli had staged disputations in Zurich in which scripture was made the standard of truth. The reason Zwingli and his allies had won these disputations was because they had demonstrated to a lay audience that they could develop a consistent argument from scripture alone, while their opponents had to fall back on tradition and authority of the church. For his Catholic opponents a disputation or council along those lines was wholly unacceptable. During the 1520s many, including most leading politicians, hoped for negotiations and a resolution; few, however, understood that the course down which Zwingli had led them rendered this impossible. Eck and Johannes Fabri, the official of the diocese of Constance, would never accept the terms of debate set down by Zwingli, nor were they prepared to come to Zurich again for stage-managed humiliation. This time, they were determined, the debate should be on their terms.

Zwingli had every reason to believe that had he dared venture into Catholic territory his fate would have been more likely that of Hus at Constance than of Luther at Worms. The Five Inner States believed that he and Zurich stood behind all the unrest in their lands, and they were well prepared to kindle the flames of his pyre. After months of rancorous negotiations, Baden was chosen as the location for a debate.[54] Zwingli and Zurich refused to accept the terms, even rejecting the offer of an armed guard. Fabri wrote an open letter to Zwingli in which he attempted both to discredit the reformer among the Confederates and to tempt him from the safety of Zurich. Zwingli refuted the claims of the Catholics in his *Friendly Letter to the Confederates*, denying that the plans of Eck and Fabri had any validity or that the Catholic states had any right to try him for a religious matter. The Confederation, he rightly argued, was a political, not a religious construct. Zwingli did not attend and Zurich took no part in the diet, which began in May 1526.

In Zwingli's absence the evangelicals were led by Johannes Oecolampadius, who knew he had walked into a one-sided debate against one of the most accomplished theologians and orators in

Europe.[55] Eck dominated proceedings: he had read the writings of Zwingli and Oecolampadius – he had just published a *Handbook of Lutheran Heresy* in 1526 which included extensive quotations from the Swiss reformers. He tore into Oecolampadius on a range of fronts, and in eighteen sessions the two men went at it hammer and tong with editions of the Church Fathers being produced as aides to the debate on authority. The final vote was a formality. It was a crushing defeat for the evangelicals; Oecolampadius had not performed badly – in fact he managed at one point to hold a three-hour oration in defence of his position – but he was no match for the subtle mind and fluid rhetoric of Johannes Eck.

Zwingli recognised the damage that had been done to the evangelical movement by his refusal to appear at Baden and take on Johannes Eck. In an attempt to make his presence felt at the debate he wrote two replies to Eck's seven theses. These pamphlets were posted on the door of the council in Baden and in the church where the debate took place. The central issue was the presence of Christ in the eucharist, and in his reply Zwingli showed himself to be much more adept than Oecolampadius in defending the Reformed position against Catholic attack. Zwingli's writings were really an attempt to repair the damage caused by the defeat at Baden. What the Catholics had succeeded in demonstrating at Baden was that the evangelicals had an insufficient understanding of the relationship between Church and scripture. Zwingli's answer would come at the Berne Disputation in 1528.

In the spirit of the disputations held in Zurich, the meeting in Baden was not about an exchange of positions on doctrinal matters. It was a demonstration of Catholic strength in response to Zwingli and the evangelical party. The latter was represented by Johannes Oecolampadius, who was hardly allowed to speak, let alone debate the positions put forward by Eck and Fabri. The meeting was beautifully orchestrated with guards posted at every gate of the city to prevent unwanted intruders entering the sessions. Curiously, there has never been an agreed account of what happened in Baden; the printed minutes were disputed by those who attended and requests by Berne, Basle, and Zurich to see the original notes from the sessions were declined.[56]

Nine of the Swiss states adopted the resolutions of the Baden diet, which called for the implementation of the Edict of Worms and declared Zwingli a heretic. Like all other institutions in the Confederation, the diet at Baden had no authority to impose its decisions, and several of the states (Basle, Berne, and Schaffhausen) refused to declare one way or the other. The reform movements in these cities were strong; the influence of Oecolampadius in Basle, as well as Berchtold Haller and Niklaus Manuel in Berne ensured that the magistrates in these cities were already minded to support Zwingli. Schaffhausen was economically dependent upon Zurich, and although the Reformation had not yet been officially adopted, evangelical ideas were preached and the religious houses were being closed.

Nevertheless Zwingli was a heretic and Zurich was isolated. The dangers posed by the resurgent Catholics were augmented by their closeness to the Habsburg dynasty, which had been recently strengthened by the victory over the French at Pavia in 1525. For Zwingli Baden was also a considerable personal failure. The Catholic theologians would certainly not have been persuaded by his theology, but Zwingli had appeared to cower at a crucial moment, to remain behind the protection offered by the Zurich magistrates when he might have taken on a more serious theological opponent than he had faced in the earlier disputations. Without question he might have been arrested, tortured, and burnt, but that would have been a risky calculation by the Catholic states, who would have created a martyr. Certainly Oecolampadius was not put in any danger, but he was not the man the Catholics regarded as the cause of the Reformation.

The disputation at Baden in 1526 pointed to two crucial truths. First, the disputation demonstrated that Zwingli's position had become entirely interwoven with the interests of the Zurich council. His theology was now part of Zurich's politics, and this would ensure that he could not become a national figure as Luther was for the Germans. Second, despite the success of the evangelical preachers in the early 1520s, the Catholics were not routed and there were theologians who could not only defend the traditional doctrines of the church but who could also underscore the weaknesses of Zwingli's own position. Their cause was aided enormously by the greatest disaster for the Reformation cause of the 1520s: the failure to agree over the meaning of one passage of scripture.

Luther and Marburg

'This is my body given for you' (Luke 22:19). What did Christ mean when he spoke to the Apostles at the Last Supper? No aspect of the Swiss Reformation has occasioned more spilling of ink than the dispute between Zurich and Wittenberg over the sacrament of the Lord's Table.[57] This was a defining issue of the early Reformation, and the psychological scars of the bitter encounter deeply affected the mentality of later Swiss reformers. The Swiss never recovered from Luther's denunciation of them as fanatics and heretics, and with his repeated assaults he succeeded in casting a shadow of suspicion over the Zwinglian teaching on the eucharist. Zwingli became a byword for a 'memorialist' view of the sacrament, a pejorative tag intended to indicate a ritual stripped of all significance, described with asperity by one critic as 'real absence'.

The accounts of the theological differences between Luther and Zwingli are legion and there is no room here for a full rehearsal of the details.[58] Until 1524 Zwingli's eucharist theology remained uncontroversial from an evangelical perspective.[59] In the eighteenth article of his *Exposition of the Articles* he had denied transubstantiation, as well as any notion of a repetition of Christ's sacrifice on the altar. In the summer of 1523 Zwingli had written a draft liturgy of the mass, *De Canone Missae Epichiresis*, in which he had proposed fairly mild alterations. A key player in the early days of the conflict was the Dutchman Cornelis Hoen, who had written a tract in which he argued that when Christ stated 'This is my body' he had meant 'This signifies my body'. A letter outlining this interpretation was sent to Luther and Zwingli: the first would have nothing to do with it, but Zwingli indicated his concurrence.

In 1525 rural unrest and Catholic opposition threatened to overturn the evangelical movement, and Zwingli faced arrest if he attempted to travel to any of the other Confederates. It is fair to say that the last thing Zwingli wanted was a quarrel with Luther. From Luther's point of view, however, the casting-out of Andreas Bodenstein von Karlstadt from Wittenberg in 1524 was linked to events in Zurich. Although Karlstadt would not arrive in the Confederation until 1530, his views on the eucharist seemed to Luther very close to what Zwingli was saying.[60] During 1525 and 1526 Zwingli's nascent ideas of a symbolic interpretation of the Lord's Supper were attacked by Catholic and Lutheran writers, and the Zurich reformer's replies became the basis of his first theological utterances on the subject. The initial debate was in Latin and largely outside the cognisance of political leaders, but by 1525 it was clear that a widespread debate over the eucharist was spreading across Germany and the Swiss Confederation.

Luther opened up against Zwingli in 1526 with his *Sermon on the Sacrament of the Body and Blood of Christ*.[61] Between 1526 and 1529 Luther and Zwingli exchanged salvos. Zwingli's most important works were *A Friendly Exegesis*, *A Friendly Answer*, *Zwingli's Christian Reply* and *Two Replies to Luther's Book*. For Zwingli, the central issue concerned the presence of the body of Christ in the sacrament of the Lord's Supper. Employing the distinction of the spiritual from the material so central to his thought, Zwingli would not permit the benefits of grace to be tied to the physical ritual of the sacrament. If Christ was present in the Lord's Supper, it had to be through the faith of the believers. Zwingli's understanding was encapsulated in the oft-quoted words of Christ from the reformer's beloved Gospel of John, 'God is spirit, and his worshippers must worship him in spirit and in truth' (John 4:24).

Zwingli pleaded with Luther that they not quarrel, but at the same time he outlined the differences between them. The reformer of Wittenberg, he was certain, had made errors in insisting upon the bodily presence of Christ in the sacrament. Nevertheless, he opined that the two were in the service of the Lord. Luther was livid with Zwingli's presumption. He did not regard the reformer of Zurich as his equal in any respect, and the spiritualist views espoused by Zwingli were nothing more than a resurrection of the heresies of Karlstadt and Thomas Müntzer. Luther associated Zwingli with heretics of the church, such as Wyclif, while Zwingli replied that Luther had remained too close to Rome.

There were, however, reasons to resolve this dispute. Luther did recognise Zwingli's learning, and it could not go unnoticed that Zwinglianism was making great progress, not only in the Confederation, but crucially in southern Germany, where Zwingli's theology had won over many in the imperial cities. The Disputation at Berne in 1528 had brought together an impressive array of theologians, and the triumph of the Zwinglian cause had sent reverberations across German lands. The great cities of Strasbourg, Ulm, Nuremberg, Augsburg, and Basle looked to follow Berne's example.

The growing rift between Zurich and Wittenberg was also crucial to the Catholic response to the Reformation. Pushed back by the exhilarated response to Luther, the Catholics quickly realised that the division over the eucharist would discredit the Protestant cause. Nothing could better illustrate the Catholic view that the evangelicals had been wrong in their claim to biblical legitimacy than an unseemly quarrel over the interpretation of a passage of scripture. Catholic recovery was best served by keeping Zwingli and Luther at odds, and the most effective way of promoting discord was to suggest that the two men were saying the same thing. This enraged Luther, who refused to have his integrity impugned through association with Zurich. To great effect, the Catholics poured oil on the fire.

Within Germany fears of a Catholic alliance against Philip of Hesse and the Elector of Saxony startled the German princes into a scramble to defend themselves. The Catholic alliance proved to be only rumour, but the point was clear: the evangelical states had to prepare for the inevitable attack. There had been ongoing discussions between the German princes, magistrates of the imperial cities, and leading reformers about an alliance. The sticking point was the dispute over the eucharist. In the empire men such as Jakob Sturm, Wolfgang Capito, and Martin Bucer pressed for co-operation. Among the Swiss the leading proponent of peace was Johannes Oecolampadius in Basle.

The strength of Charles V's position in 1529 brought matters to a head. There had been secret negotiations among the Protestants for two years prior to the emperor's return to Germany. The Elector of Saxony was hardly enthusiastic about an alliance with the Swiss, as this would do little to enhance his defensive position. It was the work of Landgrave Philip of Hesse that moved events forward. He was determined to bring the warring parties together, regardless of cost, to find a theological agreement which would strengthen his position, lead to the restoration of the duke of Württemberg, and, perhaps, result in the next emperor being a Protestant.

The Lutherans drew up their position in the *Schwabach Articles*, a document intended to separate the southern German cities from the Swiss through a clear statement of the differences between Zwingli and Luther. Philip pressed on, and invitations to a meeting at Marburg were issued in July 1529. Those on the list included Zwingli, Oecolampadius, Sturm, Andreas Osiander, Kaspar Hedio, Martin Bucer, Luther, and Melanchthon. Luther had no desire to attend, believing that reconciliation was not possible. He was essentially ordered by the Elector of Saxony to travel to Marburg.

A series of meetings at the castle in Marburg led to the confrontation of Luther and Zwingli on 2 October at 6 a.m.[62] The session was chaired by Philip of Hesse. What was actually said in the confrontation remains something of a mystery as there are eight different accounts, only some by eyewitnesses, of the exchange. Scholars, for the most part, have relied on the accounts of Kaspar Hedio and Rudolf Collin.[63] Neither Luther nor Zwingli was prepared to give ground, though there is some suggestion that Zwingli got the better of the argument. It is an appealing Romantic thought that this was the great lost opportunity of the Protestant Reformation, but it was not so simple. Both parties had made up their minds on the eucharist, and the debate had advanced to the point where both sides had too much to lose by compromising. Politics played a key role, but, in the end, there were two different theologies at work, propounded by two men of deep convictions. G.R. Potter has elegantly written:

> As darkness descended on that fatal first Sunday evening in October, it was apparent that they must agree to differ. Zwingli had not succeeded in obtaining the measure of recognition, tolerance and inter-communion for which he had hoped. Luther would not go even as far as this – he was not prepared to accept either the men of Strasbourg or the Swiss as brothers and fellow-members of a wider church. He was over-confident, then abusive: he conceded nothing that mattered, and the Landgrave had failed.[64]

It has often been noted that Marburg brought about more agreement than dissent. On large parts of Christian doctrine the two parties spoke with one voice, as on basic evangelical principles such as the rejection of transubstantiation and the acceptance of communion in both kinds. There was concord on the universal priesthood, a married clergy, the role of secular government in religion and the place of baptism. Although overshadowed by the parting of ways on the eucharist, the agreement on these points had a lasting impact on the Reformation. On virtually every substantive matter outside the Lord's Supper there was agreement; they did not anathematise each other with charges of heresy. There would be no lasting agreement, but the door remained open for future negotiations. The theological career of John Calvin, with its integration of Lutheran and Zwinglian thought, was made possible by Marburg.

The Swiss were not to be part of a German Protestant alliance. This was essentially Zwingli's project, and it had failed. The outbreak of plague in Marburg in October sent the participants scurrying from the city. When Zwingli and Luther returned to their homes they seem to have harboured better thoughts of one another in private, but publicly they denounced each other with increased vehemence. Zwinglian thought, particularly on the eucharist, continued to spread through Germany, attracting adherents with its lucidity and apparent harmony with scripture, as opposed to Luther's perplexing statements.[65] Zurich started to build alliances with like-minded cities in the southern empire, and by the Diet of Augsburg in 1530 the Zwinglians were an important presence. But returning from Marburg Zwingli was convinced that the pope and emperor stood ready to attack, and that some form of evangelical alliance was necessary. The problem was twofold: in Germany the split with the Lutherans had already scuppered political arrangements, while within the Confederation the acceptance of the Reformation in Berne had not greatly strengthened Zwingli's position, as the Bernese would not accept any foreign alliances led by Zurich. Meetings held through Germany in 1529 seemed only to underscore division in the Protestant camp.

Zwingli's theological vision

Having travelled quickly along the road leading to the implementation of the Reformation in Zurich in 1525 and the resulting disruption in the Confederation, we might pause briefly to consider a couple of crucial questions. The central argument of this book holds that the Swiss Reformation, under the guidance of Zwingli, developed a unique theological profile. What, we might now ask, was that profile as it took shape in the crucial years of the 1520s? The answer to that question is a study in itself, so we must limit ourselves to some basic principles, some of which have already been raised.

Zwingli was an engaging writer. Even to modern eyes his prose is remarkably free of the prolixity which so marks most sixteenth-century theologians. Zwingli's vast knowledge of classical authors is evident, but lightly worn, and his arguments are sharply hewn. Humour and sarcasm are found throughout, but most arresting is his driving passion and intense love for his people, whose damnation he feared. The Swiss Confederation in the form of its people and their customs, its history (even if in a humanist fantasy), and its natural wonders looms large on every page. Even in their silence the printed words convey something of the emotional and emotive preacher who moved people to abandon their old faith. Like any good teacher, Zwingli clearly wrote with the faces of his audience in his mind's eye; he knew how to speak to them and how to articulate their needs and aspirations. What he told them was that the Swiss were being punished for their carnality; their pursuit of money was a cancer which riddled the body of the whole Confederation. The Swiss had erected their golden calf and they could expect the fate that befell the faithless Israelites.

Crudely, but not unfairly, Zwingli's message boiled down to one point: a person cannot serve two masters. In the binary language which shaped his thought, a person could serve either God or the world. There was no middle ground. Anything which falls short of the pure worship of God is sin, and to break the commandments of God was, for Zwingli, an act of extreme selfishness; it reflected an obsessive relationship with the gratifications of the world, which might include any combination of sex, mercenary service, deceit, political corruption, and, crucially, false religion. To understand the depth of this conviction we need to remind ourselves that for Zwingli any thought or act which detracted, even to the smallest degree, from God's freedom, omnipotence, and goodness, constituted idolatry. Zwingli's principal objections to the mass, and the whole apparatus of medieval Catholicism, was rooted in his belief that it was idolatrous, by which he meant that humans had reduced God to material objects which could be manipulated for private ends. Against this he asserted the absolute distinction of God from humanity which he believed followed from the total sovereignty of God. Zwingli pushed God and humanity as far apart as possible as he sought to separate the material and spiritual. This distinction drew heavy criticism from Luther and others, who accused him of the early Christian heresy of Nestorianism. Zwingli refuted the accusation and was unrepentant: God is the source of all goodness, and all created things, therefore, are only good insofar as they are in relationship with him. Thus any goodness in humans exists at the pleasure of its source. This, as Gottfried Locher has pointed out, makes providence central to Zwingli's understanding of God, who is both omniscient and omnipotent. We begin to understand Zwingli's theology when we take on board that he would countenance nothing which appeared to diminish either of these divine qualities. There was a distinct flavour of the Greek Fathers in Zwingli's emphasis on the simplicity of God. From that simplicity flowed Zwingli's central premise about humanity: that those who are saved have been elected to salvation by God. Predestination formed a central plank in the thought of Zwingli, who wrote that 'providence, so to speak, is the parent of predestination'.[66] Following Luther, Zwingli rejected human free will, arguing that redemption is through grace on the basis of election.[67]

A second distinctive feature was Zwingli's attitude towards the law. He rejected Luther's opposition of law and Gospel in favour of a more positive understanding of God's will for humanity. Again the distinction between the inner or spiritual and the outer or material is asserted: the ceremonial laws of the Old Testament, which dealt with external religion have been replaced by the inner law brought by Christ. This inner law is the commandment of love, which fills all those elected by God with a desire to imitate Christ. Thus Christians, by the grace of God, have the law as guide for holy living and not simply as an unachievable standard to rebuke them. Zwingli wrote:

> The law means only what is eternally right and good; for the law is good, righteous and holy, as it says in Romans 7. Do you want to know why? It is because it is nothing other than a revelation and declaration of the will of God, and we see from the word commandment what God wants and demands. Thus it may more appropriately be called gospel rather than law. For, what man, living in human darkness and ignorance, would not rejoice if God revealed his will to him? And would that not be good news, if the will of God were made known to man?[68]

The various themes in Zwingli's thought begin to converge when we consider his understanding of the Christian life. The law is God's revealed will for humanity: it is a code for living and the basis of communal existence. God's laws must be the foundation of the positive laws of the state, for God demands total obedience to his word. Christ alone, in uniting humanity and divinity, is able to satisfy the divine commandment and is, therefore, the sole basis for human redemption. The perfection of Christ makes him the only means by which the internal and external, or the material and the spiritual, which form the polarities of Zwingli's thought, are united. Anything which deviates from a life centred on Christ is false religion. Zwingli wrote:

> There lie the altars and the idols in the temple. He who fears them now, does so not out of a steady conscience, and easily understands whether or not we once put a high value on them. This rubbish must be cast out, so that the inestimable worth which you, above all men, ascribe to these foolish idols may be ascribed to the living image of God.[69]

Thus the Christian life is an intimate relationship with Christ in which the believer is fed by the words of scripture, which nourish the inner person. Zwingli stressed that the Christian must know scripture, for not only is the Word of God therein contained, but because it is the very bread of life; it is the essential food required for the Christian life. Zwingli did not wish to confuse scripture itself with the promises of God which it proclaims: the first is a human document, while the second is from God.

The locus of this feeding is the church, which is guided by the spirit. The church of God required, according to Zwingli, the unrestricted preaching of the Word of God. Zwingli's experiences in Zurich had impressed upon him the importance of integrating the church into the political governance of the state. On the one hand, as we have seen, this was simply shrewd politics, given the small size of the evangelical party. There was, on the other hand, a more visionary explanation, and that lay in Zwingli's emphasis on personal and corporate renewal. The Reformation, for Zwingli, was the renewal of not only the church, but of the whole of society, and the magistrates, therefore, were key players. Zwingli used a variety of traditional images to describe the relationship between the church and civil government: at times he spoke of the two swords, while he also referred to them as being related as the body and soul. Zwingli looked to the kings of Israel for his polity: the king was appointed by God to rule with the sword, enforcing God's laws and ensuring true worship, but the conduit for God's will was the prophet, who had direct access to the divine will. The prophet was not to bear arms; his sword was the word of God, and he was to advise and rebuke the monarch as was necessary. The two existed together, although there was an implicit hierarchy in which the prophet, as the discerner of the spirit, had precedence over the political ruler. Zwingli articulated this view:

> In short, in the church of Christ the office of the magistrate is as necessary as that of the prophet, though the latter has precedence. For just as a man must consist of both soul and body, though the body is the humbler and lesser part, so the church cannot exist without the magistracy, even though it should take care to only dispose of the more worldly matters which have less to do with the spirit.[70]

Zwingli believed that the Reformation heralded a new age in which a truly Christian society, where God would be worshipped without idolatry and his laws would underpin the state, would be built. For the most part, he shared Luther's understanding of justification by faith alone, but his interest lay more in the regenerative power of saving grace.[71] Zwingli wrote extensively on the fruits of Christ's sacrifice, how they transformed men women into new beings who radiated with the inner presence of spirit through their good works. Zwingli's theology was largely akin to that of the other major reformers, but with his heavy emphasis on the life and work of the justified Christian he drew fire from those who believed that he was preaching a form of salvation by works.

What emerged piecemeal during the 1520s was a coherent theological vision which underpinned an ambitious, and unique, plan for the reform of the church. This was the essential character of the Swiss Reformation, and all subsequent theological, ecclesiological, and even political debates and developments were refracted through Zwingli's bold enterprise. Driven by prophetic zeal and polemical rancour, the expansiveness of Zwingli's thought, however, left many unanswered questions, and these formed a crucial part of his legacy. Zwingli did not attempt to solve the riddle of the relationship between divine omnipotence and human agency. His frequent use of the quotation from Psalms that 'all men are liars' reflected his deeply negative Augustinian anthropology, yet he was very clear on the ethical response of the Christian to election. The Christian was to face life with perseverance, steadfastness, and courage.[72] Zwingli explored what these terms meant for the individual. He went beyond most other reformers in his attention to human works, often speaking of works as signs of God's election. As Peter Stephens has commented, Zwingli recognised early on in his controversies with the Catholics that there are many more passages in the Bible that speak of salvation as a reward for works than for faith, and that scripture tells of how God rewards good works.[73] Zwingli took great pains to stress that works were not the cause of salvation but, at the same time, a true faith did not exist without the active imitation of Christ in the world. The accusation that Zwingli was attempting to restore good works, and thus undermine Luther's position, was made in his own time and has continued to find a place in Reformation scholarship. The issue goes to the very kernel of the Swiss Reformation, for Zwingli had begun his career by asserting that the Swiss were being punished by God for their evil deeds. Zwingli's obsession with the good Christian life, the life of the regenerated individual and community, seems to hold the promise of God's blessing on those who do his work. While it is only fair to Zwingli to accept his position that he did not wish to suggest that works have a role in justification, his subsequent emphasis on human ethical conduct at least suggests that his thinking on the subject was more fluid that he was prepared to admit. It was one of the many issues left unresolved after the night of 11 October 1531.

If predestination and human ethics formed one conundrum of Zwingli's theology another, arguably more serious, matter resided in the reformer's famous adoption of the Pauline language of flesh and spirit. The relationship between the material and spiritual formed, as I have frequently suggested, the absolute nucleus of Zwingli's thought. Not only was it a deeply held conviction, but it was a highly effective rhetorical device as Zwingli repeatedly contrasted the venality of the church and society with the purity and simplicity of God. The proper mediation between the spiritual and the material, according to Zwingli, was the spirit of God, and that spirit was to direct all things.

This, I would argue, was both the most compelling and subversive of Zwingli's beliefs, for it both served as the foundation of the Reformed church and society, and radically undercut it. This can be illustrated with two points: Zwingli's attitude towards human rationality, and his understanding of institutions. The first point helps to clarify our understanding of Zwingli's relationship to Erasmus. Zwingli owed a considerable debt to Erasmus: he had fully absorbed from the Dutch humanist the crucial textual and linguistic skills, and he had taken from Erasmus's *Handbook of the Christian Soldier* the military image of Christ as the captain who sacrifices himself in battle for his men.[74] But just when there seems to be agreement between the two the essential difference is revealed. Zwingli does not seek Erasmus's refinement of the inner self, an ennoblement of the soul, but rather the gutsy realisation of Christ's suffering and perseverance in human life. Christ's life becomes the ethical standard for human existence, through imitation of his suffering and obedience to his commands he becomes real in the life of the Christian. Likewise, in the end, Zwingli rejected Erasmus's programme of education as the way to the Christian life. As we shall examine later, education was very important to Zwingli, and it did have a role in shaping human conduct, but primarily as a tool for opening scripture to the people. The Christian life, for Zwingli, was growth in the life of the spirit, and not the perfection of human rationality.[75] The spirit is antithetical to human reason, which was utterly corrupted in the Fall. The two are not complementary, but embattled foes. The spirit stands in opposition to human qualities, which must be subordinated to it; not simply refined to cultivate the individual, but utterly quashed in order to allow the spirit to rule. This not only put some distance between Zwingli and Erasmus, but such a radical doctrine of the spirit threatened to undermine the institutional basis of the Christian society Zwingli strove to establish.

This problem becomes more acute if we consider the very serious matter of mediation for Zwingli, as that would continue to bedevil his successors long after his death. What Zwingli argued was that nothing human and created, such as the printed bibles produced by Froschauer, the bread and wine on the communion table, or the words spoken by the preacher, is adequate to convey the spirit of God. Ultimately there remains an absolute and profound difference between an object and the spiritual reality which that object represents. This radical diminution of the material means by which God's grace is conveyed to humanity, though rooted in a reading of Paul's letters and the Gospel of John, appeared to drive a wedge between God and the world. In what way could the spirit act through institutions? Zwingli's answer was in terms of the prophetic office, but that seemed to make spiritual authority highly individual and subjective, and this would become the most contentious issue in the years following Zwingli's death in 1531. There is a certain irony in the fact that Zwingli, the reformer most concerned with Christian living, social issues, and the reform of the community, held to a doctrine of the spirit which left it difficult to understand how institutions could function in the community. His ideas on God and humanity and on the relationship between flesh and spirit were both arrestingly fresh and deeply problematic.

Notes

1 Such surveys of the opinion of community leaders were common in the late medieval Confederation. Between 1521 and 1526 there were five surveys, whilst from 1526 to 1531 there were none. See, Karl Dändliker, 'Zürcher Volksanfragen von 1521 bis 1718', *Jahrbuch für Schweizerische Geschichte*, 23 (1898), pp. 149–225.

2 Christian Dietrich, *Die Stadt Zürich und ihre Landgemeinden während der Bauernunruhen von 1489 bis 1525* (Frankfurt-am-Main and Berne, 1985), p. 139.

3 David Nicholas, *The Later Medieval City 1300–1500* (London and New York, 1997), pp. 96–97.

4 On the uneasy situation in the city, see James C. Davis, 'Coping with the Underclasses: Venice, Lille, and Zurich in the Sixteenth and Seventeenth Centuries', *Journal of Urban History*, 19 (1993), pp. 116–122.

5 Hans Morf, *Zunftverfassung und Obrigkeit in Zürich von Waldmann bis Zwingli* (Zurich, 1969), p. 2.

6 Walter Jacob, *Politische Führungsschicht und Reformation* (Zurich, 1970), p. 4.

7 Andreas Meyer, *Zürich and Rom. Ordentliche Kollatur und päpstliche Provisionen am Frau- und Grossmünster 1316–1523* (Tübingen, 1986), p. 241.

8 Cornelis Augustijn, 'Zwingli als Humanist', *Nederlands Archief voor Kerkgeschiedenis*, 67 (1987), pp. 120–142.

9 W.P. Stephens, *The Theology of Huldrych Zwingli* (Oxford, 1986), pp. 17–21.

10 Oskar Farner, *Huldrych Zwingli. Seine Entwicklung zum Reformator, 1506–1520* (Zurich, 1946), pp. 259–281, esp. pp. 276–279.

11 On this see the fine article by James M. Stayer, 'Zwingli before Zürich: Humanist Reformer and Papal Partisan', *ARG*, 72 (1981), pp. 55–68.

12 Theodor Pestalozzi, *Die Gegner Zwinglis am Großmünsterstift im Zürich* (Zurich, 1918).

13 Valentin Groebner, '"Gemein" und "Geheym": Pensionen, Geschenke, und die Sichtbarmachung des Unsichtbaren in Basel am Beginn des 16. Jahrhunderts', *Schweizerische Zeitschrift für Geschichte*, 49 (1999), pp. 445–469.

14 Paul Klaüi, 'Notizen über Gegner der Reformation in Zürich', *Zwingliana*, 6 (1938), pp. 574–80.

15 On Zwingli's study of the Fathers, see Alfred Schindler, *Zwingli und die Kirchenväter* (Zurich, 1984).

16 The best discussion of Zwingli's 'conversion' to evangelical religion, with a comparison with Luther, is found in Gottfried W. Locher, *Zwingli's Thought. New Perspectives* (Leiden, 1981), esp. pp. 144–148. Ulrich Gäbler traces the influence of Augustine in Zwingli's 'conversion' in his useful 'Huldrych Zwinglis "Reformatorische Wende"', *Zeitschrift für Kirchengeschichte*, 89 (1978), pp. 120–135

17 Fritz Schmidt-Clausing, 'Johann Ulrich Surgant, Ein Wegweiser des jungen Zwingli', *Zwingliana*, 11 (1959–63), pp. 287–320.

18 The case for Luther's influence on Zwingli is put by Martin Brecht, see his, 'Zwingli als Schüler Luthers: Zu seiner theologischen Entwicklung', *Zeitschrift für Kirchengeschichte*, 96 (1985), pp. 301–319.

19 See summary of Zwingli's thought below, pp. 75–81.

20 The fullest treatment of Zwingli's preaching is found in Oskar Farner, *Huldrych Zwingli. Seine Verkündigung und ihre ersten Früchte* (Zurich, 1954), pp. 29–94.

21 On this point the best work is Heinrich Richard Schmidt, *Reichstädte, Reich und Reformation. Korporative Religionspolitik 1521–1529/30* (Wiesbaden and Stuttgart, 1986), esp. pp. 30–40.

22 Georg Gerig, *Reisläufer und Pensionenherrn in Zürich 1519–1532. Ein Beitrag zur Kenntnis der Kräfte, welche die Reformation widerstrebten* (Zurich, 1947), p. 8.

23 Lee Palmer Wandel, *Always Among Us. Images of the Poor in Zwingli's Zurich* (Cambridge, 1990), pp. 127–132.

24 On the relationship between spirit and flesh in Zwingli's thought, see pp. 80–81.

25 Oskar Farner, 'Anna Reinhart, Die Gattin Ulrich Zwinglis', *Zwingliana*, 8 (1916), pp. 230–245.

26 Hans Schneider, 'Zwinglis Marienpredigt und Luthers Magnifikat-Auslegung', *Zwingliana* 23 (1996) pp. 105–141; also, Peter Meinhold,

'Die Marienverehrung im Verständnis der Reformatoren des 16. Jahrhunderts', *Saeculum*, 32 (1981), pp. 43–58.

27 Emidio Campi, *Zwingli und Maria. Eine reformationsgeschichtliche Studie* (Zurich, 1997).

28 Iren L. Snavely Jr, 'Huldrych Zwingli and the Preaching Office in German Switzerland', *Fides et Historia*, 25 (1993), pp. 33–45.

29 On Jud, see Karl-Heinz Wyss, *Leo Jud, Seine Entwicklung zum Reformator 1519–1523* (Berne, 1976). Also, Bruce Gordon, 'Transcendence and Community in Zwinglian Worship: The Liturgy of 1525 in Zurich', in R.N. Swanson (ed.), *Continuity and Change in Christian Worship* (Bury St Edmunds, 1999), esp. pp. 145–150.

30 The most comprehensive study of the disputations remains Bernd Moeller, 'Zwinglis Disputationen: Studien zu den Anfängen der Kirchenbildung und die Synodalwesens in Protestantismus I Teil', *Zeitschrift der Savigny-Stiftung für Rechtsgeschichte*, 87 (Kanonistische Abteilung, 56) (1970), pp. 275–324.

31 On Fabri's role, Keith Dennis Lewis, 'Johann Faber and the First Zurich Disputation: 1523. A Pre-Tridentine Catholic Response to Ulrich Zwingli and his Sixty-Seven Articles', Dissertation, Catholic University, 1985.

32 Martin Haas, *Huldrych Zwingli* (Zurich, 1969), pp. 112–114.

33 See Heiko A. Oberman, 'Zwingli's Reformation between Success and Failure', in his *The Reformation: Roots and Ramifications* (Edinburgh, 1994), p. 190.

34 On Zwingli's thought at this point see, Keith D. Lewis, 'Unica oblatio Christi: Eucharistic sacrifice and the First Zurich Disputation', *Renaissance and Reformation*, 17 (1993), pp. 19–42.

35 Stephens, *Theology of Huldrych Zwingli*, pp. 295–300.

36 On these points, see Berndt Hamm, 'What Was the Reformation Doctrine of Justification?', in C. Scott Dixon (ed.), *The German Reformation* (Oxford, 1999), pp. 53–90. A fuller treatment is found in Hamm's excellent book *Zwinglis Reformation der Freiheit* (Neukirchen-Vluyn, 1988). Much of my interpretation is drawn from this book.

37 Hans-Christoph Rublack, 'Zwingli und Zurich', *Zwingliana*, 16 (1985), pp. 393–423.

38 See chapter 6.

39 On the second disputation, Gottfried W. Locher, *Die Zwinglische Reformation im Rahmen der europäischen Kirchengeschichte* (Göttingen and Zurich, 1979), pp. 129–136.

40 For a more detailed discussion of educational reforms, see chapter 7.

41 Lee Palmer Wandel, *Voracious Idols and Violent Hands* (Yale, 1995), p. 62.

42 On Hottinger's testimony, see ibid., pp. 73–77.

43 Ibid., pp. 81–82.

44 Ibid., p. 85.

45 Ibid., p. 101.

46 On the reform of the Grossmünster in Zurich, see p. 62.

47 Haas, *Huldrych Zwingli*, pp. 133–139.

48 The speed with which the evangelical preaching was appropriated in rural communities and joined with economic complaints is demonstrated in Peter Kamber, 'Die Reformation auf der Zürcher Landschaft am Beispiel des Dorfes Marthalen. Fallstudie zur Struktur bäuerlicher Reformation', in Peter Blickle (ed.), *Zugänge zur bäuerlicher Reformation* (Zurich, 1987), pp. 85–125.

49 Philip Broadhead, 'Rural Revolt and Urban Betrayal in Reformation Switzerland: The Peasants of St Gallen and Zwinglian Zurich', in Janos Bak and Gerhard Benecke (eds), *Religion and Rural Revolt* (Dover, NH, 1984).

50 See chapter 6 for a discussion of the rise of Anabaptism.

51 Bruce Gordon, 'Transcendence and Community in Zwinglian Worship', in R.W. Swanson (ed.), *The Church and Liturgy*, Studies in Church History (1999), pp. 96–128.

52 On Zwingli's position on baptism, see Stephens, *Theology of Huldrych Zwingli*, pp. 194–217.

53 Bruce Gordon, 'Community and Transcendence', pp. 96–128.

54 Irena Backus, *The Disputations of Baden, 1526 and Berne, 1528: Neutralising the Early Church. Studies in Reformed Theology and History*, 1 (1993), pp. 1–69.

55 On Oecolampadius, see pp. 109–110.

56 G.R. Potter, *Zwingli* (Cambridge, 1976), p. 237.

57 See Stephen Strehle, 'Fides aut Foedus: Wittenberg and Zurich in conflict over the Gospel', *SCJ*, 23 (1992), pp. 3–20.

58 A clear and sensible outline is found in Stephens, *Theology of Huldrych Zwingli*, pp. 235–250.

59 See the extensive article by E.M. Henning, 'The Architectonics of Faith: Metalogic and Metaphor in Zwingli's Doctrine of the Eucharist', *Renaissance and Reformation*, 10 (1986), pp. 315–365.

60 On Karlstadt and Zwingli, see Hans-Peter Hasse, 'Zum Aufenthalt Karlstadts in Zürich (1530–1534): Ein Beitrag zum 450. Todestag des Reformators', *Zwingliana*, 18 (1990–91), pp. 366–389.

61 A very helpful outline of the stages of the Marburg meeting is found in Locher, *Die Zwinglische Reformation*, pp. 310–318.

62 Ibid., pp. 323–327.

63 Walther Köhler, 'Das Marburger Religionsgespräch. Versuch einer Rekonstruktion', Schriften des Vereins für Reformationsgeschichte, 48 (Leipzig, 1929); more recently, Joachim Staedtke, 'Eine neue Version des sogenannten Utinger-Berichtes von Marbuger Religionsgespräch 1529', *Zwingliana*, 10 (1955), pp. 210–216.

64 Potter, *Zwingli*, pp. 328–329.

65 For the spread of Zwinglian thought into southern Germany, see chapter 9.

66 Z, III, p. 842.

67 Locher, *Zwingli's Thought*, p. 208.

68 Z, II, p. 232. Quoted in Locher, *Zwingli's Thought*, p. 199.

69 Z, VI/I, pp. 497, 3–8.

70 S, IV, p. 60.

71 Useful background reading is Alister E. McGrath, 'Justification and the Reformation: The Significance of the Doctrine of Justification by Faith to Sixteenth-Century Urban Communities', *ARG*, 81 (1990), pp. 5–19.

72 Gottfried W. Locher, 'Steadfastness. Zwingli's Final Sermon at the Bern Disputation as a Contribution to his Ethics', in his *Zwingli's Thought*, pp. 256–266.

73 Stephens, *Theology of Huldrych Zwingli*, p. 159.

74 Locher, *Zwingli's Thought*, p. 77.

75 Ibid., pp. 251–253.

3

The spread of the Reformation

The narrative of the Swiss Reformation remains reasonably straightforward until the movement spread beyond Zurich into the other states and territories of the Confederation. At that point we find ourselves confronted with coterminous events which were interconnected and interrelated to varying degrees. This chapter seeks both to address the questions of why and how the evangelical movement gained a purchase in parts of the German-speaking Swiss regions and to provide discrete, though necessarily thumbnail, accounts of those individual movements. Faced with a vast panoply of names, events, and places, it is tempting to throw up one's hands and declare the whole thing an inchoate mess, but that will not do. A more profitable line of thought is to consider how the events of the second half of the 1520s offer us a window on how a religious movement spread in the sixteenth century, and how it adapted to various political and social structures.

A few general points which arose in the previous chapter need to be recalled. The evangelical party was always a minority movement; in every case its success was dependent on winning over the magistrates, who would then impose the new religion. Apart from a brief flirtation during the Peasants' War, the reform movement was neither broad-based nor popular, and the reformers did not ever wish it to be. The evangelical movement spread in the Swiss lands through small networks of friends, most of humanist disposition, who saw themselves as a fraternity committed to the reform of religion and society. Zwingli stood at the centre of this web of contacts and all the key figures were at some point in contact with him. Most, but by no means all (Vadianus, for example), of the reformers came from the clergy and had studied at universities across Europe, frequently at Vienna, Paris,

Tübingen, and Heidelberg, before returning to the Confederation with the new religious ideas. The most significant point of contact for the future reformers, however, lay within the Confederation, and that was the relatively new university in Basle.[1] Although such distinguished scholars such as Ulrich Surgant and Thomas Wittenbach were to be found in Basle, it was not so much what was taught at the university but rather the presence of the printing industry and, more importantly, of Erasmus and his circle which made Basle so influential.[2] Virtually all the significant figures of the early Swiss Reformation either studied in Basle or spent time in the Rhenish city.

It cannot escape our notice in this respect that the influence of Erasmus and the printing culture in the city was decisive. Repeatedly, the *Handbook of the Christian Soldier* and Erasmus's paraphrases of the New Testament were cited by reformers as influential texts in moulding both their criticisms of the church and in stirring their desire for a simpler, practical spirituality based on the imitation of Christ. We must also not underestimate the impact of Erasmus's New Testament, even for those with insufficient Greek to read it. Erasmus created in Basle a circle of men of learning and zeal who would achieve great things in different fields; it was an exciting and creative place. The Dutch humanist's influence, however, extended far beyond his immediate circle; he was a powerful symbol, and the importance of his presence in Basle was understood by many who neither knew him nor could read his work. Erasmus for his part repudiated the Reformation and acrimoniously fell out with Zwingli and Oecolampadius, who ultimately came to very different theological positions than those of their erstwhile mentor. Nevertheless, they and others took from Erasmus the intellectual tools which made possible their understanding of biblical exegesis and church history. Likewise, Zwingli's emphasis on the regenerate Christian and the ethics of the Christian life, two of the key points which distinguish him from Luther, owed a great deal to the Dutch humanist. In the end, however, there was too much distance between Zwingli, and the other Swiss reformers, and Erasmus for the great man to be regarded as more than an important, if unwilling, influence.[3]

We have stressed from the outset that Zwingli's theology gave the Swiss evangelical movement intellectual coherence, but a cautionary note must be sounded. Although Zwingli was the outstanding figure, he cannot be easily compared to his contemporary Martin Luther, for the relationships of these two men to the movements they headed were strikingly different.What distinguished Zwingli from Luther, apart from the profound theological differences considered in the previous chapter, was that Zwingli's message was far more historically and politically conditioned. His theology could not be uncoupled from the historical legacy – and hegemonic reams – of Zurich, where he had forged an alliance with the magistrates by weaving together evangelical principles and worldly concerns. Zwingli was not in any sense regarded by his contemporaries as a 'Swiss' figure (except perhaps when being savaged by Luther) but rather as the preacher of Zurich, and that connection set off a series of responses. If the other Confederates felt they had spotted a Trojan horse their unease was well justified, as Zwingli had partially sold the new faith to the Zurich magistrates by appealing to their sense of pre-eminence among the Swiss. Zwingli was a powerful force, but in order for his message to take root outside of Zurich his role had to be downplayed. Thus Zwingli was attempting to mastermind a movement for which he was not regarded as an acceptable symbol. If we bear this in mind the fundamental ambiguity of the Swiss in the 1520s towards their Reformation is more understandable.

Thus a key difference between the Swiss and German Reformations was that in the Confederation the spread of the reform movement had absolutely nothing to do with any nascent sense of national identity. There was little that was 'Swiss' about its Reformation: it was not a national cause and it was not seen as the means to any form of state. This is perhaps because there was no foreign Antichrist who could be easily vilified and used to unite the Swiss. The centrality of the papacy to the German Reformation was not replicated in the Confederation. It was opposition to the Habsburgs which had given coherence to the historical evolution of the Confederation. But now the situation was different, more complex and divisive. For Zwingli the great opponents of the true faith were not the exploitative popes and their cardinals, but the Swiss themselves. It was the mercenary service, which could only be partially blamed on foreigners, which was desecrating the land and would bring divine wrath. The character of Swiss evangelical thought, with its emphasis on ethics and social renewal, necessarily led to a clash of vested interests within the Confederation. All the fault-lines conveniently masked by the vagueness of the Confederation's constitution were exposed in the noonday sun.

Printing played a crucial role in the early Swiss Reformation, particularly as it made ideas accessible to people in their own language: as Zwingli and Luther proved at Marburg, the German and Swiss Reformations were as far apart linguistically as they were theologically. Against this, however, we need to remember that printing was limited to Basle and Zurich, appearing in other centres only a good deal later. By far the most crucial factor in the success or failure of a reform movement in a locality was the presence or absence of an effective preacher. This survey of the Swiss regions brings to the fore the importance of personality to a reform movement: in this sense Zwingli was the prime example. The forces for and against the Reformation in the Confederation were finely balanced and it took a strong leader to shift events decisively. When we look at two neighbouring areas and ask why, as was often the case, one had a vibrant reform movement while the other saw barely the faintest stirrings of interest, we find that the answer has to do with the personalities involved. In Berne and Basle the evangelical parties were in an entirely different position from Zurich largely because of the weak or flawed leadership of Oecolampadius and Myconius on the one hand, and Haller and Megander on the other. In contrast, Zwingli provided a sobering lesson in the dangers of strong leadership.

Finally, something needs to be said about the mechanics of how the movement spread. It will not surprise us that the lands which first witnessed the growth of evangelical parties were those over which Zurich had the most influence, that is to say those in the eastern part of the Confederation and the Graubünden. Without Zwingli and Zurich neither of the other important Swiss cities, Berne and Basle, would have adopted the Reformation, but they had very much their own story and the results did not mirror events on the Limmat. Thus there was a certain symmetry to the events of 1525–29 as the Reformation moved from the areas where Zwingli and Zurich had the most influence to the urban centres where they had the least.

First advances in the eastern Confederation

St Gall

St Gall was a city of four thousand inhabitants, only slightly smaller than Zurich, which was distinguished by its enormous Benedictine abbey whose abbot was a prince of the empire. The abbey owned large tracts of land which ran north towards Lake Constance and the Rhine. The late Middle Ages had witnessed a drawn-out conflict between the guilds of the town and the abbey, as the merchants sought to liberate themselves from ecclesiastical rule. Both the town and the abbey were allied with the Swiss Confederation without being full members, and a principal reason for Zurich's influence in St Gall was its role as one of the four Confederates appointed to govern its affairs, such as the election of the abbot.[4] The evangelical preaching began in St Gall in 1524 and immediately found a sympathetic audience among the merchants, who had no love for the Benedictine monks and their interfering abbot.[5] The leading figure was the remarkable layman Joachim von Watt, who had been professor in Vienna from 1512, and then had read Luther during 1518–19 after his return to his native city.[6] Vadianus, as he called himself, was by far the brightest star in the firmament of Swiss humanism of the early sixteenth century, well connected with the world of learning and religious reform in the southern German cities.[7] In 1519 he married into the patrician Grebel family of Zurich, one member of which was Konrad, the future radical leader.

Vadianus's conversion to the Reformation was typical of many of the leading Swiss humanists; it developed first from reading the editions of the Church Fathers arriving from the presses of Basle. Erasmus was a towering influence in so many respects, but the Greek New Testament deserves particular mention. Vadianus, like many of his learned contemporaries, had come to a certain disposition towards Christianity and the church where Luther's writings would have maximum effect, and he was scandalised by the church's response to the German reformer. From the time of the Leipzig Disputation in 1519 Vadianus was in contact with Zwingli, and it is likely he had read Melanchthon's earliest version of the *Loci communes*. Inspired by the work of theologians, Vadianus the layman turned his hand to writing a Latin commentary on the Creed, followed by a commentary on the Acts of the Apostles. In the early 1520s it was Luther's theology which impressed itself on Vadianus; it was a relationship which would last given Vadianus's enduring contacts to the German reformers through his high standing among the humanists.[8] Although he had not taken part in the First Disputation in Zurich in January 1523, by the Second in October 1523 Vadianus was invited to preside.

Vadianus's closest colleague was Johannes Kessler, who had studied in Basle with the intention of becoming a priest. Kessler had made his way to Wittenberg with a friend to hear Luther, Melanchthon, Karlstadt, and Bugenhagen, remaining there for six months before returning to St Gall in November 1523.[9] Filled with evangelical zeal, Kessler took the lead in setting up a group of laity and clerics to discuss passages of the New Testament and Luther's theology. This group, known as the *Lesinen*, originally met in the house of a local official, but soon moved to the guildhouse of the tailors and finally to the even larger hall of the weavers' guild in order to accommodate all who wished to attend. The success of these meetings in St Gall soon attracted an opprobrious response from the diet of the Swiss Confederation, where the Confederates complained about the preaching of God's Word outside the church. Kessler was silenced by a decree of the St Gall council, but there were others to take his place. During the period 1523–25 laymen took the lead in preaching outside churches and in the rooms of the city's guilds. St Gall was a prosperous mercantile city and the guilds quickly rallied behind this religious movement which, for the most part, was led by non-clerics, a phenomenon repeated in Berne and Basle in contrast to the very clerical Zurich.[10]

The situation in St Gall was greatly influenced by the course of events in Zurich, and in particular the disputations of 1523 impressed the St Gall magistrates. Greater pressure was brought to bear by the arrival in the city of Balthasar Hubmaier in April 1523. Hubmaier, later one of the leaders of the radical movement, held open-air sermons, preaching to the faithful as they made an indulgence pilgrimage to the abbey. Hubmaier's sermons on Luke made a huge impression on his audience, and by the time Vadianus returned to St Gall in early 1523 the moment of decision had arrived. A council mandate had been issued declaring that ministers were to preach the Word of God as found in scripture. Those who resisted would have to give an account of themselves before the council. A commission was drawn up, on which Vadianus served, for the reform of the church, and its first act was to tackle poor relief. Goods for the poor were gathered in the St Laurenzen church and distributed to the needy under the aegis of the commission.

In the following years St Gall continued to follow the lead of Zurich. With Vadianus's election as Bürgermeister in December 1525 the way to reform was open. The new year brought the removal of images from the church and the establishment of evangelical services in many of the city churches, though not in the abbey, where the mass was celebrated until 1528. Although there was widespread support in the city, there was good reason for caution; this had to do with the robustness of the radical movement in St Gall, where numerous Anabaptists, including Konrad Grebel, had taken refuge following their expulsion from Zurich. Following the first evangelical Lord's Supper in St Gall at Easter 1527, a further mandate was passed requiring parish churches to keep records of baptisms and marriages, and a catechism that had been printed in Zurich was introduced in 1527 for the religious education of the youth. As in Zurich a morals mandate was brought in regulating the conduct of the people, ensuring that they attended church and making schoolmasters responsible for the moral and religious education of girls and boys.

It was not until the Berne Disputation of 1528 that the St Gall council forbade the celebration of the mass at the abbey, although the abbot had fled in 1527, taking residence in the nearby castle of Rorschach. When he died in March 1529 his death was kept a secret for a week until a successor could be elected. The council in St Gall was purged of Catholics in 1528 and in November of that year the city was admitted to the Christian Civic League as a full member, thus compensating for the fact that St Gall was only an associate member of the Swiss Confederation.

Under Bürgermeister Vadianus the cleansing of St Gall's churches proceeded apace. During 1529 the town church and the abbey were stripped and their walls were white-washed. Vadianus, according to Kessler's account, had barely finished reading the council's proclamation on images in the Münster when the people began to remove the art in a frenzied burst of iconoclasm. Much that was precious was lost, and the St Gall council was unable to impose the order exercised in Zurich, where patrons had been allowed to claim their benefactions before they were destroyed. In March 1529 the first evangelical service was held in the abbey with four thousand worshippers. The great Benedictine abbey had been secularised and was now in the possession of the magistrates. The situation was to change again following the Second Kappel War in 1531, when the abbot returned and Catholicism was restored in the abbey.[11] From 1531 until the French Revolution the abbey and its lands were divided from the city of St Gall, which remained Reformed.

Appenzell

The triumph of the evangelical cause in St Gall opened the way to other areas in the eastern part of the Confederation, and following the First Kappel War in June 1529 Zurich and St Gall embarked upon an aggressive policy of dissolving religious houses and winning over the smaller territories. The fruits of their efforts were soon evident: Toggenburg was gained in 1528. The first significant gain for the Zurich/St Gall axis was in Appenzell, where Zwingli and Vadianus were in epistolary contact with men such as Johannes Dörig, Walter Klarer, and Johannes Hess, all of whom were priests.[12] The evangelical cause, however, faced considerable opposition, led by the senior priest, Diebolt Huter. As early as 1523 the Appenzell council, following the example of St Gall, issued a decree permitting Gospel-preaching, and Huter was dispatched to attend the October disputation in Zurich, though in accordance with Catholic practice, he was not to participate. On 24 April 1524 the *Landsgemeinde* in Appenzell decided that all priests, ministers, chaplains, and assistants should not preach or teach from the pulpit anything other than what was found in scripture. The likely model for this proclamation was the St Gall mandate of 5 April 1524.

The matter was not, however, fully resolved. The magistrates, despite their preaching mandate, remained Catholics and the mass was still celebrated. The evangelicals, lacking significant popular support, had to push hard for a breakthrough, and they adopted the tactic used in Zurich of holding a religious disputation. Jakob Schurtanner, friend of Vadianus and native of St Gall, took the lead, marking out seven topics for debate: purgatory, masses for the dead, the sacrifice of Christ, the veneration of Mary and the saints, the intercession of saints, the scriptural warrant for seven sacraments, and the scriptural basis for indulgences. The day chosen for the debate was 7 July 1524. Three hundred people assembled for what turned to be a damp squib. Querulous conduct on both sides precluded any meaningful exchange and the so-called disputation never rose above rancour over points of procedure.

Nevertheless the evangelical movement did make some headway. The villages of Gais and Teufen went over to the Reformation, though as we shall see the influence of Anabaptism was very much in evidence. Men and women left religious houses in large numbers, and in the monastery of Wonnenstein, for example, there was a stir when the chaplain embraced the Reformation and married one of the nuns. But these stories can be deceiving. Within Appenzell there was no general agreement on religion, and although the Reformation had won converts in communities, those professing the evangelical faith were a minority. Violence broke out and the ruling authorities feared anarchy. The disruption led to the innovative suggestion of Joseph Schumacher that each community be allowed to choose whether it would adopt the evangelical faith or remain Catholic. There could only be one form of worship in each church and that was to be chosen by the people, with the minority being allowed to attend the nearest church of their faith.[13] This proposal, more a triumph of peacekeeping than toleration, won approval with the following results: the outer Rhoden (with the exception of Herisau) accepted the Reformation whilst Appenzell and Herisau remained Catholic. Eventually Herisau changed sides, joining the evangelical camp, and received as its minister the young Ambrosius Blarer from Constance. This creative solution, so suited to the communal nature of the Swiss states, became the model for the whole Confederation when it had to deal with the partial success of the Reformation.

The Appenzell evangelical church was closely bound to St Gall; the Appenzellers attended the St Gall synod and the St Gall liturgy for the Lord's Supper was adopted. Further, excommunication as a form of discipline, following Matthew 18:17, was used in the Appenzell churches as it was in St Gall. Zurich, however, mindful that the eastern Confederation was its natural sphere of influence, had its eyes on Appenzell and in May 1531 it commenced negotiations intended to win greater control over its churches. The Zurichers put considerable pressure on the Catholic communities to abandon their opposition to the Reformation, but without success.

The Thurgau

It was in the Thurgau more than any other region that Zurich used its force to bring about Reformation. The Thurgau had fallen under Swiss control after the Swabian War of 1499, and had become one of the Mandated Territories, as they were known, governed by a *Landvogt* (bailiff) appointed by the responsible Confederate states. For these mandated lands different Confederates were appointed to rule jointly and there was an established practice of taking turns in choosing the governor. This worked reasonably well until the Reformation placed the ruling Confederates at loggerheads over religion.

The first major controversy of the Swiss Reformation took place in the Thurgau during July 1524, when following the arrest of the priest Johannes Öchsli bells rang out in the land summoning the people to his aid.[14] About five thousand peasants gathered near the Carthusian house at Ittingen. Some of the crowd began to attack the house; but what had started as a fairly modest protest quickly grew to an onslaught and the house was sacked and its monks beaten up. The Confederate states were outraged by this pillage, and they held Zurich responsible on account of its toleration of heretical preaching. Unwilling to force a confrontation with the other Confederates, soldiers were sent from Zurich to round up the ringleaders, who were tortured and executed.

During the spring and summer of 1524 the Mandated Territories became a serious issue between Zurich and the Five Inner States of Uri, Schwyz, Unterwalden, Lucerne, and Zug.[15] The iconoclast Klaus Hottinger, who had been expelled from Zurich, had been arrested in Baden (a territory in which Zurich had joint lordship) and was burnt in Lucerne. In reply, on 24 March 1524 Zurich raised the temperature by issuing a mandate insisting that nothing be done against the evangelicals in the Thurgau without its permission. No preacher could be arrested, no one who declared him- or herself in favour of Gospel-preaching was to be prejudiced, and the free trade of meat and eggs during Lent and Advent was to be permitted.[16] Most provocatively, the bailiff, Marx Wehrli, a staunch opponent of the Reformation in the Thurgau, was seized at the end of March 1528 whilst staying at an inn in Zurich and tossed into prison for unfavourable remarks he had allegedly made against the evangelicals. After languishing in the Wellenberg, the prison tower in the middle of the Limmat, he was beheaded by the Zurich authorities on 5 May.

Zurich continued to exert pressure on the communities of the Thurgau to adopt the Reformation, and at two meetings of the *Landsgemeinde* in April 1529 it was indicated to the Thurgauers that their conversion to the new faith was crucial to Zurich's continuing friendship. The real breakthrough, however, came with the resolution of the First Kappel War in 1529. The articles of the treaty allowed individual communities in the Thurgau to decide for or against the Reformation. The Reformation mandates of the evangelical cities were declared valid in the Thurgau and no one could force Catholicism on the people. The apparent victory of the Reformation was accompanied by great unrest in the rural communities as the peasants used their new-found freedom to press their economic demands. Religious houses were sacked and there was a general breakdown of order. The evangelical states had to scramble to maintain control.

In December 1529 the first of two synods was held in St Niklaus church in Frauenfeld. About five hundred people gathered, and from Zurich came Huldrych Zwingli, who held the opening sermon in which he outlined the essential principles of Reformation. Zwingli was also present for the second synod of March 1530, during which a Reformation mandate for the reform of church and laity was drafted. It was agreed that the whole of the Mandated Territory would be reformed along the lines of the Zurich church.

Graubünden

What is now referred to as the Graubünden was in the sixteenth century three Rhaetian Leagues known as the Grey League, the League of God's House and the Ten Jurisdictions.[17] Although these leagues enjoyed close relations with the Swiss they were not part of the Confederation. Like the Swiss Confederation, the Rhaetian Leagues were a loosely bound federation of communes which had come together for mutually advantageous reasons of defence and peace-keeping. The Swiss and the Rhaetians also had much in common: they shared enemies and were built around the same principles of federalism and anti-feudalism.[18] As with the Swiss, the defeat of Emperor Maximilian I in 1499 had led to the liberation of the Rhaetians from the Holy Roman Empire, even if this was not formally recognised until 1648. Following the defeat of Milan the Swiss and Rhaetian Leagues had seized Italian lands; in 1512 the Leagues took control of the Valtelline, Bormio, and Chiavenna as mandated territories.

The evangelical movement spread from the city of Chur into the valleys of the Graubünden during the early 1520s, where it appealed to the isolated communities seeking local autonomy. The leading figure was Johannes Comander, who had studied in St Gall with Vadianus before proceeding to Basle university, where he was a contemporary of Zwingli. He returned to Chur in 1523 to serve in the church of St Martin. By the time of his return from Basle Comander was an exponent of evangelical ideas, but he was not the first in the Graubünden. Jakob Salzmann had also studied in Vienna and Basle and had corresponded with Zwingli. From 1511 he had served in the episcopal household in Chur, where there was a circle of men committed to the reform of the church. In 1522 Salzmann had read the works of Luther made available by the printing presses in Basle and this had inspired him to abandon his clerical office and to take up the position of master of the city school.

Comander's preaching in Chur turned the evangelical cause into a popular movement, but it also put him on course for conflict with the bishop, Paul Ziegler, and the abbot of the Premonstratensian house of St Luzi, Theodor Schlegel, both formidable opponents.[19] Appointed bishop of Chur in 1510, Ziegler's political sympathies lay with the Austrian Habsburgs, putting him at odds with the generally pro-French Confederation. Schlegel, a native of Chur, had studied in Tübingen and Heidelberg before becoming abbot of St Luzi in 1515; like Salzmann he was taken with the writings of Martin Luther in the early 1520s, but he could not accept Luther's break with the church.

The first fruit of the reform movement in the Graubünden was the *Ilanz Articles* of 1524.[20] As Randolph Head has noted, these articles were evidence of a strong, rurally based Reformation and they anticipated many of the demands of the German peasants of 1525.[21] Clerical courts were to be regulated, priests were to be made citizens, and parishioners were to be given the right to participate in the election of priests and lay control was granted over religious endowments. The *First Ilanz Articles* were followed by a new *Bundesbrief* of 23 September in which the relationship between the Three Leagues on matters of common action and the resolution of disputes were defined.

In Chur a battle raged between Comander and the cathedral chapter. In 1523 the Rhaetian diet had issued a mandate recognising scriptural preaching, but this was not sufficient for the evangelical camp and in 1525 Comander declared on behalf of forty clergy in the Graubünden his readiness to engage in a disputation with the Catholics on the basis of holy scripture. The Rhaetian diet determined that the religious dispute should take place on 7 January in Ilanz. Comander prepared eighteen theses for the disputation, most of which were taken from Zwingli's *Sixty-Seven Articles* of 1523.[22]

The Ilanz Disputation lasted two days and was primarily a contest between Comander and Schlegel, with the latter advancing the view that the laity were not competent to debate theological questions. Using Matthew 16:10 ('You are Peter and on this rock I will build my church…') Schlegel defended the Catholic understanding of the church and papacy. The two men also debated the issues of purgatory, the Catholic understanding of tradition, the priesthood and the eucharist. The veneration of images, however, seems not to have been touched. In the end there was no resolution and neither side could claim victory, but from the disputation came the *Second Ilanz Articles* of 25 June 1526.[23]

One reason for the failure of the disputation was the magistrates' fear of peasant revolts in the Graubünden, in particular the League of God's House. The *Second Ilanz Articles* reflected something of this concern as the bishop was relieved of all his territories, appeals to the episcopal courts were denied, and matters such as hunting and fishing rights were devolved to the communities. Despite these concessions to the communes the general spirit of the *Second Ilanz Articles* was towards the state church. Religious houses were placed under the control of political authorities, foreigners were not allowed to hold benefices in the Graubünden, and the bishop could only be elected with the approval of the League of God's House. The extent of control over the church by political authorities, as outlined in the *Articles*, was such that not only Catholic but also many of the evangelical clergy were left feeling unsettled.

In Chur from 1527 the majority of the council supported Comander in his struggle against the Catholic hierarchy, and this brought about a breakthrough. The mass was abolished, and by late March images were removed from the principal churches. The victory, however, was not complete. Opposition to the reforms ran deep in the city and a highly visible symbol of resistance was the high altar in the church of St Martin, which remained intact until 1529.[24] Unlike most of the Swiss cities, Chur witnessed an open battle between the evangelical and Catholic parties. Catholic opposition dug in around Abbot Schlegel in the cathedral chapter and religious houses. In the summer of 1528 the council ordered the religious houses to cease celebrating the mass, but its threats went unheeded; in St Luzi, Catholic worship remained untouched in defiance of the decrees of the council. In the rural areas the evangelical party made limited, but unspectacular gains, as many areas remained staunchly Catholic. Outside the city of Chur, the most fertile ground for the Reformation was in the Ten Jurisdictions, where in communities such as Klosters, Davos, and Malans evangelical churches were established, generally as a result of energetic preaching and local leadership.[25] In the League of God's House, in contrast, there was little success. The story was similar in the Grey League.

With its religious situation precariously balanced, the Graubünden found itself in 1528 drawn into the growing hostilities between the Catholic and evangelical states of the Swiss Confederation. The particular event was the so-called 'Musso' War. Musso was the name taken by Gian Giacomo de' Medici, who had acquired a castle on the border between the Graubünden and Milan. He was a minor figure, but one with powerful connections to important Catholics in the region who were working to reverse the Reformation in Chur. A quarrel had broken out between Musso and the Rhaetian Leagues, and when two of their emissaries were killed, tensions heightened. Musso, emboldened by his Catholic allies, made impossible demands and then followed these up with an invasion of the Valtelline, which belonged to the Graubünden. The Swiss, as sworn allies, were bound to defend the Rhaetian Leagues and troops were sent from all the Confederates except the Five Inner States.

The incident was in itself quite forgettable, and the military action was minor, but the reactions of the various parties demonstrated the fragility of the Confederation. Zurich believed that the disturbances in the east were part of a plan by Archduke Ferdinand of Austria to attack and the refusal of the Catholic states to send troops was interpreted as complicity in this invasion. In truth, Ferdinand was far more concerned with the dire situation in Vienna, where the Turks were hammering at the door. In the spring of 1531 Musso's troops were driven from the Valtelline and his castle was destroyed by Zurich artillery. Terms were agreed which were favourable to the Graubünden and the evangelical cause; and the principal consequence of this little war was that the Reformation in the Graubünden and its southern Italian valleys was secured.[26]

Glarus

In the eastern land of Glarus the evangelical party had particular hopes for success as did Zwingli, who had served as *Leutpriester* from 1506–16.[27] Even after his moves to Einsiedeln and Zurich he had retained close friendships and connections in Glarus, most prominently with his former student Valantin Tschudi, a priest and historian. Following his studies in Italy, Basle, and Paris Tschudi had returned to Glarus as Zwingli's successor in 1518. Tschudi was a humanist and one of the most important of the Swiss historians of the period, but Zwingli's hopes that his student would lead the Reformation in Glarus were to be disappointed; Tschudi was a moderate whose religious views fell somewhere between the Catholic and evangelical parties, perhaps more akin to those of Erasmus, whom he had known in Basle. He wrote Zwingli a long letter on 15 March 1530 in which he defended himself and his actions. He had concocted for himself a unique mixture of Catholic and evangelical theology which reflected his daily routine, when as a priest he would celebrate mass in the morning before holding an evangelical sermon in the afternoon. His priestly duties remained undisturbed until 1530, when he married, though he seems never to have fully embraced the Reformation or left the Catholic church, retaining a highly individual form of religion until his death at the hand of a plague epidemic in 1555. He was described by the principal reformer of Glarus, Fridolin Brunner, as a 'windbag'.

Brunner was an entirely different sort of man. Like most Swiss reformers, he had studied at Basle and had taken many of the reform ideas back to his native land. Brunner arrived in Glarus as a priest in 1521 or 1522.[28] During the time of the disputations in Zurich he had converted to the evangelical camp, claiming to be the first in Glarus so to do. There is some evidence of Brunner's evangelical activity in Glarus around 1523, but the political uncertainty in the region made an open declaration of beliefs far too dangerous. He attended the disputation in Baden in 1526, but did not speak out against the powerful Catholic forces arrayed there. The turning point came with the Berne Disputation of 1528, which Brunner attended. The conversion of Berne and the likelihood that Basle would soon follow enabled men like Brunner to return to their homelands and preach openly. This emboldened preaching spawned acts of iconoclasm in numerous parish churches, all of which led to a meeting of the *Landsgemeinde* on 15 March 1528. Representatives from the Catholic and evangelical states were sent to Glarus to influence the situation, but there was no real resolution when the two sides clashed. A vote of the delegates indicated that the evangelical sympathisers were a minority, but as sporadic iconoclasm in the parishes around Glarus indicated, there were enough supporters to cause a considerable amount of unrest.

At a second *Landsgemeinde* on 3 May 1528 another vote was held. This time it was not only citizens but also those resident on the land and in the city but without citizenship (the *Hintersässen*), among whom the evangelicals had a majority, who were allowed to vote.[29] The outcome was different, but no less fractious, for as the representatives sought to hold elections to offices, the meeting descended into chaos and violence, and had to be abandoned. The evangelicals held the upper hand and managed, with considerable support from Zurich and Berne, to secure for themselves the key offices whilst the Catholics, unable to draw upon the same level of support from the Five Inner States, retreated.

The situation in Glarus posed a great danger to the Swiss Confederation. The violence and disorder which raged during 1528–29 resulted in the destruction of altars and church art of great spiritual significance to Catholics. Although the Swiss diet still contained a majority of Catholic states, it was powerless to deal with the situation; the opposition of Zurich and Berne was enough to secure a stalemate. The only way forward was a local solution, and this came in May 1529, when the *Landsgemeinde* decided that each community should be allowed to choose its form of worship. The resolution was weighted in the evangelicals' favour, for the mass was to be permitted as long as the majority wished to retain it.[30] When this majority was lost the Reformation would be introduced. In communities where the mass had already been abolished, however, no further change was envisaged. The articles of Reformation offered protection to clergy of both parties, reduced the number of saints' days and declared that neither side could openly denounce the other as heretical. This principal of parity was used on various occasions in the eastern part of the Confederation and it formed a uniquely Swiss resolution to the problems posed by Reformation in the communes. One must not idealise it, as there were serious political and religious constraints imposed, but the concept of parity came from a long tradition of communal rule. It provided a *modus vivendi,* which was the logic behind all communal agreements in Swiss history.

In the wake of the First Kappel War in 1529 Zurich, under the influence of Zwingli, for whom the notion of parity was nothing less than accommodation with idolatry, pushed forward the Reformation in Glarus.[31] There were renewed attempts to hold disputations in order that the Catholics might be roundly defeated, but the priests were too canny to be drawn into the trap. Nevertheless, Zurich was successful in leaving its stamp on the new evangelical order in Glarus; the *Landsgemeinde* set up a commission to cleanse the churches of images and by 1530 a marriage court (*Ehegericht*) was created after the model of Zurich.

This was reversed by the disaster of the Second Kappel War. The Five Inner States (*Fünf Orte*) demanded a return to the old religion and Glarus, unable to obtain support from the humiliated Zurich, gave way. The Second Peace of Kappel brought the recatholicisation of the Freiamt, Toggenburg, Gaster, Weesen, and Rapperswil, all lands bordering Glarus with the consequence that in the communities of Linthal, Schwanden, and Näfels religious images and altars were restored. The evangelicals were not vanquished but their position was greatly weakened; they were still in the majority but lacked crucial external support. The depth of the division was underscored in 1532 when the Catholics and evangelicals parted ways: they met in separate *Landsgemeinden.* Despite the religious hostility, however, both sides acknowledged that peace was essential, and this was reflected in the thirteen articles of the First Glarus Peace of 1532. Catholics and evangelicals, it declared, were not to preach against each other; marital disputes in Catholic or mixed marriages were to be resolved in the episcopal court, while for evangelicals such cases were to be heard in a secular marriage court. Only the village of Linthal was to return to the Catholic religion; in Schwanden and Glarus the principle of parity was to remain. The other villages which had previously chosen one of the confessions would remain as before.

The principal urban Confederates

Berne

In December 1518 Luther's first writings arrived in Berne, brought by a bookseller. From the early 1520s there were isolated voices supporting the evangelical cause, but otherwise Berne was a thoroughly ordinary Catholic city.[32] In early 1522, however, things became more polemical. Georg Brunner, the inflammatory preacher in Kleinhöchstetten, where there was a beloved image of the Mother of God popular with pilgrims, described the pope in a sermon on John 16:5 as Antichrist. Brunner was a talented preacher and showman who could work a crowd, and he delighted in shocking those making the pilgrimage to the Madonna with his anti-Roman sentiments. The local clergy sought to have Brunner removed, or at least transferred to another chapter, but the Berne council was not persuaded. The magistrates in the city had their own agenda; they were concerned with curtailing the power of the clergy, and the Brunner case allowed them to demonstrate their resolve not to kow-tow to priests. It was arranged that a trial would be held before sixteen officials, lay and clerical, of whom eight were clear supporters of the evangelical faith, three were Catholics and the remainder, somewhere in between. The form of the trial was indicative of what was to come: the fiery Brunner lambasted his opponents and defended himself with reference to biblical texts. His opponents had neither the time nor the skill to contest Brunner's interpretation of the texts, and the effect was a decisive victory for the evangelical party. At this early date the Bernese council had demonstrated at least tacit support for the Reformation.

An even more remarkable scene took place at the Cistercian nunnery at Fraubrunnen, where a large number of clergy had gathered to celebrate the feast of St Anna on 26 July 1522. During the meal, and no doubt emboldened by the wine, several of the clergy fell into discussion over the 'new religion'. Some Catholics, men like Bendicht Steiner, attacked humanism, blaming it for the evils which had befallen the church. The evangelicals present responded, saying that the Lord's Supper was a memorial and that Christ had taught the priesthood of all believers. Sebastian Meyer, the distinguished evangelical preacher, found himself in dispute with his neighbour at the table over the subject of Martin Luther. When Meyer sought to correct a wrong-headed interpretation of Luther, another chimed in that where Jan Hus held one heretical view, Luther held ten. Then another said that Luther, like Hus, should be burnt. Meyer retorted that it had been wrong to burn Hus. Provokingly, his neighbour asked Meyer if the Bernese council had erred in burning the monks following the

Jetzer case. Meyer fell into the trap, replying that this was indeed an error.[33]

Meyer's indiscretion nearly doomed the evangelical cause in Berne before it had even really taken shape. The magistrates were furious at his suggestion of error; they were in no mood to be upbraided by clerics, and only an abject apology spared Meyer. His contrition was crucial, as Meyer was the principal voice for the evangelicals in Berne, and by 1522 he was already putting his thoughts in print in the form of commentaries on the Pauline epistles and the Apostles' Creed. This brought him into conflict with the Dominican Wilhelm Zieli, who launched a vicious polemical counterattack. The council was once again drawn into religious debates and this time sided with Meyer, largely, one suspects, because it wanted to put an end to the war of words which was dividing the community. Following the resolution of this dispute the Bernese council, against the wishes of the Swiss diet, declared on 27 December 1522 that it wished its ministers to be free to preach the Word of God without restriction.

The Catholics began to fight back. In the autumn of 1522 the Dominican Hans Heim von Mainz was summoned to Berne to refute the 'Lutheran' views being propagated there. Sebastian Meyer sought to take him on, and indeed he managed to counter Heim's influence, but there were strong forces within the city opposed to the Reformation. Meyer was a foreigner and hardly a charismatic man, and in the face of the lucrative mercenary business, which lined the pockets of many in the city and ensured that many families had a vested interest in the failure of the evangelical party, he made little impression. As in Zurich, the situation required a more powerful personality to push the Reformation forward, a person with influence who could capture the public mood. The role fell to Niklaus Manuel.

The *Fastnacht* (carnival) plays of Niklaus Manuel, held in 1523, did more than any sermon or tract to mobilise evangelical sentiments in Berne.[34] Manuel's plays were anticlerical, humorous, and poignant. They were performed in the Kreuzgasse and satirised the venality of the papacy, warmongering cardinals, and avaricious clerics (monks in particular).[35] In contrast, the simple people (beggars, peasants, women, and children) were idealised, presented by Manuel as true adherents of the Gospel of Christ, able to confound the corrupt hierarchy with their faith. We know from the chronicle of Anshelm that a great number of people attended these productions in the streets of Berne, taking in Manuel's evangelical message of Christian freedom.

The Berne council was moved to proclaim the mandate *Viti et Modesti* on 15 June 1523 in which the clergy were instructed to preach nothing other than the Gospel and God's teaching, though exactly what was intended by these terms was unclear. It was certainly not the wish of the council to sanction Luther's views, which were expressly condemned: the vague formulations employed stated that preaching from the Bible was to be open and unequivocal and not dependent upon human sources. This preliminary position, commonly found in the German imperial cities, was virtually unworkable. For the evangelical party there was no question of not reading Luther, who for many was the father of the movement. The Catholics, on the other hand, understood very well that the Gospel alone offered little support for their essential forms of worship and devotion. The mandate of 1523 was the response of a civic council unable and unprepared to deal with doctrinal issues.[36] Although the evangelical party had made inroads in the early 1520s, Catholic resistance was by no means broken, as powerful families in Berne had no interest in abandoning traditional religion. Each side interpreted the mandate as best served their purposes: the evangelicals continued to propagate the teaching of Luther, and later Zwingli, under the shield of Gospel-preaching, whilst Berne officially remained Catholic. Outrages against Catholic practices were punished, such as in the case of a man in Hindelbank who was fined ten pounds for breaking a fast in July 1524.

Between 1524 and 1528 the situation in Berne remained unresolved. Evangelical ideas were spreading, particularly in the religious houses, where monks and nuns eagerly read Zwingli's work on the religious life.[37] His teaching on the freedom of the Christian inspired many to abandon the religious life and to marry. Yet at the same time, devotion to Mary, the Mother of God, continued to hold the affections of most Bernese. Politically, the magistrates were concerned to maintain stability within a Confederation increasingly riven by the religious dispute, for peace was essential to Berne's realisation of its territorial aspirations in the west. Although there were strong evangelical sympathies in the city, and Zwingli's influence was growing, there was no interest among the magistrates to fall in line with Zurich, their old rival.[38] The Five Inner States were putting great pressure on Berne to declare for the Catholic side in order to prevent a civil war, and in response the Bernese magistrates undertook a survey of public opinion (*Volksbefragung*) in 1524, and the results were fascinating. The rural communities voiced their desire to remain with the old religion, citing fasting and the veneration of Mary and the saints as their principal grounds. The communities felt themselves incapable of rendering judgement upon the new faith, which few understood, and many replied that Luther's teaching had only brought confusion and disruption.

A balance had to be struck. Evangelical ideas were popular in the city and among members of the religious houses, but not in the rural communities. At the same time, many of the magistrates were sympathetic to the new faith, but Berne understood itself as the key broker in the split between Zurich and the rest of the Confederation. A second mandate was issued in November 1524 which reiterated the view that scripture was to be proclaimed without reference to any human authority, but this time Luther was not named, indicating a slight but significant shift in the council's position. Nevertheless, traditional practices of the church, such as clerical celibacy, images in church, fasts, and the veneration of saints, remained unimpugned. Further, in the spring of 1525 the council sought to halt the haemorrhaging of the religious houses by ordering monks and nuns to stay put and not to marry.

In April 1525 came a third mandate, but this time the tone was more favourable to the Catholics, reflecting the fact that the text was a reworking of the mandate issued by the Catholic Confederates at Lucerne on 28 January. The seven sacraments, the veneration of saints, purgatory, monastic houses, pilgrimages and fasts were all explicitly endorsed, making Berne most Catholic. There were some alterations, for instance all marital and disciplinary cases were put in the hands of the magistrates, who were to decide whether a matter should be referred to an ecclesiastical or secular court. Where the Confederates had banned all writings by Luther and Zwingli, however, the Bernese excluded from this ban works which pertained to the Bible, a conceit by which virtually all of the reformers' works could continue to be circulated in the city, for what did they write about if not the Bible? At the same time that indefatigable figure, Georg Brunner, was exiled from Bernese lands for refusing to celebrate the mass. It was a time for contradictions: a reformer was banned for not celebrating the mass, but literature attacking the mass was tolerated. The key point, of course, was that the magistrates wished to remain in control of events, and to ensure that any attempt to force the pace of change would be punished.

The Baden Disputation of May 1526, at which the Catholics were led by the shrewd and talented Johannes Eck, who was more than a match for the leaders of the evangelical delegation, Johannes Oecolampadius and Berchtold Haller, was an extremely difficult moment for the Reformation cause in Berne. As Irena Backus has argued, Eck knew his Bible better than the reformers present and was able to turn their own arguments against them in order to prove that they were simply reviving ancient heresies.[39] Faced by this skilled and subtle debater, Oecolampadius and others often had to resort to arguments from tradition and philosophy and were unable to employ their own principle of scripture alone. Eck trapped and demolished them. Oecolampadius was at least given some respect by Eck on account of his learning; Haller, the priest from Berne, was treated with derision by the Catholics, who had really wanted to take on Zwingli. Haller, aware of his precarious position in Berne, refused to debate, and when Eck asked him whether he believed Christ to be present in the eucharist he gave no answer. Eck, with his superior learning and sardonic wit, made mincemeat of Haller, who retreated humiliated to Berne, where the prospects for the Reformation now seemed, in light of this Catholic triumph, very gloomy indeed.

Haller, as his performance at Baden made all too clear, was a kindly, devout man but without the theological acumen or personality to carry forward a reform movement. In the face of the defeat in 1526 it was the guilds in Berne who kept the fires burning. They were inspired by the evangelical teachings and eager to take control of the church; they were also opposed to the patrician families who so favoured the old faith for various reasons, including the mercenary service. It was the guilds in 1527, and not the rather hapless Berchtold Haller, who urged the magistrates to hold a disputation in the city in order to resolve the religious question. Unlike Zurich, where the Reformation was essentially a clerical movement, in Berne it was the laity, beginning with Niklaus Manuel, which drove the movement forward. The result of this was that the Bernese church never acquired a distinct theological voice.

Berne was not only awash with *Flugschriften* (mostly from Zurich as there was no printing press in the city until 1537), but it is clear that men were preaching in homes and taverns, and that evangelical ideas were being widely discussed. The situation was so volatile that the council decreed in 1525 that no one, whether a citizen, guest or servant, was to insult another person on account of his religion. The terms evangelical (*Lutersch*) and Catholic (*bäpstisch*) were not to be used in the marketplace, tavern or street, either publicly or privately.[40] The following year another mandate indicated that the singing of songs which parodied both sides of the religious debate was widespread.

The low level of popular support for the Reformation in the rural areas was made evident by a survey of February/March 1526 when only one community from eighteen indicated any enthusiasm for change. The reason given by this one community was what had been achieved in Zurich was the replacement of a bad system with a better one, and that this must be a good thing. The response gave no indication of particular attachment to any evangelical ideas. It was in the city alone that the new beliefs were taken up seriously.[41] Five thousand city dwellers who were themselves not in agreement on religion were wholly unable to impose their will on 70,000 rural subjects.

By 1527 it was evident to all in the Confederation that the divide between Zurich and the Five Inner States was not to be bridged, though the Bernese continued to mediate.[42] Within the city most of the magistrates continued to believe that the preaching of the Gospel was not incompatible with the celebration of the mass. There was pressure for a clear statement on religion, and following the February survey the council issued its fifth mandate in May 1527. This mandate revoked all the previous mandates with exception of the *Viti et Modesti*, and although they still strove to maintain a cautious position, the magistrates now indicated a change of direction. Instead of affirming the traditional forms of religion, the mandate of 1527 opened the way to the Reformation by stating that no one, on his own, had the right to abolish the old rites or to remove images from the church. This had to be done in agreement between the council and the burghers. Clearly opinion in the city was running well ahead of the rural parishes, where in 1527 public sentiment was strongly in favour of retaining the old religion.

A major change came during 1527 as the large council in Berne changed in character. Many who had opposed the religious developments had left when Berchthold Haller had his post changed from mass priest to civic preacher. Further, the large council came ever more under the control of the guilds and mercantile families, who were the primary supporters of the evangelical movement. The large council also contained representatives of the rural communities who, largely incorrectly, understood the evangelical biblicism as support for communal autonomy, and thus they gave their support at a crucial moment.[43]

The Bernese council acceded to the wishes of the guilds and set the date of 8 January 1528 for a religious disputation. Invitations were sent to the bishop, all the Confederates, Charles V, and many of the south German imperial cities. Eight of the Confederates refused the invitation, whilst the emperor objected that such a disputation in advance of the next imperial diet was untimely. In preparation for the disputation Franz Kolb and Berchthold Haller wrote ten propositions, nearly all of which came from earlier debates between evangelicals and Catholics. Theses 1, 2, 4–6 had been penned by Johannes Comander for the Ilanz Disputation of 1526, while 3 was from Zwingli's *Sixty-Seven Articles* of 1523. The final two propositions were taken from a 1524 debate in Basle over marriage.[44] The role played by Zurich in the preparations is seen in the fact that the theses were printed by Froschauer for distribution among the participants.

The disputation ran for almost three weeks (6–26 January) and was held in the Franciscan church under the watchful eye of Vadianus, who served as president.[45] Over 250 theologians took part, including all of the leading evangelicals in the Confederation, although the Catholic representation was rather low voltage, led by Diebolt Huter from Appenzell, the head of the Augustinian Hermits in Freiburg and Alexius Grat, the Bernese Dominican. The debate focused on the first five theses, with the principal issue being the authority of scripture vis-à-vis the church. The evangelicals always had the upper hand, and their position was strengthened immeasurably by the presence of Zwingli in Berne, where he and a number of other leading reformers (Ambrosius Blarer, Johannes Oecolampadius, and Martin Bucer) preached in the Münster.

Finally, the theses were accepted by a vote of 200 to 48 and Vadianus was charged with preparing the acts of the session for presentation to the Bernese council. On 2 February the citizens and inhabitants of Berne gathered in the Münster to discuss whether they would accept the council's decision on religious matters. When it came to a vote, the majority of hands indicated that the people would be obedient to the position taken by the magistrates, and five days later the Reformation Mandate was issued.

Irena Backus has argued that the Berne Disputation of 1528 saw the emergence of a confident Zwinglian church which was no longer on the defensive but was certain of its arguments. Although the Catholics were wholly outgunned at Berne, the Zwinglians showed themselves to be subtle humanists who could manipulate texts with great skill to defeat their opponents. The Zwinglians placed themselves explicitly in the tradition of Augustine, and they claimed the bishop of Hippo as their inspiration, though they were careful to ground their arguments in scripture. The Berne Disputation, however, marked an important stage in the development of Swiss evangelical thought. It was the reply of the Swiss reformers to the charges levelled by Eck at Baden. As Backus has written: 'What the reformers in fact did was simply to substitute their own Church of largely Zwinglian and Bucerian inspiration for the Church of Rome. This is what gave their arguments a fundamental unity and coherence against which the Roman Catholics found themselves powerless.'[46]

The mandate was an extensive document which laid out not only the principles of the new church order, but also the details. The authority of the bishops of Sitten, Lausanne, Basle, and Constance, in whose dioceses the Bernese lands fell, was annulled and the magistrates were put in control of all ecclesiastical matters. Forms for the liturgy of baptism and Lord's Supper were outlined and clergy were instructed in their duties. On 23 February the council put the new Reformed order to the rural communities for a vote. The results have been lost, but a letter from Berchthold Haller to Zwingli indicated that most of the communities had given their approval.

Some of the communities he listed in the letter were ones which had only recently indicated their preference to remain with the Catholic faith, giving the impression that there was considerable confusion in the rural areas about the difference between the two religions. What did occur without delay was the removal of images from the church; across the city and rural areas during the winter of 1528 churches were stripped of their altars, wall paintings, liturgical goods, and pictures. It has recently been discovered that in contrast to Zurich, where most of the artefacts from the churches were destroyed, many of these precious goods in Berne were buried in the square beside the Münster. Many of the parish churches were badly damaged as the council struggled to maintain control.

The superficial nature of the reforms of 1528 was soon revealed. In the Bernese Oberland it was not long before the mass was reintroduced, as priests returned from the Five Inner States. Many sought to return pictures and altars to the churches in defiance of the Bernese authorities. In all of this the locals were supported by clergy and soldiers from Unterwalden. Bernese troops had to restore order by forcing the Unterwalden forces to retreat, and the council demanded reparations on the part of the Catholics. The leader of the revolt in the Oberland was beheaded, but Berne remained nervous about its tenuous hold on rural areas; a factor which proved crucial in the Second Kappel War, where Berne, on account of its delicate situation at home, was unwilling to support Zurich.

Basle

Although Basle did not officially adopt the Reformation until 1529, its role in the early years was crucial. The affluent mercantile city on the Rhine had, as we have noted previously, opened its pockets frequently to support the endeavours of its fellow Confederates. Yet Basle's position within the Confederation bespoke an Olympian distance from the other more rustic members. Basle was far and away the most sophisticated urban centre; it had hosted the most sensational church council of the fifteenth century and it possessed a university of at least middling quality. These were important background points, but what raised the city to the first rank of Reformation centres was its printing industry. Through men such as Johannes Petri, his nephew Adam, Thomas Lampater, Pamphilus Gengenbach and, most famously, Johannes Froben, Basle, with its easy access to both France and the empire became the most important point of diffusion for the works of Martin Luther in the 1520s.

Luther's vernacular pamphlets, printed in the city, stimulated the spread of evangelical ideas in Basle. The most important early figure was the Franciscan Konrad Pellikan, who would later serve in Zurich as a distinguished Hebraist. Parallel to events in Zurich, Basle saw the outbreak of protests against the established church. The lower clergy attended a dinner held at the local castle of Klybeck on Palm Sunday 1522 where suckling pig was served in contravention of the ecclesiastical ordinances. Wilhelm Reublin, whom we have encountered in Zurich, was an early leader of resistance: he made his sentiments public by carrying a copy of the Bible during a Corpus Christi procession instead of the relics of his parish church of St Albans.[47] For his efforts Reublin was dismissed as *Leutpriester* by the Basle council. He quit the city and headed into Zurich territory, where he took up the post of minister in Witikon, from where he would play an important role in the advent of the Anabaptist movement.

Reublin's departure in the summer of 1522 was closely followed by the arrival of Johannes Oecolampadius, the diffident, scholarly figure who would ultimately lead Basle to adopt the Reformation. Oecolampadius has received scant attention from historians: he had neither Zwingli's flair for preaching nor his polemical style. Cursed with a tremulous voice, there were frequent complaints in the Basel Münster that Oecolampadius could not be heard above the usual din. His writings were scholarly and, for the most part, Latinate. Greatly admired by his contemporaries, including opponents, for his learning, the legacy of this man is largely invisible. His major contribution was in his biblical commentaries, where he explored ideas which were later to come to fruition in the work of better-known writers such as John Calvin.

A native of neighbouring Swabia, Oecolampadius had studied under the great south German humanist Jacob Wimpfeling at Heidelberg before studying Greek and Hebrew at Stuttgart and Tübingen. During this period he became acquainted with important humanists in the region: Johannes Reuchlin, who was his teacher, Philip Melanchthon, with whom he remained a lifelong friend, and Wolfgang Capito, who brought the young Oecolampadius to Basle in 1515 when he took the chair of theology. During the winter of 1515–16 Oecolampadius assisted Erasmus on his edition of the Greek New Testament.

Oecolampadius's career led him through a variety of positions in southern Germany during the heady days of the early 1520s. During his time as a monk at the Brigittine house at Altomünster in Bavaria he wrote two pamphlets which indicated his adherence to the view of justification propagated by Martin Luther.[48] In the autumn of 1522 he returned to Basle where Cratander offered him a post as corrector in his print shop. During this time Oecolampadius returned to his work on editions of the Church Fathers, a task he had begun before his departure to Augsburg in 1518. His learning was quickly recognised and Oecolampadius was appointed to the university as a professor of theology in 1523, alongside Konrad Pellikan.[49]

It was during these months that Oecolampadius began to correspond with Zwingli. It is useful to reflect upon the shared intellectual and spiritual ideals of these two men. For in neither was there a dramatic conversion experience. Rather, for both the road to the evangelical cause was mediated through the world of south German humanism and, in particular, the presence of Erasmus in Basle. For both the edition of patristic texts was of paramount importance, and if we are to identify an intellectual core to the Swiss Reformation, it must be located in the editions of the Latin and Greek Fathers which issued from the presses of Basle, Nuremberg, and Augsburg. Alongside the theological and spiritual insights of the Church Fathers must be placed the humanist exegetical techniques advocated by Erasmus, the continuing hold of scholastic thought and a vernacular tradition of mysticism. None of these can be separated from one another, and together they formed the spiritual world of men such as Zwingli, Oecolampadius, and a cast of others in the Confederation.

Events in Basle bore a strong resemblance to what was happening in Zurich and Berne. Oecolampadius's preaching had brought a considerable following to the evangelical movement among both clergy and laity, but had also stirred resistance among the patriciate. The small council was dominated by the more conservative magistrates who wished to eschew religious controversy. Religious instability was bad for trade. Following the lead of other imperial cities, the Basle council issued a mandate in the spring of 1523 enjoining the clergy to preach from scripture, but not to mix in the teachings of Luther.

Although the response of the Basle council to the evangelical preaching followed along familiar lines, there was much in the city to distinguish it from events in the other Confederate states.[50] Basle was riven by internal conflict. The magistrates were locked in a struggle with the bishop over the extent of his role in civic affairs. The adoption of the Reformation in 1529 would be the final act of a struggle for liberation from episcopal jurisdiction. In economic matters there was also trouble. We have spoken about Basle's position as an important trading centre, seated on the Rhine facing both the empire and the French kingdom. The powerful guilds in the city were very much the motor of religious change.[51] The effective linking of the evangelical agenda to the aspirations of the rank-and-file guild members for social and religious change was the force which ultimately cowed the small council. During 1525 as the peasant armies reached the gates of the city there were riots within Basle which revealed the extent of adherence to radical religious ideas among the guilds.[52] The greatest hostility was reserved for the religious houses, which were seen as privileged competitors, and protests against the ecclesiastical order were voiced by the wool-weavers, masons, carpenters, coopers, and cabinet-makers. The response from the city council was the trade constitution of 1526 under which merchants were forbidden from selling foreign goods which could be made in Basle. It was a triumph for the artisans over the merchants and a clear sign of their growing power within the city. The peasants, having taken control of almost all of the Basle countryside, were only mollified by promises from the council that their demands would be met.

The energy of the Basle Reformation came from various forms of conflict within the city which brought about a chorus of calls for change. On 8 February 1529 eight hundred guildsmen met in the Franciscan church to elect representatives to go before the small council of the city to demand constitutional and religious change. Their demands focused on two principal ideas: that guild leadership should be more reflective of the membership and that the small council should be elected from the large council of the city. In other words, guilds had risen up against oligarchy within the city. Events quickly turned violent with men taking up arms and many acts of iconoclasm in the churches. The small council caved into the demands of the mob.[53]

Hans Guggisberg has argued that Oecolampadius did not play a central role in the events of 1528–29, although preaching was central to the Basle Reformation. Other figures, Wolfgang Wissenburg, Johann Lüthart, and Thomas Girfalk, about whom we know very little, are recorded in the documents of the council as the primary agitators.[54] These men seem to have mediated the message of the reform pamphlets to those urban groups unable to read, and they were responsible for directing the social unrest so characteristic of the Basle Reformation. Unlike Zurich, where Zwingli controlled the agenda, the reform movement in Basle was much more inchoate. The key was the power of the guilds, who had been struggling since the early decades of the fifteenth century for political control in the city, and now they had their chance.

The churches of the city were quickly and systematically stripped of their goods and the council declared that all pulpits were to be occupied by supporters of the evangelical cause. The former bishop and cathedral preacher Tilman Limperger delivered the first Reformed sermon in the city on 14 February, a week later the first Reformed baptism took place in the church of St Theodor, across the Rhine. On 1 April, the Thursday after Easter, the Reformation mandate was passed by the Basle council. The document was divided into two parts: the first dealt with the clergy and professors of the university, while the second addressed the reform of morals. The services of the church were regulated, as were the sacraments of baptism and the Lord's Supper. Infant baptism was embraced and the Lord's Supper was to be celebrated three times a year at Easter, Pentecost, and Christmas. Ministers in rural areas were required to hold communion more frequently; in addition to the three principal celebrations they were to celebrate the Lord's Supper every three to four weeks as a concession to those unable to make it to the church regularly. The morals mandate which formed part of the Reformation decree contained the familiar strictures on marriage, orderly behaviour, and the requirement to attend church.

Although the new church order in Basle closely resembled those in Zurich and Berne, there arose in Basle a heated discussion over discipline, in particular the use of the ban. It had been proposed that a disciplinary body consisting of clerical and lay members be created in order that the ban might be effectively employed. Oecolampadius supported the use of the ban as a power of the church, but there was little support for this position in the other evangelical states. Zwingli was of the opinion that it belonged to the authority of the Christian magistrates and should not be exercised by the church. In Berne, Kaspar Megander was in sympathy with Oecolampadius, but despite a speech before the synod, he was unable to persuade the Bernese magistrates to grant this power to the church. The importance of the issue was that it stood as a stumbling-block to Burgrecht between the evangelical states.[55] The only solution was to agree to disagree and Basle was left to take its own path in this matter. On 14 and 15 December the Basle council issued its mandate on ecclesiastical discipline; the result was not as Oecolampadius had wished – discipline of the clergy and laity in the city and rural areas was entirely in the hands of the magistrates or their appointed officials. The ministers were to have no say. In Zurich, despite his view that these powers properly belonged to Christian magistrates, Zwingli had carved out a place for the clergy in the running of the church. This was to prove more the exception than the model as other evangelical churches found themselves wholly under the thumb of their political masters.

Schaffhausen

The publication of Luther's works in Basle in 1518 had an immediate impact on the small city of Schaffhausen, perched on the northern tip of the Confederation. Michael Eggenstorfer, the abbot of the Benedictine monastery of All Saints, was an enthusiastic reader. This man, who was filled with ideas for church reform, had already in 1520 sent some of his young monks to Wittenberg to study with Luther.

Although Eggenstorfer left the Catholic faith, he was not the man to lead the Reformation in Schaffhausen. Following the introduction of the Reformation in 1529 Eggenstorfer retired to private life, married, joined one of the guilds, and lived quietly until his death in 1552.[56]

The man responsible for introducing the Reformation was the native son Sebastian Hofmeister, who had been educated by the Franciscans and obtained the degree of doctor of theology in Paris in 1519. He returned to Schaffhausen and during various trips to Zurich came to know Zwingli. When Hofmeister went to the Franciscan monastery in Constance, he began an exchange of letters with Zwingli and Luther. By 1523 he was in the Franciscan house in Lucerne as a preacher, and we know that his sermons raised accusations of heresy. This led to a legal process against him and his return to the Franciscan house in Schaffhausen. The extent to which he had imbibed the evangelical message along the way became apparent in his preaching in Schaffhausen, where he expounded Zwingli's views on the eucharist.

It is hardly surprising that the outbreak of the Peasants' War in south-western Germany should have profoundly affected the neighbouring city and rural territories of Schaffhausen, where during 1524–25 unrest was endemic. As we shall see later, the rural areas of Schaffhausen became a hotbed of Anabaptist activity, but we should be careful about making connections between the Peasants' War and religious dissent. There was an overlap between the evangelical ideas and the economic and social demands of the peasantry and the guilds, but these were only vaguely conceived. Nevertheless, Hofmeister was removed from his post in Schaffhausen by the council in an attempt to quell the troubles. He travelled to the Graubünden for the Ilanz Disputation and then to Berne for the crucial meeting of 1528.

Despite the close links between the cities, the Reformation mandate of Easter 1525 in Zurich was rejected in Schaffhausen, where the council had already declared in February that the mass was to be celebrated, the Ave Maria sung, and the offices of the church recited. With Hofmeister's departure, the evangelical sympathies in the city remained leaderless until the Berne Disputation of 1528. With the conversion of Berne and Basle, there was little doubt that Schaffhausen would follow suit, and in September of 1529 representatives from the cities of Berne, Basle, Zurich, St Gall, and Mülhausen arrived to put pressure on the council to bring about Reformation. Under the leadership of Bürgermeister Hans Peyer the Reformation was duly adopted and a commission was set up to remove the images from the churches.[57]

Although the form of the Reformation adopted in Schaffhausen was closely modelled on Zurich, the city did not possess anyone of the stature of Zwingli to lead the church. Instead Schaffhausen fell victim to the least attractive aspect of the evangelical Reformation: its vulnerability to personality conflicts in the absence of established lines of authority. The two leading ministers were Germans, the Bavarian Erasmus Ritter and Benedikt Burgauer from St Gall in the Rheintal, who detested each other. For eight years the people of Schaffhausen had to endure the bitter rivalry between Ritter and Burgauer until finally in 1534 the council declared that both had to go. Ritter went to Berne, where he remained a keen supporter of Zwingli, while Burgauer served in a number of southern German cities. The disruption caused by their enmity was such that it was only with their deposition in 1534 that reform of worship and restructuring of the rural churches was implemented.

The international front: union and division

The influence of Zurich was to be found in varying measures in each of the Reformations between 1525 and 1530. It was, however, a mutually dependent relationship, for as Berne, Basle, St Gall, and Schaffhausen adopted the evangelical religion it was the Zurichers who found themselves rescued from the wilderness, where they had wandered as a result of their opposition to the French alliance, mercenary service, and their heretical faith. But all of this raised the very serious question of whether there was any future for the Confederation. Brought together for purposes of defence and commerce, the Confederates were now faced by an issue so divisive that civil war, perhaps along the lines of the Old Zurich War of the previous century, seemed likely. The formation of alliances was the lifeblood of the Confederation, but the revolution brought about by the changes in Zurich, Berne, and Basle during the 1520s meant that religion had to be considered an essential component of any agreement. Whereas all the previous alliances had been made on grounds of mutual interest (commerce and defence), what Zwingli now envisaged was an aggressive religious bond between the states, not for defence, but for the propagation of the evangelical faith. The first of these was formed between Zurich and Berne in June 1528, with St Gall following in November, and it was known as the Christian Civic Union. During 1529 the Civic Union was extended to Biel, Mülhausen, Basle, Schaffhausen, and Strasbourg. Delegates would frequently meet in Aarau, near Zurich, to discuss matters of religion and politics. For Zwingli, it formed the basis of an evangelical Confederation which would ally itself with the Protestant leaders in the empire. The admission of Strasbourg to the Civic Union in January 1530 reflected the close relationship between that city and the Swiss Confederation. Under Bucer, Capito, and Sturm, the Strasbourg church was neither entirely Lutheran nor Zwinglian, but these reformers had largely eschewed the enmity stirred by Luther against the Swiss and had been crucial participants at the Berne Disputation of 1528. From Zwingli's perspective, Strasbourg offered the Swiss a crucial line of communication to Philip of Hesse.

During 1529–30 Zwingli sought to expand the Civic Union into Germany to bring in cities such as Lindau, Constance, and others where Swiss evangelical ideas had gained a purchase. Yet there remained for Zurich an insurmountable problem, and that was the total unwillingness of Berne to be drawn into German affairs. For Berne, as we shall see in the next chapter, the only real issue was expansion towards Geneva and the defeat of the Savoyan threat. Old rivalries were very much alive as the Bernese were not prepared to provide the military muscle for Zwingli's ambitions for Zurich. Although Berne and Zurich were the two powerhouses of the Swiss Reformation, they had little in common. Zurich wanted to vanquish the remaining Catholic states and impose the evangelical faith; Berne was content to negotiate with them. The Zurichers looked north and east, the Bernese west and south. Zwingli's plans in Germany came to little and the best he could obtain was the 'Christian Agreement' of November 1530, a vague arrangement whereby Zurich, Basle, Strasbourg, and Hesse swore to defend themsleves, but as G.R. Potter noted 'without Berne [the agreement] was of little use to either Philip or Zwingli, who both wanted action'.[58]

In the four years between 1525 and 1529 the Reformation made impressive progress in the Confederation, but with the First Kappel War of 1529 came a sense of stalemate. The evangelical movement had become entangled in the traditional politics of the Confederation. It was isolated from the empire on account of its sacramental theology and the Diet of Augsburg. The Anabaptist threat had revealed serious internal problems of theology and church polity and many communities remained unmoved by its message. All of these factors, together with a providential conviction that victory was within reach, pushed Zwingli and Zurich to the brink. The bitter memories of Zurich's role in the civil wars of the fifteenth century had done much to retard the growth of the Reformation; this nightmare was about to be revisited and the consequences would shape Swiss politics and religion for centuries.

Notes

1 Conradin Bonorand, 'Die Bedeutung der Universität Wien für Humanismus und Reformation, insbesondere in der Ostschweiz', *Zwingliana*, 12 (1964–68), pp. 162–180; Marc Sieber, *Die Universität Basel und die Eidgenossenschaft 1460 bis 1529: Eidgenössische Studenten in Basel* (Basle, 1966).

2 On Erasmus and his circle in Basle, see Léon-E. Halkin, *Erasmus. A Critical Biography*, transl. John Tonkin (Oxford, 1993), pp. 171–181.

3 See Cornelis Augustijn, *Erasmus. His Life, Works, and Influence*, transl. J.C. Grayson (Toronto, 1991), pp. 147–152.

4 Kurt Spillmann, 'Zwingli, Zürich und die Abtei St Gallen' *Zürchen Taschenbuch*, 20 (1965), pp. 385–390.

5 C. Arnold Snyder, 'Communication and the People: The Case of the Reformation in St Gall', *Mennonite Quarterly Review*, 67 (1993), pp. 152–173.

6 The standard work on Vadianus remains the two-volume Werner Näf, *Vadian und seine Stadt* (St Gall, 1957).

7 On this point, see chapter 10.

8 Ernst Gerhard Rüsch, 'Um das Abendmahl: Vadians Brief an Luther vom 30. August 1536', *Theologische Zeitschrift*, 39 (1983), pp. 284–293.

9 Ingeborg Wissmann, *Die St. Galler Reformationschronik des Johannes Kessler (1503–1574)* (Bielefeld, 1972). See esp. pp. 1–20 on the life of Kessler.

10 Ernst Gerhard Rüsch, 'Politische Opposition im St. Gallen zur Zeit Vadians', *Schriften des Vereins für Geschichte des Bodensee und seiner Umgebung*, 104 (1986), pp. 67–113.

11 On the Kappel Wars, see chapter 4, pp. 122–135.

12 Huldreich Gustav Sulzberger, *Geschichte der Reformation im Kanton Appenzell* (Appenzell, 1866), p. 163.

13 A good example of this is the community of Arbon. Willy Wuhrmann, 'Die paritätische Kirchgemeinde Arbon', *Arboner Tagblatt* (1925).

14 John P. Maarbjerg, 'Iconoclasm in the Thurgau: Two Related Incidents in the summer of 1524', *SCJ*, 24 (1993), pp. 577–593.

15 See Randolph C. Head, 'Shared Lordship, Authority, and Administration: The Exercise of Dominion in the Gemeine Herrschaften of the Swiss Confederation, 1417–1600', *Central European History* 30 (1997), pp. 489–512.

16 Rudolf Pfister, *Kirchengeschichte den Schweiz* (Zurich, 1974), II, p. 115.

17 Traugott Schiess, 'Die Beziehungen Graubündens zur Eidgenossenschaft, besonders zu Zürich, im XVI. Jahrhundert', *Jahrbuch für Schweizerische Geschichte*, 27 (1902), pp. 29–183.

18 Randolf C. Head, *Early Modern Democracy in the Grisons: Social Order and Political Language in a Swiss Mountain Canton* (Cambridge, 1995), pp. 57–65.

19 Oskar Vasella, 'Der Bruch Bischof Paul Zieglers von Chur mit den Drei Bünden im Jahre 1524' *ZSKG*, 23 (1943), pp. 271–278.

20 Oskar Vasella, Zur Entstehungsgeschichte des 1. Ilanzer Artikelbriefes vom 4. April 1524 und des Eidgenössichen Glaubenskonkordates von 1525', *ZSKG*, 34 (1940), pp. 182–192.

21 Head, *Early Modern Democracy*, p. 67.

22 Pfister, *Kirchengeschichte*, p. 127.

23 Emil Camenisch, 'Mitarbeit der Laien bei Durchführung der Bündner Reformation. a. Das Ilanzer Religionsgespräch', *Zwingliana*, 7 (1941), pp. 431–436.

24 Ibid., p. 129.

25 Emil Camenisch, 'Mitarbeit der Laien bei Durchführung der Bündner Reformation', *Zwingliana*, 7 (1942), pp. 431–436.

26 Werner Graf, 'Die Ordnung der evangelischen Kirche in Graubünden von der Reformation bis 1980', *Jahresbericht der Historisch-antiquarischen Gesellschaft von Graubünden*, 112 (1982), pp. 7–93.

27 Fritz Büsser, 'Zwingli als Pfarrer in Glarus', in his *Zwingli und die Zürcher Reformation 1484–1984* (Zurich, 1984), pp. 5–17.

28 Jakob Winteler, *Geschichte des Landes Glarus*, 2 vols (Glarus, 1954), II, p. 297.

29 Wolfgang Amadeus Liebeskind, 'Die Hintersässen in Glarner Landrecht des 16. Jahrhunderts' *Beiträge zur Geschichte des Landes Glarus* (1952), pp. 72–99.

30 Winteler, *Geschichte*, p. 313.

31 Ibid., p. 320.

32 On the religious background, see Kathrin Utz-Tremp, 'Gottesdient, Ablasswesen und Predigt am Vinzenzstift in Bern (1484/85–1528)', *ZSKG*, 80 (1986), pp. 31–98.

33 Kurt Guggisberg, *Bernische Kirchengeschichte* (Berne, 1958), pp. 70f.

34 Peter Pfrunder, *Pfaffen Ketzer Totenfresser. Fastnachtkultur der Reformationszeit – Die Berner Spiele von Niklaus Manuel* (Zurich, 1989), pp. 154–158.

35 See Glenn Ehrstine, 'Of Peasants, Women, and Bears: Political Agency and the Demise of Carnival Transgression in Bernese Reformation Drama', *SCJ*, 30 (2000), pp. 675–697.

36 Heinrich Richard Schmidt, 'Stadtreformation in Bern und Nürnberg – ein Vergleich', in Rudolf Endres (ed.), *Nürnberg und Bern. Zwei Reichsstädte und ihre Landgebiete* (Erlangen, 1990), p. 89.

37 A highly instructive study of an early supporter of the Reformation in Berne, the humanist and cleric Heinrich Wölfli, see Rapp Buri, Anna Rapp Buri and Monica Stucky-Schürer, 'Der Berner Chorherr Heinrich Wölfli (1470–1532)', *Zwingliana*, 25 (1998), pp. 65–105.

38 See Hans Rudolf Lavater, 'Zwingli und Bern', in *450 Jahre Berner Reformation* (Berne, 1980), pp. 60–103.

39 The best work on the Baden Disputation is Irena Backus, 'The Disputations of Baden, 1526 and Berne, 1528: Neutralising the Early Church', *Studies in Reformed Religion*, 1 (1993), pp. 1–78.

40 Pfrunder, *Pfaffen*, p. 147.

41 Schmidt, 'Stadtreformation', p. 111.

42 Leonhard von Muralt, 'Berns westliche Politik zur Zeit der Reformation', in his *Der Historiker und die Geschichte* (Zurich, 1960), pp. 88–96.

43 Schmidt, 'Stadtreformation', p. 115.

44 Pfister, *Kirchengeschichte*, p. 73.

45 Dan L. Hendricks, *The Berne Reformation of 1528: The Preacher's Vision, the People's Work, an Occasion of State* (Ann Arbor, MI, 1981). A theological interpretation is found in Gottfried Locher, 'Die Berner Disputation 1528: Charakter, Verlauf, Bedeutung und theologischer Gehalt', *Zwingliana*, 14 (1978), pp. 542–564.

46 Backus, 'The Disputations', p. 98.

47 Christoph Dejung, 'Neue Gedanken zu Rolle und Person von Wilhelm Reublin', *Zwingliana*, 17 (1987), pp. 279–286.

48 Ernst Staehelin, *Das theologische Lebenswerk Johannes Oekolampads* (Leipzig, 1939), pp. 120ff.

49 Thomas A. Fudge, 'Icarus of Basel. Oecolampadius and the Early Swiss Reformation', *Journal of Religious History*, 21 (1997), pp. 268–284.

50 Julia Gauss, 'Basels politisches Dilemma in der Reformationszeit', *Zwingliana*, 15 (1982), pp. 509–548.

51 Hans Füglister, *Handwerksregiment: Untersuchungen und Matrialen zur sozialen und politischen Struktur der Stadt Basel in ersten Hälfte des 16. Jh.* (Basle, 1981). Also, Hans R. Guggisberg and Hans Füglister, 'Die Basler Weberzunft als Trägerin reformatorischer Propaganda', in *Stadt und Kirche* (Gütersloh, 1978), pp. 48–56.

52 Guggisberg, *Basel in the Sixteenth Century*, p. 27.

53 For a more detailed account, see Lee Palmer Wandel, *Voracious Idols and Violent Hands. Iconoclasm in Reformation Zurich, Strasbourg and Basel* (Cambridge, 1995), pp. 167–173.

54 Guggisberg, *Basel in the Sixteenth Century*, pp. 31–32.

55 On the nature of a Burgrecht, see pp. 114–115.

56 Jakob Wipf, 'Michael Eggentorfer, der letzte Abt des Klosters Allerheiligen und die Anfänge der Reformation in Schaffhausen', *Zwingliana*, 4 (1922), pp. 97–111.

57 Ernst Gerhard Rüsch, Die Schaffhauser Reformationsordnung von 1529', in *Schaffhauser Beiträge zur Geschichte* 56 (1979).

58 G.R. Potter, *Zwingli* (Cambridge, 1976), p. 387.

4

War and disaster 1529–34

The failed Reformations

In our overview of the various Reformations in the Confederate states and their territories we have noted that success depended upon certain constellations of political, religious, and social elements. An effective preacher and strong personality was crucial, but not always enough. Likewise, traditions of communalism or of growing guild power did not necessarily lead to a successful Reformation. Opposition to the Reformation was powerful and complex; local conditions determined allegiances, a point best illustrated by an examination of several regions where the evangelical movement took root but ultimately withered and died: the cities of Lucerne, Zug, Solothurn, and Fribourg. In each of these cases reform movements emerged and engaged in activities similar to those we have observed in other parts of the Confederation. Yet, with the exception of Solothurn, progress was modest and, ultimately, easily quashed. Why? Above all, it was the lucrative business of mercenaries that proved most effective in defeating the Reformation; in all of these cities the income from military pensions formed a crucial part of the local economy. At every level of society, from the magistrates whose pockets were lined with French money to the rural youth hungry for adventure and wealth, the allurements of mercenary service beguiled, silencing the censorious sermons of the evangelical preachers.

Nevertheless, there were groups of evangelicals in the four cities by 1522. In Lucerne and Zug especially the leading figures were humanists closely connected with Zwingli. Oswald Myconius, Sebastian Hofmeister, the canon Johann Xilotectus (a friend of Vadianus) and the priest Jodocus Kilchmeyer led the movement in Lucerne, but were forced out by anti-Reformation propaganda in 1522. Those sympathetic to the cause who remained in the city were largely scattered among the clergy, deprived of any organised body and vulnerable to hostile magistrates. Likewise Werner Steiner in Zug, and Peter Falk, Pierre Girod, and Cornelius Agrippa in Fribourg, were clergy belonging to humanist circles. Solothurn, as we shall see, differed in that evangelical support developed in the guilds, and not among the clergy. In each case, again with the exception of Solothurn, the evangelical circles were small, without strong leadership, and unable to penetrate either the council chambers or the guildhalls. In Lucerne, Zug, and Fribourg evangelical preaching was unequivocally condemned in 1522 and the magistrates were resolute in their rejection of the new learning; they were not even willing to issue the preaching mandates which appeared in Zurich, Berne, and Basle. It was not just the magistrates who were hostile. From Zug Bartholomäus Stocker wrote to Zwingli in 1522 that the people were utterly uninterested in the evangelical ideas.[1] And when Stocker advocated marriage to his fellow priests, he noted, he was derided as a fool. This impression of resistance was corroborated four years later when a survey of popular opinion in Zug revealed negligible support for the evangelical faith. Lucerne, which emerged as the leading Catholic state (*Vorort*) during the 1520s, had at least some evangelical activity which led to clashes between groups of lay sympathisers and the authorities, and arrests were made. Such incidents, however, were rare and isolated, for the expulsions of Hofmeister, Kilchmeyer, and Xilotectus had effectively crippled the movement.[2]

The magistrates in these cities made some canny decisions. Their calculations were based on religious conviction as well as an assessment of what was transpiring in the Confederation. Not only did they, above all in Fribourg, depend upon the money from mercenaries, but they feared the political hegemony of Zurich and Berne. In Fribourg the magistrates took the lead in suppressing a reform movement which had appeared in 1522–23. Luther's ideas were condemned and house-to-house searches were conducted to root out sympathisers and pamphlet literature. Tavern-owners were encouraged to report anyone who voiced pro-evangelical sentiments. Further, the council appointed two men, the Alsatian Hieronymous Mylen and the provincial of the Augustinians in the Rhenish-Swabian province, Konrad Treger, to use the pulpit against the evangelicals. The Fribourg council received little support from either the bishop of Lausanne or any other member of the ecclesiastical hierarchy; its campaign against the Reformation was of its own initiative, driven by a rejection of the evangelical message, the need to suppress dissent, and the preservation of good relations with the French. Indeed, French diplomats played a crucial role in shoring up the rulers of these states with money and offers of support.[3]

The greatest loss to the evangelicals was Solothurn, traditionally an ally of Berne.[4] Again French influence was key as Solothurn was the residence of the French ambassadors in the Confederation, and they worked hard to retain the sympathies of the magistrates. As a result, Solothurn had resisted falling into the Reformed camp in the wake of the Berne Disputation of 1528 and remained neutral during the First Kappel War. With the greatest reluctance, and under pressure from Berne, it sent some troops in the Second Kappel War.[5] The Reformation had come late to Solothurn, largely because the main influence was Berne, not Zurich. Solothurn was not a centre of learning and there were few humanists or clerics driven by ideas of reform; the Reformation was imported through pamphlet literature and taken up by the laity, especially certain guilds. These guilds found themselves in conflict with Solothurn magistrates, who banned all form of evangelical activity, such as the removal of images from the churches. But the strength of Berne was hard to resist, and by 1529 evangelical ideas were disseminated through the city and rural areas. Two surveys of popular opinion revealed in 1529 that support for the Reformation was still small, but it was growing. By 1531 the evangelicals were in the majority in the rural areas and Solothurn was confessionally divided and poised for religious war. The situation was exacerbated by the arrival of Anabaptist groups in the Solothurn rural areas; most of these radicals had been driven out of Basle. The situation was only resolved with the Second Kappel War. The defeat of the Reformed Confederates led to the collapse of the Reformation in Solothurn. Berchtold Haller wrote to Bullinger in 1534 of the desperate plight of those evangelicals left in Solothurn who were being persecuted by the magistrates.[6] As Hans Guggisberg has argued, had Zwingli and his supporters won, Solothurn would certainly have adopted the Reformation.[7]

The failure of the Reformation in these states cast in relief the hostile attitudes held by many in the Confederation towards the evangelical movement. The opposition was not simply on account of Mammon; trade and the mercenary service were important considerations, but the most effective resistance to the evangelical faith arose from the unwillingness of many to part with the Catholic religion. An intense distrust of Zurich, a desire to maintain the Confederation as it was, and a sense of solidarity with the original Confederates were joined with a flat rejection of the evangelical faith. The preaching which had proved so potent in other areas fell on deaf ears, and issues such as clerical marriage stirred no hearts. A letter of 1529 from the Bernese council to Zurich stated that the people of the Catholic inner states wished to remain with the old religion out of 'real piety'. At the same time, the ruling authorities in these states possessed sufficient control over their churches to retain a hold on the events. The Reformation had little to offer magistrates who had already a firm grip on the religious life of their states. Indeed, these rulers stole a march on the reformers by demonstrating how effective the Christian ruler could be in suppressing heresy while the magistrates of Zurich, Berne, and Basle prevaricated.

The Kappel Wars 1529–31

The adoption of the Reformation in Berne and Basle in 1528 and 1529 left the three most powerful members of the Confederation outside the Roman church and facing an uncertain future. Following the decisive Disputation of Berne in 1528, Zwingli's theology defined the profile of the Swiss Reformation. Forged in the fires of conflict with Johannes Eck, the Anabaptists, and Luther, Zwinglianism, as it now could be named, took shape as a coherent body of thought, readily identifiable by friend and foe alike. That said, we should not be tempted into thinking that Zwingli stood at the front of a unified movement. During the 1520s Zwingli had real political power in Zurich, and in the lands over which Zurich exercised influence, but nowhere else. The spectacular successes of 1528–29 were the results of long processes within Basle, Berne, and the other states in which religious, political, and economic forces were transforming the communities. Zwingli and his allies, through preaching, writing, and close co-operation with magistrates, had proved the decisive catalysts in bringing about the Reformation, but the highly individualistic nature of the Confederates, with their disparate interests, remained unaltered. The personal and charismatic nature of Zwingli's authority in Zurich was not sufficient to hold together a collection of states with few shared aspirations. What Zwingli demanded of the Swiss in the late 1520s was a change of mentality and historical purpose; for just over two hundred years the Confederates had understood their connectedness in terms of defence and the maintenance of peace. Zwingli sought to redefine the Confederation as a religious body, held together by a common adherence to the Gospel in opposition to the Roman church. Instead of governance through mutual consent, he envisaged a Confederation led by Zurich, and he was highly successful in redirecting Zurich's age-old hegemonic aspirations to serve the spread of the Reformation. The marriage, however, was to prove disastrous. The collapse of the Swiss Reformation between 1529 and 1531 is a tale of fatal political compromises and bloodlust. It is surprising that the Confederation survived at all.

There were two crucial issues that dominated the Confederation in the immediate aftermath of the Reformation. First were the alliance systems created between 1527 and 1529, the Protestant Christian Civic Union and the Catholic Christian Union, concluded between the Five Inner States and Ferdinand of Austria in April 1529. The second issue was whether Confederates divided by religion could continue to administer jointly the Mandated Territories.

At some point after 1525 Zwingli began to consider the possibility of a religious war. His *Plan for a Military Campaign*, which has no date but is thought to have been written around 1527, was a shrewd assessment of the political situation in the Confederation. The work is one of the few places where Zwingli spoke openly of war as a godly means of furthering the Reformation.[8] Zwingli's military and political plans are laid out in detail. The key, he argued, was for Zurich to overcome Berne's tendencies towards neutrality in the religious conflict. Glarus, Basle, Appenzell, and Solothurn were likewise considered potential allies who had to be won over, while Zwingli believed that Schaffhausen was hostile to Zurich's cause. In the east, Zwingli wrote, Zurich should forge an alliance with St Gall and ally with the Graubünden to liberate the Tyrol, thus destroying the power base of the great enemy of the Reformation, Austria. The Mandated Territories should be claimed by Zurich through military force while the hostile states such as Schwyz should be neutralised. In order to achieve this, Zwingli argued, Zurich should make alliances with Constance, Strasbourg, and Lindau.

Zwingli's blueprint, although never employed militarily, became the basis of Zurich's external relations between 1527 and 1529, as alliances were made with Constance, Berne, Basle, Schaffhausen, St Gall, Biel, and Mülhausen. The terms of the alliances promised military support should one of the members be attacked and the purpose of the union was said to be the protection and propagation of the true religion. On the Catholic side, the Five Inner States concluded an alliance with Ferdinand of Austria in which the king promised six thousand foot soldiers and four hundred cavalry should any of his Swiss allies be attacked.

Both of these alliances served one purpose and that was to ensure control over the Mandated Territories, and from 1528 Zurich was adamant that no alterations were to be made in the jointly administered lands without its permission. The Catholics were eager to punish the evangelicals in the territories as heretics, but Zurich insisted that religious belief was not grounds for action against any individual. At a meeting of the diet in Baden in September 1528 Zurich and Berne advocated that the free preaching of the Gospel be permitted in the Mandated Territories. It was a highly sensitive moment as Berne was facing a revolt in its Oberland which had been supported by Catholic Unterwalden. Zurich was attempting to broker a peace between the two states and it was within this context that Zwingli proposed a new constitution for the Swiss Confederation. He put forward a position, which was supported by Berne, that in the Mandated Territories the evangelical faith should be established where desired by a 'majority of hands'.

The Catholic states responded that all the Swiss Confederates, with the exceptions of Zurich and Schaffhausen, had in 1524 sworn to abide by the old religion, and that this was reason enough to punish those priests in the Mandated Territories who had preached heresy. The complexity of the argument lay in the fact that the Reformed states insisted upon the principle of majority voting in the establishment of religion in a territory, but they were not prepared to accept the principle of majority voting in the diet of the Confederation, where the Catholics held a majority.

The question of whether the individual communities had a right to choose their faith and how this was to be weighed against the rights of the Confederate members was utterly unclear as the Confederation had no written constitution. The argument made by Zurich was that the alliances which constituted the Swiss Confederation touched only on political and external matters, not religion, and this left each community with the right to choose its faith. This position reflected the rapid progress the evangelicals were making in the Thurgau and other Mandated Territories, where during late 1528 and early 1529 numerous communities had declared themselves for the new religion. Against this, the Catholics charged that Zurich and Berne were using their strength to apply a principle of minority rule.

Whilst Zwingli was embroiled with Luther in the months leading up to Marburg, in May 1529 Zurich was in dispute with the Catholic states over evangelical preaching in the Mandated Territories and the lands of the Abbot of St Gall. After the success of the Reformation in St Gall Zwingli had sought to promote the conversion of the abbot's lands, and this led the Catholic states into negotiations with Ferdinand of Austria. For the first time since the start of the Reformation movement the threat of civil war hung in the air, and both sides were desperate. The loss of Berne and Basle left the Catholic Confederates virtually surrounded, while the Reformed states were increasingly frustrated by their inability to obtain an all-out victory. In a letter seized by some evangelical supporters, Thomas Murner, a leading Catholic writer, wrote that the Catholics were preparing to fight: both sides awaited a provocation, and it was not long in coming. In May 1529 in the Mandated Territory of Gaster the evangelical minister Jakob Kaiser was arrested and taken to Schwyz, where he was burnt as a heretic.

Zurich mobilised for war, despite the arrival of a delegation from Berne led by Niklaus Manuel seeking to stay the hand. Military banners were unfurled across the land, and by 8 June four thousand men from Zurich stood on the field at Kappel.[9] The previous day Basle, Schaffhausen, Solothurn, and Glarus had likewise sought to mediate between Zurich and the Five Inner States, but to no avail, and war was declared. On 9 June from Kappel Zwingli wrote his assessment of the situation. He hoped that the show of force would suffice to intimidate the Catholic states into submission. He regretted that it had come to a possible clash of arms, but the people of the Five Inner States, he wrote, had remained ignorant of the true faith on account of the rapacity of those who received pensions for mercenaries.[10] Zwingli maintained in his text that he did not wish to crush the Catholic states militarily, but they would have to agree to certain conditions: the free preaching of the Gospel was to be permitted, they would have to abandon their alliance with Austria, outlaw pensions, punish those who received pensions, and the Five Inner States would have to pay war reparations. Zurich was well prepared to fight when the two sides came face to face near the monastery at Kappel-am-Albis, its troops greatly outnumbered the Catholic forces, who were under the command of Hans Äbli of Glarus. Zwingli's principal role in accompanying the Zurich soldiers to Kappel was as a military chaplain and each day the men would gather to hear him preach. His last military venture had been at the battle of Marignano in 1515, where the slaughter of Swiss soldiers had traumatised him into a lifelong campaign against the mercenary system.

Äbli wisely opted for negotiations over combat and the result was the First Peace of Kappel of 26 June 1529. The unwillingness of the soldiers to fight was expressed in the famous, if apocryphal, account of the men from both sides gathering on the field at Kappel to share their milk soup, with each side only allowed to dip from its half of the pot.[11] The terms of the peace were based on the principle that each state could abide by its own faith, while in the Mandated Territories the confessional orientation of each village was to be determined by the will of the majority. Zurich and the other Reformed states insisted that the Catholic alliance with Ferdinand of Austria be dissolved and that reparations be paid. Should the payments not be made, the Reformed states threatened, they would use their geographical advantage to impose an economic blockade.

Despite the fairly rapid concession by the Catholic states, the result was a defeat for Zwingli. Not only had he failed to persuade the other Reformed states, most notably Berne, to carry on the war to complete victory, but he had not been able to keep the support of the Zurich council. The Zurich magistrates, according to Zwingli, had chosen compromise at a crucial moment, thereby divesting themselves of their role as bearers of the sword. As far as Zwingli was concerned, the disputations had taken the cause as far as they could; what was now required was action on the battlefield, as the Catholics were prepared at all costs to thwart the Reformation. Berne, however, demurred. Led by Niklaus Manuel, the Bernese were not prepared to impose the three key conditions insisted upon by Zurich: the freedom of preaching in Catholic lands; the abolition of mercenary service; and the payment of reparations to Zurich. Zwingli made various attempts to involve himself in the negotiations, but with little success. Manuel was the one leader among the evangelicals who offered a genuinely alternative vision to Zwingli's; like the Zurich reformer he had seen with his own eyes the slaughter of Swiss soldiers in Italy. Manuel understood that greed, and not anything found in the Gospels, drove the interests of those with power.[12] He also understood the concerns of the rural population in a way that Zwingli never did; he had served as a local governor and he knew that in these communities practical matters of existence prevailed over ideology; farmers were not about to kill their neighbours, with whom they traded, for being Catholic. Manuel was fully aware of the fundamental problem for the Reformed states, that Zwingli's warmongering had no public appeal. Manuel, in a flurry of diplomatic activity between Berne and Zurich, sought to defuse the situation. As a leading politician in Berne, Manuel was arguably one of the most influential men in the Confederation and his opposition to a religious war was more than sufficient to counter Zwingli. It would, however, be misleading to contrast Zwingli and Manuel in terms of their fundamental principles: it was not a case of the ideological preacher against the wily, pragmatic politician. Manuel was no less committed to the evangelical cause, and although like Zwingli his conversion to the Reformation had arisen from the horrors of military conflict, his spiritual development had followed a different path. He would, and could not accept that coercion in matters of religion had any positive effect.[13] That truth would prevail in the end he did not doubt, but it would occur through God's providence, not the rash actions of men. Niklaus Manuel died in 1530, depriving the Confederation of his powerful voice of moderation. Had he lived, the Reformation might well have taken a different course and religious war might have been avoided, as his stature among the leaders of the evangelical states was greater than Zwingli's. His legacy, however, proved enduring. Under Heinrich Bullinger, even during the most bitter confessional disputes, the Reformed churches recoiled in horror from the prospect of armed conflict in the name of religion.

The period following the First Kappel Peace in 1529 was full of bad-tempered communications between the Reformed states. Two distinct visions of the way forward had emerged; visions which hung on the answer to the question of which came first, religion or the Confederation? Many, including Zwingli and the young Bullinger, believed that the religious divide had made the survival of the Swiss Confederation impossible. How could a political body exist with two religions? Others, particularly among the political leaders in Zurich, Berne, and Basle, were not prepared to dissolve the Confederation; they did not see the religious divide as final and they were encouraged by the prospect of a general council of the church in the empire to resolve the Reformation question.

Zwingli the firebrand, determined to punish the recalcitrant Catholics, could not win the support of the warlike Bernese for the cause of the Reformation. In truth, however, Zwingli was no fanatical warrior, and despite posterity's desire to portray him with a sword in one hand and the Bible in the other, he never lost his revulsion of warfare and the hardships it brought upon the ordinary people in terms of lost lives, disease, and moral degeneracy. At the same time, Zwingli was no pacifist. He adhered to the Thomistic doctrine of the just war, and argued that the cause of the Gospel was sufficient grounds for an attack upon the Catholics. He saw this as preferable to the Bernese solution of an economic blockade, which in place of a decisive victory would result in the slow starvation of the common people. His view did not carry the day and he was bitter. In the spring of 1529 Zurich imposed the blockade and issued a mandate forbidding its rural subjects from trading with their Catholic neighbours.[14] By the summer of 1529 the Reformation had hit an Alpine wall, and within Zwingli himself there was a clash of contradictory impulses. His theology had always worked through the dialectical relation of opposites: the Reformation had come to a point where Christian freedom would have to be won by military coercion.

If the way south was blocked Zwingli was still committed to a Protestant alliance which could extend north to the Baltic. After the failure of Marburg, Zwingli remained directly involved in German affairs through contact with Philip of Hesse, a deeply ambitious prince opposed to the emperor and desirous of expanding his territory. Following the Protest of Speyer in 1529 the German princes feared that the return of Charles V would bring religious war. Charles had calmed the papacy and suspended hostilities with France and seemed ready to respond to the challenge thrown down by the German princes, who, in turn, needed the support and money of the southern German cities and the Swiss if they were to defend themselves. Philip and Zwingli dreamt of an anti-papal and anti-imperial alliance which stretched from the Mediterranean to Scandinavia.

From the Swiss perspective this grand scheme foundered on account of the implacable opposition of Berne. In many respects the real story of the failure of the Swiss Reformation was the rivalry of Zurich and Berne. Zwingli had played an important role in 1528, and he had sent his good friend Kaspar Megander to Berne to ensure that the two churches remained in harmony. Nevertheless, the contrasts between the two were always more prominent. Berne had its eyes to the west, in particular the French-speaking lands of the Pays de Vaud. It had not the slightest interest in financing either Zurich's expansion in the east of the Confederation or north of the Rhine in Germany. Historically, Berne had always taken its role within the Confederation more seriously than had Zurich; the Bernese magistrates were not prepared to permit the whole structure to collapse on account of religious quarrels; the defensive and economic aspects of the alliance were too important. Further, whereas Zurich controlled its rural areas with an iron fist, Berne had a much larger rural population which was by no means cravenly subordinate. In Berne there was a delicate balance between the rural and urban powers which was best served by peaceful relations with Catholic neighbours.

Zwingli also looked to France for possible support, despite Zurich's refusal in 1521 to renew its alliance with France, and in April 1531 he met with the French representatives in the Confederation, Lambert Maigret and Louis Dangerant. Zwingli saw Francis I as the crucial weapon in the struggle against Charles V, while the French saw the Swiss Confederation, along with the cities of Constance and Strasbourg, as a way of attacking the empire from the south. However, the French only wanted to form an alliance with Zurich and did not want to have to negotiate between the confessional sides in the Confederation, so the alliance discussions came to nothing.

To the north Zurich had little cause for optimism. Neither Basle nor Constance, the city which Zwingli once referred to as the 'key to the Confederation', were prepared to offer needed support. In the spring of 1530 Zurich agreed to co-operation with Philip of Hesse, Duke Ulrich of Württemberg, Basle and Berne. The arrangement, however, was short-lived as Berne refused to join in any alliance with Philipp on the grounds that it had other priorities. In Germany events were dominated by the summoning of the Diet of Augsburg (April–September). Philipp took the lead in attempting to hold the Protestant parties together in the wake of the Marburg disaster. The Protestants were invited to state their case to the diet, and Philip Melanchthon developed the *Confessio Augustana*, which emphasised the points of difference from Zwinglian theology. Martin Bucer, Wolfgang Capito, and Jakob Sturm attempted a compromise confession in July 1530, known as the *Confessio Tetrapolitana*, which was roundly dismissed by the Germans and Swiss alike. Zwingli, who had been prepared to attend the Diet of Augsburg, wrote a text for submission.

The *Fidei Ratio* was Zwingli's confession of faith, hurriedly prepared between 24 June and 3 July, it remains the most lucid explication of his theology. Such diverse figures as Martin Bucer and Johannes Eck recognised the maturity of the work, and both referred to it as 'Zwingli's Confession'. Zwingli set out twelve articles following the structure of the Apostles' Creed in order to emphasise the antiquity of his thought. The *Ratio* was written in Zwingli's best Latin and he displayed the breadth of his humanist learning as Cicero, Ovid, Homer and the Church Fathers were either cited or emulated in style. The ancient church, Zwingli wrote, had not been destroyed by the Reformation, but had been restored to its essential unity as the body of all in the world who professed Christ. He took the article 'I believe in One, Holy, Catholic and Apostolic church', the statement of the Nicene and Athanasian Creeds, and declared that the foundation of this statement was Christ, the source of all belief. From this view of the church's catholicity Zwingli attacked the rituals and traditions which had been used to define the true church in the world. The central theme of the first part of the *Ratio* was the majesty and sovereignty of God and the salvation of humanity through the sacrifice of his Son Jesus Christ. Zwingli stressed both that God is the source of all goodness and that the elect know that they are saved. He wrote:

> The [church] is known to God alone, for ... he alone knows the hearts of the children of men. But, nevertheless, those who are members of this church, since they have faith, know that they themselves are elect and are members of this first church, but are ignorant of the members other than themselves.[15]

The *Ratio* was an anti-Lutheran work, and, although Zwingli had been warned by his friends that Charles V would tolerate no attack on the mass, he wrote a full justification of his views on the Lord's Supper against both Wittenberg and the Roman church. At the same time he declared himself to be the first to have stood against the Anabaptists. In the final part of the text Zwingli wrote an extensive account of his views on the relationship between the church and secular authority. He reiterated his view that God sanctioned disobedience and resistance towards those rulers who set themselves against the faith.[16] Thus the role of the prophet (as Zwingli saw himself) was crucial, for the prophet had the task of ensuring that all things were ordered according to God's will.

Zwingli's *Ratio* was brilliant and bold, one of the great writings of the early Reformation, but it was never going to have any effect on the proceedings in Augsburg. Whether the emperor even saw it or not is unclear. Johannes Eck wrote an extensive refutation, demonstrating point by point that Zwingli was a heretic. The Lutherans were no less hostile; Luther himself asked whether the Germans wanted to make an alliance with people with such ideas, while Melanchthon wondered aloud whether Zwingli had gone mad.

Between 1529 and 1531 in the Swiss Confederation there was a slow accretion of conflict. Zurich was alarmed at the international situation, where it was believed that Charles V would act against Protestantism in Germany and the Swiss lands. To defend itself Zurich prepared to pre-empt the emperor with an attack against Austria with the support of France, the old enemy of the Habsburgs. None of the other Reformed Confederates (Basle, Berne, Schaffhausen, Fribourg, Biel, Solothurn, St Gall, Glarus, and Constance) was prepared to lend a hand in this venture; only Philip of Hesse offered any encouragement. At a meeting of the evangelical diet in Zurich in April 1531 Berne refused outright to become involved in any military campaign. A month later on 12 May when Zurich brought forward a plan for war it stood alone. The other Reformed Confederates were only prepared to go as far as enforcing the economic blockade.

By April 1531 Zwingli had begun to speak of war, having lost all confidence in the readiness of the Catholic states to honour the First Kappel Peace of 1529. In particular the Catholics had shown no willingness to permit evangelical preaching in their lands. The Catholics had a distinct advantage in the Mandated Territories; they were in the majority and thus had the right to appoint the local governor year after year for up to ten years. Thus they were in a position to complicate life for the evangelicals in these lands by appointing hostile officials. For a meeting at Bremgarten in August 1531 Zwingli wrote his *Counsel* in which he offered, as it turned out for the last time, an assessment of how the Confederation might be salvaged.[17] Part of the text was a reiteration of familiar themes: the Confederation could only be saved by the abolition of mercenary pensions and the establishment of evangelical preaching. It was wrong, he wrote, that the Five Inner States should be permitted to thwart the Reformation in the Mandated Territories by means of their majority on the governing bodies. Berne and Zurich between them had more responsibility for the Mandated Territories than any of the Catholic states and should, therefore, be accorded greater weight. Most interestingly we encounter Zwingli's historical analysis of the Swiss dilemma; he poses the question of whether sovereignty lay entirely with the individual Confederates, or whether the union as a whole existed as a sovereign body. Zwingli was a federalist, and his proposals argued for the restructuring of the Confederation in order that Berne and Zurich alone might administer the Mandated Territories. This would lead to the establishment of an evangelical Swiss Confederation, which was Zwingli's goal.

What was Zwingli's role in the actual government of Zurich? He described himself as a 'prophet', declaring God's Word to the faithful. In Zurich and abroad, however, many were utterly persuaded that Zwingli was in fact calling the political shots. In the large council there was still opposition to his reforms, while the small council, which was responsible for church affairs was firmly evangelical. The sensitivity of the issues debated meant that the most important decisions were made behind closed doors by the Bürgermeister and his most trusted counsellors, among whom was Zwingli. Indeed we know that Zwingli often wrote reports and the formal correspondence which came out of Zurich. It was through this circle of about six men that all the negotiations with the other states were conducted, and Zwingli wrote most of the letters to Philipp of Hesse, Berne, Strasbourg, and the French representatives.

There was, however, opposition in the city. Not many of Zwingli's opponents remained on the councils but they came from influential quarters and were not afraid to raise their voices in dissent. In particular these opponents objected to Zwingli's harsh demands that the blockade against the Catholic states be strictly enforced. The damage this was doing to fellow Confederates was considered unacceptable; there was little desire to consider these people as enemies. Secondly, Zwingli's intractable demand that evangelical preaching be permitted in the Mandated Territories was believed to be so divisive that it was tearing the Confederation apart. On 26 July 1531 a petition was presented to the Zurich council calling for Zwingli's dismissal. It decried the manner in which Zwingli's religious views were determining the external relations of the city. The council rejected the petition, but there could be no disguising the reality that Zwingli no longer commanded the same level of respect in the city. Many questioned his motives and were suspicious of his role in government. The opposition was not strong enough to dislodge him, but resentment was everywhere, ensuring that when the fall came it would be brutal.

Even among his supporters, however, there was disquiet that Zwingli was driving Zurich towards a war it could not win. The rejection of mercenary service in 1521 may have been a high-minded act of principle, but it had seriously damaged Zurich's military strength. When the flow of pension money into the city stopped Zurich had turned to other ways of making money. Its soldiers were no longer trained and they had little experience in comparison to the Catholic forces, which had fought at Bicocca and Pavia. Finally,

Zurich simply did not have the financial resources to carry out a military campaign against the Catholic states; in any such endeavour the resources of Basle and Berne would be required, and there was no support from those quarters.

There were other problems. If there were those in the city who had not been converted by Zwingli's preaching, without doubt the vast majority of men and women had little interest in or understanding of his political agenda. What did the farmers along Lake Zurich care about alliances with Hesse or Strasbourg, or the rights of the abbot of St Gall, or whether the Gospel was preached in some Mandated Territory? The call to arms issued by the Zurich council in late summer 1531 fell on deaf ears as most inhabitants of Zurich's rural territories prepared themselves for the harvest.

The blockade, meanwhile, was highly effective. It forced the Catholic states to take counter-measures; they mobilised their forces in an effort to break the wall that had been erected around them. Within Zurich and Berne there was discord on the subject of sanctions as consciences were troubled by the prospect of victory by the starvation of fellow Confederates; the only possible result, it was argued, was the destruction of the union. The opposition was sufficient to cause Zwingli to threaten to leave Zurich; a threat he quickly retracted. Where he might have gone is an interesting question to ponder. In any case, repeated attempts by Zurich's allies to persuade the city to lift the economic blockade failed. In the Catholic states deprivation was making the subjects restless; and on 21 September 1531 the Catholic Confederates armed for war.

In Zurich the mobilisation of the Catholic states had been anticipated since the middle of September, but the situation in the city was not good. Zwingli's hard-line attitudes had exposed fault-lines among the influential families in the city and there was growing mistrust of the leading politicians. Distrust mixed with indecision as the Zurich magistrates wrestled with how to respond to the declaration of war issued by the Catholic states on 9 October. They were divided on the seriousness of the threat and could not agree to a military plan. Their military leaders were not experienced and the troops extremely reluctant to risk their lives for a cause they hardly believed in. Uncertainty, weakness, and fear marked Zurich's response to the Catholic threat. However, the Swiss historian Leonhard von Muralt has cautioned that we must not overplay the chaos of Zurich's military campaign, for well-ordered military campaigns were never the Swiss method of fighting wars. Men, horses, and other resources would always appear at the last minute as communities rallied to the war effort.[18]

Once again part of the Zurich forces made their way to Kappel, but they were betrayed by one of their own, who stole across the lines to inform the Catholics that the Zurich force was weak. Indeed, those gathered around the Zurich banner were the commander Caspar Göldli, Huldrych Zwingli and his friends, and a large number of preachers – hardly a serious military threat. By late afternoon on 10 October the Catholic forces had decided to delay their attack until the next day. What then transpired was unexpected by both sides; a band of Catholic troops made its way through the woods near the Zurich camp and launched a surprise attack. With the clash of arms the remaining Catholic forces joined in the assault. The Zurich forces were taken unawares and badly outnumbered. Zwingli did not attempt to flee but took up his sword. How he died, we do not know exactly, but his body was quartered and burnt. The chronicler Johannes Stumpf provides a graphic account of how Zwingli's body was treated.[19] The corpse was found in the field and the troops immediately rejoiced that the 'heretic' was dead. What then followed was a form of juridical humiliation. According to Stumpf a large number of men, women, and children had come from the rural areas of Zug to witness the trial of the body. The body was propped up and interrogated. 'Are you an honest man and a good Christian? Then stand up! But if you are a traitor and heretic, then fall down.' When the body slumped heavily to the ground Zwingli was sentenced to death with the judgement which had been given against him years earlier in Lucerne. As a traitor he was to be quartered, and then as a heretic burnt. Before he was quartered, however, they cut off the head – an act which allowed Stumpf to compare Zwingli with John the Baptist and Cicero. The Catholics had their revenge on the man they accused of having destroyed the Confederation. In all five hundred men from a force of two thousand died on 11 October, while the Catholics lost about eighty from seven to eight thousand.

The defeat was decisive, but not final. Two days after the battle at Kappel Zurich summoned a force of twelve thousand men, while near by eight thousand soldiers, reluctantly sent by Basle, Berne, Solothurn, and Mülhausen, approached the Catholic army. The Bernese forces, however, were so unwilling to be involved that many of the soldiers simply drifted away back home, and by the end of October the Bernese army had withdrawn from any engagements. Meanwhile, things went from bad to worse. At the battle of Gubel on 24 October forces from Zurich, Schaffhausen, Berne, and the eastern Swiss states were surprised and overrun by soldiers from Zug. The complete indiscipline of the evangelical soldiers led to a rout by an inferior force. The commander Jakob Frei and eight hundred men fell. Zurich and her allies fled home humiliated; Zurich's territories were utterly unprotected and the Catholic forces poured across the borders.

Far too late the incompetent leaders of Zurich's forces, Hans Rudolf Lavater and Caspar Göldli, were replaced by Hans Escher, a man with proper experience. The situation, however, was not to be saved.

The concern raised by the war was such that mediators began arriving from Appenzell, Solothurn, Neuchâtel, the southern German cities (Augsburg), and France. Zurich immediately sought peace after the defeat at Gubel, and the chronicler Johann Stumpf reported that many leading citizens in the city declared their intention to return to the Catholic faith.[20] God had revealed the true religion. With the defeat at Gubel the will of Berne and Basle to be involved in a religious war quickly evaporated. Both sued for peace and withdrew from Catholic lands. Zurich was crippled and was forced to abandon immediately its allies in the Mandated Territories and St Gall. The Catholics took control of the Freiamt and restored the mass.

The collapse of the political regime in Zurich meant that the peace negotiations were carried out by the military leaders, and on 20 November a document signed by Zurich and the Five Inner States was sealed and proclaimed.[21] Both sides declared their desire for peace, but the Catholics had very specific demands: the Freiamt, Bremgarten, and Mellingen were to be theirs. The terms of the First Kappel Peace were abrogated, while in the Mandated Territories the majority were to decide on their faith, but where this was in favour of the Reformed religion Catholics were to be guaranteed the right to hear mass and receive the sacraments. Such privileges were not extended to communities where the evangelicals were in the minority. Zurich was to abandon all foreign alliances and to pay war reparations. Toggenburg, although divided confessionally, had to reaccept the authority of the abbot of St Gall. For the Catholics the Second Kappel Peace essentially protected the Confederation against further expansion by the heretics. The Reformed religion was permitted within specific circumstances, but there was no recognition of equality. Crucially, Catholics in Reformed areas were protected, while no such protection was extended to the evangelicals.

The Second Kappel Peace became a central constitutional document of the Confederation, remaining unaltered until the Third Peace of 1656. It was a realistic document which reflected the wisdom of the Catholic victors; they knew that the Reformation was not going to be rolled back in the large urban states. The central issue was the protection of their faith in their own lands and in those Mandated Territories which they jointly administered. By securing the Catholic religion in territories such as Rapperswil, Sargans, Weesen, Bremgarten, Zurzach, and Brugg they secured trade and travel routes from their central position to Austria in the east, Milan in the south, Wallis in the west, and the Austrian lands north of the Rhine. Thereby they secured their independence within the Confederation and their connections with Catholic Europe.[22]

In the eastern parts of the Confederation, where the Zurichers had traditionally exercised influence, and where they had supported the evangelical preachers, there was little left after the Kappel War to show for their earlier efforts. Much of the Thurgau returned to the Catholic fold. The Second Peace of Kappel introduced the principle of each state abiding by its own faith, though the terms of the peace referred to Catholicism as the true religion. This division along religious grounds anticipated the *cuius regio, eius religio* of the Peace of Augsburg in 1555. Although the Catholics did not conceal a sense of triumph, the Second Peace of Kappel sought to establish a way forward by removing religion from the equation of daily life in the Confederation. The Confederation had shown itself incapable of dealing with religious matters, and it is hardly surprising that the Peace was negotiated by Berne, the most reluctant of the evangelical states to fight for religious reasons. The Second Peace of Kappel was an attempt to hold the Confederation together, and little more than that: it enshrined no principles of religious toleration or acceptance. The evangelical states were exhausted, defeated, and disorganised. Communications between Berne, Zurich, and Basle virtually ceased as the whole movement was riven by recriminations; old wounds were opened as each of the Reformed city states was badly affected, and forced to pay steep reparations. The Catholics, for their part, harboured dreams of rolling back the Reformation all together.

Backlash

The defeat had its most dramatic consequences in Zurich. The chronicler Johann Stumpf reported that many in the city saw the catastrophe as divine punishment for the introduction of a false religion; some said that the Mother of God of Einsiedeln had led the Catholic forces to victory and that the Zurichers should return to her care. Mostly, however, the hatred was directed towards the Zwingli party, which was held directly responsible for leading the city into an unnecessary and humiliating disaster. Leo Jud, Zwingli's closest friend and colleague, had remained in the city; his supporters begged him to dress in woman's clothing, leave his home and hide with friends whilst gangs rampaged through the city looking to lynch those associated with Zwingli. Courageously, Jud opted to preach, declaring that Kappel was indeed a punishment, not for abandoning Catholicism but rather for the weakness of the Zurichers in not following the Gospel.

While Jud attempted to rally the evangelicals in the city the defeated Zurich army, under the leadership of the Zwingli-hater, Hans Escher, was returning along the Lake of Zurich. Escher had negotiated with the Five Inner States a peace in which the Catholic faith was recognised as the true religion. He also boasted that when he returned to the city he would run a sword through Jud and all the other troublesome priests. To avoid the outbreak of civil war, the Zurich council hastily sent negotiators to meet the returning forces, making them swear to peace before they could enter the gates of the city. Escher reluctantly agreed, but the troubles were not over; forces from Schwyz took up position outside the walls of Zurich. Jud, Oswald Myconius, and the other members of the Zwingli circle prepared for the worst, but fortunately the Schwyzer troops moved off the following day, unwilling to storm the city.

Zurich felt that it had been abandoned by its Reformed allies, and even those political leaders in the city who had opposed war railed against the putative unfaithfulness of the Bernese and Baslers. In the immediate aftermath of the defeats Zurich swung from a policy of confrontation to seeking peace at any cost. Although Philip of Hesse had offered military assistance, it had been refused, and now the Swiss connections with German Protestantism were severely weakened. Philip hoped at least to preserve the alliance with Basle, but this too proved impossible. All of the Reformed states were faced with the enormous punitive damages claimed by the Catholic victors, and they could not pay. Berne sought a loan from Strasbourg while Zurich borrowed 6,000–8,000 gulden from Augsburg. In order to finance these loans both cities had to use the income derived from the secularisation of the religious houses; money that had been intended for the building of churches and schools. Helmut Meyer has estimated that the burden laid upon the Reformed states by the war reparations was evident for at least ten years after the Kappel War.[23]

Despite their weak position, the Reformed states sought to have Constance admitted to the Confederation as part of the Kappel Peace. In January 1532 the Bernese delegates described Constance as the 'key to the Confederation', and indeed there was a great deal of logic in this view. Constance offered important protection against Habsburg Austria as well as a crucial link with southern Germany. The Catholic states were not in principle opposed to admitting Constance as a Confederate; however their Austrian allies, who remained their insurance against further religious war, insisted that no arrangement with Constance be made. The moment passed and the city of Constance, which had desperately wanted to join the Confederation, had to look elsewhere for support against Austria. The city was increasingly drawn away from the Swiss towards the Schmalkaldic League.

The most controversial subject remained the war reparations. The Five Inner States wanted 20,000 gulden from Zurich and Berne each. In the end they received 8,200, which was still more than three times the amount they had been forced to pay in 1529. Zurich and Berne had the greatest debts, with each owing 2,500. Basle had to pay 1,200 and Schaffhausen 1,000. St Gall and Mülhausen each owed 400 gulden. Zurich accepted the negotiated settlement first, Berne a few days later. None of the Reformed states quarrelled with the amounts; the arrangement had been sorted out by the traditional use of mediators.

Heinrich Bullinger, who was just taking up his position in Zurich, was deeply sceptical that the Confederation could survive the war. He wrote a text in which he argued the case for Zurich's withdrawal from the Confederation on the grounds that peace with the Catholic states was impossible.[24] The Catholic states, he argued, had interpreted the agreements of the Confederation to their own advantage and further association with them would be of no use to Zurich. Further, the situation of the evangelicals in the Mandated Territories was hopeless; Zurich could no longer help them. Finally, he argued that remaining confederates with states which opposed God's Word was contrary to the divine will.

It is unclear to what purpose Bullinger wrote this work, and he certainly did not pursue the ideas he laid out to the Zurich council. The work does, however, highlight the isolationist sentiments in the city after the defeat. Zurich continued routine trade with Basle and Berne, and the three cities continued to share information, but such was the depth of resentment that nothing, not even the dissolution of the Confederation, was unthinkable.

While the political leaders and churchmen attempted to come to terms with defeat the restive stirrings of the rural populace made themselves felt. Largely ignored by Zwingli, the rural communities believed that they had been pushed into a military conflict that they had consistently opposed from the start. The degree of rural alienation reflected Zwingli's belief that the Reformation would only take hold in the city and would have to be imposed upon the subject lands. Between 1521 and 1526 at least six surveys of rural opinion had been carried out by the council on matters such as the mercenary service and the evangelical religion, but between 1526 and 1531 there were none. The reason for this was arrestingly simple: Zwingli knew that the evangelical religion had not been enthusiastically received in the villages of Zurich's rural territories, and further surveys would only yield up inconvenient answers. The religious situation in the villages was much more fluid than in the cities; the borders between the Confederate states were notional to farmers taking their goods to market. Catholics and Protestants mixed easily, and all of the surveys of public opinion (*Volksanfragen*) taken in the period before Kappel reflected the prevalent view in hinterlands of Zurich and Berne that whilst the people accepted the Reformed faith, they were not prepared either to die or kill their neighbours for their religion. The resistance to religious war was absolute, and the response to Kappel was a wave of anticlericalism directed at those in the city held responsible. On 28 November representatives of the rural communities in the Zurich lands gathered at Meilen on Lake Zurich to present a petition to the Bürgermeister and council consisting of eight articles outlining their grievances. The petition included requests that the urban leaders not undertake war without the consent of the rural communities; that foreign clergy and persons be excluded from influence on the council; that only native sons be appointed as ministers or rural officials; and that the communities be permitted to regain their old rights.[25] Although there was no call for a return to the old religion, the petition was a damning indictment of Zwingli's polity and role in Zurich.

In Berne, although the state had not suffered anything like the humiliation of Zurich, the rural communities spoke out against the presence of 'foreign' clergy and their bellicose sermons. The centre of the controversy in Berne was Kaspar Megander, Zwingli's ally and the principal theologian in the city. After the defeat at Kappel he had preached against the Bernese magistrates, denouncing them for their mendacity in not supporting Zwingli and Zurich. Megander was suspended from office, and was forced to remain silent until the Synod of Berne in early 1532. Berchtold Haller, Megander's colleague, was far too ill to assume his preaching duties. While in Basle, Johannes Oecolampadius, whom many regarded as Zwingli's natural successor, lived for barely another month, leaving yet another urban church rudderless. During the fraught months from October to December, while the Reformed churches were rocked by attacks from the Catholic states and internal critics, there was no leadership. Relations between Zurich and Berne had been poisoned to the extent that there was virtually no contact between the two states. The breakdown of the Reformation was such that rumours flew that Zurich was about to restore the mass.

In truth, there was never much chance of a return to the old faith. Although Catholicism retained its supporters, particularly in Basle, the consolidation of authority which had accompanied the religious changes of the 1520s had gone too far for the magistrates to turn back the clock. They were not about to reopen religious houses, redecorate the churches, or give back the money to the Grossmünster chapter. There had been a deeply bitter response to the defeat at Kappel. What became apparent was that resentments against Zwingli and his followers which had remained suppressed while the Reformation was successful, were unleashed in the wake of the disaster. The rural communities voiced their protest, but they did not demand the restoration of the old religion. Even if, as many believed, the evangelical ministers in the cities had betrayed them with their ill-advised political sermons, neither the urban or rural populations evinced a strong desire to return to the Catholic faith. In truth, the Reformation had moved so quickly that most people were unclear on the differences between the two faiths, but they seemed content to remain with the new arrangement as long as certain terms were applied.

The most important issue of the Swiss Reformation through the early 1530s, the years directly after the defeat at Kappel, was the freedom of the Gospel. Zwingli had argued that the minister, as interpreter of scripture, had a prophetic role in the community declaring God's will. This was the essence of the Zwinglian ministry. Yet it was the preaching which had landed these ministers in such trouble, and not just the political sermons of Zwingli in Zurich and Kaspar Megander in Berne. In villages across the land ministers ill-trained in preaching or scriptural exegesis caused an uproar in their communities by using the pulpit to berate the faithful. One Johannes Ammann, minister in Rifferswil, railed against his congregation, accusing them of being murderers and thieves. When his livid parishioners demanded that he either substantiate his charges or be punished for slander he simply replied that it was his duty as a minister to use the pulpit to excoriate the faithful. Ammann was eventually fined by the local bailiff for his misuse of authority.[26] Such incidents were legion and symptomatic of a larger issue, that the Reformed churches had little control over their clergy, most of whom had little knowledge of the new faith and even less sense of how to preach. What was clear, however, in light of the political catastrophe of Kappel, was that political leaders were no longer prepared to give ministers a long lead. Preaching was dangerous and had, therefore, to be controlled. The fourth Meilen Article read:

> Gracious lords, it is our friendly entreaty and desire that preachers no longer be accepted in our city save those who are peaceable and generally orientated towards peace and quiet. We further wish that those provocative ministers who publicly are wicked from the pulpit be sent away by you and us together, who wish only peace and quiet. Eventually, let the preachers in the countryside say only that which is God's Word expressed in both Testaments. Let the clergy, as already notified, not undertake or meddle in any secular matters either in the city or the countryside, in the council or elsewhere, which they should rather allow you, our lords, to manage.[27]

This article contained the seeds of a debate which would run through the sixteenth century: what should a minister preach? The articles made it clear that ministers were to stick to the Word of God and not involve themselves in politics. Indeed, Kaspar Megander in Berne, had been suspended from office for having the temerity to scold the magistrates. But was not this what Nathan had done before the adulterous King David? Zwingli's Old Testament model of the relationship between prophet and monarch was founded on the belief that one spoke with the authority of God's Word, whilst the other bore the sword. Inherent in this model was a notion of the superiority of the prophet over the king. Zwingli had concealed this problem through his concessions to the Zurich council through the 1520s – which had lost him the support of the radicals - but when it had come to the matter of war against the Catholic states, an issue on which Zwingli was deeply passionate, it had all gone wrong. He misused the power he had accrued and now the church had to pay the price.

Heinrich Bullinger

The Zurich council might have appointed Leo Jud as Zwingli's successor, but there were problems. Jud was a foreigner, and xenophobia was running high in 1531. More importantly, Jud was suffering a personal crisis; he had become so depressed after the death of Zwingli that he was unable to accept any leadership role. There were others, however, who wanted the position. Kaspar Megander, long unhappy in frosty Berne, wanted to return to his native city. Megander, along with Oswald Myconius, stood for a continuation of the war against the Catholics; a view anathema to humbled Zurich, which was concerned to maintain control over its rural areas. Jud suggested the young Heinrich Bullinger of Bremgarten. A talented theologian, educator, and preacher, Bullinger was known to oppose religious wars. In fact, Bullinger received offers from Berne and Basle as well, but he clearly wanted to come to Zurich.

Bullinger was elected on 9 December to the position of minister in the Grossmünster. On account of the Meilen Articles, whose terms so limited the role of the minister, he asked for time to consider his position. A week later he gave a written reply to the council. He was prepared to agree that ministers should avoid political comment in their sermons, as this was dangerous to the state, but in return he demanded that they retain the right to preach against blasphemy and profanity in the community, as these directly threatened the spiritual health of the faithful.[28] This he understood to be the freedom of ministers to proclaim the Gospel without fear of recrimination. The council, desperate to have Bullinger, agreed to his terms. Over the next couple of years Bullinger would set himself to the development of a polity which retained the preaching of the Word as its spiritual foundation, but within an institutional framework. Like Zwingli he worked closely with his political masters, keeping sensitive issues for discussion behind closed doors. Basically, Bullinger was to be allowed to run the church as he thought best, as long as he kept the ministers under control. It was an arrangement to which Bullinger would devote his forty years as chief minister of the Zurich church. Never a brilliant theologian, Bullinger was an educator and a 'bishop', concerned for the pastoral welfare of his clergy and the laity. His deepest concern remained for the cultivation of piety and godly living, and these, he believed, only took root in an ordered society.

In Berne the council had passed a mandate on 6 December 1531 stating its intention to abide by the Reformed faith, but the situation in the church was hardly encouraging. The strife caused by Megander's preaching had torn the city apart and no ready solution appeared. Even before the Second Kappel War Megander had fallen foul of the Bernese magistrates with his incendiary preaching, but his accusations from the pulpit of indolence were too much and the minister was suspended from office. The perilous state of the church in Berne after Kappel was exacerbated by the fact that its leading ministers were either ill or disgraced. Help was required from outside, and as Zurich was in no position to act, it arrived from Strasbourg when Wolfgang Capito entered Berne on 29 December. The situation he found was deeply troubling; although Berne had suffered little in the military débâcle, the mood in the land was ugly. Those who had called for war (the *Kriegshetzer*) were roundly denounced, and as in Zurich this meant specifically the foreign clergy. Similar demands to those made by the rural communities in Zurich at Meilen were presented to the Bernese council: no more foreign preachers who would lead the people into war; no more wars against the will of the rural communities; no more political preaching, etc.[29] The Bernese council moved to meet the demands of the people by issuing a decree in which a synod of the clergy was called for January of the new year. Capito had impressed the Bernese rulers in 1528 and now in the midst of this crisis they turned to him once again. The Strasbourg reformer began by persuading the magistrates to lift Megander's suspension, arguing that in private conversation the disgraced reformer had indicated remorse and declared that he had not intended to offend the civic rulers. Berchtold Haller wrote to Bullinger providing an account of the Megander case and requested, most likely out of fear for his position in Berne, that the head of the Zurich church burn their correspondence concerning the affair.[30]

It was of course a fiction, but all sides were eager to get out of this mess as no one knew where it might lead. Capito then proceeded to write twenty-two articles for the January synod in which he outlined a polity for the Reformed church which gave the magistrates control over all spiritual affairs. As in Zurich, the central question remained the meaning of the freedom to preach the Gospel. Capito, against Megander and others, argued that such a freedom did not extend to the unfettered expression of political views or criticism of secular rulers. The realities of the post-Kappel world required a diminution of Zwingli's concept of the ministry as a prophetic office. The articles, known as the *Synodus*, became alongside the articles of the 1528 Disputation the foundation of the Bernese church. The articles are of considerable importance for several reasons. First, they mark the painful stage, which we have already seen in Zurich, of the Reformed church coming to terms with the new political reality. The leaders of the Reformed church had to articulate how their central ideas of *sola scriptura* and *sola fide* squared with the functioning of an early modern state. Unlike in the heady days of the 1520s this was no longer undertaken from a position of strength but rather as an emergency response to a humiliating defeat. The boundaries of Christian freedom were being set. The Reformation had survived, barely, but the bill had now to be paid, and the price was full subordination to the state.

The loss of Zwingli

The disaster of the Second Kappel War had first befallen Zurich, and the city reacted with the stunned disbelief of one suddenly informed of an unexpected death. There was great shock, but the grief was not for the loss of a beloved son: if there were tears, they were bitter, as the response in the city and rural areas was of anger. The fragility of the Zurich Reformation was laid bare. Zwingli, like Savonarola, dealt in the currency of human emotion; from the pulpit he had relied upon his ability to rouse the faithful to the cleansing of the temples. The prophetic voice which had promised the restoration of true religion had brought humiliation and disgrace. It did not matter who actually was responsible for the military débâcle; the violent and shocking death of Zwingli could hardly be anything other than the visitation of divine punishment on a false prophet. How else could it be interpreted? Even for his most devoted followers, the story of Zwingli's violent death on a battlefield was hard to reconcile with any tradition of martyrdom or sanctity.

It is impossible in a few words to provide any meaningful assessment of what Zwingli had achieved in just under ten years. This book is unapologetic in its view that Huldrych Zwingli was the dominant force in the Swiss Reformation: without his vision, his preaching, his theological profundity and dexterity, and his political acumen, there would have been no Reformation in the Swiss Confederation. It would be impossible to sustain that Zwingli himself was the author of the Reformations in Berne, Basle, or Schaffhausen; events in these states were dictated by local events and characters, and had their own logic, but he was responsible for what happened in Zurich, and without Zurich there would have been no other Reformations.

Through ransacking scripture, the Fathers, and even the medieval scholastics, Zwingli sought to create a church faithful to the apostolic witness, but what emerged was a vision of arresting originality, which he expressed with imagination and eloquence. In contrast to Luther, Zwingli had set before his countrymen a picture of what God's kingdom on earth would look like, and he encouraged them to believe that they would be its subjects. Yes, only the elect would inherit the kingdom, but Zwingli, perhaps too audaciously for many of his contemporaries, was optimistic about salvation for most men and women. He was an indefatigable scholar and churchman, a charismatic preacher, and a lucid thinker. His theology was written in the heat of polemical battles; he spoke and often wrote in paradoxes, using the language of polarity common to both the academic discourse of his age and to the words of his beloved St Paul. Zwingli used contrarieties, such as flesh and spirit or material and spiritual, to great effect, and with a profound sense of drama, to make a point. He often threw out his views with haste and emotion to meet particular circumstances, and there were obvious contradictions, as his opponents never ceased to declare. These contradictions were an amalgam of unresolved tensions in his thought and, despite the boldness of his rhetoric, he recognised clearly that certain things were beyond human comprehension and articulation. Zwingli's motivation was his unshakeable belief that the faithful have access to the salvation conferred by Christ's sacrifice, not through any human instrument or ritual, but through the grace of God conferred as a gift. Zwingli believed that others had to be imbued with faith in the incredible events of Christ's life and it was his life's work to make that faith available to the wider community. This faith made people pure, as God is pure. It alone washed away the filth which Zwingli saw everywhere in the human condition; it alone provided the comfort he had struggled to find after the horror of Marignano. A community which discovered faith, Zwingli declared, had the means to share the death and resurrection of Christ and the unexpressible benefits which they brought, which was the friendship of God. That meant above all the proper worship of God. At the core of all that Zwingli sought was the desire to cleanse the temple and have the people adore their God with pure hearts.

Zwingli had wanted his fellow Confederates to be holy. The preaching, pamphlets, and the politics were directed to that purpose. It was a vision, but Zwingli was also an efficient administrator and he worked hard to make it happen. He understood politics and compromise and, although this proved damaging, he recognised that the movement would have to sustain losses. It was ultimately a vision, however imperfectly formulated, for which he was prepared to die. The death of a reformer in armour on a battlefield was hard to place in biblical or church history; Zwingli's controversial career as a preacher and theologian had been ended in the most spectacularly controversial manner imaginable. Was this a glorious stand or punishment for hubris? Was he a hero or a demon? In the sixteenth century nothing was thought to just happen; there was always some underlying meaning. Luther was in no doubt when he coldly commented that 'those who live by the sword, die by the sword'. Oswald Myconius went to other extreme with a gushing biography which retold the story of how Zwingli's heart would not burn when the Catholics sought to dispose of his remains. The contested and divisive legacy of Huldrych Zwingli would hang over every aspect of the Swiss Reformation for the next half-century.

Notes

1 Hans R. Guggisberg, 'The Problem of "Failure" in the Swiss Reformation: Some Preliminary Reflections', in E.I. Kouri and Tom Scott (eds), *Politics and Society in Reformation Europe. Essays for Sir Geoffrey Elton on his Sixty-Fifth Birthday* (London, 1987), p. 196.

2 André Zünd, *Gescheiterte Stadt- und Landreformationen des 16. und 17. Jahrhunderts in der Schweiz* (Basle, 1999), pp. 37–49.

3 Ibid., pp. 70–71.

4 On the development of Solothurn as an imperial free city in the late Middle Ages, see Rainer Christoph Schwinges, 'Solothurn und das Reich im Späten Mittelalter', *Schweizerische Zeitschrift für Geschichte*, 46 (1996), pp. 451–473.

5 Johannes Stumpf, *Schweizer- und Reformationschronik*, 2 vols, ed. Ernst Gagliardi, Hans Müller and Fritz Büsser (Basle, 1953/1955), II, pp. 292–293.

6 *HBBW*, 4, 21 March 1534, pp. 92–94.

7 Ibid., p. 201.

8 The text is found in Z, III, pp. 539–583.

9 Rudolf Braun, 'Zur Militärpolitik Zürichs im Zeitalter der Kappeler Krieg', *Zwingliana*, 10 (1958), pp. 537–573.

10 Z, X, pp. 152–159.

11 See Georg Kreis, 'Die Kappeler Milchsuppe: Kernstück der schweizerischen Versöhnungsikonographie', *Schweizerische Zeitschrift für Geschichte*, 44 (1994), pp. 288–310.

12 See Glenn Ellis Ehrstine, 'Of Peasants, Women, and Bears: Political Agency and the Demise of Carnival Tradition in Bernese Reformation Drama', *SCJ*, 30 (2000), pp. 675–697.

13 Bruce Gordon, 'Toleration in the Early Swiss Reformation: The Art and Politics of Niklaus Manuel of Berne', in Ole Grell and Bob Scribner (eds), *Tolerance and Intolerance in the European Reformation* (Cambridge, 1996), pp. 128–144.

14 Stumpf, *Reformationschronik*, II, pp. 136–137.

15 W.P. Stephens, *The Theology of Huldrych Zwingli* (Oxford, 1986), p. 105.

16 Ibid., pp. 302–304.

17 Printed in *EA*, 4 1b, no. 540, pp. 1041ff.

18 Leonhard von Muralt, 'Renaissance und Reformation', in *Handbuch der Schweizer Geschichte*, 2 vols (reprint Zurich, 1980), I, p. 521.

19 Stumpf, *Reformationschronik*, II, pp. 185–186.

20 Ibid., p. 246.

21 Helmut Meyer, 'Krisenmanagement in Zürich nach dem Zweiten Kappeler Krieg', *Zwingliana*, 14 (1977), pp. 349–369.

22 Von Muralt, 'Renaissance und Reformation', p. 525.

23 Helmut Meyer, *Der Zweite Kappeler Krieg* (Zurich, 1976), p. 306.

24 The text is entitled 'Rahtschlag wie man möge vor kriegen syn und der V orten tyranny abkummen' and is found in the Zentralbibliothek Zürich, ZBZ F 95, 122ff.

25 Pamela Biel, *Doorkeepers at the House of Righteousness. Heinrich Bullinger and the Zurich Clergy 1535–1575* (Berne, 1991), pp. 52–53.

26 Bruce Gordon, 'Preaching and the Reform of the Clergy in the Swiss Reformation', in Andrew Pettegree (ed.), *The Reformation of the Parishes* (Manchester, 1993), p. 75.

27 *Aktensammlung zur Geschichte den Zürchen Reformation in den Jahren 1519–1533*, ed. Emil Egli (Zurich, 1879), p. 769.

28 Biel, *Doorkeepers*, pp. 80–81.

29 T. de Quervain, *Kirchliche und soziale Zustände in Bern unmittelbar nach der Reformation (1528–1532)* (Berne, 1906), pp. 231–235.

30 *HBBW*, 2, pp. 30–32.

5

Consolidation and turmoil 1534–66

The *First Helvetic Confession*

The events of early 1532 revealed the total disarray in the Swiss Reformed churches. The correspondence between the reformers from this period underlined the extent of the breakdown in communication between the erstwhile confessional partners. Bullinger had not yet stamped his authority on the Zurich church; in Basle the rather weak Oswald Myconius was despised by his fellow churchmen; and in Berne the church was beholden to the goodwill of the visitors from Strasbourg. In all three cities, the magistrates had lost confidence in the Reformed theologians, who not only had brought about the war but were now demonstrating that they did not really agree with one another.

Capito's articles in Berne were the first theological work following the Kappel War, and they formed an impressive outline of subjects ranging from preaching to the sacraments and the Christian life, but there was no doubt that they reflected the Lutheran positions current in the Strasbourg of Martin Bucer.[1] Capito so impressed the Bernese magistrates, who much preferred him to the insolent Megander, that the Strasbourg theology gained a perch in the Confederation. The Bernese were occupied with their plans for expansion in the west and the attempts by Capito and Bucer to bring about a reconciliation between the German Lutherans and the Swiss sounded very attractive. Peace rather than conflict with Luther offered the Bernese security in the east while their eyes were turned to the west. Also, any reconciliation with the Lutherans would certainly diminish the role of Zurich as leader of the Reformed church.

In Basle Oswald Myconius was also increasingly persuaded by the need for a *rapprochement* with the Lutherans. During the early 1530s he was caught up in settling the dispute over excommunication in the church, which was finally resolved along the Zurich model. More unpleasant however was his struggle with Karlstadt, who was without doubt the leading theological figure in Basle. Karlstadt did not attempt to conceal his contempt for Myconius, who did not possess a higher degree in theology. Understandably, Karlstadt would have nothing to do with Luther. In order to bring some order to the church's teaching in the city Myconius prepared a confession of faith in 1534, known as the *First Basle Confession*, which was printed with a preface by the Bürgermeister Adelberg Meyer.[2] It was laid before the guilds of the city and accepted; it became the basis for the first general confessional statement of the Swiss Reformed churches.

The situation among the churches remained unclear until 1536. The repeated attempts by Bucer and Capito to bring the Swiss reformers back into dialogue with Luther achieved only limited success.[3] Every ladder was followed by a snake, and in 1535 Luther's commentary on Galatians was printed with a preface in which he denounced the Swiss and their theology. Bullinger was outraged, though he had not yet abandoned hopes of some form of agreement with the Germans. Luther, somewhat ironically, did the Swiss a great favour by prodding them out of their morose introspection following Kappel. The key figure at this moment, however, was Martin Bucer. Bucer has not enjoyed a good reputation for his efforts to harmonise Lutheran and Zwinglian thought, but it cannot be denied that his endless travels in search of reconciliation forced the Swiss to reflect on Zwingli's ambiguous theological legacy and to begin to think conceptually about their theology as a coherent body of beliefs. Such a shift required the Swiss churches to start talking to one other again and it soon became their practice to hold meetings in Aarau, which lay at a crossroads in the Confederation. At one of the first meetings in December 1535 Leo Jud, Konrad Pellikan, and Theodor Bibliander from Zurich met with Oswald Myconius and Simon Grynaeus from Basle. Zurich's frosty relations with Berne, partially on account of Megander's resentment of Bullinger, resulted in Bullinger's letter of invitation to Aarau arriving too late for any representative to be dispatched. At Aarau five articles touching on the key issue of the Lord's Supper were agreed upon and sent back to the principal cities for ratification. Bullinger was in agreement, and through Martin Bucer the articles made their way to Luther, who also signalled a softening of his view towards the Swiss. To the outrage of Megander and his hard-line Zwinglian followers, the Bernese magistrates likewise welcomed the articles.

This initial agreement opened the door for more wide-ranging discussions designed to establish the theological direction of the

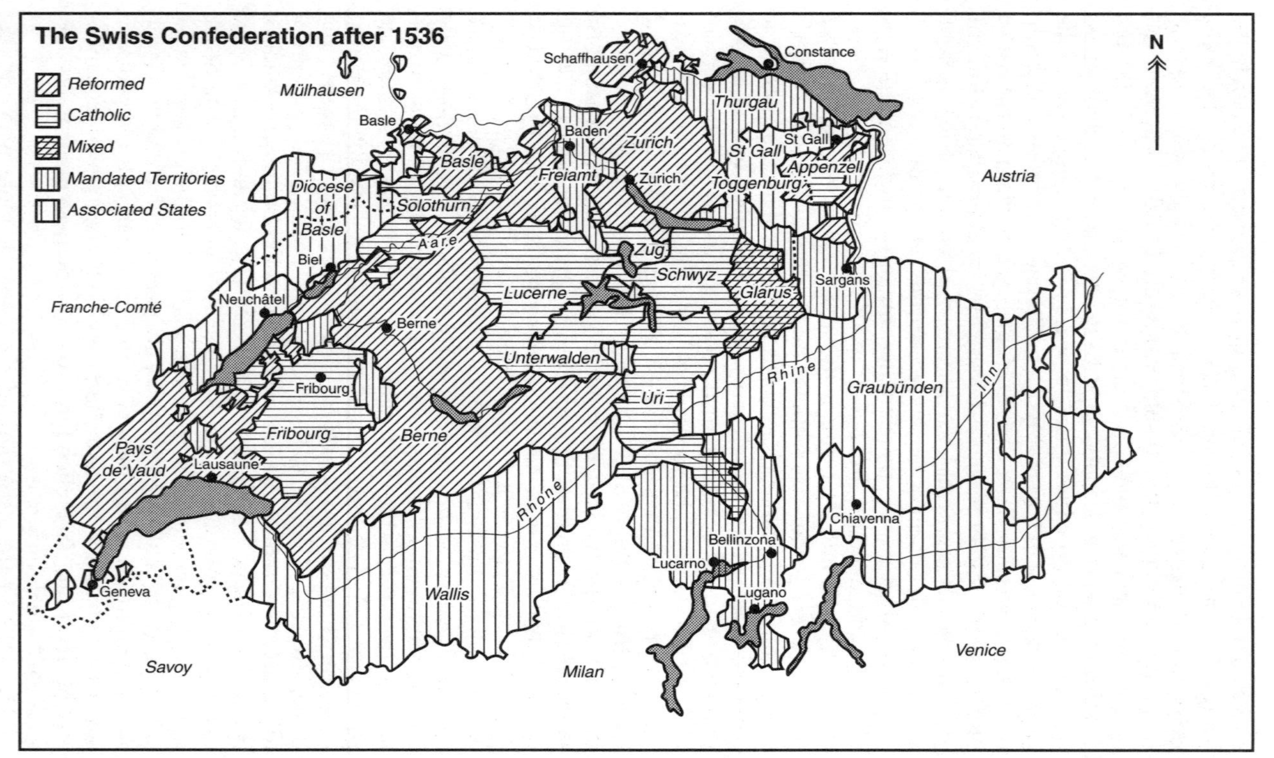
The Swiss Confederation after 1536
Reformed
Catholic
Mixed
Mandated Territories
Associated States
N
Mülhausen
Basle
Schaffhausen
Constance
Thurgau
Baden
Zurich
St Gall
St Gall
Appenzell
Basle
Freiamt
Zurich
Toggenburg
Austria
Diocese of Basle
Solothurn
Aare
Zug
Biel
Schwyz
Sargans
Glarus
Neuchâtel
Lucerne
Franche-Comté
Berne
Unterwalden
Rhine
Graubünden
Inn
Fribourg
Uri
Fribourg
Berne
Pays de Vaud
Lausaune
Rhone
Chiavenna
Bellinzona
Lucarno
Lugano
Geneva
Wallis
Venice
Savoy
Milan

Swiss Reformed churches. The first council of the Reformed churches (*Conventus generalis*) was summoned by the Basle magistrates and lasted from 30 January until 4 February 1536. Bürgermeisters and theologians from Zurich, Basle, Berne, Schaffhausen, St Gall, Biel, Constance, and Mülhausen were in attendance and even Heinrich Bullinger made one of his rare sojourns outside Zurich to take part in the theological discussions. Glarus, Appenzell, and Graubünden were unable to attend on account of their bi-confessional religious settlements.

The sessions took place in the former Augustinian monastery in Basle and Bucer and Capito arrived to aid in drafting a document which they hoped would serve as a bridge to Wittenberg. Bullinger, Grynaeus, and Myconius were primarily responsible for the theological orientation of the text, but Bucer and Capito had a hand in the formulation of the article on the Lord's Supper. The text was written in Latin and it fell to Leo Jud to prepare a German translation of the text for dissemination among the churches of the Reformed states; he used the opportunity to give the articles a distinctly Zwinglian flavour. Jud's translation of the *First Helvetic Confession* of 1536 was part of a wider offensive on the part of Zurich to reassert the authority of Zwingli's theology. In the same year Theodor Bibliander had edited four volumes of Zwingli's correspondence, while Oecolampadius and Bullinger had prepared Zwingli's last theological work, the *Fidei Ratio*, for publication, which Jud translated into German.

The 1530s was a confusing period of conflicting impulses. Bullinger had to attend to serious internal matters before he would emerge as the guiding hand of the Swiss Reformed churches. Towards Wittenberg the Swiss felt both revulsion and a tremulous need for reconciliation. There were serious theological differences, particularly over the Lord's Supper and Christology, but the shadow of Martin Luther fell unavoidably across the Confederation and the consciousness of its leading churchmen.

The expansion of the Reformation into French-speaking lands

During the Berne Disputation of January 1528 one day was set aside for a debate in French on the ten articles drafted for the event. Guillaume Farel, who had translated the articles from Latin, was opposed in the disputation by four theologians sent by the bishop of Lausanne. Naturally no agreement was reached, but this debate marked the beginning point of Farel's missionary work in the French-speaking communities around Lausanne.[4] His first success was in the village of Aigle, where a Reformed order was established with the support of the Bernese authorities. The work of converting the community was greatly aided by the arrival of French-speaking refugees who had been living in Strasbourg, Basle, and Zurich. Farel's eyes, however, were on a greater prize, the city of Neuchâtel, which he entered on 1 December 1529.[5] With the force of the Bernese council behind him, he demanded that evangelical preaching be permitted by law. During his first visit Farel established a circle of friends in Neuchâtel upon whom he depended for support and who kept the evangelical movement going until he returned to the city in July 1530 with Antoine Froment. The two men preached in the local hospital, in private houses and in the streets; they produced pamphlets denouncing the mass and they drew up propositions for debate. A legal process was launched against Farel by the clergy of the city, but with little success. The support from Berne was crucial.

In 1530 events turned violent. On 23 October Farel preached in the Collégiale against the veneration of saints and the congregation began to demolish the images in the church. Paintings, including the famous *Notre Dame de Pitié*, as well as a huge crucifix, and statues of Mary and of John the Baptist were destroyed or badly damaged; the evangelical party raged through the city destroying religious art in a number of the churches. Chaos reigned. On 4 November 1530 the council summoned the citizens of Neuchâtel for a vote on the Reformation. With a majority of only eighteen the Reformation was accepted, largely on account of the tremendous pressure exerted by Berne. The remaining pieces of devotional art were stored in a local castle and peace returned to the city in early 1531, when Farel had departed. The church was left in the hands of Antoine Marcourt, who was chief minister until 1537.[6] The new evangelical order was established in Neuchâtel and the city became a crucial base for missionary work in the surrounding countryside. During those early years of the 1530s crucial figures of the French-speaking Reformation worked together in Neuchâtel, establishing bonds which would remain important to subsequent events in Geneva and France. In 1533 a printing press was established in Neuchâtel by Pierre de Vingle, who immediately began producing Marcourt's works. The most important work to come from the press was the *Bible de Serrières*, which was printed on 4 June 1535 and contained a preface by the young John Calvin.

The other crucial centre for the Reformation in French-speaking lands was the city of Biel in the Bernese Jura.[7] The city belonged to the diocese of Basle, and its most important contribution to the intellectual and religious life of the Confederation was made by Thomas Wittenbach, a distinguished theologian who had taught in Basle and whose lectures on Romans were profoundly influential on the young Huldrych Zwingli and Leo Jud. By 1520 the master had become the disciple as Wittenbach had returned to his native Biel, where he preached in the Benedictine house against the mass, purgatory and clerical celibacy. Wittenbach was a much beloved figure in Biel, and it is no exaggeration to say that it was on account of his efforts that the majority of the council became friendly to the evangelical cause. The matter was helped by long-standing disputes with the distant bishop of Basle and the generally indifferent quality of the local clergy. Wittenbach was on close terms with the Bernese reformers Haller and Meyer, and although he died in 1526, Biel quickly followed Berne's adoption of the Reformation and by the summer of 1529 the city was firmly in the evangelical camp. Biel was not a Confederate and its position was rather uncertain following the break with its bishop. To compensate, like St Gall, it was admitted in 1529 to the Christian Civic Union, which had emerged as an alternative confederation.

Biel was a tremendous gain for the evangelicals, for with its political influence, combined with the might of Berne, the Reformation advanced through Erguel, Tessenberg, Neuveville, and Moutier-Grandval. All of these areas were visited by Farel on his preaching tours and he was able to convert notable locals, generally priests, who then became advocates of the Reformation. It would be wrong, however, to assume that these communities embraced the evangelical cause with open arms; resistance from clergy and laity, particularly among the peasants, was strong and persistent. The established pattern of holding disputations was not generally very effective. In Tessenberg, for example, a vote was held and the evangelical order was adopted, but by no means unanimously and there was considerable ill will. Provision had to be made in all the communities for those who wished to attend Catholic services, while those clergy who refused to convert were pensioned off. In almost every case, the preaching of the evangelical message was reinforced by veiled threats from Berne and Biel, whose magistrates were in no mood to tolerate opposition to their hegemonic aspirations.

It was during this period that many of the preachers first travelled to Geneva, where a Confederate army had been in 1530 to quash the renewed threat of episcopal and ducal rule in the city. The Swiss forces from Berne, Neuchâtel, Fribourg, and Solothurn had imposed upon the duke of Savoy the Peace of St Julien (19 October) which allowed the Swiss to occupy the Vaud in order to protect Geneva. Kaspar Megander, the controversial minister in Berne, had been with the Swiss soldiers in the city and had preached in the cathedral of St Pierre. The most important moment came on 16 January 1536 when Berne finally realised its ambitions in the west by launching an army of six thousand men, including one thousand from Biel, Neuchâtel, Aigle, and Lausanne, against the duke of Savoy. The commander was

Hans Franz Nägeli, and his army was so well equipped that the Catholic Five Inner States did not dare attempt to come to the aid of Savoy. By 2 February the Bernese had marched virtually unopposed through the Pays de Vaud and were at the gates of Geneva. By the end of the month all the land north of Lake Geneva was in Bernese hands and all pockets of resistance had been overcome.[8] On 31 March the Bernese entered Lausanne.

The Reformation of the French-speaking lands

During his preaching tours Farel became acquainted with a twenty-year-old young man who had at one point planned to become a priest but had been won over to the evangelical cause during his studies in Paris. Through Farel's patronage Pierre Viret became preacher in Orbe, holding his first sermon on 6 May 1531. From Orbe he travelled into the neighbouring lands of Grandson, Avenches, and Payerne, where he preached in homes and taverns. In 1534 he was sent by the Bernese to support Farel in Geneva, where he remained for most of the year, surviving an attempt on his life by poisoning.[9]

Lausanne was closely connected to Berne through an alliance struck in 1525, but when the powerful Confederate adopted the Reformation in 1528 it did not prove possible to carry the French-speaking city with it. Three visits by Farel to the city were not able to overcome Catholic resistance and the situation remained unchanged until the Bernese troops entered the gates on their return from the siege at Yverdon. In late March Pierre Viret came to Lausanne from Orbe and began preaching from the pulpit of the church of St Francis. The bishop had left the city but there were still powerful clergy, notably the Dominican Dominique de Montbousson, a preacher in the cathedral, who spoke out against the evangelical religion. Viret pursued his established tactic of preaching in the streets and taverns, whipping up the people against the 'idolatry' of the mass. The evangelicals gained a foothold and were able to hold their services in the former Dominican church of the Madeleine, but this did not satisfy Viret, who appeared before the council in early April to demand the abolition of Catholic worship and a disputation with Montbousson. The council did not agree and arrangements were made for the Dominican's departure from the city.

There were, however, plans to hold a disputation in the Pays de Vaud, as the Bernese fully intended using the Reformation to strengthen their hold on the French-speaking lands. The issue was not whether the Reformation would be adopted – that matter was settled as soon as Berne had won control over the region. Rather, a disputation was required for more pedagogical reasons, to persuade the reluctant Vaudois that they should accept the evangelical faith, and therewith Bernese authority.

There were powerful attempts to stop the disputation. Emperor Charles V wrote to the Bernese council forbidding them from holding the event, arguing that no decisions about the faith should be made before the council planned for Mantua in May 1537.[10] A polite rejection was sent to the emperor, then residing at Savigliano, and plans continued apace with Farel being summoned from Geneva to Berne to prepare the theses for discussion. Ten articles were put forward: justification by faith alone; Jesus Christ as the only Lord, redeemer and mediator of his church; the church as the community of believers, saved alone through the blood of Christ, and based on the Word of God; that the members of the church are known to God alone, and that there are two sacraments as visible signs of God's mercy; confession and absolution through the Word of God alone; that worship must be regulated by scripture and external ceremonies are to be rejected; that secular rulers are ordained by God and are responsible for freedom and peace; that marriage is not contrary to holiness; and concerning matters indifferent (*adiaphora*).

Bernese interests were represented by Kaspar Megander, who was accompanied by various members of the council, while Farel came from Geneva accompanied by John Calvin. Of the 337 clergy summoned from the Pays de Vaud, however, only 174 appeared in Lausanne, whilst a mere quarter of the forty religious houses sent representatives. The bishop, Sébastien de Montfalçon, gamely indicated his willingness to participate, but a fall from his horse made that impossible. This crucial first disputation in French was opened by sermons from Farel and Antoine de Marcourt.[11] Farel took the lead in debating with the Catholic opponents, though he was assisted by Pierre Viret. For the Catholics there was a team of priests and laymen led by Dominique de Montbouson. The Catholics only debated certain issues, taking on, for example, the evangelical principle of *sola scriptura* but not justification by faith alone. The theological level of the debate was modest, as Farel was far more comfortable as a reformer of worship and practice than he was with dogmatic formulations, but scholars have noted that the disputation marked a shift in theological emphasis.[12] It seems that Farel's arguments owed much to Calvin and Melanchthon and less to the Zwinglian tradition. It was a nuance but indicative of the fact that, although Berne was in control politically and militarily, the French churches were to develop their own theological voice. In truth, however, the Reformed side was well prepared and organised, supported by the resources of Berne, and there was never any question about the outcome. On 24 December 1536 the Reformation edict was pronounced in the Pays de Vaud.

Discord in the conquered lands

The comfortable victory at Lausanne was not, however, a good indication of what was to happen in the French-speaking lands, where for the next thirty years there were to be bitter rivalries and conflict. The first conflict came when the Bernese council made Pierre Caroli, a French refugee who was a doctor of the Sorbonne and a supporter of Faber Stapulensis, first minister in the Pays de Vaud over the native Pierre Viret. The two men despised each other, and things were not helped by the fact that Viret was paid about a third of what Caroli received. Both men were in Neuchâtel, and when Viret went to Geneva for three weeks Caroli used the opportunity to undermine not only his rival, but the men with whom he was associated. Caroli wrote to Berne making accusations of Arianism against Viret, Farel, and Calvin, and to substantiate his allegations he included passages carefully selected from Calvin's *Institutes*, which had been published in Basle that year. At the end of February 1537 Calvin, Farel, and Viret had to appear before the *Chorgericht* in Berne to answer the charges. The matter was then pursued at a synod in Lausanne in May, presided over by the Bernese theologians Kaspar Megander and Peter Kunz and attended by members of the Bernese council. The synod cleared the men of the accusations and recommended that Caroli be dismissed from his office. Caroli was banished, and he left Lausanne and returned to France where he reconverted to Catholicism.

The May synod was important for a number of reasons. Megander wrote to Bullinger describing the events and vouching for the orthodoxy of Calvin's theology. There was unease among the German-speaking reformers, who neither spoke nor read French, that heretical tendencies were detectable among the preachers in the Pays de Vaud. Calvin was still unknown and Megander's recommendation did much to persuade Bullinger at a crucial moment that the Frenchman was a good thing.[13]

The synod was also a decisive moment in the establishment of the type of church in the Pays de Vaud to which Calvin would so strongly object. Bernese control was absolute. The parishes were divided into six classes (chapters), each with a dean who was responsible for the life and learning of the clergy. The classes were to meet regularly for fraternal admonishment. In the parishes the minister was to sit with the elders of the community and the local bailiff (*Vogt*) on the morals court. This tribunal was limited to admonishment and recommendation; it was not to use force. The Bernese magistrates alone were to administer punishment and they retained complete control over who was appointed minister in the parish.

Confessional strife in Berne 1538–48

At the moment when Berne was seeking to extend its control over the French-speaking lands, a bitter dispute broke out in the city over the nature of the new religious polity. From 1532 until 1548 the urban church was riven along ideological lines, alienating Berne from Zurich and Basle and profoundly influencing its response to events in Geneva. The bitter theological disputes between Kaspar Megander and Erasmus Ritter on one side and Sebastian Meyer and Peter Kunz on the other paralysed Berne and the magistrates grew impatient. Meyer and Kunz preached Luther's views on the sacrament of the Lord's Supper, while Megander and Ritter saw themselves as true disciples of Zwingli. On 21 May 1537 the Bernese council summoned the clergy to a synod at which they were instructed that no one, either in preaching or in teaching the catechism, was to use the divisive phrase 'real presence'.[14] The council wanted peace at any price and it believed, strangely, that by suppressing emotive language it could resolve the deep-seated animosities.

Centre stage was an open battle between Kaspar Megander and Martin Bucer for control of the Bernese church. It is hard to imagine two more different men. Megander was the loyal defender of Zwingli who had denounced the Bernese magistrates from the pulpit as having 'picked cherries' while Zurich struggled alone in the Kappel War of 1531. He was the first leader of the Reformed churches to be disciplined by civil magistrates, and he had Capito to thank for his return from disgrace.

But Megander was no fool. He was a highly efficient church organiser who had achieved a great deal in Berne following his arrival in 1528; he had undertaken several visitations of the rural parishes, and the ministers in the countryside were loyal to him. He had written ordinances and biblical commentaries, but it was his 1537 catechism which caused a storm. After repeated visits to Berne, Bucer managed to persuade the magistrates that Megander's catechism, with its strict Zwinglian position on the sacraments, made reconciliation with German Protestants impossible. Megander was instructed to revise certain articles of his catechism, which he reluctantly agreed to do, but before he had a chance Bucer produced a wholly reworked version of the text which had not only excised the those passages which he had found unacceptable, but had added numerous others.[15] Megander was outraged to find himself outmanoeuvred, and he sought to rally the church against Bucer, but the magistrates trusted the Strasbourg reformer. To the utter consternation of Heinrich Bullinger and John Calvin, Kaspar Megander was given a bitter choice: either he had to accept the new catechism or leave the city. In

January 1538 Megander rode from Berne to return to his native Zurich, where Bullinger offered him a post as preacher.

There was no doubt that Megander was a difficult person, but his deposition raised serious problems for the new Reformed churches. The Bernese magistrates had made it clear that they could decide a theological question, and when required they were prepared to remove an ordained minister. This was a cold wind for the leaders of the other churches, who were struggling with the issues of evangelical preaching and magisterial control. Calvin wrote an excoriating letter to Martin Bucer denouncing his mendacity in the removal of the legitimate head of a church. The Bernese magistrates ignored petitions from the other Reformed churches with the result that Zwinglian theology had lost its perch in the city. Megander's supporters remained in the rural parishes, but the Strasbourgers had prevailed and now had the ear of the secular authorities.

The expulsion of Megander did not, however, bring the desperately sought harmony for the Bernese church. The removal of the Zwinglians simply opened an old wound; the rural clergy believed that their interests had been ignored and that the Strasbourg/ Lutheran theologians had been foisted on them. They had admired Megander, who had been a welcome visitor to the rural parishes during his numerous visitations. He was plain speaking and his theology was comprehensible, unlike these new men in the city.

Things got worse. The council issued a degree that the rural clergy should not teach anything which had not first been approved by the city ministers. In the city Megander's chair had hardly cooled when he was replaced by men much more sympathetic to Luther's theology. The principal figure was Simon Sulzer, a native son of Berne who had been educated by Myconius in Lucerne, by Bucer and Capito in Strasbourg, and by Simon Grynaeus and Sebastian Münster in Basle. He was among the most learned figures to come out of Berne, and he would play a leading role in Swiss religious politics as head of the churches in Berne and Basle. In 1540 Sulzer was appointed professor of theology in Berne and then preacher in the Münster.

Sulzer had personally known Luther, and soon after his appointment to the Münster he began introducing a number of Lutheran practices, such as private confession, emergency baptism, and private communion for the sick. His theology of the Lord's Supper was derived from Luther, and in the celebration of the sacrament he insisted upon the use of the best gold and silver vessels and plates and not the wooden dishes favoured by the Zwinglians. In all that he did he gave the impression that the idea of transubstantiation was being revived. But Sulzer was a shrewd politician; he dealt skilfully with the Bernese politicians, who were relieved not to be at war with one of their leading ministers. Sulzer, for his part, did not openly polemicise against the Zwinglians or Zwingli's theology, for he knew that Megander's supporters were numerous.

This policy of proceeding carefully, favoured by Sulzer and Kunz, was not to the liking of Sebastian Meyer, who left Berne in 1541 gravely disappointed by the council's decree that no innovations be introduced into the worship of the church. Meyer believed that the time had come for Berne to reject its Zwinglian legacy and embrace Lutheranism. He returned to Strasbourg, leaving Sulzer and Kunz to follow a different tactic. This was a strategy of appeasement, and Kunz, with deft servility, prepared a statement on church discipline in which the ministers placed themselves under the control of the magistrates. It was this position which so shocked Calvin, who thought that it was an offence against nature that theologically illiterate magistrates should declare on God's Word.[16]

The Lutheran position in Berne was dependent on the fragile relations between the Swiss Zwinglians and the German Protestant churches. As Luther and the Swiss began to quarrel again in the early 1540s hopes for any sort of reconciliation began to fade. In Berne, Peter Kunz died on 11 February 1544 and Sulzer took over his position in the Münster. From the rural parishes voices began to accuse Sulzer of being Luther's minion in Berne, and it was Luther who had so insulted the Swiss. At the same time the council, which sought to avoid theology as much as possible, found itself having to investigate the views of several ministers whose ideas about the Lord's Supper jarred with the Berne Disputation of 1528 and the *Synodus* of 1532. One minister from the parish of Wynigen was found to have maintained that Christ was 'substantively' present in the Lord's Supper. Suddenly, it seemed that Sulzer's crypto-Lutheranism was having an effect on the clergy and the council felt impelled to act. Bush fires were breaking out all over, as Zwinglians and Lutherans in Berne clashed over biblical interpretations and practices such as communion for the sick. One of the most effective charges shouted out by the Zwinglians was that Sulzer, through his closeness to Luther and the Strasbourgers, had divided Berne from her Confederate allies Zurich and Basle. The Bernese council reacted with the only tool it knew how to use, it attempted to silence both parties by decreeing that certain issues were not to be mentioned. Needless to say, that had no positive effect and the fuse continued to burn.

Erasmus Ritter had remained in Berne as the sole voice of Zwinglianism among the leading ministers, but he had been effectively silenced by the powerful Kunz and Sulzer. Ritter died in 1546 and was replaced by Jodocus Kilchmeyer, who had been a student of Vadianus in St Gall. Kilchmeyer was appointed against the will of Sulzer, but the magistrates had been attracted to him on account of his scholarly achievements. They were eager to boost the reputation of their theological college. Kilchmeyer was a Zwinglian and his presence in the city turned the tide.

The defeat of the Schmalkaldic League at Mühlberg in 1547 brought home to the Bernese magistrates their reliance on close relations with Zurich and Basle, and how damaging the theological alienation following Megander's departure had been. The next battlefield in the city was the theological school, where in 1546 a student named Peter Keller had written a song in praise of Luther's views of the eucharist. The song also criticised the magistrates in Berne. Keller and other students were severely punished for their insolence; the student was expelled from Berne. More importantly, this case caused the magistrates to investigate more closely what was going on in the school, and they did not like what they found. Thomas Grynaeus, nephew of the great scholar in Basle, was forced in 1547 to resign as professor because he was found to have brought Lutheran views into the school, and he was replaced by the avowed Zwinglian Eberhard von Rümlang. At the same time Berne summoned home all of its students who were studying in Lutheran universities in Germany.

Sulzer tossed aside his mask in 1548 and openly attempted to bring about a full Lutheran reform of the city. He failed. In April 1548 Sulzer and his two colleagues Beat Gering and Konrad Schmid were deposed from office and asked to leave the city. Sulzer went to Basle where he was immediately made professor of theology and preacher in the church of St Peter's. Within five years he would be head of the Basle church.

Sulzer was replaced by Johannes Haller, whose father had fallen alongside Zwingli at Kappel. Haller had served as a preacher in Augsburg before being driven out by the Interim in 1548. Kilchmeyer and Rümlang were instrumental in having Haller appointed, and when he arrived in Berne among his first acts was to lead a meeting of the synod in rejecting Charles V's Interim. Calvin and the Genevan church leaders welcomed Haller's appointment, even though he was clearly Zwinglian in his theology. It was hoped that Haller's dependence on Bullinger would increase Zurich's influence in Berne to Geneva's benefit. Indeed, Haller ensured that the *Consensus Tigurinus* of 1549 was accepted and implemented in Berne. His experiences in Germany, however, deeply influenced Haller and he was determined that the Swiss churches should make no accommodations with the Lutherans. As Calvin sought to bring the Swiss and German churches back into conversation, he found that the Bullinger–Haller axis was immoveable. Under Johannes Haller Lutheranism lost its foothold in the Swiss Confederation outside

Basle and Bullinger's Zurich was firmly back in control of the theological agenda.

Opposition to Calvin in the Pays de Vaud

Although the Caroli affair had been resolved in favour of Calvin and his colleagues, relations between Geneva and Berne over the next thirty years were marked by a profound sense of difference inflamed by a series of conflicts.[17] Essentially, Geneva depended upon the Bernese for its independence and, although it was not part of the Confederation, all of its affairs during the sixteenth century were bound up with the Swiss. Calvin's position in Geneva was never as strong as his opponents suggested; until perhaps the final years of his life Calvin needed the support of the Swiss Reformed churches both to secure his own authority in Geneva and to undertake his missionary work in France. Yet he was not a great admirer of Zwingli's theology, nor did he share the Swiss republican ideology of men such as Viret.[18] Calvin understood the world of French aristocrats and court culture, and he held bourgeois magistrates, such as those of Berne, in contempt, deeply resenting their aspirations to control Christ's church.

Some of the points of difference seem now to be very small. In Berne certain of the old feast days (Christmas, the Annunciation, the Ascension, and the Circumcision of Christ) were retained, whilst Calvin argued only Sundays were to be marked. There was a similar disagreement over where the baptismal font was to be placed in the church and whether unleavened bread (as was the case in Berne) was to be used for the Lord's Supper. In Berne it was the tradition to conclude the Sunday sermon with a reading of the names of those who had died in the previous week.[19] Calvin objected to this as too close to the Catholic notion of intercession for the dead. There was also disagreement over baptismal names: Calvin insisted that only biblical names were to be used, while in Berne, as well as in Zurich and Basle, the traditional names associated with local saints continued to be used.

From the Bernese perspective, the Reformation in Geneva had only been possible on account of their military might and their support of evangelical preaching in the French-speaking areas. It was expected, therefore, that Bernese liturgical forms and practices would be adopted. Berne certainly did have the political and military power, but Calvin, crucially, had more influence over the clergy of the Pays de Vaud. Calvin believed that it was Peter Kunz in Berne who had poisoned the magistrates against him, and he visited the city in order to resolve the differences, but without success. Berne attempted in vain to mediate in the dispute in Geneva which led to Calvin and

Farel being expelled in 1538.[20] But the departure of these two men made little difference as the Bernese found to their consternation that the Genevans without Calvin were no more pliable and certainly not inclined to accept their practices. From Strasbourg Calvin opined that he did not wish to return to Geneva for he believed that he had been vilified by the Bernese, and in particular Peter Kunz, to whom Calvin had sent an excoriating letter on account of his role in the dismissal of Megander. It took the intercession of Heinrich Bullinger to overcome Calvin's reservations, and the Frenchman returned to Geneva on the condition that the leader of the Zurich church would support him.[21]

The *Ecclesiastical Ordinances* in Geneva made clear a decisive difference between Calvin and the Bernese over church discipline and the use of the ban. This subject has been treated extensively over the years, and Calvin's teaching does not need to be repeated here, but in Berne the matter of discipline and excommunication lay in the hands of the magistrates. The church could only advise and recommend. This was also the situation in Bullinger's Zurich. In the Pays de Vaud, however, the leading minister, Pierre Viret, sided with Calvin, and was viewed by the Bernese with great suspicion. Viret spoke out against the magistrates' appropriation of church goods and their control of the selection of ministers. At the May synod of 1548 in Lausanne Viret preached that the clergy should have greater independence from the magistrates. The 'new papists' (the authorities in Berne) were worse than the old, according to Viret, who never missed the opportunity to use inflammatory language. The Bernese, having dealt with Megander ten years previous, were outraged, and they moved to strip Viret of his office. Farel was regarded as equally subversive as he too had argued for the church's independent use of the ban. Calvin had to use all his diplomatic tact to defuse the situation at the 1549 synod in Berne.[22] The situation did not remain calm for very long, however, as the Bernese sought in 1552 to impose their own French liturgy. Most of the clergy in the Pays de Vaud objected and once again there was a stand off.

The 1550s brought more serious divisions, this time doctrinal rather than ecclesiastical. In 1551 the French medical doctor and former monk Jérome Bolsec accused Calvin of heresy in his doctrine of double predestination.[23] Calvin sought support from the other Swiss churches, but what he received disappointed him. Bullinger was not a supporter of double predestination, and in Berne Wolfgang Musculus likewise refused to give unqualified support.[24] The Bernese were not prepared to support Calvin's attempts to have Bolsec executed or declared a heretic. '

The question of predestination touched a raw nerve among the Swiss Reformed churches. In Zurich the matter had been prevalent from the mid 1530s on account of Theodor Bibliander, who more or less argued for a universalist variation on Zwingli's teaching; for Bibliander, God wills the salvation of all, and no one is damned by God's will, but rather by his or her rejection of God's grace.[25] It was a position which owed much to Erasmus's teaching on free will. In 1535 Bibliander had had an epistolary debate with Oswald Myconius in which the Basle reformer had strongly defended Zwingli's view on predestination. Bibliander went quiet on the subject after accusations against him in Zurich that he was a Pelagian, meaning that he attributed too much to human merit, but the Bolsec affair in Geneva reopened the discussion and once more he and Myconius debated the matter.

Bolsec was expelled from Geneva on 23 December 1553 on account of his errors, but it was clear that Calvin's position had little support in the Pays de Vaud. The Bernese authorities, sensing the divisive nature of the dispute, forbade any discussion of predestination among its clergy or laity on pain of banishment.

The unedifying series of disputes between Berne and Geneva did have the positive effect of bringing to the fore one of the most remarkable figures of the period, Nikolaus Zurkinden (1506–88).[26] A layman and important official of the Bernese government, Zurkinden had already raised eyebrows with his rather tolerant attitude towards the Anabaptists in his region. He was also something of an amateur theologian, and Celio Secundo Curione, about whom we shall hear more in the next chapter, dedicated to Zurkinden his *Paradoxa*, a rather oblique critique of the doctrine of the Trinity. Zurkinden had a profound interest in the Trinitarian theological debates which were dividing Calvin from so many of the Italian religious figures who had come to Geneva. Zurkinden's open-mindedness on the subject – he disliked rigid dogmatic formulations – made him a patron of men with more radical tendencies. Yet, at the same time, he developed an enduring friendship with John Calvin. The correspondence between the two formed a dialogue on the issue which consumed them both, the unity of the church. Zurkinden rejected Calvin's teaching of double predestination and he could not accept the justification of Servetus's execution, yet both men explored in their letters how the church could find unity in the midst of endless quarrels and division. It was a touching friendship which stretched across a bitter frontier.

Charles V and the Council of Trent

By the early 1540s most of the first generation of reformers had gone. Bullinger was firmly in control of the Zurich church, but in Basle and Berne the situation was far from settled. The plague carried away

Karlstadt and Grynaeus in Basle, and in Berne the internecine warfare between the Zwinglians and Lutherans raged unabated, while the bitter quarrels in Geneva were a great concern to the whole Reformed community in the Confederation. The 1540s, however, brought more serious challenges from beyond the borders of the Confederation. War clouds gathered in the empire and the long-promised council of the Catholic church had become a reality. Within the Confederation the Catholics, very much on the defensive despite their victory at Kappel in 1531, achieved some significant victories which brought into sharp relief the fragility of the Reformed churches.

Following the Peace of Crépy in 1544 between Charles V and Francis I the emperor was in a position to do something about German Protestantism. The peace had also made possible the summoning of a council, Charles's cherished dream, and Paul III was cajoled into issuing the bull *Laetere Jerusalem* on 30 November 1544 calling all the Catholic church to Trent in northern Italy. The imperial diet at Worms in March of 1545 rejected the possibility that German Protestants might participate in the Council and war between the emperor and the Schmalkaldic League seemed unavoidable.

The Swiss were extremely nervous about events in the empire. Their most vulnerable point was the imperial city of Constance, which although not part of the Confederation, was a close friend. Only the objections of Lucerne and the Five Inner States had prevented Constance from becoming a Confederate after the Kappel War of 1531. In 1545, recognising its precarious position, the magistrates of Constance sent a delegation to meet with the representatives of Zurich, Berne, Basle, Schaffhausen, St Gall, and Mülhausen on 7 September 1545 at a secret conference. Berne, in a reversal of the position it took in the late 1520s, alone among the Reformed states favoured Swiss participation in a German war. Six weeks later the Swiss diet at Baden declared that the Confederation would remain neutral, not permitting foreign troops or weapons to travel its roads. Nevertheless, despite official neutrality, thousands of Swiss soldiers crossed over the Rhine to join the Protestant forces. Constance was a member of the Schmalkaldic League and when the emperor's army entered southern Germany in 1548 the city fell into his hands. Once again, Lucerne thwarted the efforts of the Reformed states to send military assistance. In 1548 Constance was made part of the Habsburg lands, its Reformed order was abolished, and it became a Catholic city lost to the Swiss for ever.

The defeat of the Schmalkaldic League at Mühlberg in April 1547 was especially traumatic for Basle, which was closely allied to Strasbourg.[27] The fall of the Alsatian city left the Baslers, who still officially acknowledged the emperor as their sovereign, fearing the worst.[28] Any invasion of the Confederation by Charles to avenge the humiliation of his grandfather Maximilian I would start with Basle. The leader in Basle, Bernhard Meyer, frantically sought to rally the Confederates, Reformed and Catholic, to a new front which would defend the Confederation against the old enemy, the Habsburgs. He also attempted to win support from the German imperial cities so that Basle might be included in any post-war agreement guaranteeing their freedoms. The response he received from his efforts tells us much about the state of the Confederation in the late 1540s. The Catholic Confederates abhorred the religion of the Reformed states and they clearly felt that there was nothing to fear from any possible invasion by Charles and his Spanish troops. Basle, Zurich, and Berne were keenly aware that any declaration of hostilities against the emperor would both cause a civil war in the Confederation and likely lead to the loss of the lands west of Berne, so recently obtained.[29] Nevertheless, Basle opened up its pockets and gave generously, and privately, to the imperial cities in Germany.

The defeat and the Interim of 1548 brought waves of refugees into the Confederation, perhaps most prominently Count Georg of Württemberg and his family. The streets of Basle were full of men, women, and children from German lands, while the council wrestled with how to respond to the demands from the emperor that the city accept the Interim. The situation was dangerous and frightening. In a highly risky move, Basle broke with Zurich and Berne and joined with the Catholic States in renewing an alliance with the French king in 1549.[30] It refused to adopt the Interim and staked its future on French support. In the end the gamble was never tested; with Charles V's spectacular defeat in 1552 and his abdication four years later, Basle's position within the Confederation and outside the empire was secured.

This raises the question of whether Charles had any real intention of pressing the Habsburg claim to Swiss lands. Up until 1538 Charles V had kept a permanent representative in the Confederation in order to recruit soldiers, but by the middle of the 1530s he had lost interest in the Swiss following his terrible defeat in southern France. The one place where the emperor remained interested in the Swiss was not along the Rhine, but in northern Italy, where he had consolidated his territorial control. Charles wished, for the sake of security in Italy, to remain on good, if rather distant, terms with the Swiss. Above all he was more interested in ensuring access to the Gotthard Pass than in military conflict. Unlike for his grandfather Maximilian I, the old Habsburg lands of the Swiss Confederation had no spiritual or dynastic significance for Charles, and he did not see his prestige in any way connected to their recovery. He had much bigger interests in

Europe. If the Catholic states were to find any Habsburg support, they would have to turn to Ferdinand, not Charles.[31]

In the period before the opening of the Council of Trent powerful forces were at work to ensure that the Swiss would participate. The papal legate in the Confederation was Girolamo Franco, who travelled extensively through the lands with his companion Albert Rosin, a native of Zurich who although a Catholic was made a citizen of the city in 1543. The two men sought to persuade the Catholic and Reformed diets, meeting separately in Lucerne and Baden, that the council was a genuine gathering of the whole church. The Swiss hesitated, but there was genuine support, and from an unlikely quarter. The council in Zurich put the invitation before the ministers and asked for a response; Bullinger had to scramble to persuade his political masters that this was a poisoned chalice. He wrote a long tract against the Council of Trent which was essentially a tract against the papacy. The response of the Swiss Reformed theologians to the Council of Trent was a joint work by Bullinger and Calvin, the first of a series of co-operative efforts which would last for the next ten years.[32] Representatives of Zurich, Berne, Schaffhausen, and Basle met in Basle to discuss the invitation and agreed that it was to be rejected. In January 1549 the four Reformed cities replied to the other Catholic Confederates that they could not accept and it was decided at the federal diet at Baden that the Swiss would not send representatives to the first session of the Council of Trent. Neither the Reformed nor Catholic states were enthusiastic; the former for obvious reasons, but the latter demurred on account of their alliance with France, which had no desire to see Trent succeed.

French support ensured that the Swiss Confederates did not attend the second session from 1551. Bullinger was able to rally the Reformed states against participation, despite a renewed charm offensive of Franco and Rosin. This time, however, Charles V had ordered the ecclesiastical princes of the empire, which included figures like the abbots of St Gall and Einsiedeln and the bishops of Constance, Chur, and Basle, to attend, so for the first time there was some Swiss representation. It was only in 1561 that the Swiss Catholic states agreed to send a delegation, though some, in particular Fribourg, refused to agree on account of French opposition.[33] In March 1562 a large Swiss delegation departed over the Alps to attend. The success of the Council was to mark a watershed in Catholic fortunes in the Confederation. In the remaining decades of the century the Catholic Reformation, led in the Confederation by men such as Carlo Borromeo, saw the revitalisation of the religious orders, the arrival of the Jesuits, the founding of schools, and the reform of clergy and laity. Its successes were dramatic, but that story will have to be told elsewhere.

Confessional hot spots: the Graubünden, Glarus, St Gall, Locarno, Saanen

During the 1550s, while the Swiss were debating their participation at the Council of Trent, a series of confrontations took place between the Reformed and Catholic sides which reminded the Swiss of the fragility of the Second Kappel Peace. While the prospect of a civil war between the Catholic and Reformed states was slight, the ferocity of these local conflicts was a harsh reflection of the visceral hatred which the confessional differences could arouse.

Following the execution of Abbot Schlegel in 1529 and the conclusion of the Musso War in 1531 the religious situation in the Graubünden remained uncertain. The peace which concluded the war, however, had greatly enhanced the territorial jurisdiction of the leagues by bringing Chiavenna, Valtelline, and Bormio more firmly under their control. In 1537 the first evangelical synod was held, establishing the Rhaetian church. All the ministers of the three leagues were required to attend and it was decreed that only those who had appeared in person before the synod to receive their appointment would be considered legitimate clergy of the Reformed church. By this measure the synod of the Rhaetian church had removed from the communities their right to choose their minister.

On 27 December 1537 until 4 January 1538 a disputation took place in the Engadin town of Susch to discuss the issue of lay baptism. The issue had arisen from the sad case of Ulrich and Serena Campell, whose new-born daughter was not expected to live more than a few days. Campell, who was an important figure in the Engadin Reformation, was not present for the birth. The mother did not wish the local Catholic priest to baptise the child so the sacrament was performed by the baby's grandfather. The grandfather had been encouraged by his absent son to perform the rite, and the biblical texts I Corinthians 14:33–35 and I Timothy 2:11–12 were cited in support.[34] The child was given the name Anna and then buried following her brief life. The incident caused a storm, for when the Catholics found out what had happened they insisted that only a midwife was qualified to carry out a lay baptism. Soon the matter became a confessional issue as representatives of the Catholic and Reformed churches gathered in Susch to debate the sad case. What united the two sides was their disapproval of lay baptisms, which they feared would lead to Anabaptism. However, in emergencies the Catholics held that the midwife was competent. The Reformed preachers, who included such notable figures as Philipp Gallicius and Blasius from Chur, were insistent that only a minister of the church could perform the sacrament of baptism. The spread of radical ideas had, even at this early date, made the Reformed church highly clerical.

The Reformed church in the Graubünden had more immediate contact with both Catholics and radicals than any of the other Swiss churches and this was reflected in the development of its confessions and worship. The strong Catholic presence in the Graubünden, along with the proximity of Austria, formed one pole, while the flow of Italian religious refugees with their unorthodox views into the southern part of the Confederation constituted the other. At the Rhaetian synod of 1552 Philipp Gallicius and Johannes Comander wrote a confession which clearly demarcated the Reformed faith from Catholic and antitrinitarian positions.[35] The confession was resisted by several of the Italian immigrants, notably Camillo Renato, who had openly rejected Bullinger's theology of the Lord's Supper. Undaunted, the leaders of the Rhaetian church imposed the confession at the synod meeting in the autumn of 1553. Together with the *Rhaetian Confession,* Bullinger's Zurich synodal ordinance of 1532 was made the law for the Reformed churches of the Graubünden. The *Rhaetian Confession* of 1553 was largely drawn from the writings of Heinrich Bullinger with the slight modification that double predestination was affirmed.[36]

Ulrich Campell, the father of baby Anna, emerged as one of the leading figures in the Rhaetian church during the middle decades of the sixteenth century.[37] During the 1550s he succeeded in winning over a number of communities in the Engadine to the Reformation, not least his own town of Susch. From 1571 he was minister in Chur and then in Schleins. Not only was Campell an effective preacher and reformer, but he was the most distinguished author among the Rhaetian reformers. Among his learned works were the *Topographia Raetica* and the *Historia Raetica,* descriptions of the mountains in the Graubünden as well as a history of the Rhaetian peoples written in collaboration with Josias Simler in Zurich. Campell's dedication to his own culture was seen in the hymn book and psalter which he produced in the Romansch language. Campell was one of the first to produce Reformed literature in both Romansch and other dialects of his region. The money for printing his vernacular catechism for adults came out of his own pockets.[38]

The Italian refugees played a crucial role in the Reformation of the southern part of the Graubünden. Particularly notable were Francesco Negri and Agostino Mainardo, who was active in Chiavenna and lived to be eighty-one years of age. Mainardo closely followed the *Rhaetian Confession,* a line which was followed by his successor Girolamo Zanchi, who had come to know Peter Martyr Vermigli in Lucca, and was a distinguished scholar who had spent time in

Geneva, Strasbourg, and England.[39] Heinrich Bullinger had wanted Zanchi to succeed Mainardo in order to keep a weather eye on heresy among the Italian churches.

Another important figure was the former bishop of Capo d'Istria, Pietro Paulo Vergerio, who had fled Italy and arrived in Poschiavo in 1549. Vergerio was closely involved with Giulio Milanese in the activities of the Landolfi printing house in Poschiavo which produced large amounts of literature for distribution in Italy and the Graubünden. In addition Landolfi also specialised in Romansch translations of the works by reformers. In his theology, however, Vergerio was not in sympathy with the *Rhaetian Confession* and during a stay in Germany he translated the Lutheran *Württemberg Confession* into Italian and took it back to the Graubünden. Bullinger was deeply suspicious of Vergerio and worked hard to thwart the Italian's attempts to spread Lutheranism in the Graubünden. Nevertheless, Bullinger did admire the brave decisions Vergerio had made for his faith.

The next explosion came in Glarus, which according to the peace treaty of 1532 had divided itself between Catholic and Reformed communities. This arrangement remained intact until 1555 when Reformed worship was established in the Catholic village of Linthal in the absence of a priest to celebrate mass. Naturally, the Catholics were outraged by this breach of the agreement, and after complex negotiations and manoeuvres the Five Inner States prepared themselves for war. They were not hesitant to use this incident as grounds for launching the recatholicisation of Glarus. By 1559 plans were in place for military action. Pressure was put upon the assembly (*Landsgemeinde*) in Glarus to agree to the expulsion of the Reformed. They were to leave Glarus within fourteen days; those who opted to remain were to be humiliated by the requirement to pay a special tax to fund the re-establishment of Catholic worship.

Once again the Confederation stood on the brink of war. The key figure was the distinguished Catholic humanist and politician Aegidius Tschudi, who had been waging a campaign for the return of the old faith.[40] Tschudi had important connections with Rome, above all the knight Melchior Lussy from Unterwalden, who had been handsomely rewarded by Pope Pius IV for various services, including the provision of a troop of soldiers who later became known as the Swiss Papal Guard. Lussy was sent by Pius IV to deal with the heretics in Glarus. For four years (1560–64) the Five Inner States refused to acknowledge the Reformed parts of Glarus, and troops stood on the borders between Schwyz, Unterwalden, and Glarus, ready to suppress the Reformed communities. In the end, it was the intervention of France and Zurich to persuade Lucerne and Zug to work towards a resolution of the matter which ended this phoney war. Glarus was restored to the terms agreed in 1532, but it was a sobering reminder that neither side felt especially bound by the terms of the Peace of Kappel. There was no toleration, both sides simply awaited the right moment to act against the other.

Throughout the eastern part of the Confederation there were endless skirmishes in the localities, as bad-tempered quarrels broke out between Catholics and the Reformed, though for the most part there was little violence. Relations between the Catholic and Reformed states were so tense that every seemingly minor infraction could have disastrous consequences. Both sides believed, quite reasonably, that the other was plotting against them, and even the smallest hint of subversive activity rattled nerves. In Bremgarten in the Freiamt the Catholic priest converted to the Reformed religion and expressed his desire to marry. He was immediately imprisoned. A foreigner in Baden was reputed to have blasphemed Mary the Mother of God and had a nail put through his tongue.[41]

More serious was the situation in the Thurgau, which was now deeply sensitive territory following Constance's forced reconversion to Catholicism in 1548. The Catholic majority in the Swiss diet demanded that in this Mandated Territory all the faithful, both Catholic and Reformed, had to present themselves to their local priest or minister during Lent to be examined on the essentials of the faith. There was an agreement that these essentials consisted of the Lord's Prayer, the Apostles' Creed, the Ten Commandments, and the Ave Maria. The mandate requiring this examination was read out from all the pulpits in the land on 15 December 1548, but the Reformed ministers took exception to the requirement that they should include the Ave Maria in worship. Many refused to obey and the civil authorities were required to take action.

Similarly in St Gall, which had been divided between the Catholic abbey with its extensive lands and the city, which was Reformed, there were endless disputes about what was required. The abbot sought to make the Reformed mark Catholic feast days, which, of course, they resisted. These spats lumbered on until there was a general agreement in 1558 which resulted in a wall being erected around the abbey sealing it off from the town. The abbey and the Reformed church of St Laurentius, only about fifty metres apart, were separated by a stone wall without gates. Catholics made their way in and out of the abbey through a separate entrance; the two communities were utterly segregated, though the Protestants upon leaving the city had to pass through the abbey's lands before reaching friendly territory.

Perhaps the most important confrontation came in the Mandated

Territory of Locarno, which was administered by the seven Catholic states and four Reformed cities. The Catholics were deeply concerned about the appearance of a Reformed community in 1549 which numbered around 200 people. This new community was a violation of the 1531 Peace of Kappel, which made provision only for those communities in existence in 1530. The Catholics proposed a disputation, but it was hardly a success. The Reformed church was represented by the former priest Giovanni Beccaria and the medical doctor Taddeo Duno. The debate never got past the first article on the papacy and had to be abandoned. The principal theological force, however, was Heinrich Bullinger in Zurich, who took a great interest in the Italian community.[42]

In 1554 the Catholics turned up the heat by requiring all people living in Locarno to attend confession and the eucharist. It appears that most of the evangelicals in the community obliged the authorities, but the matter was not settled. During a December meeting of the Swiss diet a commission prepared a report, likely written by Aegidius Tschudi, who would later cause so much trouble in Glarus. The commission managed to avoid a religious war between the Confederates, but the price was that the Reformed states recognised that a community of co-religionists on the other side of the Alps was beyond their help. During the summer of 1554 the members of the community were examined and it was found that 211 men and women declared themselves for the evangelical faith. In March 1555 over a hundred people were expelled from Locarno and had to make their way over the snow-bound mountains and across Lake Zurich, arriving on 3 May in Zurich, where they were met by Heinrich Bullinger and leading members of the council.[43] Bullinger alone among the Reformed leaders had supported the Locarnese out of a sense of confessional solidarity. The cities of Basle, Schaffhausen, and Berne were not prepared to put anything on the line for a community of people they could not save; these cities readily accepted the enforcement of the Catholic religion in Locarno on the grounds that it should not be undertaken in any of the other Mandated Territories. In the middle decades of the century there was no common will for missionary work by the Reformed states. The same old principles applied: agreement and unanimity for the Swiss was always a defensive measure.

Berne, the only Reformed state which realistically could have exercised any influence in the Locarno case, had not made any noise on account of its own delicate negotiations with Catholic Fribourg. In 1555 the impecunious Count Michael von Greyerz sold his lands jointly to Berne and Fribourg. The land was amicably divided, with Fribourg taking possession of the castle, but the complication was that the lands which Berne had acquired were Catholic, wholly untouched by the Reformation. The Bernese found themselves having to force a reluctant population to convert to the Reformed faith, an undertaking which was rewarded with a small uprising.[44] The Bernese allowed those who wished to leave to cross the border into Fribourg, but on account of economic and social concerns many remained, and the records reveal that most people's adherence to the Reformed religion was at best perfunctory. Large numbers continued to go on pilgrimages and attend mass across the border. This situation continued for most of the sixteenth century, and the Bernese authorities, sharply aware of the loose grip the Reformed faith had on many of their rural subjects, had to act with circumspection.

There were numerous other flare-ups, in Zug on 14 March 1556 the Catholic authorities burnt Protestant bibles in response to the work of an evangelically minded minister called Marx Seiler.[45] A document was drawn up by Reformed opponents seeking redress and there was outrage throughout the Reformed churches, but in the end, nothing came of it. By the middle of the century the confessional reality was that the Reformed states had little sense of corporate identity and no one was inclined to press their case too far. The Reformed churches harboured no hopes of a Reformation in Zug, and they were not about to upset the relative stability of the Confederation for a minor irritation. As we shall now see, this overriding concern for stability could lead to some strange arrangements.

Basle and its bishops

For all the skirmishing between the Catholic and Reformed states it is fair to say that apart from a few zealous partisans no one in the Confederation wanted war, largely because it was unwinnable without external support and no European power wanted to become enmeshed in the tribal politics of the Swiss. Charles V had demonstrated that he had other priorities, while the French king was perfectly content to have his agents recruit Swiss mercenaries. Within the Confederation the Second Peace of Kappel had provided a framework for the states to begin consolidating their control over their urban and rural communities, and although we should shy away from involving the concept of toleration, interesting local arrangements sprung up which speak for the pragmatic spirit which dominated the lives of most Confederates.

Perhaps the most striking example of the practical nature of confessional relations in the Confederation was in Basle, the only Swiss city to have been an episcopal seat and whose reformation was the culmination of a long struggle between the magistrates and the bishops. The revolution of 1529 saw the Basle council relieve Bishop

Christoph von Utenheim of all remaining authority over the clergy in the city and rural territories. The departure of the bishop and the cathedral chapter from the city did not, however, diminish the force with which they defended their rights and privileges, particularly with regard to income from benefices. Between 1529 and 1531 opinion among the Basle magistrates was divided between those who wanted to put an end to the claims of the bishop and chapter by military force, and those who believed that the city's interests were best served by coming to some sort of contractual arrangement.[46] The defeat at Kappel, however, left only one way forward. Although no longer resident in the city, the bishop remained a territorial lord, controlling a large piece of land which now forms the modern canton of Jura, stretching from just outside the walls of Basle to Neuchâtel. The principal intention of the Basle council after the Reformation was to ensure its influence over this region by keeping the bishop bound to the city by treaty. In order to achieve this the Reformed city had to retain and honour the legal bond between Basle and its bishop developed in the Middle Ages, but as a political and financial contract stripped of all spiritual duties and obligations.

During the 1530s and 1540s the bishops struggled to control the communities in the diocese. Resistance to tax collection was robust as the inhabitants of the Jura looked to the Swiss Confederates to defend them against their despised overlord. They might have been successful in their resistance, for the bishops were extremely weak, had it not been for the support given by Reformed Basle to the bishops. As Ferdinand and Charles demanded that the Turkish tax be levied Bishop Philipp could have found himself in trouble with the *Reichskammergericht* had not the city intervened to loan him the money. Basle had no intention of using the financial troubles of the bishops to press territorial or confessional claims.[47] In 1547 the city and the bishop signed a contract which gave the magistrates the right to intervene militarily in the territory if necessary and valuable market rights in the region. It would, however, be wrong to view the contract as one step on the city's path to acquiring the bishop's lands. Rather the pragmatic Baslers were prepared to honour the old canonical rights and to prop up the bishop in his lands in order to create a buffer zone between themselves and hostile Catholic territory in Germany. By making the bishops financially dependent on the city's largesse Basle sought to exclude other regional powers from exerting influence in the Jura.

This strategy was immediately tested with the imposition of the Interim in 1548. In January 1549 Bishop Philipp was instructed by the emperor to implement the Augsburg Interim. The bishop passed on the imperial request to the city. As we have already noted, Basle feared that it would suffer the fates of Strasbourg and Constance, and the magistrates reacted nervously. They wrote to the bishop reminding him that the 1547 contract guaranteed each party full religious rights in their part of the old bishopric. Basle also expressed its belief that it was not bound by the terms of the Interim. To this the bishop replied that he by no means desired a dispute, but was simply fulfilling his obligation to convey the emperor's request, so that the city could not claim that it had not seen the document. In the end, despite the formal request, Charles V made no move against Basle, nor did he offer the bishop any assistance.[48] Catholic leaders in the Confederation had harboured secret hopes of Spanish troops crossing the Rhine, but the reality was that they would have to fight their own battles.

The crucial role played by the city of Basle in propping up the Catholic parts of the diocese was underscored in 1553 following the death of Bishop Philipp. While the cathedral chapter dithered over whether it possessed legitimate authority to elect a successor, large numbers of subjects saw this moment of weakness as the opportunity to increase their resistance to the bishop's authority. Once again the Reformed city did not seize the opportunity to wrest control of the lands and expand the Reformation. Rather, in order to limit the damage caused by the instability, the council pressed the chapter to move quickly towards the election of a new bishop. Somewhat bizarrely, the Reformed council of Basle had to persuade the Catholic cathedral chapter that it was legitimately empowered to elect a bishop.

Between 1525 and 1575, apart from the removal of the bishop and chapter from the city, the rulers of the city of Basle and the bishops of the diocese of Basle had a remarkably cordial relationship grounded on the legal and financial agreements developed in the late Middle Ages. The bishops, naturally, had no authority over the city and its territories, but in those parts of the diocese which remained Catholic they continued to rule, supported by the financial and military resources of a Reformed Confederate. As Hans Berner has argued, there may have been many in Basle who believed that ultimately the bishop's lands would pass to them, but the city was not prepared to press the cause of the Reformation. The arrangement brought stability during the uncertain decades of the middle of the century.

The bishops of Basle remained content with the relationship with Reformed Basle; both sides accepted that the two religions were officially recognised and that it was to the benefit of both that they be allowed to pursue their own consolidation, rather than rivalry. By the 1570s, however, the Tridentine winds were blowing through the Confederation, and the new bishop, Jakob Christoph Blarer, who was elected in 1575, dreamt of restoring the old diocese to Catholicism and had a zealous ally in the Lucerne politician Ludwig Pfyffer. In 1579 Blarer concluded an alliance with the seven Catholic states (Lucerne, Unterwalden, Schwyz, Zug, Lucerne, Uri, and Fribourg) which committed him, among other things, 'to bring the flock of Christ back into the fold'. Blarer believed that it was his pastoral duty to cleanse his lands, and felt that the Second Peace of Kappel did not apply to the diocese. Immediately, with the support of the papal nuncio, Francesco Giovanni Bonhomini, Blarer declared that the evangelical subjects in his lands would either have to convert or leave their communities. He replaced Reformed ministers with Catholic priests in the parish churches.

In December 1580 the four Reformed states, meeting in Aarau, demanded the revocation of this decree and insisted upon the rights of the evangelical faithful in the diocese. Crucially, the Catholic states did not support the bishop and he had to back down immediately, although he was offered a face-saving agreement. The Reformed states prevailed upon their Catholic Confederates to use their influence to temper the views of the bishop; they were to demand that Bonhomini never again appear in Swiss lands. The Catholic states were not willing to fight the Reformed states, nor were they willing to do Rome's bidding.

The skirmish had not, however, been an unqualified success for Basle and her Reformed allies. When the rights of the evangelicals in the diocese were restored it was found that many who had been forced to convert to Catholicism chose to stay with their new faith. Over the next two decades of Bishop Blarer's rule he was remarkably energetic in winning back most of the evangelical communities in his lands, and for this he was heavily dependent upon the Jesuits. By the end of the century the last of the evangelicals had left the diocese and the bishop had achieved his goal of purifying the lands.

Theological and political developments

By the 1540s the Zurich church had lost interest in any reconciliation with the Lutherans in Germany. Repeated insults from Luther, both real and imagined, poisoned the waters. Most dramatically, Luther had spat in the face of the Swiss with his rejection of a copy of the Zurich Latin Bible which the printer Christoph Froschauer had sent him in 1543. Luther thanked Froschauer in a letter but added that as the Zurichers had placed themselves outside the church of God on account of their heresy, he could have no contact with them. He regretted that the men in Zurich had gone to such efforts when they would all be damned for their false teachings. He could not accept the gift, he wrote, and requested that there be no further contact.[49]

Bullinger was incandescent with rage at this snub and he wrote to many leading reformers in the empire outlining his objections to Luther's reply. There was, however, worse to come. Luther wrote his *Short Confession on the Lord's Supper* in which he rejected, for the final time, any association with the Zwinglians, who, he insisted, had been admonished enough times about their errors and must now be abandoned to their perdition. He made no distinction between Zwingli and Oecolampadius, whom he named, and Karlstadt and Schwenckfeld. He admitted that there had been some agreement at Marburg, but only because the Zwinglians had given ground. Zwingli's death at Kappel followed by Oecolampadius's only a few weeks later were, according to Luther, divine warnings that the Swiss had fallen into error.[50] The prominence of Karlstadt in the Swiss churches from 1530 until his death must have angered Luther beyond all reason; he could never have made peace with those who had provided sanctuary to his most hated opponent.

The Swiss reply came in 1545 from the pen of Heinrich Bullinger, his *True Confession*, in which he refuted point for point all of Luther's allegations. Bullinger's reply highlighted the most significant differences between the two men. What Bullinger most objected to was not the theological disputes between the two men, but rather the contumelious nature of Luther's writings. Bullinger had a profound sense of order and dignity in the church, that all things should be done properly and in the spirit of Christian love. There would be disagreements, he readily accepted, but the greatest sin, and here he echoed Zwingli, was self-love. Those who care not for their neighbour cannot be called followers of Christ. Bullinger wrote in his *True Confession* that the world was grateful for what God had done in Luther, and that the Zurichers had always acknowledged his achievements, but the Wittenberg reformer had abused his position to denigrate and vilify fellow Christians, thus breaking the bond of charity between churches. There was a great deal of Erasmus in Bullinger, for peace and concord were for him true signs of the church, and he was shocked by Luther's crudeness.

By the mid 1540s, however, John Calvin was looking for a broader European Protestant consensus and he understood that this meant some sort of reconciliation between the Swiss and the German Lutherans. Calvin wanted the Swiss to renew their alliance with France in light of the defeat of the Schmalkaldic League at Mühlberg. Bullinger was adamantly opposed, but in Zurich itself there was some sympathy. King Henry II of France had invited the Swiss Confederates to be supporters at the baptism of his daughter Claudia, a clear sign that they were being courted by the French, whose ambassadors travelled to Zurich to meet with Bullinger to persuade him to change his mind. By the middle of the 1540s Bullinger was acknowledged as the most important religious figure in the Reformed Swiss churches, and one reads accounts of the French representatives discussing politics and religion with the reformer in the bath waters at Baden. Bullinger held firm and Zurich and Berne did not join the other Confederates in renewing the French treaty in 1549.

Among the refugees who came into the Confederation following the Interim were Johannes Haller and Wolfgang Musculus. These men were very close to Bullinger and their appointments in Berne raised hopes that relations between Zurich and Berne, soured by the domination of the Lutheran party in Berne, would be improved, and that this would alleviate the problems between Berne and Geneva. Johannes Haller, who had been cast in a virtually impossible role, was torn between the unreasonableness of the two parties. On the one hand, the desire of the Genevans to debate theology openly was extremely divisive, whilst on the other he found the Zwinglians in the rural areas, who continued to plague Calvin, extremely difficult to rein in.

Calvin knew that if there was to be any hope for Protestant unity the strife between the Lutherans and Zwinglians over the Lord's Supper would have to be buried. He undertook with a reluctant Bullinger a series of negotiations which he hoped would establish a united Reformed position. In 1547 Calvin had received a copy of Bullinger's *On the Sacraments*, in which the leader of the Zurich church had shown that he was willing to move beyond Zwingli's theology of the eucharist. Bullinger, however, did not wish to be drawn into discussion on the point; he was aware that Calvin was unsympathetic to Zwingli and he did not wish to damage the church with another public quarrel. Bullinger insisted that he and Calvin keep their disagreements to private correspondence. Calvin, however, wanted more. He continued to write to Bullinger urging him to discuss the matter, for he was certain that agreement was possible. Calvin had to persuade Bullinger that his language about the presence of Christ in the bread and wine was not similar to the Lutheran view. The Genevan reformer travelled to Zurich and an agreement was reached in 1549, known as the *Consensus Tigurinus* or *Zurich Agreement*, in which the two reformers discreetly omitted points on which they did not concur.[51] The *Consensus* was testimony to the respect, even friendship, which existed between Bullinger and Calvin. It was a symbolic act in which Geneva and Zurich could finally lay Zwingli to rest, and in that sense it opened the way forward. But it was no theological agreement. The differences were real, but the two friends decided that it did not serve the church to continue the debate.

The *Consensus Tigurinus* aroused deep suspicion among the other Swiss Reformed churches, who felt they had been excluded from the discussions. Berne felt it was being outmanoeuvred by Calvin, who was seeking a Zurich alliance for support in his quarrels with them. Others felt that Calvin was dragging the Swiss towards the German Lutherans, that Zwingli's heritage had been betrayed. Following the 1549 *Consensus Tigurinus* things did not get much better. Calvin's relations with Berne went into free fall as the two sides quarrelled over an endless series of issues. There were, of course, the Bolsec and Servetus cases, but the Lutherans in Germany also provided trouble.[52] In 1554 Bullinger informed Calvin that Joachim Westphal in Hamburg had published a tract against the *Consensus Tigurinus*. Bullinger asked Calvin to write a defence on behalf of the Swiss churches, and by October 1557 Calvin's *Defensio* was ready. He sent it to Zurich for approval, but his assessment of the Swiss churches in a letter to his friend Farel made it clear that things were not well.

> It pleases me greatly that the defence of our Consensus meets with your approval. If only the Zurichers will judge it in a similar manner! By the way, I see that they have become so mild that I have an almost certain hope that they will not delay with their signature nor make any difficulties. I do not trust the Bernese, they will likely provide the usual excuse that their council will not allow them to sign ... The Baslers will follow Sulzer's pliable art.[53]

Calvin's *Defensio* was never sent to Berne or Basle, it was purely an arrangement between Zurich and Geneva. In the last decade before his death Calvin had forged a close relationship with Bullinger; it was a relationship in which clear differences were acknowledged.[54] They corresponded frequently about theology and events across Europe, with Calvin keeping Bullinger informed about events in France, while Bullinger's close connections to England meant that information from the north was relayed to Geneva. There were, however, some serious glitches along the way, such as when Theodor Beza and Guillaume Farel suggested at the Worms Colloquy of 1557 that the Swiss churches could accept the *Confessio Augustana*. Farel suggested a new confession which more closely approached Lutheran thought and he issued it on behalf of the Swiss churches without their knowledge or consent. Bullinger was furious and Calvin, embarrassed by this rash act, calculated by the French reformers to win German support for the Huguenot cause in France.

However, things were changing in the Swiss churches. In 1556 Peter Martyr Vermigli, a native of Florence who had been in Strasbourg and Oxford, was appointed to the chair of Old Testament in Zurich following the death of Konrad Pellikan.[55] Vermigli was a Calvinist and he held to Calvin's view of double predestination. This brought conflict with Theodor Bibliander, who had taught in Zurich for thirty years and was an opponent of Calvin's teaching on predestination. In February 1560, following a controversy unleashed by Vermigli's first lectures, the Zurich church had to decide which way it would go theologically. The ministers and theologians supported Vermigli over Bibliander, who had to resign his office. Officially, Bibliander had been retired on grounds of mental illness, but in fact the change reflected a shift in Zurich's theology towards Geneva.

In Berne the dominant theological force was Wolfgang Musculus, who had arrived from Augsburg in 1549 with a wife and eight children. He had been invited by Thomas Cranmer to become minister to the German-speaking refugees in London, but had refused on account of his age. He really wanted to go to Berne, where his good friend Johannes Haller was chief minister. Musculus was invited, but there were problems; he was reputed to be a Lutheran, and to have given his support to the *Wittenberg Accord* of 1536.[56] In truth, Musculus's reforms in Augsburg had infuriated Luther, who believed that the Zwinglians were in charge of the city.[57] It was Bullinger's intervention which made the appointment possible; he wrote to the Berne council a strong reference supportive of Musculus's theology. His principal work, written after his arrival in Berne, was his *Loci Communes* of 1559.

Musculus was very much an independent thinker whose theological formulations fell somewhere between Zurich and Wittenberg.[58] In the conflict with Calvin over the role of the magistrates in the affairs of the church Musculus very much sided with the Bernese council, developing a concept of the state church in which the magistrates were equated with the father of the household. Like Zwingli before him, he took the Old Testament kings as his model. The church was not to have independent authority, but was to be governed as a flock is ruled by the shepherd. The shepherd was the secular rulers.[59] Musculus's views influenced Rudolf Gwalther, who would succeed Bullinger in 1575. The two men held to a strong view of the magisterial church, a position which irritated the Genevans to no end.

Lutheran Basle

By 1535 Basle had weathered two serious storms: the first was the dispute over the use of the ban, while the second surrounded the reopening of the university. Erasmus, who had returned to the city in 1535, had withdrawn to a small group of close friends, eschewing any contact with the Reformed church in the city. It was during this year that Calvin lived in the quarter of St Alban under the pseudonym

'Martianus Lucianus'.[60] During these years leading to the publication of the first edition of the *Institutes of the Christian Religion* Calvin kept company with a group of distinguished scholars who would exercise a profound influence on his thought. Calvin had little contact with Erasmus: the crucial figures in Basle for the Frenchman were Simon Grynaeus, who became his trusted mentor, and Sebastian Münster, under whom he studied Hebrew. Despite the disaster of Kappel, Basle recovered quickly and the reopening of the university in 1532 led to an explosion of printing and intellectual activity in the city. With the death of Simon Grynaeus during the plague of 1541, Calvin lost his closest friend in the Confederation. He knew Oswald Myconius, the head of the Basle church, to whom he had been introduced by Grynaeus, but relations were neither warm nor close. The correspondence between the two men seems to have been wholly initiated by Myconius, and for the most part was newsy and full of minor complaints and troubles. Intellectually, Myconius was not Calvin's equal.

Under Myconius's leadership the Basle church was essentially Reformed, grounded in the Basle Confession of 1534, but its exact theological profile remained unclear. Myconius relied on the advice of Grynaeus, Bucer, and Bullinger, and there was a strong feeling that his views reflected those of the last person he had spoken to or corresponded with. In fairness, his theology was probably most akin to Bucer's, and like the Strasbourg theologian he believed that the positions of Zwingli and Luther could be reconciled. Myconius, as a teacher in the Fraumünster in Zurich, had played an important role in Zwingli's early years, and for this he retained the respect and gratitude of men like Bullinger, who otherwise found this timid and awkward man deeply frustrating. He was waspish and easily offended; his extensive correspondence with Bullinger is filled with the repeated attempts of the Zurich church leader to reassure Myconius that he was an esteemed colleague who had the support of the other Reformed churches. Myconius, however, was not entirely useless – though Erasmus had named him 'homo ineptus'. He was an effective pastor, who had devoted enormous energy to the reform of the clergy and the provision of pastoral care in the parishes.

The situation in Basle changed radically with the arrival of Simon Sulzer in 1548 following his dismissal in Berne. Sulzer sympathised with the theology of Martin Bucer and Wolfgang Capito; he had studied in Strasbourg during the 1530s and had supported the 1536 *Wittenberg Accord*. Following the triumph of the Zwinglians in Berne in 1548 Sulzer returned to Basle, the native city of his wife and the place where he had studied before his call to Berne. In Basle Sulzer had powerful patrons, mostly men who had been his teachers, such as

Myconius, Münster, the Amerbach family, and the printers Thomas Platter and Johannes Oporinus. Sulzer also came to Basle with the full support of Calvin, who was deeply grateful for Sulzer's support for Pierre Viret and other allies in the Pays de Vaud who had found themselves in hot water with the Bernese council.

If Myconius had been indulged as a difficult but loveable old uncle, Simon Sulzer was treated with cool suspicion. Bullinger had long ago washed his hands of the Strasbourg theologians, and the final flurry of vile exchanges between Wittenberg and Zurich had utterly poisoned the waters. There was no sympathy for what Sulzer had done in Berne and his return to Basle was regarded as highly unfortunate. These suspicions were quickly confirmed by Zwinglian ministers in Basle who complained of Sulzer's attempts to introduce the 'Lutheran' practices of organ-playing and polyphonic music during worship.[61]

The rupture came with the *Consensus Tigurinus* in 1549. Although it was essentially worked out between Bullinger and Calvin some effort was made to consult the other Reformed states (notably Berne and Schaffhausen), but not Basle. Great offence was taken, even though Calvin wrote to Myconius in attempt to assuage the Baslers. The letter simply poured oil on the fire and the Basle church leaders bided their time for their revenge, which they took a few years later in the Bolsec controversy. At the same time a circle of men such as Sebastian Castellio, Celio Secundo Curione, and Lelio Sozzini (who operated largely out of Zurich), together with other Italian refugees, began to take shape in Basle, and at the core of their thought-world was opposition to the theology of John Calvin.[62]

By the early 1550s, as Sulzer was elected head of the Basle church, Basle was flourishing. It had survived the Schmalkaldic War and the Interim. On the one hand, its place within the Confederation was secure, while, on the other, its face was turned towards the wider European stage. Basle university now had an established reputation in the Reformed and Lutheran worlds and students from Scotland to Poland came to study. The university matriculation lists for this period indicate the large number of nationalities represented in the university. Simon Sulzer reported to Bullinger in a letter that Basle was full of students.[63] The university was led by Martin Borrhaus and boasted such figures as Sebastian Castellio and Celio Secundo Curione. From the Basle presses came a torrent of work by authors such as Münster, Curione, Bibliander, and Guillaume Postel, all of whom, with the exception of Sebastian Münster, were regarded by the Genevans as suspect writers. These were the men who would voice their opposition to Calvin first in the Bolsec affair and then after the execution of Servetus. By the middle of the 1550s there was an all-out polemical war between Basle and Geneva; Simon Sulzer did not conceal his opposition to Calvin's theology, especially his doctrine of double predestination, and the head of the Basle church protected those figures such as Curione and Castellio who were writing against Geneva. The relationship between Calvin and Sulzer, once warm, went cold, and their letters were restricted to formal exchanges of information.

Basle was also deeply implicated in the deteriorating relationship between Berne and Geneva. The 1526 pact between Berne and Geneva was to last twenty-five years, and in 1551 it was extended for five years, but in 1556 the situation was so dire that any further extension seemed unlikely. Under the terms of the agreement mediators in any dispute between the two cities were to be appointed by the Basle council. When Basle entered the Swiss Confederation in 1501 it had taken on the role of mediator (*Schiedsrichter*) in inter-state disputes, and it had taken this role very seriously. Over the decades since 1526 Basle had successfully settled a number of disagreements between Berne and Geneva, but now Berne wanted to free itself of this third party in order to exercise direct control over the troublesome French-speaking city. Through a series of labyrinthine negotiations, largely organised by Bullinger, the Reformed states succeeded in having the two cities resume negotiations. The thorn in the side, however, was the Perrinist party, those defeated by Calvin and driven from Geneva, which continued to agitate from Bernese and Catholic lands.

As Amy Nelson Burnett has shown, a meltdown in the relationship between Sulzer and Heinrich Bullinger came in 1562 after a sermon had been preached in Basle in which a minister had referred to those who rejected Christ as the 'papists, Jews, Turks, and the Schwärmer'. This was incendiary language as Luther had used the term 'Schwärmer' (fanatics) to describe Zwingli and his followers, and Bullinger was highly offended. Sulzer claimed the event was of little consequence and that the Basle ministers had a policy of avoiding doctrinal quarrels. Bullinger was not satisfied with this trite response and he effectively terminated communication with the head of the Basle church. Bullinger wrote to Calvin that 'Sulzer in Basle is slowly trying to lead that church from the true doctrine established there by Oecolampadius to the Lutherans. He has now joined himself to Marbach and his party, in open opposition to our churches, and subscribed to the *Augsburg Confession* and its Apology.'[64] Bullinger set about working to isolate Sulzer in the Confederation and his plan had two willing collaborators, Johannes Haller in Berne and Theodor Beza in Geneva, who mocked Sulzer's Lutheran views by referring to him as the 'flesh eater'.

Bullinger's campaign against Sulzer was not limited to letter-writing, he worked through the civil governments. He used his influence with the Zurich council to have a formal complaint written to Basle about Sulzer's participation in the *Strasbourg Consensus* of 1563, where there had been an attempt to heal the breach between Lutheran and Reformed positions. At a meeting of the evangelical states in Baden in July 1563 Bullinger was instrumental in having a letter drafted by Zurich, Berne, and Schaffhausen to the Basle council expressing concern about Sulzer's activities. Schaffhausen and Berne were not willing to follow Bullinger's lead in demanding a process against Sulzer; despite his removal from the post as chief minister in Berne, Sulzer retained close connections in the city. The problem for Bullinger was twofold: first he believed that Sulzer's acceptance of the *Strasbourg Consensus* was an acceptance of the Lutheran views of the *Augsburg Confession*, which Bullinger categorically rejected, and, second, he believed that Sulzer was lying about his intentions. In Basle Sulzer was fully supported by the magistrates, who willingly chose to deceive the other Reformed states about the degree to which Lutheran theology was now accepted as the standard. The magistrates prevaricated by arguing that they were not aware of the theological implications of the *Strasbourg Consensus*. Bullinger made full use of the situation, by openly declaring that Sulzer had lied to Berne about what he had agreed to and duped the Basle council by not telling them about the nature of the *Consensus*. Zurich and Berne were not willing to fall out with Basle, so Sulzer had to take the full blame for what happened.[65]

During the autumn of 1563 there was a struggle in Basle between the pro-Zurich party, led by Wissenburg and the pro-Sulzer party. Bullinger followed the events closely and wrote a series of works defending Zurich's theological position and refuting the argument of some in Basle that his theology was not in agreement with the *First Basle Confession* of 1534. In particular many in Basle believed that Bullinger and the Zwinglians had rejected any notion of Christ's presence in the eucharist. Bullinger argued his position from the *Consensus Tigurinus* of 1549 to indicate that he was by no means opposed to Christ's presence.[66]

In October 1563 the Basle council issued its response to the event. It maintained that neither had it departed from the 1534 confession nor had it accepted the *Augsburg Confession*. Sulzer was not censored. Although this was only a minor victory for Sulzer and a defeat for Bullinger, it has been argued 'the protracted conflict within Basle and between Basle and the other evangelical cities is significant, however, for it drew attention to Basle's growing theological and political independence and laid the foundation for its further alienation from the other evangelical Swiss churches.'[67]

The *Second Helvetic Confession*

The greatest theological work to emerge out of the Swiss Reformation was the *Second Helvetic Confession* of 1566. It has been called by one scholar 'a dogmatic work of magnificent and impressive completeness'.[68] According to an entry in his diary from 1565, Bullinger had written an *Expositio Brevis*, a short confession of faith, in reply to a request from the Palatine elector Frederick III. The request arose out of the troubled confessional situation in the Palatinate, where the 1564 attempt to unite the Reformed and Lutheran parties had collapsed under attack from Lutheran theologians. The emperor Maximilian II hoped that the religious quarrels would force Frederick to abandon the Reformed religion, which was not part of the Peace of Augsburg. Thomas Erastus, the elector's physician, went to Zurich and Geneva in search of aid; the elector wanted a confession of faith which he could present to the imperial diet. Bullinger obliged and wrote his confession and sent it on 18 December 1565 to Heidelberg.

When the theologians in Heidelberg acknowledged receipt of Bullinger's hand-written confession the Zurich church leader began to revise the text, which he then sent to the churches of Geneva, Biel, and Berne. The Bernese pronounced themselves satisfied with the text with the exception of two items: first, the vessels used at communion, and, second, Bullinger's position on liturgical vestments. The first point referred to the continued use in Berne of silver and gold vessels for communion in the city churches while Bullinger argued, following Zwingli, that only wooden ones were appropriate. It was a small, but not unimportant, disagreement and Bullinger rewrote the twenty-first chapter of the confession to accommodate the Bernese views.

Bullinger was eager that this work appear as a confession of the whole Swiss church and it fell to his colleague and close friend Rudolph Gwalther to win the agreement of the other Reformed Confederates. The time was short, but Gwalther travelled through Schaffhausen, Basle, and Mülhausen seeking acceptance of Bullinger's statement of faith. Basle, under Simon Sulzer, could not, on account of its Lutheran sympathies, accept this Reformed document. From Geneva came a very different response: Beza and Nicholas Colladon rode to Zurich to request that Geneva be permitted to sign the document alongside the Swiss churches. The Reformed churches in Glarus, Appenzell, and in the Mandated Territories of Thurgau, Rheintal, and Toggenburg were so closely connected to Zurich that they simply accepted what Bullinger wrote.[69] Neuchâtel signed up in 1568 and Basle eventually put its name to the document in 1644.[70]

The text was quickly translated into German by Bullinger himself and printed by Froschauer in Zurich in March 1566. Beza took responsibility for the French translation, and the work appeared in 1566 from the press of François Perrin. The work was then quickly disseminated throughout the Reformed world, appearing in Latin at the Scottish Synod of St Andrews in September 1566, with an English translation completed two years later. In eastern Europe the Confession was adopted by the Calvinist Synod of Debrecen in Hungary in February 1567, and by the Polish Synod of Sendomir in spring 1570, where it was adopted as the *Confessio Polonica*.[71]

Within the Swiss Confederation the authority of the *Second Helvetic Confession* was somewhat unclear. The text made no reference to the *First Helvetic Confession* of 1536, while in the Graubünden, although the Bündner signed the *Second Helvetic Confession*, the *Confessio Rhaetica* of 1552 continued to be the official statement of belief. Further, Basle, as noted above, did not accept the *Second Helvetic Confession* until well into the seventeenth century. For the Bernese there were other complications, as they were bound by the acts of the 1528 Disputation and the 1532 *Synodus*. Until well into the seventeenth century every minister's house would have copies of all three statements of faith. Throughout the late sixteenth and early seventeenth centuries the *Heidelberg Catechism* of 1563 was also widely used and highly regarded. Thus, although the *Second Helvetic Confession* found widespread acceptance, it was never used exclusively, but rather it had to take its place alongside other confessional documents which had shaped the Swiss churches during the sixteenth century.

It is generally accepted that the *Second Helvetic Confession* is a mature expression of the theology of Heinrich Bullinger, leader of the church in Zurich and the dominant churchman of the Swiss Reformation from 1532 until his death in 1575. The *Confession* brings to the fore Bullinger's passionate belief in the catholicity of the Reformed church. By this he meant that the Reformed churches of the sixteenth century stood in direct theological continuity with the apostolic church and the Fathers of the early church.[72] Bullinger saw himself as a latter-day Church Father struggling against heresy, as Augustine had against the Donatists and Pelagians. Bullinger had a profound belief in the historical continuity of the church, he was by no means an opponent of tradition. The great enemy was not the Roman Catholic church, whom he freely admitted was full of fellow Christians, but the papacy, which he readily identified with Antichrist.

The *Second Helvetic Confession* sets out Bullinger's understanding of creation, sin, and salvation. Its thirty articles follow the structure of the Apostles' Creed, beginning with holy scripture and its interpretation. Chapters 3 to 10 treat God the creator, the Trinity, revelation, sin and predestination, while in chapters 11 to 16 we find Christology, the law and Gospel, rebirth and good works. Chapters 17 to 23 handle the church; 23 to 28 concern various practices of the church; 29 contains Bullinger's views on celibacy, marriage, and the family, and the final chapter discusses the role of the Christian magistrates.

Scholars of Reformation theology have detected subtle shifts in emphasis in Bullinger's thought in his treatment of the order and structure of Christian doctrine.[73] Underpinning the *Confession* is a pronounced Christocentrism, much stronger than we find in Bullinger's earlier writings. Further, we find the head of the Zurich church treating predestination as a discrete topic. This, no doubt, owed much to the unpleasant quarrel over predestination which had taken place in Zurich following the arrival of Peter Martyr Vermigli and the forced retirement of Theodor Bibliander, who had not only opposed Calvin's teaching of double predestination, but who seemed to favour a form of universalism.[74] Bullinger once again rejected Calvin's view that God chooses specifically to decree the damnation of an individual as well as to decree the election of the chosen. Bullinger refused to consider the problem of reprobation.[75] Rather, he emphasised that those who are the elect are the faithful; indeed at moments he seems to suggest that the elect are chosen on account of their faith, but he did not wish to go that far. Election, for Bullinger, was the basis of human regeneration, and faith was God's gracious gift to humanity. Those who are in Christ have been elected to eternal life, while those outside Christ will perish. But unlike Calvin, Bullinger refused to speak of God electing the damned to their fate. Rather, at every turn, he emphasised the goodness of Christ. In all his theological formulations Bullinger sought to present their pastoral aspects, stressing that election was part of God's will to save his people. In this sense, Bullinger's work was similar to the writings of Wolfgang Musculus.

The *Second Helvetic Confession* is the work of a man who had laboured for thirty-five years as head of the church in Zurich. He had weathered innumerable theological controversies, pastoral and administrative problems, personal losses, and betrayals. But from the pages of this elegantly written text emerges the wisdom of experience and a lifetime of study; for Bullinger, the matters of greatest import were the redemptive work of Christ and the unity of the church. These, as Richard Muller has argued, were grounded 'in the reality of Christ's humanity and the eternal union of Christ's human nature, in its integrity, with his divine nature'.[76] In asserting the clear distinction of Christ's two natures within their union, Bullinger saw himself as not only defending the tradition of Zwingli against the attacks of Luther and his followers, but he felt himself standing shoulder to shoulder with the Fathers of the early church, refuting the old heresies.

The 1560s brought to an end the great theological flowering of the Swiss Reformation. Bibliander and Vermigli died in 1562, Musculus a year later, and Calvin in 1564. Bullinger would live until 1575, but the *Confession* of 1566 was his last major work, and it was by far the fullest statement of his theology. The passing of these men marked the terminus of a period of theological development which extended back to the early work of Zwingli, in particular to his *On True and False Religion*. During this period the leading figures began the process of codifying Reformed doctrine, delineating its aspects and working out the relationships between the different parts. In the work of Bullinger, Vermigli, Musculus, and Calvin there was a search for a system of thought, grounded in scripture and a desire for the renewal of piety, which would elucidate the Bible itself. There were considerable variations and disagreements, but at the centre of Swiss Reformed thought stood Christology and election. All set forth Christology as the fulfilment of divine grace in human history; this for Musculus and Bullinger was expressed in terms of the continuity of the historical covenant from Abraham to Christ.[77]

Predestination became the foundation of Swiss Reformed thought in the generation after Zwingli (it was for Zwingli as well, as we have noted in chapter 2) as Bullinger and others sought to construct a theology faithful to their emphasis on the sovereign grace of God.[78] Richard Muller has commented that the Swiss Reformed theology of the period lasting until the death of Bullinger concerned itself above all else with the 'historical-causal pattern of man's redemption'.[79] This meant the role of Christ in the fulfilment of God's will in this world. What distinguished the Swiss theologians, if we include Musculus in their number, was an emphasis upon the historical dimension of God's salvation, the working out of God's eternal covenant.[80]

Building on the work of Erasmus, Luther, Zwingli, and Oecolampadius, the Swiss theologians of the middle decades of the sixteenth century set about constructing a theological system. At the centre of this system was an emphasis on the saving work of Christ and of faith alone, which was guaranteed by God's eternal election. Although there was some disagreement among the principal figures on certain points, they were united on the key issues of their theology. They constructed a thorough biblical theological system using the tools of humanist scholarship and intended to serve the pedagogical interests of the Reformed churches. The faith was to be taught and it was to be lived, thus the emerging theology of the Swiss reformers was didactic and pastoral. It was not in itself a finished project, rather it was one step along the path of theological development. By the last years of Bullinger's life the winds of change were blowing. The Swiss reformers had made extensive use of medieval scholastic theology in their thought, but the polemical war with the Roman church precluded open acknowledgement of their debts. The next generation, often referred to as the Reformed scholastics, would take the work of Bullinger and Calvin and use it as the basis for a more openly scholastic approach to theology, with an emphasis upon greater definition and precision. Aristotle, never fully dislodged from his place as the teacher of human reason, would soon openly return to the work of Reformed theologians. It would have shocked and appalled Zwingli, but it reminds us of the fundamental point about the Swiss Reformation. Despite its polemic against the Roman church, the theological structures which emerged in the Swiss Reformation stood firmly on the traditional teaching of the church. Certain of the Church Fathers, such as Augustine, Chrysostom, and Cyprian, were taken as authoritative voices when their views were found sympathetic (when not they were ignored as 'secondary authorities'), whilst medieval scholasticism, often *sotto voce*, continued to exert considerable influence. Zwingli and the Swiss followed Luther in proclaiming something bold and new in their vision of *sola fide*, but the subsequent theology which they derived from this principle owed a great deal to tradition. From the 1528 Disputation of Berne onwards the Swiss reformers set about replacing the medieval Catholic church and its systems of authority with their own edifice, which reflected their own understanding of authority and tradition. This was achieved through a deliberate appropriation of the early church and a good deal of the medieval church. The Swiss reformers' theology was grounded in a sense of historical continuity and purpose. The Swiss Reformation was based on a series of theological and historical assumptions, and it was through the lens of these assumptions that scripture was read and interpreted. Without doubt, it was a radical reconstruction of the theological foundations of the church, but the Swiss reformers shared with their Roman Catholic opponents an unshakeable belief that the church in this world required structures, order, authority, and systematic theology. The story of the period 1532 to 1575 is how this took shape within the framework of a shaky Confederation which no longer had a clear sense of purpose.

The death of Bullinger marked the end of the Swiss Reformation. He had been in Zurich in the1520s, known Zwingli, and ultimately saved the movement. He had been the most influential churchman in the Confederation and its most prominent figure abroad. He died a disappointed, but not bitter, old man, sensing that he had failed to restrain the demonic forces in the world. In accordance with his wishes, he was given a simple funeral and buried in an unmarked grave. The length of his life had certainly extended the influence of the Swiss Reformed churches longer than might otherwise have been the case, for the centres of the Reformed faith had shifted west to Geneva and north to the Low Countries, England, and Scotland. The Swiss would continue to make contributions, but in a minor key. Their period of prominence, which had begun on the battlefields of the fifteenth century and continued in the tumultuous religious upheaval of the sixteenth, was now at an end.

Notes

1 Ernst Saxer, 'Capito und der Berner Synodus', in Gottfried W. Locher et al. (eds), *Der Berner Synodus von 1532. Edition und Abhandlungen zum Jubiläumsjahr 1982*, 2 vols. (Neukirchen-Vluyn, 1988), II, pp. 150–166.

2 Richard Stauffer, 'Das Basler Bekenntnis von 1534', in H.R. Guggisberg (ed.), *Ecclesia Semper Reformanda* (Basle, 1980), pp. 28–49.

3 Hans Georg Rott, 'Martin Bucer und die Schweiz: Drei unbekannte Briefe von Zwingli, Bucer und Vadian (1530, 1531, 1536)', *Zwingliana*, 9 (1978), pp. 461–492.

4 Louis-Edouard Roulet, 'Farel, agent bernois? (1528–1536)', in P. Barthel, R. Scheurer, and R. Stauffer (eds), *Actes du Colloque Guillaume Farel* (Geneva and Lausanne, 1983), pp. 99–105. On Farel's early thought, see Hans Helmut Esser, 'Die Stellung des "Summaire" von Guillaume Farel innerhalb der frühen Reformierten Bekenntnissschiften', *Zwingliana*, 19 (1992), pp. 93–114.

5 On Farel's missionary work, the best source is still *Guillaume Farel, 1489–1565* (Neuchâtel and Paris, 1930); also, Roulet, 'Farel, agent des Bernois?'.

6 See Gabrielle Berthoud, *Antoine Marcourt* (Geneva, 1973).

7 W. Bourquin, 'Die Reformation in Biel', in *Gedenkschrift zur Vierjahrhundertfeier der Bernischen Kirchenreformation* (Berne, 1928), pp. 347–388.

8 The best account of the conquest is Charles Gilliard, *La Conquête du Pays de Vaud par les Bernois* (Lausanne, 1985).

9 Heiko A. Oberman, 'Calvin and Farel: The Dynamics of Legitimation in Early Calvinism', *Journal of Early Modern History*, 2 (1998), pp. 32–60.

10 R. Pfister, *Kirchengeschichte der Schweiz* (Zurich, 1974), p. 165.

11 A detailed account of the disputation is found in Henri Vuilleumier, *Histoire de l'Eglise réformée du Pays de Vaud sous le régime bernois* (Lausanne, 1927), I, pp. 148–183.

12 David N. Wiley, 'The Disputation of Lausanne and the Theology of William Farel: The Doctrine of Justification and its Sources', in Eric Junoud (ed.), *La Dispute de Lausanne 1536. La théologie réformé après Zwingli et avant Calvin* (Lausanne, 1988), pp. 142–148.

13 B. Gordon, 'Calvin and the Swiss Reformed Churches', in Andrew Pettegee, Alistair Duke, and Gillian Lewis (eds), *Calvinism in Europe* (Cambridge, 1994), pp. 64–81.

14 K. Guggisberg, *Bernische Kirchengeschichte* (Berne, 1958), p. 204.

15 Rainer Henrich, 'Ein Berner "Kunzechismus' von 1541: Bucers verloren Geglaubte Bearbeitung des Meganderschen Katechismus', *Zwingliana*, 24 (1997), pp. 81–94.

16 Ibid., p. 208.

17 Some of the best literature on this subject is very old: C.B. Hundeshagen, *Die Conflikte des Zwinglianismus, Lutherthums und Calvinismus in der Bernischen Landeskirche von 1532–1558* (Berne, 1842); also, E. Bähler, 'Der Kampf zwischen Staatskirchentum und Theokratie in der welschbernischen Kirche im 16. Jahrhundert', *Zeitschrift für Schweizerische Geschichte*, 5 (1925), pp. 1–61, 129–191.

18 Georges Bevaud, *Le Réformateur Pierre Viret (1511–1571). Sa Théologie* (Geneva, 1986).

19 Guggisberg, *Bernische Kirchengeschichte*, pp. 214–215.

20 Frans Pieter van Stam, 'Farels und Calvins Ausweisung aus Genf am 23. April 1538', *Zeitschrift für Kirchengeschichte*, 110 (1999), pp. 209–228.

21 Gordon, 'Calvin and the Swiss Reformed Churches', p. 69.

22 Ibid., p. 218.

23 Philip C. Holtrop, *The Bolsec Controversy on Predestination from 1551–1555: The Statements of Jerome Bolsec, and the Responses of John Calvin, Theodore Beza, and Other Reformed Theologians* (Lewiston, NY, 1993).

24 On Bullinger, see Peter Walser, *Die Prädestination bei Heinrich Bullinger im Zusammenhang mit seiner Gotteslehre* (Zurich, 1957).

25 Joachim Staedtke, 'Der Zürcher Prädestinationsstreit von 1560', *Zwingliana*, 9 (1953), pp. 536–546. Staedtke provides a full account of Bibliander's teaching.

26 The key work is E. Bähler, *Nikolaus Zurkinden von Bern 1506–1588. Ein Vertreter der Toleranz im Jahrhundert der Reformation* (Berne, 1912).

27 Paul Burckhardt, 'Basel zur Zeit des Schmalkaldischen Krieges', *Basler Zeitschrift für Geschichte und Altertumskunde*, 38 (1939), pp. 5–103.

28 Paul Burckhardt, *Geschichte der Stadt Basel* (Basle, 1942), p. 35.

29 Ibid., p. 36.

30 On 7 June 1549 eleven of the Confederates, as well as the abbot and city of St Gall, Mülhausen, Wallis, and the Graubünden renewed the treaty providing soldiers to the King of France. Only Berne and Zurich refused.

31 On this topic, see Bettina Braun, 'Die Eidgenossen und das Politische System Karls V.', in Horst Rabe (ed.), *Karl V. Politik und politisches System* (Constance, 1996), pp. 257–278.

32 A very useful summary of the differing positions of Calvin and Bullinger is found in Gottfried W. Locher, 'Bullinger und Calvin: Probleme des Vergleichs ihrer Theologien', in U. Gäbler and F. Herkenrath (eds), *Heinrich Bullinger 1504–1575* (Zurich, 1975), I, pp. 1–33.

33 Pfister, *Kirchengeschichte*, p. 267.

34 Ibid., p. 133.

35 Essential work on Comander remains Wilhelm Jenny, *Johannes Comander: Lebensgeschichte des Reformators der Stadt Chur*, 2 vols, (Zurich, 1969/1970).

36 Emil Camenisch, 'Die Confessio Raetica: Ein Beitrag zur bündnerischen Reformationsgeschichte', *JHGG* (1913), pp. 223–260.

37 On the Graubünden reformers in this period, see Conradin Bonorand, *Die Engadiner Reformatoren Philipp Gallicius, Jachim Tütschett Bifrun, Durich Chiampell: Voraussetzungen und Möglichkeiten ihres Wirkens aus der Perspektive der Reformation im allgemeinen* (Chur, 1987).

38 Albert Frigg, 'Geschichte der evangelischen rätoromanischen Bibelübersetzungen', *Bündner Monatsblatt* (1958), pp. 35–40.

39 Christopher J. Burchill, 'Girolamo Zanchi: Portrait of a Reformed Theologian and his Work', *SCJ*, 15 (1984), pp. 185–207.

40 Frieda Gallati, 'Die Rolle des Chronisten Aegedius Tschudi im Glarnerhandel oder "Tschudikrieg"', *Beiträge zur Geschichte des Landes Glarus* (1952), pp. 100–148.

41 Pfister, *Kirchengeschichte*, p. 254.

42 Mark Taplin, 'The Italian Reformers and the Zurich Church, *c.* 1540–1620' (PhD Dissertation, University of St Andrews, 1999), pp. 58–69.

43 Pfister, *Kirchengeschichte*, p. 257.

44 Ibid., pp. 258–259.

45 Christine Göttler, 'Die Zuger haben das Wort Gottes verbrannt – Strategien der Konfessionellen Polemik am Beispiel einer reformatorischen Schmähschrift vom Jahr 1556', *Zwingliana*, 18 (1989), pp. 69–119.

46 Hans Berner, *'Die gute Correspondenz'. Die Politik der Stadt Basel gegenüber dem Fürstbistum Basel in den Jahren 1525–1585* (Basle, 1989), pp. 40–41.

47 Ibid., p. 55.

48 Ibid., p. 57.

49 Mark Edwards, *Luther and the False Brethren* (Stanford, CA, 1975), p. 185.

50 Ibid., p. 190.

51 Paul Rorem, 'Calvin and Bullinger on the Lord's Supper. Part I: Impasse', *Lutheran Quarterly*, 2 (1988), pp. 155–184, and , 'Calvin and Bullinger on the Lord's Supper. Part II: The Agreement', *Lutheran Quarterly*, 2 (1988), pp. 357–389.

52 On Bolsec and Servetus, see chapter 6.

53 Gordon, 'Calvin and Swiss Reformed churches', p. 77.

54 These differences are highlighted in Wilhelm Neuser, 'Calvins Kritik an den Basler, Berne und Zürcher Prädikanten in der Schrift "De praedestinatione" 1552, in Oberman, Schindler, and Stucki (eds), *Das Reformierte Erbe*, 2 (Zurich, 1992), pp. 237–243.

55 Marvin W. Anderson, 'Peter Martyr, Reformed Theologian (1542–1562): His Letters to Heinrich Bullinger and John Calvin', *SCJ*, 4 (1973), pp. 41–64.

56 On the *Wittenberg Accord*, see below pp. 290–292.

57 On Augsburg and Musculus, see chapter 9, pp. 293–295.

58 Craig Farmer, 'Eucharistic Exhibition and Sacramental Presence in the New Testament Commentaries of Wolfgang Musculus', in Rudolf Dellsperger, Rudolf Freudenberger and Wolfgang Weber (eds), *Wolfgang Musculus (1497–1563) und die oberdeutsche Reformation* (Berlin, 1997), 299–310.

59 Pfister, *Kirchengeschichte*, p. 301.

60 U. Plath, *Calvin und Basel in den Jahren 1552–1556* (Zurich, 1974), p. 21.

61 Amy Nelson Burnett, 'Simon Sulzer and the Consequences of the 1563 Strasbourg Consensus in Switzerland', *ARG*, 83 (1992), p. 156.

62 On these figures, see chapter 6, pp. 217–221.

63 Plath, *Calvin und Basel*, p. 50.

64 21 May 1563. Quoted from Burnett, 'Simon Sulzer', p. 159.

65 Ibid., pp. 163–164.

66 Paul Sanders, 'Heinrich Bullinger et le "zwinglianisme tardif" aux lendemains du "Consensus Tigurinus", in Oberman, Schindler, and Stucki (eds), *Das Reformierte Erbe*, 1, pp. 307–323.

67 Ibid., p. 175.

68 Ernst Koch, *Die Theologie der Confessio Helvetica Posterior* (Zurich, 1968), cited in Edward A. Dowey, 'Heinrich Bullinger's Theology: Thematic, Comprehensive, Schematic', in John H. Leith (ed.), *Calvin Studies V* (Davidson, NC, 1990), p. 43.

69 Pfister, *Kirchengeschichte der Schweiz*, p. 305.

70 Hans Berne, 'Basel und das Zweite Helvetische Bekenntnis', *Zwingliana*, 15 (1979), pp. 8–39.

71 Ibid., p. 306.

72 On this subject see Scott H. Hendrix, 'Deparentifying the Fathers: The Reformers and Patristic Authority', in Leif Grane et al. (eds), *Auctoritas Patrum: Zur Rezeption der Kirchenväter im 15. und 16. Jahrhundert* (Mainz, 1993), pp. 55–68.

73 Richard Muller, *Christ and the Decree. Christology and Predestintion in Reformed Theology from Calvin to Perkins* (Grand Rapids, MI, 1988), pp. 44–47.

74 Joachim Staedtke, 'Der Zürcher Prädestinationsstreit von 1560', *Zwingliana*, 9 (1953), pp. 536–546.

75 Ibid., p. 44.

76 Ibid., p. 46.

77 Ibid., p. 68.

78 Mark S. Burrows, '"Christus inter nos Vivens": The Peculiar Genius of Bullinger's Doctrine of Sanctification', *Zeitschrift für Kirchengeschichte*, 98 (1987), pp. 48–69.

79 Ibid., p. 71.

80 Cornelis P. Venema, 'Heinrich Bullinger's Correspondence on Calvin's Doctrine of Predestination 1551–1553', *SCJ*, 17 (1986), pp. 435–450.

6

The radical challenge

We have already touched on the explosive elements of Zwingli's thought: his emphasis on the utter distinction of spirit and flesh, the possibilities of regeneration in the world, a vision of a Christian community, and so on. This entrancing alternative to the worldly church of the sixteenth century was magnetic, attracting disgruntled peasants in the rural areas as well as humanist-minded readers south of the Alps in Italy. Yet our brief discussion of Zwingli's theology suggested that there was an unresolved tension between spiritual purity and institutional articulation. In other words, Zwingli pried God and world apart without a complete sense of how they might be brought together in a new relationship. That tension was crucial to the development of what might be called religious radicalism in the Swiss Confederation. This chapter explores that development without attempting anything of a comprehensive treatment of Anabaptism, which was a complex, diverse movement with a wide range of sources outside the Confederation.[1]

The provenance of the radical movement in Zurich was a revolt within the circle of close friends around Huldrych Zwingli. For the most part these men were clerics and humanists who, with Zwingli, had been gripped by the New Testament polarity of spirit and flesh. They shared the vision of a spiritual renewal centred on the person of Christ and of a life in the world led by the Holy Spirit and revealed by scripture, rejecting all human attempts to achieve God's favour. Without doubt these men shared Zwingli's most profound spiritual convictions – this was the message which had turned Zwingli into a reformer – but it was the flesh, not the spirit which ultimately divided them. They could not agree on accommodation with the world; spiritual purity could not be sullied by politics, and thus Zwingli the politician became Zwingli the apostate. Swiss evangelical thought was cleft at its most vital point; the radical spiritualism inspired by Paul and the Gospel of John could only be realised in the world at a cost, and those for whom that price was too high found themselves vilified, banished and even executed by the new church. Within a couple of years of declaring in his sermons that God is spirit Zwingli had begun to speak of the need for heretics and dissenters to be punished. This cruel irony haunted the Reformed church through the sixteenth century, for as the initial Anabaptist threat faded a long line of figures emerged to remind the reformers of some uncomfortable first principles.

In an age which spoke in polemical tones this was a particularly hurtful split, for it arose from the very thing which united these men – the reading of scripture. The visceral nature of the dispute owed a great deal to a deep-seated sense of betrayal on both sides. Konrad Grebel and Simon Stumpf had been among Zwingli's earliest supporters, but the decision to leave the matters of iconoclasm and the mass in the hands of the magistrates following the disputation of October 1523 was, for these two men, unacceptable. The failure to abolish idolatrous religion with a single stroke was a fatal error, they argued, and Zurich would be made to pay for its compromises. During 1524 the situation worsened as the Grebel circle came to view the magistrates' treatment of the faithful in the rural areas, where communities had begun calling for local autonomy in religious matters, as evidence that they were anti-Christian. There were, however, additional issues. From the start of evangelical preaching in the early 1520s some priests had been calling for the abolition of the tithe, a subject close to the hearts of those living in the rural communes

The origins of the movement

The origins of this radical circle in Zurich very much paralleled Zwingli's own experiences. Fired by the publication of Luther's works in Basle, the writings of Karlstadt and Zwingli's own *Sixty-Seven Articles*, groups of laymen and clerics met in private houses to study the Gospel. One such group met in the house of Klaus Hottinger, who had been involved in the iconoclasm at Stadelhofen, and included Andreas Castelberger, who frequently travelled between Basle, Zurich, and Glarus. Castelberger led a study of Paul's Epistle to the Romans in a circle which included Heinrich Aberli, Lorenz Hochrütiner, and Bartlime Pur, all of whom would be important figures in the dissemination of Anabaptist thought.[2] These men quickly came into contact with the priests Simon Stumpf, Felix Mantz, and Wilhelm Reublin, who were preaching against tithes and advocating communal control of the church. By Christmas 1523, under the leadership of Grebel, the group had rejected Zwingli as a true prophet, but their resistance had not yet extended to breaking with the church; they were considering their next move.[3] Although personalities played a role, the root cause of the rupture was divergent interpretations of key biblical passages. Grebel held Bible studies on the Gospel of Matthew, and he wrote a concordance of biblical passages, which appeared in 1525 under a pseudonym, dealing with the issues of faith and baptism in order to prepare his followers to debate the question of infant baptism.

Converted to the evangelical cause in 1522, Konrad Grebel came from a Zurich patrician family which had profited greatly from the mercenary business, and he had belonged to Zwingli's sodality which had studied Erasmus's Greek New Testament. He had once had a great love for Zwingli, reflected in a Latin poem he wrote about the reformer, and he threw himself into the Reformation cause in Zurich, interrupting sermons and calling for the removal of images from the churches. Grebel was a man of unflinching confidence, full of prophetic visions of the scourging of the church and its clergy, and it was hardly surprising that his zeal could not be contained within Zwingli's measured pace of reform. During 1524 it became apparent that the break was not simply on account of the pace of reform, but was due to a fundamentally different theological perspective which had taken shape, and Grebel had emerged as the principal advocate of an alternative Christian community. He rejected Zwingli as a true messenger of the Gospel on account of the reformer's dependence upon the enemies of God – the magistrates.[4] The defining issues in the break were the removal of images, the tithe, the eucharist, the role of civil authority in religion, and holy scripture. By the summer of 1524 the radicals in Zurich had gained an identity as a group whose central belief was articulated in the statement 'what we are not taught with clear scriptural examples shall be to us as if it were forbidden, as if it were written not to do'.[5] They considered themselves the 'poor in spirit', sent into the world to suffer as Christ had done.

Grebel's theology emphasised the transforming power of the spirit. The true Christian, he argued, was utterly changed by the inner working of the Word, a perceptible process in which the believer was led by the spirit into a life of moral purity in accordance with the teaching of scripture.[6] The link between belief and outward conduct was, of course, pronounced in the writings of Erasmus and Zwingli. For Grebel, however, there was different emphasis: there was an absolute correlation between the power of the spirit and external conduct. He rejected any watering down of the faith for those of tender conscience; anything less than total obedience to the Word was a sham, hypocritical religion based solely on externals. This was a conclusion which Zwingli, mindful of the Augustinian principle that Christians remain capable of sin, was not prepared to draw. Clearly Grebel had a more sanguine view of human perfectability, which he derived from Erasmus, and this was central to his understanding of the Christian life. Where the two men parted company was in Zwingli's understanding of Christian society as a mixed body in which the elect and the damned live together indistinguishable to the human eye. God alone, Zwingli declared, knows the identity of the faithful, though the elect themselves are secure in the knowledge of their salvation. For Zwingli, the freedom of the Christian was paramount and he refused to accept that Christian faith could in any way be measured by either external appearances or actions. Human judgement is not competent for the task. Grebel, whose theology had similar contours in that it was shaped by the dichotomy between inward and outward realities (or spirit and flesh), laid greater emphasis on the need for moral rectitude and purity of life. Increasingly, he came to believe that this life was only to be found in separation from non-believers.

What made the radical challenge in Zurich so complex and painful was that both sides thought they were accomplishing the same thing. Zwingli and Grebel were utterly convinced that they were privileging the spiritual over the material and worldly. The problem was that they approached the issue from different angles. For Zwingli, the spirit is beyond human comprehension and discernment and therefore it is God's sovereign will that must ultimately prevail. Society must be made as Christian as possible but in every community the elect and the damned live alongside one another, perhaps even in marriage, harbouring spiritual gifts and lusts of the heart invisible to minister and magistrate. Grebel saw this so-called confidence in God's providence as spiritual lassitude, as a compromise with the forces of the world for personal gain. He had greater faith in human achievement in that believers could serve the spirit in removing themselves from all contamination. The difference was not a matter of semantics or a theological quibble; it was something for which very ordinary men, women, and children were prepared to risk everything, even their lives.

With his emphasis on the spirit, Grebel not only stole some of Zwingli's fire, but he was able to harness the energy of the reform movement in Zurich by linking his ideas about spiritual freedom to the aspirations for local autonomy rife in the rural areas. In his letters to Thomas Müntzer from the autumn of 1524 Grebel outlined the nature of his beliefs in a somewhat autobiographical manner.[7] He believed in *sola scriptura* and had supported Zwingli's initial advocacy of the right of the laity to read and interpret the Bible but he could not accept the limitations placed upon scriptural interpretation implicit in Zwingli's conception of the Christian minister. The principal qualification for understanding the Bible should be neither office nor ordination, but a personal disposition which Grebel referred to as being 'poor in spirit'. It was faith, a work of the Holy spirit, which opened scripture, not clerical privilege or university learning.[8] He dismissed all traditions of the church as 'human wisdom'. The return to a community of the 'poor in spirit' was envisaged as the restoration of the witness of the apostolic church.

For Grebel, the Lord's Supper was the central act of witness; it was the gathering of the elect, whose spiritual renewal was evident in their way of living, to remember Christ's passion, the ultimate suffering. Those unable to maintain the required level of moral purity were to be excluded from the meal, a practice known as the ban. church discipline was crucial, for it was the means by which the church was to remain clean. It was a fraternal rule to be applied by the community of believers in order to maintain the 'rule of Christ' in accordance with the strictures of Matthew 18:15–18.

The issue of infant baptism first arose in 1523, and by Easter 1524 it had become a major talking point when in Witikon, encouraged by the priest Wilhelm Reublin, several parents refused to have their children baptised. Baptism for the Grebel circle was the act of recognition of one's salvation in this world. 'Inner baptism' was God's saving action in Jesus Christ, while 'outer baptism' was the rite by which a candidate was received as a member of the body of Christ (congregation), placing him- or herself under its authority. The baptised person was joining the visible community of Christ, which was marked by the 'rule of Christ' and existed through a regime of moral rectitude reinforced by excommunication and absolution.[9] The slogan 'first faith and then baptism' was taken by their opponents to mean that the radicals required a test of faith before baptism could be administered; that was why they insisted on adult baptism. Goertz has argued that this was never the view of Grebel and his supporters, for whom baptism was 'an initiation which opened up to baptised persons the congregation of Jesus Christ as a reality in which their faith could grow and be proven and in which their life could be sanctified'.[10] This view, however, seems to suggest that for the Anabaptists baptism was no mere outward sign, but more of an event in which something took place.

Andreas Bodenstein von Karlstadt, who became the primary theological voice for many of the radicals, played a crucial role in formulating the attack on infant baptism.[11] Karlstadt's writings had begun circulating in Swiss lands in 1524. Infant baptism was linked in the minds of many rural people to the tyrannous rule of the clergy, who exacted payment for the sacrament or were indolent in its performance, and control over baptism was soon joined to the demand for authority over the local church.[12] The matter was of such importance that on 17 January 1525 a disputation was held in Zurich between Zwingli, Jud, and the other reformers, on the one hand, and the radicals led by Grebel, on the other. By 21 January the radicals had held their first rebaptisms and thus signalled their break with the church. From that moment they were branded 'Anabaptists' by their opponents, and by March 1526 the persecutions had begun. The Zurich council issued a mandate which threatened punishment by death for anyone who was rebaptised.

Banned from the city and refuted in their attempts to reform the community along the lines of scripture, the Anabaptists took to the countryside to fulfil their ideal of Christian renewal. Grebel himself went briefly to Zollikon, a village just outside Zurich, before moving on, leaving behind his colleagues to establish an Anabaptist order. Grebel's intention was to convert Schaffhausen, where he had strong family ties on the council. Once in the city he sought to work with local spiritualist leaders to bring about a reform of the community, but it did not come to fruition. Grebel was thrown out of Schaffhausen and travelled to St Gall, where there was both an active Anabaptist community and another influential relative, Vadianus.[13]

Following their expulsion from Zurich the radicals abandoned all hope of participation in the urban reformations in the Confederation; their future lay in association with the concerns of the rural communities. The peasant rebellions of 1525 in Germany had spilled into the Swiss Confederation, meeting with local anti-clerical sentiments. In the rural areas of Zurich the catalyst was the preaching of Wilhelm Reublin, who demanded the abolition of the tithe, the rejection of infant baptism, and the right of communities to elect their own minister. The Zurich council, advised by Zwingli, rejected these claims. Although there was considerable overlap between those holding Anabaptist views and those involved in the peasant revolts, it would be wrong to assume an automatic connection between the two. At different moments the evangelical ideas came into contact with a wide range of political and social concerns, and temporary alliances were formed. The radical circle in Zurich found itself aligned with the aspirations of the rural communities, where sympathy for the demands of the German peasants was rife. As the first acts of rebellion began to take place in communities such as Hallau and Grüningen it was virtually impossible to distinguish between the rebellious peasants and those who would emerge as Anabaptists in 1525.[14]

With the defeat of the peasants in 1525 the Anabaptist movement no longer enjoyed broad popular support, and it was driven away from towns and villages to ever more remote corners of the forests and hillsides, where it developed a sense of purpose in the light of growing persecution. The Reformation in Zurich, it became very clear, would not embrace the reforms regarded by the radicals as absolutely vital. The clergy, according to the Reformation Mandate in Zurich, were to retain their benefices and Zwingli had defended the tithe, so reviled in endless sermons by the radicals, as a Christian institution. Further, the ban was not to be introduced into the community according to scriptural principles and the removal of images was to remain a gradual, and partial, process.

Grebel and his circle had sought to rescue the Reformation from the false turn it had taken under Zwingli's leadership. Zwingli, as we have seen, had played the anticlerical card from the pulpit until about 1522, and he continued to stir the people of Zurich in order to pressure the magistrates. Inevitably this had created a panoply of diverse expectations, but for Zwingli himself the matter of Reformation was linked to political possibilities. He had reserved to himself the role of a prophet endowed with the authority to admonish and even threaten the ruling lords, but this was to the exclusion of any notion of authority for the communities. Martin Haas has rightly argued that in these years of the 1520s few people understood the major theological issues in which Zwingli was increasingly wrapped up, but they did understand the link between the attack upon the beneficed clergy and Zwingli's anticlerical statements.[15] The main thrust of the Anabaptist agenda appeared to most people as entirely consistent with the early evangelical preaching in Zurich. What was incomprehensible to many was why, after Zwingli had fired the people with a clarion call to return to the vibrant faith of the apostolic church, they were being offered a compromise – a privileged clergy, mass baptism which seemed to take no account of faith, and an open Table of the Lord which made no real demands upon a person's love of Christ or neighbour.

After the leaders of the Grebel circle were expelled from Zurich, Anabaptism gained its first stronghold in the village of Zollikon on Lake Zurich. James Stayer has demonstrated that a defining aspect of early Swiss Anabaptism was the community of goods, taken from Acts 4:32–35 where the Apostles declared that all things should be held in common. Johannes Kessler in his *Sabbata* wrote:

> Now because most of Zollikon was rebaptised and held that they were the true Christian Church, they also undertook, like the early Christians, to practice community of temporal goods (as can be read in the Acts of the Apostles), broke the locks off their doors, chests and cellars, and ate food and drink in good fellowship without discrimination. But as in the time of the apostles, it did not last long.[16]

Not for the first time Zwingli found himself counting among the offences of the Anabaptists a principle he had once espoused from the pulpit as a Christian ideal. Now that it had been adopted by his opponents he turned it against them as one of their errors. He wrote that they had misunderstood the scriptural passage from Acts. Whatever shifts had taken place in Zwingli's own theology, the principle of the community of goods had been jettisoned as soon as he had sought to win over the propertied magistrates of the city. But for the Anabaptists, as Stayer has written, the text from Acts could be given a fairly accommodating interpretation. The community of goods did not mean going beyond the household as the focus for living; what was intended was a sharing of goods and capital in order that a fund be established to alleviate poverty and hardship.[17] The members of the congregation should look after the old, ill, and those unable to work. It was, in the beginning, part of the Anabaptists' plan for a reform of society, but in the wake of their rejection in 1525 and the persecutions from 1526 it became part of their vision of a separated community. This view, however, was not universally shared by early Swiss Anabaptists, for in 1527 several figures under interrogation in Berne stated that while they rejected usury and the tithe they did not reject the idea of property.[18] This was an indication of what would take shape in the future: property-holding Anabaptist communities.

Two key protagonists in this early period of Anabaptism were Wilhelm Reublin and Johannes Brötli, who was the priest at Zollikon.[19] Following their banishment from Zurich in the aftermath of the rebaptisms of January 1525, they moved to Klettgau, a centre of the Peasants' Revolt where they may well have come into contact with Thomas Müntzer.[20] They settled in the village of Hallau in a territory recently conquered by Schaffhausen for the Swiss Confederation, which had relieved the bishop of Constance of this part of his lands. In 1525 the rural subjects of Schaffhausen had convened in Hallau to present their grievances against serfdom, tithes, and compulsory labour services.[21] Brötli preached in Hallau whilst staying in the local inn, and Reublin played a crucial role in the dissemination of Anabaptist ideas by travelling through the region baptising the burghers of Schaffhausen and Waldshut. In these two towns a pair of important figures were won over to the cause: Sebastian Hofmeister, minister of Schaffhausen, and Balthasar Hubmaier, minister of Waldshut.[22] There were mass baptisms in Hallau and Waldshut, where at Easter in 1525 Hubmaier and sixty others accepted baptism from Reublin.[23] As long as the Peasants' War raged the rulers in Schaffhausen were powerless to counter the movement, but once events turned against the peasants the Schaffhausen council exiled Hofmeister. Hallau submitted to Schaffhausen only after the locals sought to protect Reublin and Brötli from the soldiers, but with the defeat of the peasants in Klettgau and the capture of Waldshut by the Austrians in December 1525 the fate of the movement was sealed. Hubmaier, Reublin, and Brötli fled to Moravia, and the abandoned people of Hallau were heavily fined for their connivance in the Anabaptist insurrection.

It is striking how many of the important early Swiss Anabaptists found refuge among the rebels. James Stayer has drawn our attention to the case of Hans Rüeger, who was executed in Schaffhausen in 1527.[24] Rüeger was an important local figure in Hallau who had participated in the deposition of the priest to make way for Reublin and Brötli, and he had been part of the delegation which had submitted on behalf of the town to the Schaffhausen forces at the end of 1525. In 1518 he was listed among those receiving papal pensions in the Schaffhausen area in return for recruiting young men to fight in the Italian wars. He is an example of the sort of lay person attracted to the mixture of Anabaptist theology with local aspirations for the removal of Schaffhausen's overlordship.

The figure of Balthasar Hubmaier rose above the other Anabaptist preachers as a first-rate theologian. In an age of multiple ironies, Hubmaier had been the student of Johannes Eck, who had worked hard to promote this gifted young man.[25] He was educated at Freiburg-im-Breisgau and then at Ingolstadt, where he held an important office in the university before taking up a preaching office in Regensburg. Like most of the leaders of religious movements in this period, Hubmaier did not fear controversy, in fact he seemed to court it. He had left Regensburg in a storm of controversy after his promotion of a Marian cult in the city. He arrived in the relative obscurity of Waldshut, a minor town in Austrian lands. Again, as was so often the case, it was contact with Basle humanists, above all Erasmus, which concentrated his mind on church reform and he was soon in contact with Zwingli, whom he met when he attended the October disputation of 1523 in Zurich. He reformed the mass in Waldshut with the support of the local council, but soon the town was engulfed in the Peasants' War and threatened with attack by Archduke Ferdinand; Hubmaier took refuge in Schaffhausen. Although he saw himself as a disciple of Zwingli, he also read the works of Karlstadt and Müntzer which questioned infant baptism.[26] As the new Reformed order was established in Zurich at Easter 1525 the peasant armies triumphed at Waldshut and three hundred people, including Hubmaier, were baptised by Reublin.

Hubmaier was a sophisticated theologian with a profound sense of the interiority of religion; he was also one of the few in the Confederation who could match Zwingli theologically blow for blow in debates on the sacraments.[27] In his 1525 work *On the Christian Baptism of Believers*, Hubmaier argued that the sacrament is a public confession which marks a person's entry into the church; it is the visible sign of an inward transformation of that person through the Word of God. It is, in a sense, a second baptism, for Hubmaier spoke of the initial 'baptism of the spirit' which came through the preached Word. The second baptism demonstrates that the believer stands apart, but not separated from the world. The inevitable consequence of this baptism is persecution at the hands of non-believers. Closely linked to baptism was the Lord's Supper, which Hubmaier interpreted as a communal meal of remembrance which stirs the hearts of believers to an intense experience of Christ's passion. This memory fires the believer to love of neighbour and to a life of Christian witness which may lead to hardship and death. What distinguished Hubmaier from the views of Grebel was his belief that Christian government was a realistic goal and that the political rulers would be able to bring about a world where Christians could carry out their ethical duties.[28] For Hubmaier, the Christian life consisted of a dynamic relationship between an intense inner spirituality derived from Christ's passion and a total commitment to ethical conduct in the world.

With the fall of Waldshut to Austrian forces Hubmaier fled to Zurich in December 1525, where he stayed with Anabaptist friends. He was imprisoned and forced to recant, but when he spoke in favour of believers' baptism he was tortured and brought once more to a recantation of his views. He left Zwingli's city in April 1526 and made his way to Moravia, where he was arrested in 1527 and taken to Vienna to be burnt as a heretic. His wife was drowned in the Danube three days after his execution. Drowning Anabaptists was seen as an appropriate punishment for those who mocked the sacrament of the church, and it was used in Catholic and Reformed lands. Thus the man who had so often spoken of martyrdom had himself experienced the baptism of blood and fire.

A final figure who should mentioned is Ludwig Hätzer, a native of Bischofszell in the Thurgau, who was drawn to Zurich in 1523 by Zwingli's preaching. He had studied in Basle and imbibed humanist influences without ever taking a degree and, no doubt, he made contact with Zwingli's friends whilst at the university. Shortly after his arrival in Zurich he entered the debate over religious images in the autumn of 1523 by publishing a book, printed by Froschauer, in which he encouraged the council to take drastic action and have the churches stripped. Hätzer was a strong supporter of Zwingli and he recorded his feelings about the reformer in the printed record of the Second Zurich Disputation, which he edited. Like Grebel and Mantz, however, Hätzer came to question the pace of reform during 1524. Hätzer did not join the Grebel circle, and he was not rebaptised, but was involved in the discussions between Zwingli and the radicals. He turned against infant baptism and was expelled with the other radicals in January 1525.

Hätzer was reconciled with Zwingli in 1525 but he moved back to Basle where he met Johannes Oecolampadius, who took him into his house. The friendship between the two humanists proved fruitful as Hätzer undertook translations of Oecolampadius's works on the eucharist into German. Hätzer was a restless soul and he shifted from one southern German city to another. Although he continued to support Zwingli against Luther, he had moved away from the biblicism of the Swiss reformers towards mysticism and spiritualism. He found a kindred spirit in Hans Denck, and the two translated the Old Testament prophets into German. It was a highly influential work, used by the Zurich scholars in the preparation of their 1531 Bible. Hätzer's own fate was fairly gruesome: whilst in Constance in 1529 he was accused of fornication, tried, and executed. It has been suggested by several scholars that this energetic and creative man, who sailed very close to religious radicalism, was seen as a trouble-maker and therefore eradicated. Hätzer's religious views are difficult to map, but his spiritualism was encouraged by Zwingli's theology. Ultimately he moved beyond that theology to a more mystical position, but the inspiration clearly came from Zurich.

Schleitheim Articles

The important distinctions within early Swiss Anabaptist thought reflected the varied circumstances from which it had emerged. The crucial moment in the evolution of Swiss Anabaptism came with the *Schleitheim Articles* of February 1527. Schleitheim was one of the rebellious villages in Schaffhausen territory, and it is likely that Reublin baptised the people there. It was located within the lands of Schaffhausen and Klettgau, which Hubmaier, Brötli, and Reublin had turned into the principal base of Anabaptist activities in the Swiss Confederation during 1525.

There are seven articles which treat the subjects of baptism, the ban, the Lord's Supper, separation from the world, the election of ministers, the sword, and the oath. They are the first systematic statement of Swiss Anabaptism, and Arnold Snyder has called them the 'crystallization point for the Swiss movement'.[29] The first three articles drew upon general agreement among the early Swiss Anabaptists: only adults should be baptised and the rite should follow a confession of faith. Those who were baptised had indicated that they accepted the discipline of the community and that they alone could participate in the Lord's Supper. The point of departure, however, came in the radical separation of the church from the world. Articles 4 to 7 were not universally accepted among later Anabaptists and would lead to a considerable diversification of the movement. What gave the Swiss Anabaptists their distinctive character from 1527 was their strict ideal of separation. Anabaptism in the Swiss lands had moved from having territorial aspirations to a rejection of the world.

The *Schleitheim Articles* were drafted by Michael Sattler, who had come from Strasbourg at the beginning of 1527.[30] Sattler introduced into Swiss Anabaptism a new tone: no longer was there to be any identification with the social-revolutionary message of the peasants. The way forward lay between the magisterial reformation of Zwingli and the revolt from below of the peasantry.[31] The *Schleitheim Articles* were an apocalyptic document, reflecting the Anabaptist desire to preserve the purity of the Body of Christ from contamination by worldly forces. Their basic premise was that the world was about to be punished for its sinfulness; the kingdom of darkness was to be destroyed leaving the kingdom of light. The crucial tenet of Schleitheim was separation. The *Schleitheim Articles* made clear that the ban and baptism were external symbols of the true church and that a minister was to live without tithe or benefice. The separation from the world was to be absolute, embracing all aspects of life, such as church, work, taverns, and homes.

St Gall

The Anabaptists found a secure perch in the eastern part of the Confederation in St Gall, where radical influence arrived from Zurich in the person of Lorenz Hochrütiner, a native of St Gall who had been a citizen of Zurich since 1520.[32] Hochrütiner had been an early convert to the Reformation and had involved himself in many of the most notable incidents of iconoclasm in Zurich, such as the destruction of the crucifix at Stadelhofen. He had been banned from Zurich in the summer of 1524 and when he returned to St Gall he immediately joined the *Lesinen*, the circles of laymen and clerics reading scripture, and stirred up a debate over the baptism of infants. With the arrival of Konrad Grebel in March of 1525 the situation became more confrontational as Grebel led a group of enthusiasts in disrupting a baptismal service on Palm Sunday.[33]

Grebel's appearance in St Gall forced Zwingli once again to tangle with his erstwhile friend and now reviled enemy. Vadianus and Zwingli began a detailed epistolary discussion of infant baptism, and by the end of May 1525 the Zurich reformer had written his *Concerning Baptism, Rebaptism, and Infant Baptism*, which was sent to St Gall to bolster the defences. The council in St Gall wished to resolve the matter by disputation, and it demanded that the preachers and the Anabaptists present their views for public consideration. The event took place in the St Lawrence church on 5–6 June. Zwingli's book on baptism was read from the pulpit to the assembled company, which included the Bürgermeister, members of the council, the clergy, and many members of the public. The Anabaptists present quite reasonably objected that scripture, not Zwingli's writings, should form the basis for debate. Their chances of victory, however, were slight as the political rulers in St Gall, as in Zurich, perceived the Anabaptist rejection of the tithe and the swearing of oaths as sedition. Following the disputation the council forbade believers' baptism along with other tenets of Anabaptist belief, threatening sympathisers with heavy fines. Nevertheless, unlike in Zurich, there remained in the city considerable sympathy for the Anabaptist cause among both the general laity and the politicians, and although the movement was officially proscribed, St Gall was the only city in the Swiss Confederation in which the Anabaptists retained an identifiable presence.[34]

From its base in St Gall Anabaptism spread into nearby Appenzell, in particular into the communities of Teufen and Tablat. An important figure in this regard was Hans Krüsi of the parish of St George in Tablat, who was likely converted to Anabaptism while Grebel was in St Gall. Krüsi came to Tablat as a minister and immediately embarked on acts of iconoclasm in the local church. Soon afterwards he was arrested by the authorities in St Gall. Directly upon his release he resumed preaching Anabaptist ideas in the rural areas of St Gall before being seized again and taken to Lucerne, where he was burnt at the stake after Catholic officials had extracted a full confession. What makes Krüsi a significant figure was his book, printed in Augsburg in 1525, in which he listed under the headings 'faith' and 'baptism' all the biblical passages he deemed relevant knowledge for a Christian. It was a compendium of proof texts for the Anabaptist communities in the eastern part of the Swiss Confederation and it offers one of the few pieces of information on what was taught by the itinerant preachers.[35] In Appenzell a disputation was held in October 1529 in Teufen with several of the *Schleitheim Articles* forming the basis of the debate. There was no resolution and the attempts of the authorities to deal with the Anabaptists in the land were of little effect. Ultimately, many of the Anabaptists, encouraged by Wolfgang Uolimann, left Swiss lands and travelled to Moravia.

Basle

In 1525 the first Anabaptists appeared in Basle, gathered around the tailor Michael Schürer.[36] The Basle council responded quickly by expelling four members of the group and threatening the others with execution if they did not refrain from baptising adults and holding clandestine meetings. The four men thrown out of the city had actually performed the baptisms, and Oecolampadius began corresponding with Zwingli on the matter. In August 1525 a small disputation was held in St Martin's church in Basle between the preachers and the Anabaptists, led by Lorenz Hochrüter, who had been part of the radical circle around Castelberger in Zurich. Oecolampadius put the case for infant baptism, but his opponents seem to have prevailed on the day. The learned Oecolampadius was perhaps the greatest scholar of the early Swiss Reformation, but, as we have seen, he was neither an effective preacher nor debater. To counter the Anabaptist success Oecolampadius had his defence of infant baptism printed. This did not prove a success. In the text he employed arguments which his Catholic opponent Johannes Eck wryly noted could have been used to support other traditional Catholic practices not explicitly sanctioned in scripture, such as auricular confession, celibacy, and the use of Latin in worship.[37] From the Anabaptist camp Balthasar Hubmaier wrote a comprehensive refutation of Oecolampadius's tract. This defeat of the magisterial reformers highlighted the extreme difficulty they had in defending the practice of infant baptism. For men who had declared that the Bible alone was the true authority this was a point for which they could find no warrant in scripture. The debate over baptism was a fundamental turning point in the Swiss Reformation; it marked the moment when it had to shift grounds towards the acceptance of extra-biblical authority. Although Zwingli had defended the practice by associating baptism with circumcision, it was not entirely persuasive. In truth the Swiss reformers had no desire to abandon this long-standing practice of the church.

During 1526–27 the situation in Basle was extremely uncertain. Inflammatory language led to trials as the Lucerne Anabaptist Hans Altenbach was called to account for his remarks that the Lord's Table in St Martin's and other Basle churches were 'abominations to God'. From Zurich came Karl Brennwald, who engaged the Basle preachers in a disputation before the council in June 1527. Facing, on one side, theologians (including Oecolampadius) representing the evangelicals and, on the other, a party of Catholic churchmen, Brennwald placed before the council his rejection of infant baptism, the role of political authorities, the taking of oaths, and coercion in matters of faith. Most of his theses were from the *Schleitheim Articles*. The council, not surprisingly, ruled against the Anabaptists and a mandate was issued proscribing their activities. The introduction of the Reformation in Basle brought renewed measures against the Anabaptists; the mandate of 1 April described the Anabaptists as despisers of the sacrament of baptism on account of their insistence upon believers' baptism. The Anabaptists themselves were described as those who preached in the woods, fields, and private houses, and they were threatened with imprisonment. Those who returned to Anabaptism after punishment were to receive the sword.

In December 1529 another disputation was held in Basle between the Anabaptists and the preachers of the new Reformed church. This resulted in the arrest of Anabaptists in the city and rural areas, causing many to flee from Basle to relative safety in Solothurn territory. There were executions in the city during 1530 as the magistrates tightened their grip on dissent; not only men but women, including the seventy-year-old Anna Hüdeli, were either drowned or put to the sword.[38] The harshness of the council's response was rewarded. By the end of 1531 Anabaptism had more or less lost its footing in Basle; executions and exile had depleted the communities as most had made their way towards Berne, which for the remaining part of the sixteenth century was the centre of Swiss Anabaptism.

The radicals in Berne

Anabaptism arrived in Berne in 1525 as an import from Zurich following the expulsions after the first rebaptisms. There has been an attempt in the historiography to argue for an independent tradition of radicalism in Berne descended from the Waldensians, but there is no hard evidence that Bernese Anabaptism predated the genesis of the movement in Zurich.[39] What is true, however, is that following the spread of Anabaptism into Basle, Schaffhausen, and Waldshut, Zurich was not the only source of radical thought. Although in areas such as the Aargau the pattern of iconoclasm, sermon interruptions, the breaking of the Lenten fast and the circles of Bible-reading owed much to Grebel and his supporters, the preaching of Balthasar Hubmaier in Waldshut, which offered a variation on Grebel's message, reverberated across Bernese lands.

Wherever the initial impulses came from, the movement quickly took root in Berne and by August 1525 Hans Meyer and a hat-maker who lived in a village near Zollikon were baptised. Both later appeared in Zurich and were involved in disturbances in the parish of Hinwil in the Zurich Oberland. Bernese Anabaptism was divided between its Zurich and Waldshut branches; the principal distinction resided in their differing attitudes towards secular authority. Whilst the Zurich radicals rejected the idea of a Christian magistracy, those from Waldshut, under the influence of Hubmaier, recognised the possibility of Christian secular authority. Waldshut's capitulation to Austrian forces had brought many of Hubmaier's supporters into Bernese territory.

The correspondence of Zwingli, Oecolampadius, and Berchtold Haller in Berne offers the earliest information on Anabaptist activity in Berne. Jakob Groß had been sent from Waldshut to preach in Aargau, while a native of Aarau, Hans Meyer, (known as Pfistermeyer), was baptised in Lake Zurich at Zollikon. Later he participated in the disputation between Zwingli and the radicals on 22 December 1525 before returning to his native land, where he was welcomed by the Bernese council with the news that he was banished from its territory, a courtesy extended to the other radicals. In the spring of 1527 Lorenz Hochrütiner and Hans Hausmann arrived in Berne from Basle, and according to Berchtold Haller, won over twenty people to the Anabaptist cause in a very short time. Hochrütiner, whom we have encountered in Zurich, St Gall, and Basle, was described as man with a biting wit who could stir an audience with his oratory.[40]

In August 1527 Zurich, Berne, Basle, and several other states issued an *Anabaptist Concordat* in which the activities of the radicals were prohibited. This agreement was ratified in September by a vote of the people in Berne. This only served to expand the movement as many moved into the territories of Zurich and Basle and began active missionary work. The consequence was the development of flourishing communities along the borders between Berne, Basle, and Solothurn which were supported by local nobles, not because they ascribed to the radical religious polity but rather as an effective means of irritating the urban magistrates.

Pfistermeyer was a fascinating and shadowy figure who moved covertly between communities finding protection in the households of sympathisers. The authorities hunted him down and occasionally, as in 1529, he found himself languishing in prison in Berne, only to return undaunted to his work. In the Freiamt, the Mandated Territory, a large Anabaptist community had sprung up largely on account of Pfistermeyer's zeal and inspiration. He was a charismatic preacher whose invectives against the injustice of the tithe found eager audiences. The young Heinrich Bullinger, minister in Bremgarten, found himself in 1530 having to deal with Pfistermeyer, who was easily able to draw an audience of two to three hundred faithful. After many threats the Bernese authorities intervened in the Freiamt in March 1531 and seized Pfistermeyer, tossing him once more into prison. Such was the breadth and depth of Pfistermeyer's support in the rural areas, however, that the Bernese magistrates knew that they had to proceed with caution. They did not wish to create a martyr; rather they chose the route followed in Zurich during the 1520s of holding a disputation. Although no disputation of the early Swiss Reformation was held without the results being a foregone conclusion, it was, nevertheless, in the interests of all that this meeting be properly constituted and ordered. Only then could the outcome be put beyond dispute. It was a triumph for the magistrates and the reformers as Pfistermeyer renounced his Anabaptism. The disputation records were printed for distribution among the people.

Encouraged by the success of Pfistermeyer's conversion, the Bernese magistrates sought another disputation with the Anabaptists, although the reformers in the city did not share their enthusiasm. The magistrates insisted, and the town of Zofingen in Aargau was chosen because of its location in the centre of an Anabaptist stronghold; the magistrates wanted to demonstrate that they were not simply a distant authority issuing mandates, but that they were prepared to take the fight to the people and defeat the movement on its home ground.

The major problem for the Bernese authorities was their inability to control the flow of Anabaptist sympathisers into their lands. Since 1527 Anabaptists had been arriving from Basle, but by 1530, following repressive measures in the Rhenish city, the stream had swollen, and the Bernese authorities, struggling against rural dissent throughout their vast territories, were unable to respond. Many Anabaptists also came from Solothurn and this proved a particular headache for the Bernese as neither Basle nor Solothurn had been party to the 1527 mandate issued by Zurich, Berne, and St Gall proscribing Anabaptist activities. Large numbers were arrested but they had to be released with a warning that if they returned they would be executed. There was a large Anabaptist community in Erlinsbach in Solothurn territory which nurtured numerous groups in the Bernese countryside. The Solothurn government was confessionally split and not especially willing to cooperate with Reformed Berne, and Bernese soldiers and officials were not allowed to cross the border in pursuit of Anabaptists. The radical preachers, men such as Christian Brugger, Marti Weniger (known as Lincki), and Hans Landolt from Zurich, developed strong followings in these rural communities among which they moved with impunity.[41]

In an attempt to deal with the problem of porous borders and the itinerant nature of the movement, the Bernese magistrates extended their invitation to a disputation at Zofingen to men from Solothurn. Mandates and executions had failed abysmally to halt the movement; it was now hoped that a public debate in which Anabaptist views were convincingly refuted in front of the people in their own language would help to turn the tide. The disputations were to serve a didactic purpose for clergy and laity alike, for the ministers of the Bernese church were required to attend in order to be instructed in how to respond to a member of the Anabaptist sect about fundamental questions of the faith. In the end, the Zofingen disputation of

1–9 July 1532 was a great disappointment, serving only to underscore the differences between the two sides.

At the time of the Zofingen disputation the Bernese magistrates were alarmed to learn that the Anabaptist movement had spread through their lands as far as the Emmental. It was evident that the disputations were not working and that the clergy were not proving effective agents against the Anabaptists, so the magistrates turned to more draconian measures – they began executing the radicals. From almost every parish reports came from the rural ministers that they were dealing with Anabaptists and patterns began to emerge. The central issues raised by the radicals were whether a Christian could serve as a magistrate and whether the Old and New Testaments were to be accorded equal value.[42] Although these questions dated back to the earliest days of the Anabaptist movement, there was a new influence detectable in the Swiss lands, the writings of the Silesian nobleman Kaspar Schwenckfeld. Schwenckfeld's tracts put into print the criticism found on the lips of most Swiss Anabaptist leaders: he wrote in the vernacular and gave poignant expression to a spirituality unfettered by the coercive forces of the state.[43] Perhaps most damning was Schwenckfeld's assertion that the arguments put forward by men such as Zwingli and Bullinger in defence of the church, sacraments, political authorities, and the oath were derived from the Old Testament in the absence of support from the New. Schwenckfeld and others argued that the New Testament was the only foundation of the church, and that the Gospels and Epistles provided precious little to support the type of churches being constructed in Zurich, Berne, and Basle. Schwenckfeld hit a raw nerve. There was no doubt that major tenets of Zwinglian theology were drawn from the Old Testament: the concept of the covenant, infant baptism as the new form of circumcision, the prophetic role of ministry, and the godly prince fashioned after the example of the Israelite kings. The battle over the place of the Old Testament in the Christian church formed a crucial front for the Swiss Reformers in the struggle against the Anabaptists and spiritualists. Zwingli and Bullinger understood the logic behind the arguments of their opponents, and they were aware that their own positions often owed more to tradition than any precise passage in scripture It was for that reason that they placed such a premium on refuting accusations that their theology was extra-biblical. They repeatedly hammered home the centrality of the Old Testament to the Christian life and there were some successes. Important conversions from the Anabaptist camp were achieved; in 1535 Lincki returned to the Reformed church.

During the 1530s Berne was in a difficult position as the leading ministers in the city warred over the influence of the Strasbourg reformers while in the countryside Anabaptism remained unchecked. In the midst of this Berne had launched its long-awaited expansion into the French-speaking lands of the Pays de Vaud. The Bernese magistrates were desperate to silence the theological quarrels which were tearing the fabric of the new Reformed order. Gloomily Berchtold Haller wrote to Bullinger on 17 March 1533 seeking advice on biblical grounds for punishing the Anabaptists.[44] There were no further conversions and the Anabaptist hold on the rural communities was not shaken by either disputations or thunderous edicts. Apart from the sacramental questions, there were two aspects of Anabaptist belief which were especially unpalatable to the Bernese magistrates; they would neither swear the oath of obedience to the state nor do military service. Death sentences and deportations brought hardship and suffering but also a heightened sense of spiritual progress and communal identity, and for four decades after the Reformation in Berne the Anabaptists remained. In 1566 it was decreed that those who refused to take the oath were to be expelled and forced to swear that they would not return to Berne. Representatives of the council were sent to all of the regions where Anabaptists were known to live and conducted a house-to-house search for those unwilling to declare their obedience to the state. Those who refused to comply were banished, while those who were married by an Anabaptist preacher and not by the parish minister were decreed to have committed adultery and their children declared illegitimate.

Torture and execution were not uncommon, but generally reserved for leaders of the movement. Typical of these men was Wälti Gerber of Röthenbach, who had preached that all mandates of the state were contrary to the Christian religion, that no Christian could be a citizen, and that no minister of the church was a Christian. Gerber, who had been arrested twenty years earlier for his radical views and had fled from Berne, was executed on 30 July 1566.[45] Hans Haslibacher, who was executed on 20 October 1571, became one of the best known of the Anabaptist martyrs on account of a song about him which became part of popular culture, reflecting a degree of popular sympathy for the movement.

The obvious consequence of repeated attempts to crush the movement with force was that the communities became highly adept at moving about to avoid detection. It was clear that by the end of the sixteenth century there had been little success in combating the movement in Berne, and reports spoke of how respectable people continued to join Anabaptist communities. On 3 September 1585 a new mandate was issued stating that Anabaptist beliefs contravened the *Second Helvetic Confession* of 1566 and that they posed a threat to the well-being of the state. The mandate, which was reissued in 1597, required all people to take the oath of obedience to the state, to attend church on Sundays, to bring their new-born child to church for baptism within eight to fourteen days, to attend the Lord's Supper, and to avoid all Anabaptist meetings.[46] Those who returned to the Anabaptists were threatened with torture and death. Leaders of the Anabaptist movement were to be executed, and those who attended meetings of the sect were to be fined one hundred pounds. The mandate concluded with an expression of the magistrates' contempt for the indolent clergy of the Reformed church whose pathetic performance in the parishes was the principal cause for the flourishing of the Anabaptists.

Bowed but not defeated, many Anabaptists were driven from their homes in the sixteenth century. It is hard to speak in terms of numbers, but clearly many returned in violation of the oaths imposed upon them by the Bernese officials, while others found refuge in distant lands. It has already been mentioned that several notable leaders made their way to Moravia, where they found protection under Leonhard von Liechtenstein. Some came under the leadership of Jacob Hutter from the Tyrol, forming a group which became known as the Hutterites. Between 1573 and 1576 the Hutterites sent missionaries into Bernese lands seeking recruits, and there is evidence that a good number of people left and travelled east. In 1585 there was a report that more Swiss Anabaptists arrived in Moravia than the local communities could handle. Their travels would take them to many lands, finally to the New World, and among the descendants of the Moravian Anabaptists familiar Bernese family names are still to be found.

Bullinger against the Anabaptists

For Bullinger, the principal threat to the Swiss Reformation after 1532 was the Anabaptists, not the papists; he saw the radicals as wolves among the sheep, often invisible to the eye, who had to be driven out before they could destroy the faith of true Christians. For all of the Reformed churches the major question after 1531 was the relationship between state and church. Leo Jud, Zwingli's friend and colleague, as well as Kaspar Megander in Berne, had both come to the opinion during 1533 that magistrates were nothing more than heathens determined to destroy the church. The situation was so precarious that Bullinger, who preferred never to travel, went directly to Constance to speak with the Blarer brothers. The influence of Schwenckfeld and his work was being felt everywhere among the Swiss churches and Bullinger knew that his 1532 arrangement with the Zurich council was in trouble. Numerous ministers from the rural areas wrote to

Bullinger declaring that they were under severe pressure from the Anabaptists, who questioned the fundamentals of the faith. One of the tactics employed by Bullinger was to ensure that those who renounced their Anabaptist views were well treated by the council in Zurich. An example of this is the former Anabaptist leader Wilhelm Reublin, who came to Bullinger when he had financial difficulties. Bullinger was most helpful in interceding with the council.[47] The winning back of Anabaptist leaders was a key defensive strategy of the Reformed churches during the 1530s and 40s.

Bullinger involved himself in the debates with the Anabaptists which took place in Berne during 1532. He did not attend, but he sent letters and texts which were intended to bolster the Bernese preachers in their discussions. For the most part, Haller and Megander in Berne favoured a milder approach, while Bullinger, who fully supported the execution of Anabaptists in Zurich, took a harder line. The principal issue was the link between the Old and New Testaments. Bullinger continued to stress the continuity of the covenant of God with the Israelites with that of the new covenant in Christ. In all the discussions the Reformed preachers relied on a 1531 work by Bullinger with the catchy title *Four Books to Warn the Faithful from the Shameless Disturbance, Offensive Confusion, and False Teachings of the Anabaptists* (Zurich, 1531) as the basis for their arguments, and whenever Bullinger sought to help an embattled minister or church leader, he would send a copy of the book.[48]

In Schaffhausen the situation was unique. Alone among the Reformed states the council was more favourable towards the Anabaptists, largely because the Bürgermeister, Hans von Waldkirch, was through his wife distantly related to Konrad Grebel. Although he was not rebaptised, as his sister had been, he remained sympathetic to the movement; this may also have been on account of his anti-clericalism. He did little to assist the Schaffhausen clergy in their confrontations with the Anabaptists, and in 1535 they wrote to Bullinger beseeching his intervention with the Schaffhausen council. Bullinger obliged, but to little effect as von Waldkirch replied that he was simply ensuring that the church believed 'in Christ alone and was built on his holy Word'.

A similar situation arose eight years later and it was clear that von Waldkirch was still tacitly supporting the Anabaptists. Bullinger wrote again, and it was a sign of his authority and standing in the Swiss churches that the Schaffhausen council replied saying that a mandate against the Anabaptists would be issued.[49] Nevertheless, the situation did not change and a disputation with the Anabaptists in Schaffhausen did not take place until 1559. It did not go well for the Reformed ministers. Bullinger was deeply troubled when he read the account of the debate and no doubt the unsettled situation in

Schaffhausen encouraged him to revise his early work against the Anabaptists.

The result was his massive work *On the Origins of Anabaptism*, which appeared from the press in 1560. The book is a monument to how Bullinger's mind worked. It was divided into six parts, with the first two books covering the history of the movement and its fracture into different groups. Books 3 to 6 form Bullinger's refutation of Anabaptist beliefs. Bullinger readily took to the role as defender of orthodoxy, seeing himself as standing in the tradition of the Church Fathers (above all Augustine) in exposing the errors of the heretics. Bullinger believed that God's will for the Church was revealed in human history, and his own struggle with the Anabaptists was portrayed as part of the larger picture of the dualistic battle between truth and falsehood. Heresy and orthodoxy, for Bullinger, were historical concepts with long lineages which can only be understood through a thorough study of the past. The shadow of Augustine's *City of God*, with its historical perspective on the struggle between God and the devil, falls across Bullinger's historical writings. In *On the Origins*, every aspect of Anabaptist thought was carefully detailed in order to be refuted with appropriate references to scripture and the Fathers. In book 3 Bullinger treated the natures of the church, preaching, and scriptural exegesis. Book 4 covered soteriology, ethics, eschatology, the works of Christ, human works, the law and the relationship between the Old and New Testaments, love as the foundation of the New Testament, and the sleep of the soul. Bullinger devoted all of book 5 to political authority and the final book dealt with the Anabaptist understandings of baptism, the Lord's Supper, and the ban. It is particularly striking that Bullinger begins with the church. For Bullinger, the church and its catholicity, revealed in history, was absolutely central, and it was of the greatest importance for him to demonstrate that the Reformed faith was consistent with the witness of the Church Fathers. The worst offence committed by the Anabaptists, according to Bullinger, was that they had divided the church, and that is why he devoted much of his career to proving that Zwingli and the reformers had not done the same.

Spiritualists, Antitrinitarians, and dissemblers

The Anabaptist movement, in all its forms, arose out of a fundamental tension within early Swiss evangelical thought – the radical opposition of spirit and flesh. This polarity was part of the Augustinian tradition which so greatly influenced Zwingli and his followers, and it was the defining idea of the Swiss Reformation. Although extremely attractive as slogans, biblical texts such as 'the spirit alone gives life, the flesh is of no avail' (John 6:63) proved to be stumbling-blocks when the reformers came to demonstrate how the flesh and the spirit could be reconciled in order to form human communities. Luther had argued that Zwingli had a false understanding of Christ's two natures, and that he tended towards the Nestorian heresy. Zwingli, and later Bullinger, robustly denied the charge, but there could be no denying that the Zurich reformer's work had proved influential upon those whose thought became increasingly radical. One of the most effective weapons against Zwinglianism in the sixteenth century was that it engendered heresy, and while Zwingli and later Bullinger fervently denied this accusation there is no doubt that for many the radical nature of Zwingli's theology, with its stress on the role of the spirit, was its most striking quality. Zwingli's unequivocal rejection of the mass as a materialistic corruption of the Lord's Supper may have condemned him in the eyes of Luther and Eck, but it was highly attractive to those who saw authentic Christian living in the inner, spiritual reality of Christ, and not in the outer rituals of the church. In Zurich, Basle, and the Graubünden, radical thought flourished at moments during the sixteenth century, testing the boundaries of the Reformed church, particularly on the sacraments, Christology, and the Trinity. In order to explore the diversity of radical thought which existed in the Confederation, or just on its borders, let us turn to several of its key exponents.

Kaspar von Schwenckfeld

The radical thinker who most profoundly influenced, and was influenced by, the early Swiss Reformation was the Silesian nobleman Kaspar von Schwenckfeld (1489–1561). By 1525 the works of Zwingli and Karlstadt on the eucharist were readily available in Silesia and Schwenckfeld had become well acquainted with their arguments, even if he did not entirely share their experiences. Zwingli was a powerful influence on Schwenckfeld, particularly in his emphasis upon the inner reality of the spirit over external forms. Schwenckfeld, however, took Zwingli's argument and mixed it with elements drawn from Luther and the German mystical tradition to arrive at a point far beyond Zwingli. Whilst acknowledging the force of Zwingli's thought, Schwenckfeld kept a critical distance, disapproving strongly of the Zurich reformer's entanglement in hair-splitting theological debates. Nevertheless, there was a genuine empathy between the two men. By 1525 Schwenckfeld had parted company with Luther over the latter's doctrine of the eucharist. Although approving of Zwingli's attack on Luther's view of the real presence, Schwenckfeld developed his own highly spiritual teaching on the sacrament and by 1526 he had ceased partaking of the Lord's Supper altogether. He finally broke with Luther in 1527 and by 1529 he had left his native Silesia for Strasbourg, where he was very much within the orbit of the Swiss Reformation world. From 1529 until 1534 he remained in Strasbourg, where he enjoyed a good reputation among many of the leading citizens, despite the aggressive opposition of Martin Bucer, who sought to demonstrate that despite his discreet silence in the city Schwenckfeld was an Anabaptist. Schwenckfeld certainly did mingle with Anabaptists and he had a particular influence on Wolfgang Capito, with whom he lodged.

Although there was some common ground, Schwenckfeld was deeply critical of the Zwinglian polity emerging in the Swiss Confederation and southern German cities. His position on baptism was perhaps most controversial; he rejected Zwingli's equation of infant baptism with the rite of circumcision. He felt that Zwingli and Bucer were still privileging the external over the internal with their adherence to water baptism for infants. No outward act could confer grace, and in retaining the sacrament the Swiss theologians were committing idolatry on the same level as the mass. At the same time, Schwenckfeld rejected the Anabaptist rebaptisms as these placed too much worth on the external symbol.[50] As Emmet McLaughlin has written, 'Schwenckfeld's focus was on individual faith, individual self discipline, and individual salvation. He simply lacked any sympathy for the ideal of the *corpus christianorum* which ran throughout Zwingli's and Bucer's thought.'[51] Baptism was for Schwenckfeld not an institutional act, but a personal confession of one's faith in Jesus Christ.

Nevertheless on the relationship between the Word and spirit Zwingli and Schwenckfeld were broadly in agreement, but with some important differences. Both men spoke of faith as the gracious gift of God unmerited by any individual, and both spoke of a grace which precedes any encounter with God's written word. For Zwingli, however, this initial grace opened the eyes of the believer to God's revelation in the Bible. Thus he could speak of the dynamic relationship between the believer and the written Word of God (Bible). Schwenckfeld, however, emphasised the sufficiency of God's grace which is poured into the heart of the believer. This grace does not need to be fed by the outer Word. The inner Word, which for Schwenckfeld was the glorified Christ, works upon the soul, while the outer Word, the Bible, points towards the inner but neither conveys nor augments it.

Schwenckfeld was critical of the Swiss on a number of fronts. He believed that Zwingli's doctrine of predestination, by which the seed of faith was present in the righteous, was an unacceptable diminution of Christ's salvific power. Schwenckfeld also rejected Zwingli's emphasis upon the church as the body of the faithful; he could not accept the Zurich reformer's position, greatly strengthened in the theology of his successor Heinrich Bullinger, that Christians are defined by their membership in the invisible congregation of the faithful. Schwenckfeld, in contrast, stressed the place of the individual believer over corporate identity. The root of his objection lay in what he termed the 'Judaising' of the Reformed church, whereby the laws and forms of the Old Testament were used to construct a polity in which authorities could coerce Christians into obedience. There was no more graphic example of this in Schwenckfeld's eyes than the execution of Anabaptists in Zurich by drowning them in the Limmat. Schwenckfeld's position was a frontal assault on the Zwinglian understanding of the church with its communal nature. It was not a popular teaching in that it did not attract widespread support, but Schwenckfeld's ideas were taken up by influential individuals who found satisfaction in his spiritualism.

Schwenckfeld's influence and standing among the Swiss was evident from an early point. Just as his initial ideas had been influenced by reading Zwingli and Oecolampadius, these reformers demonstrated their respect by preparing editions of his works: in 1527 Oecolampadius produced an edition of Schwenckfeld's *Course of the Word of God*, and a year later Zwingli edited the *Instruction*.[52] In both cases Schwenckfeld had refused permission and the unsanctioned editions remained a source of irritation. Nevertheless, Schwenckfeld's spiritualism, his rejection of the real presence in the eucharist and, perhaps not of least importance, his falling out with Luther, had endeared him to the Swiss, who in this period of theological fluidity had not really digested the full implications of his thought. The connections, however, went deeper. Leo Jud, Zwingli's closest friend and ally, was profoundly influenced by Schwenckfeld's writings, and in the period following Kappel he came to espouse the Silesian's views on baptism, the role of civil government and the eucharist.[53] There was an exchange of letters between Jud and Schwenckfeld in 1533–34, and even though Jud was persuaded back into the fold by Bullinger, there can be no doubt that the intense interiority of his spirituality owed much to Schwenckfeld. Both men shared a deep attachment to the German mystical tradition of the later Middle Ages as well as to the spirituality of the *Devotio Moderna*. During the 1530s Jud followed Schwenckfeld in producing an edition of Thomas à Kempis's *Imitation of Christ* and in writing a passional, a meditative work on the sufferings of Christ. Schwenckfeld's thought was also a strong influence on Sebastian Castellio, who also produced editions of the *Imitation of Christ* and of the mystical text the *German Theology*.

After his stay in Strasbourg Schwenckfeld travelled through southern Germany where he built up a strong following, as men and women from all levels of society were attracted to his spiritual message, which they favoured over the moralistic preaching of the reformers. A particularly strong community formed in Augsburg, giving Schwenckfeld access to printing presses which greatly facilitated the dissemination of his thought through Germany. Much of his success had to do with his personality: a nobleman of great refinement, he was gentle, learned, and extremely pastoral. People wanted to be around him and talk to him. He was often invited into the homes of patricians, and the conventicle meetings which he held in the German cities of Ulm, Strasbourg, Augsburg, Landau, and Speyer, amongst others, were like family prayer evenings.[54] McLaughlin has written:

> Schwenckfeld's ideas offered the perfect mix, and this explains his popularity and success. Many of Schwenckfeld's closest friends and followers in Augsburg were former Anabaptists. They were attracted to his near-Zwinglian eucharistic position, his opposition to state churches, and his spiritualistic emphasis. During his stay in Augsburg conventicles flourished once again. In addition, his conservative social outlook and his anticlericalism were attractive to the city councillors caught in the cross fire of Lutheran sacramental dogmatism, Zwinglian political-social radicalism, and the Catholic imperial threat.[55]

Schwenckfeld was, however, among the most reviled figures of the sixteenth century and his theology was repeatedly condemned by the reformers, including Bullinger, who tangled with the Silesian nobleman over Christology in the 1540s. In 1542 Bullinger prepared his *Grüntlicher Bericht* in which he attacked Schwenckfeld's putative conflation of the two natures of Christ. This was a highly sensitive issue for the Swiss reformers as Luther had landed a punch when he accused Zwingli of having pulled Christ's natures too far apart. Schwenckfeld's profound spirituality combined with his genial manner had won him the goodwill of important figures in the Confederation, and men such as Bullinger and Vadianus found themselves having to assert rather abstract theological verities in order to discredit him.[56] The laity were hardly impressed by these preachers who now seemed to find the letter preferable to the spirit. As with Zwingli's denunciation of the Anabaptists, the ferocity of the polemic was a good indication of how close to the bone Schwenckfeld's ideas were. He was not a Zwinglian, never resident in the Confederation, nor was he ever a member of the Reformed Churches, but this man who was so influential in German Pietism and religious movements in the New World, shared a great deal with Swiss evangelical thought. The legacy of Zwingli was by no means confined to the confessions and catechisms of the established churches.

The Italians

Following 1542 and the establishment of the Roman Inquisition hundreds of religious refugees made their way north to find security in the Swiss Confederation. Many settled in the Rhaetian-ruled territories of the Valtellina, Bormio, and Chiavenna, where they were able to live in relative peace. Some, however, found that their ideas of apostolic Christianity did not square with the established Reformed Churches of the north, and soon doctrinal conflict broke out. The first battle erupted in Chiavenna around the figure of the Sicilian Camillo Renato, a man accused by his opponents of holding Anabaptist and extreme sacramentarian views.[57] These radical figures were not prophets in the wilderness; rather, they were deeply wedded to Zwingli's theology, in particular to his call for scriptural purity and a symbolic understanding of the Lord's Supper. When they arrived in the Confederation the Italian evangelicals were appalled by the level of what appeared to be compromise on the part of the Reformed church leaders. Bullinger and others had watered down the purity of Zwingli's thought in order to retain the support of the magistrates. It was a confrontation of cultures. There had never been an evangelical church in Italy; those who had converted to the cause were largely drawn to the principles of *sola scriptura* and *sola fide*, and they viewed ecclesiastical bodies and regulations with deep suspicion. In the face of persecution they developed strategies to conceal the exact nature of their beliefs. All of this proved extremely uncomfortable for the Swiss Reformed churches, which were obsessed with establishing public order and determined to demonstrate with their doctrinal formulations that their faith was consistent with the theology of the early church. Although the Swiss churches gave refuge to the Italians fleeing north, and although they avowed many of the same beliefs, the religious mentalities of these two groups were entirely different, and this led to some of the most painful episodes of the Swiss Reformation in the middle decades of the century.[58] It should be pointed out that only a minority of the Italian exiles, although one that included a significant proportion of their intellectual leadership, were unable to reach an accommodation with the Swiss churches.

A leading figure among those Italians who settled in Swiss cities was Celio Secundo Curione, a schoolmaster from Piedmont who claimed to have been converted to the Reformation by Zwingli's writings.[59] Curione became professor of Rhetoric in Basle and was a leading figure in the flourishing community of humanists in the city. It was the connection between humanism and Christian faith in Zwingli's writings which Curione most cherished and he became alarmed by the growing influence of Calvin over the Swiss churches during the 1540s. Curione shared Renato's view of the sacraments and as a humanist believer in free will he was repelled by Calvin's teaching of double predestination. In his principal work, *De Amplitudine Beati Regni Dei*, Curione limited himself to saying, in accordance with Zwingli, that the number of the elect was greater than that of the damned.[60] His emphasis was on the abundance of God's grace. Curione wrote to Bullinger expressing his worries about the authoritarianism and doctrinal rigidity of the Genevan church. Luca D'Ascia has recently argued that Curione sought to unite philosophy and theology in his writings and that he was profoundly influenced by Zwingli as well as Italian Neoplatonism.[61] Curione absorbed Zwingli's teachings on faith alone and predestination and his rejection of a mediating role for the church. D'Ascia has argued that in attempting to demonstrate the unity of religion and philosophy Curione had no intention of being bound by dogmatic positions. Curione was typical of many of the Italians living in the Swiss cities; he sought to remain faithful to his evangelical and humanist principles whilst not alarming the leaders of the established churches, who were their hosts. The *modus vivendi* was dissimulation. Works critical of key doctrines such as the Trinity were circulated among the circles of radical Italian thinkers, most of whom kept a public face of loyalty to the worship and discipline of the Reformed churches. This primarily took place in Basle, but it was also to be found in Zurich.

The defining moment for many of these Italians was the execution of the antitrinitarian Michel Servetus in Geneva in 1553.[62] This truly remarkable Spaniard, whose anatomical work was revolutionary, incurred the wrath of both Catholics and Protestants alike with his radical theological views. When he published *De Trinitatis Erroribus* (1531) and *De Trinitate* (1532) he was forced to assume the name of Michel de Villeneuve, from his family home, Villanueva, and to spend some time in Lyons, working on an edition of Ptolemy's geographical and other scientific works, then in Paris studying medicine. It was in Paris that he first met John Calvin. In his most radical work, the *Christianisimi Restitutio* (1553), Servetus developed a mature refutation of orthodox Christian theology. That same year the Spaniard, who was in the city in disguise, was apprehended in Geneva whilst attempting to make his way to Italy. He was tried and executed. Following his trial, the Genevan syndics declared:

> The sentence pronounced against Michel Servet de Villeneufve of the Kingdom of Aragon in Spain who some twenty-three or twenty-four years ago printed a book at Hagenau in Germany against the Holy Trinity containing many great blasphemies to the scandal of the said churches of Germany, the which book he freely confesses to have printed in the teeth of the remonstrances made to him by the learned and evangelical doctors of Germany. In consequence he

> became a fugitive from Germany. Nevertheless he continued in his errors and, in order the more to spread the venom of his heresy, he printed secretly a book in Vienne of Dauphiny full of the said heresies and horrible, execrable blasphemies against the Holy Trinity, against the Son of God, against the baptism of infants and the foundations of the Christian religion. He confesses that in this book he called believers in the Trinity Trinitarians and atheists. He calls this Trinity a diabolical monster with three heads. He blasphemes detestably against the Son of God, saying that Jesus Christ is not the Son of God from eternity. He calls infant baptism an invention of the devil and sorcery. His execrable blasphemies are scandalous against the majesty of God, the Son of God and the Holy spirit. This entails the murder and ruin of many souls. Moreover he wrote a letter to one of our ministers in which, along with other numerous blasphemies, he declared our holy evangelical religion to be without faith and without God and that in place of God we have a three-headed Cerberus.

And then the judgement:

> For these and other reasons, desiring to purge the Church of God of such infection and cut off the rotten member, having taken counsel with our citizens and having invoked the name of God to give just judgement … having God and the Holy scriptures before our eyes, speaking in the name of the Father, Son and Holy spirit, we now in writing give final sentence and condemn you, Michael Servetus, to be bound and taken to Champel and there attached to a stake and burned with your book to ashes. And so shall finish your days and give an example to others who would commit the like.[63]

Many of the Italians, perhaps mindful of experiences in their homeland, were shocked by the brutal death of a heretic as an act of the state. It was made worse by the news that Servetus had been tried and executed in accordance with rules employed by the Inquisition.[64] Texts were circulated which denied the right of the magistrates to put a man to death for his beliefs. At the centre of the debate was the Savoyard Sebastian Castellio, from 1552 professor of Greek in Basle, who anonymously published his work *On Heretics*, in which he compiled texts from authors ancient and contemporary as witness against the execution of Christians on account of their beliefs. Curione likely assisted in the work, which unleashed a torrent of vitriol from Geneva.

Calvin was persuaded that the Italians were all secret heretics, and following his battle with Giorgio Biandrata, who had questioned the doctrine of the Trinity, the Italian church in Geneva was purged. Most of the community ultimately conformed, while a few went east to Poland, where an antitrinitarian church was founded. Calvin wrote to the other Swiss churches warning them about the Italians, but in the cities of the Confederation their reception had been rather better. The leading figures of the Zurich church, Bullinger, Theodor Bibliander, Konrad Pellikan, and Rudolf Gwalther had, in contrast to Calvin, enjoyed good relations with many of the scholarly Italian refugees who had come north. Bibliander, for example, had no sympathy for Calvin's theology and he was more in tune with the Italian humanist emphasis on free grace and the perfectibility of the human will.[65] Also, the Italians' loyalty to Zwingli was clearly in their favour when dealing with the Zurich church. Calvin had blotted his copybook long before with uncharitable remarks about the Zurich reformer.

In 1549, whilst in Geneva, the Sienese Lelio Sozzini (1525–62) had written *On the Resurrection* in which he had questioned the immortality of the soul.[66] During travels through Germany (Wittenberg), Poland, and Italy he came in contact with men who were deeply influenced by the antitrinitarian thought of Michel Servetus. Like many of his contemporaries he was shocked by the execution of Servetus in Geneva, but he continued to remain on good terms with Calvin and Bullinger. After a time in Poland he returned to Zurich in 1559, where he wrote his most famous work, *A Brief Explanation of the First Chapter of the Gospel of John*, a work naturally on the Trinity. It is striking that one of the most influential works of antitrinitarian thought in the sixteenth century was written in Zurich. Sozzini essentially argued that Christ was a man to whom God had given divine qualities; the idea of Christ's pre-existence was wholly denied. The work remained in manuscript form and was circulated among sympathisers, particularly in Basle.

Lelio's nephew, Fausto, arrived in Zurich after his uncle's death in 1562 and read the text, which changed his whole theological perspective. Fausto wrote works building upon Lelio's thought and a distinctive theology emerged which he took to eastern Europe, where he became involved with the antitrinitarian churches.[67] Lelio's ideas, however, had already from 1560 been circulated in Moravia, Poland, and Transylvania by the Italians Nicolo Parita and Biandrata, and were then printed in an antitrinitarian anthology of 1568.[68] Lelio and Fausto, in contrast to Servetus, completely denied Christ's divinity and sought to portray him as a historical figure. Although influenced by other Italians such as Renato and Bernardino Ochino, they did not share in the illuminism or mysticism of these men, which in the case of Ochino was derived from his Capuchin background. Lelio had enjoyed a life of great favour, for despite Calvin's doubts he continued to be well treated by men such as Bullinger and Philip Melanchthon, who clearly had a great deal of affection for the Italian. Lelio was the master of dissembling, masking his radical thought behind questions and rhetorical devices. Because of this, it came as a terrible shock to Bullinger when he discovered that he had been harbouring a heretic in his home.

Bullinger had supported the execution of Servetus and he had not permitted Biandrata to remain in Zurich, but he was not by nature disposed to force people to reveal the extent of their beliefs or doubts. He was for the most part satisfied if they complied with the public face of the Reformed church and did not bring scandal or attempt to teach heresy. The thoughts of the heart, according to Bullinger, were for God to judge. This was to change with the arrival of Bernardino Ochino in Zurich.[69] The former head of the Capuchin order was one of the most spectacular converts to the Reformed church, but there were suggestions that his religious beliefs were far more radical than might have appeared to be the case. After a turbulent stay in Geneva Ochino arrived in Basle in 1544 where he came to know Curione and Castellio. He continued his peregrinations through Germany, England, and the Swiss Confederation before returning to Geneva on the day of Servetus's execution. Finally he came to Zurich where he was given the post of minister to the Italian community. Through his close contacts in Basle, including the Lucchese printer Pietro Perna, known for his radical sympathies, he published widely whilst in Zurich, but the content of his work caused unease.[70] There was the suggestion that behind his elegant prose, which appeared to argue for orthodox Reformed theology, lay a radical agenda along the lines of those living in Basle. Nothing happened until 1563 when Ochino was warned by Bullinger not to publish any more texts. By that point, however, Ochino, with the help of Curione and Castellio, had published his *Dialogi XXX*, which contained among other things repudiations of force against heretics and of monogamy. Bullinger had resisted any action against Ochino, but when some Zurich merchants in Basle were told by a Nuremberg nobleman of rumours that heretical books were being written by leading figures of the Zurich church, trouble was imminent. To prevent scandal Ochino was dismissed from his post and banished from the city. He denied the charges, but was forced to leave with his four young children and ultimately found his way to Moravia, where he died in 1564, or possibly early 1565.[71]

The Ochino affair was a turning point for the Swiss churches. Bullinger believed he had been duped; his hospitality had been abused by men who had turned out to be heretics sheltering under his wing. By the mid 1560s the Zurich church had grown impatient with radical dissent: in 1564 Antonio Mario Besozzi was expelled from the city as a supporter of Ochino. In 1571 the Italian radicals living in Rhaetian territories, especially in the Valtellina, were driven out. It was only in Basle that the radicals could find a home, and by the final decades of the sixteenth century there was little life left in the radical movement. The encroaching orthodoxy of the Genevan church was taking hold.

David Joris in Basle

The intensity of the persecution of Anabaptists in Basle in the years following the Reformation in 1529 meant that there were few radicals left in either the city or the rural areas by the early 1530s. Most, as we have seen, made their way towards Berne. Within the city, however, although it would be wrong to speak of toleration in the modern sense, religious refugees of various persuasions (including, for example, the young John Calvin) began from the mid 1530s to find a home, and no trouble was made for them as long as they remained quiet. One such example was the circle of Anabaptists who arrived with David Joris from Antwerp in 1544.[72] Joris presented himself to the Basle magistrates as one Johann van Brugge, driven from his native land on account of his evangelical beliefs. Joris lived in patrician style in the city and the Netherlandish refugees ingratiated themselves with the locals by their fine conduct and generous charity. Joris forbade his followers from revealing his true identity, and he soon became friends with other important religious dissidents in the city, such as Sebastian Castellio.

Castellio and Joris were both avid readers of the work of Sebastian Franck, from whom they both drew deeply in their thought on matters such as doctrine and the treatment of heretics. The two men worked closely together – and certainly Castellio knew van Brugge's true identity – but they did not entirely agree on matters of theology. Joris's adherence to the mystical tradition led him to a far more radical critique of Christian doctrine, and when he began to espouse antitrinitarianism his Savoyard friend had no sympathy.

By the 1550s divisions began to emerge in the Netherlandish circle in Basle as some started to lose faith in Joris's teaching. Financial difficulties were a worry, but more serious were reports from the Netherlands that van Brugge was not a nobleman, but a heretic on the run. Both Joris and his wife died before the truth was revealed but the matter was soon investigated in Basle and the faculties of law and theology declared that heretics, whether alive or dead, should be burned. Joris, as van Brugge, had been accorded a fine burial in one of the Basle churches.[73] The houses of Joris's supporters and friends (including Castellio) were searched and incriminating evidence was found. Castellio was forced to renounce any association with Joris, and along with the other professors, including Curione, he had to submit a document declaring that articles taken from Joris's writings were heretical. The primary offence was Joris's denial of the divine and human nature of Christ, although a catalogue of other heretical ideas were also attributed to his writings. Joris's followers, most of whom had disguised themselves as his household servants, were required to make a public recantation in the Basle Münster and were let off fairly lightly. On 13 May 1557 a great crowd gathered at the Steinentor in Basle for the burning of the remains of David Joris. Three weeks later, at the public recantation by thirty of Joris's supporters, Simon Sulzer preached, reminding the community and the penitents of how benevolently the council had acted when heresy had been uncovered.[74]

Sixteenth-century Basle developed a reputation, beginning in the time of Erasmus, for openness and toleration, and we cannot doubt that part of the legacy of the Dutch humanist was the radical humanist thinking which ultimately had little in common with the Reformed theology of the Swiss churches. Basle's humanist culture certainly contributed to an atmosphere of intellectual openness which was not to be found in the other cities of the Confederation. But this should not surprise us, as Basle was always different from the other Confederates; it many ways its natural terrain was the Rhineland of Germany and the Alsace. It alone had been a university city and its prominence in the fifteenth century was without rival in the Swiss lands. In 1557 Guillaume Farel wrote to Bullinger that 'what you did not allow to be published in Zurich, has been published in Basle without any difficulty'.[75] The reason for this is partly theological and partly economic: under the Lutheran-leaning Simon Sulzer in Basle, critics of Calvin and the Genevan theologians were allowed to gather in the city and their publishing activities were only moderately restrained. Essentially Sulzer turned a blind eye to the activities of Curione, Perna, Castellio, and others because it suited his purposes to do so. Alongside this mentality was the economic reality that the printing business of Basle was enormously important, and that the Europe-wide distribution of books was conducted according to laws of commerce and trade which had nothing to do with religious confession. The economic contribution of the foreigners in the city was considerable and the status brought by their presence was not something to be quickly disregarded. The convergence of these forces made Basle, for a period, a centre of critical theological thought which was most unwelcome in the Reformed churches. Soon the mood would change and such ideas would no longer find a home in the Rhenish city, but for a while Basle was perceived by some as a dangerous nest of heretics – a refuge for those who would destroy the Reformed religion in the name of a return to the Bible. Bullinger and Calvin did not find the irony amusing.

The experience of radicalism in the Swiss Reformation, whether in the form of Anabaptism or the intellectual dissent of the Italians, challenges us to reflect upon the fundamental religious character of Zwinglianism. Anabaptism broke out in Zurich at a very early date precisely because there was a radical agenda in Zwingli's thought. He had placed scripture against the established church, but had then pulled back from that polarity as soon as he realised he had to carry the magistrates with him. By that point, however, Pandora's box was open and (quite frankly) his most popular idea had spread its wings. Zwinglian theology, which privileged spirit over flesh, never sat comfortably with institutionalisation. Many of those who read Zwingli were profoundly influenced by the spiritual nature of his message, and even among the leaders of the Swiss Reformation, in men such as Leo Jud and Theodor Bibliander, the spiritualist side of Zwingli was strongly represented. It would be misleading to suggest that these important thinkers simply derived their ideas from Zwingli, for clearly they opened up lines of thought which he would never have pursued. Nevertheless, Zwinglian theology was built upon a series of dualisms and the tradition of Anabaptist, spiritualist, and radical thought in the sixteenth century bore witness to the powerful reaction countering attempts to harness that polarity by placing religion under the control of the magistrates.

Notes

1 On the origins of the movement and its relationship to other radical movements, see the important article by James M. Sayer, Werner O. Packull, and Klaus Depperman, 'From Monogenesis to Polygenesis: The Historical Discussion of Anabaptist Origins', *Mennonite Quarterly Review*, 49 (1975), pp. 83–121. Also, James M. Stayer, 'The Swiss Brethren: An Exercise in Historical Definition', *Church History* 47, (1978), pp. 174–195.

2 G.R. Potter, *Zwingli* (Cambridge, 1976), p. 176.

3 Hans-Jürgen Goertz, '"A Common Future Conversation": A Revisionist Interpretation of the September 1524 Grebel Letters to Thomas Müntzer', in Werner Packull and Geoffrey Dipple (eds), *Radical Reformation Studies. Essays Presented to James M. Stayer* (Ashgate, 1999), p. 75.

4 Ibid., p. 76.

5 Ibid., p. 78.

6 On the theology of Grebel, Mantz, and Sattler, see Hans-Georg Tanneberger, *Die Vorstellung der Täufer von der Rechtfertigung des Menschen* (Stuttgart, 1999), esp. pp. 32–76.

7 Leland Harder (ed.), *The Sources of Swiss Anabaptism: The Grebel Letters and Related Documents* (Scottdale, PA, 1985). James Stayer discusses the relationship between Müntzer and Swiss Anabaptism in his 'Saxon Radicalism and Swiss Anabaptism: The Return of the Repressed', *Mennonite Quarterly Review*, 67 (1993), pp. 5–30.

8 Goertz, '"A Common Future Conversation"', p. 83.

9 Tanneberger, *Die Vorstellung der Täufer*, pp. 43–68.

10 Goertz, *The Anabaptists*, p. 73.

11 Calvin Pater, *Karlstadt as the Father of the Baptist Movements: The Emergence of Lay Protestantism* (Toronto, 1984), pp. 117–169.

12 Peter Blickle, *The Communal Reformation* (Atlantic Highlands, NJ, 1992).

13 W. Näf, *Vadianus und seine Stadt*, 2 vols (St Gall, 1944–57), II, pp. 192–194.

14 Ibid., p. 11.

15 Martin Haas, *Huldrych Zwingli und seine Zeit* (Zurich, 1969), p. 78.

16 James M. Stayer, *The German Peasants' War and Anabaptist Community of Goods* (Montreal and Kingston, 1991), pp. 95–96.

17 Ibid., p. 98.

18 Ibid., p. 104.

19 James M. Stayer, 'Reublin and Brötli, the Revolutionary Beginnings of Swiss Anabaptism', in Marc Lienhard (ed.), *The Origins and Characteristics of Anabaptism* (The Hague, 1977), pp. 83–102.

20 See the essay by James M. Stayer, 'Anabaptists and Future Anabaptists in the Peasants' War', *Mennonite Quarterly Review*, 62 (1988), pp. 100–113.

21 Stayer, *German Peasants' War*, p. 63.

22 Torsten Bergsten, *Balthasar Hubmaier: Anabaptist Theologian and Martyr*, transl. Irwin J. Barnes and William R. Estep (Valley Forge, PA, 1978), pp. 210–214.

23 Ibid., p. 64.

24 Ibid., pp. 64–65.

25 Walter L Moore Jr, 'Catholic Teacher and Anabaptist Pupil: The Relationship between John Eck and Balthasar Hubmaier', *ARG*, 72 (1981), pp. 68–97.

26 On Hubmaier and Zwingli, see Eddie Mabry, *Balthasar Hubmaier's Doctrine of the Church* (Lanham, MD, 1994), pp. 39–45.

27 Tanneberger, *Die Vorstellung der Täufer*, pp. 97–119.

28 Mabry, *Hubmaier's Doctrine of the Church*, pp. 45–46.

29 C. Arnold Snyer, *Anabaptist History and Theology. An Introduction* (Scottdale, PA, 1995), p. 61.

30 On Sattler see C. Arnold Snyder, *The Life and Thought of Michael Sattler* (Scottdale, PA, 1984), and John H. Yoder, *The Legacy of Michael Sattler* (Scottdale, PA, 1973). Also helpful is Sean F. Winter, 'Michael Sattler and the Schleitheim Articles: A Study in the Background of the First Anabaptist Confession of Faith', *Baptist Quarterly*, 34 (1991), pp. 52–66.

31 Hans-Jürgen Goertz, *The Anabaptists* (London, 1996), p. 14.

32 Heinold Fast, 'Die Sonderstellung die Täufer in St Gallen und Appenzell', *Zwingliana* 11 (1960), pp. 223–240.

33 Fast, 'Die Sonderstellung', p. 234.

34 R. Pfister, *Kirchengeschichte der Schweiz* (Zurich, 1974), p. 175.

35 Ibid., p. 176.

36 Hanspeter Jecker, 'Die Basler Täufer. Studien zur Vor- und Frühgeschichte', *Basler Zeitschrift für Geschichte und Altertumskunde*, 80 (1980), pp. 5–131.

37 Ibid., p. 177.

38 Claus-Peter Clausen, 'Executions of Anabaptists, 1525–1618: A Research Report', *Mennonite Quarterly Review*, 47 (1973).

39 Isaac Zürcher, *Die Täufer um Bern in den ersten Jahrhunderten nach der Reformation und die Toleranz* (Berne, 1986); Ulrich Gerber, 'Berner Synodus – Berner Täufertum: Gemeinsames und Trennendes', in *Anabaptistes et dissidents au XVIe siècle* (Neukirchen, 1987), pp. 285–296.

40 Kurt Guggisberg, *Bernische Kirchengeschichte* (Berne, 1958), p. 229.

41 Arnold Snyder has studied the modes of communication employed by Anabaptist communities. His important conclusions are found in C. Arnold Snyder, 'Orality, Literacy, and the Study of Anabaptism', *Mennonite Quarterly Review*, 65 (1991), pp. 371–392.

42 Martin Haas (ed.), *Drei Täufergespräche*. Quellen zur Geschichte der Täufer in der Schweiz, IV, p. xvii.

43 See below, pp. 213–216.

44 *HBBW*, 3 (1533), pp. 83–84.

45 Guggisberg, *Bernische Kirchengeschichte*, p. 360.

46 Ibid., p. 361.

47 Heinold Fast, *Heinrich Bullinger und die Täufer. Ein Beitrag zur Historiographie und Theologie im 16. Jahrhundert* (Weierhof, 1959), p. 35.

48 J. Staedtke (ed.), *Heinrich Bullinger Werke* (Zurich, 1972), I/1, 28, p. 18.

49 Ibid., p. 41.

50 R. Emmet McLaughlin, *Caspar Schwenckfeld. Reluctant Radical. His Life to 1540* (New Haven and London, 1986), pp. 134–136.

51 Ibid., p. 126.

52 Ibid., p. 111.

53 Klaus Deppermann, 'Schwenkfeld and Leo Jud on the Advantages and Disadvantages of the State-Church', in Peter C. Erb (ed.), *Schwenkfeld and Early Schwenkfeldianism* (Pennburg, PA, 1986), pp. 211–236.

54 McLaughlin, *Caspar Schwenckfeld*, p. 161.

55 Ibid., p. 167.

56 R. Emmet McLaughlin, 'The Schwenkfeld–Vadianus Debate', in Erb (ed.), *Schwenkfeld and Early Schwenkfeldianism*, pp. 242–243.

57 George Williams, 'Camillo Renato (c. 1500–?1570)', in J. Tedeschi (ed.), *Italian Reformation Studies in Honor of Laelius Socinus* (Florence, 1965), pp. 105–183.

58 The most recent study is Mark Taplin, 'The Italian Reformers and the Zurich Church, c. 1540–1620' (PhD dissertation, University of St Andrews, 1999).

59 Markus Kutter, *Celio Secondo Curione: Sein Leben und Sein Werk (1503–1569)* (Basle, 1955).

60 Luca D'Ascia, 'Celio Secundo Curione, erasmista o antierasmista?', in Achilla Olivieri (ed.), *Erasmo Venezia e la cultura padana nel' 500* (Roviga, 1995); also, Uwe Plath, 'Der Streit um C.S. Curiones "De amplitudine beati regni Dei" im Jahre 1554 in Basel', in *Eresia e riforma* (Florence, Chicago, 1974), pp. 271–281.

61 Luca D'Ascia, 'Tra Platonismo e Riforma: Curione, Zwingli e Francesco Zorzi', *Bibliothèque d'Humanisme et Renaissance*, 61 (1999), pp. 673–699.

62 Roland Bainton, *Hunted Heretic* (Boston, 1953).

63 Cited from Charles A. Howe, *For Faith and Freedom: A Short History of Unitarianism in Europe* (Boston, 1997), p. 156.

64 Marian Hillar, *The Case of Michael Servetus (1511–1553) – The Turning Point in the Struggle for Freedom of Conscience.* Texts and Studies in Religion, 74 (Lewiston, NY, 1997). Also, Jerome Friedman, *Michael Servetus: A Case Study in Total Heresy* (Geneva, 1978).

65 Emil Egli, 'Biblianders Leben und Schriften', in his *Analecta Reformatoria II: Biographien* (Zurich, 1901), pp. 1–44.

66 John Tedeschi (ed.), *Italian Reformation Studies in Honor of Laelius Socinus* (Florence, 1965). See also, Edward M. Hulme, 'Lelio Sozzini's Confession of Faith', in *Persecution and Liberty: Essays in Honor of George Lincoln Burr* (New York, 1931), pp. 211–225.

67 Antal Pirnát, *Die Ideologie der Siebenbürgher Antitrinitarier in den 1570er Jahren* (Budapest, 1961).

68 Most recently, see Mihály Balász, *Early Transylvanian Antitrinitarianism (1566–1571): From Servet to Palaeologus* (Baden-Baden and Bouxwiller, 1996).

69 Karl Benrath, *Bernardino Ochino of Siena: A Contribution towards the History of the Reformation*, transl. Helen Zimmern (London, 1876).

70 Hans R. Guggisberg, 'Pietro Perna, Fausto Sozzini und die Dialogi quatuor Sebastian Castellios', in S. van der Woude, *Studia Bibliographica in Honorem Herman de la Fontaine Verwey* (Amsterdam, 1967), pp. 171–201.

71 Taplin, 'The Italian Reformers', pp. 107–161.

72 Gary K. Waite, *David Joris and Dutch Anabaptism 1524–1543* (Waterloo, Ont., 1990), pp. 178–187.

73 Ibid., p. 186.

74 On Joris in Basle, see Hans R. Guggisberg, *Sebastian Castellio 1515–1563. Humanist und Verteidiger der religiösen Toleranz im konfessionellen Zeitalter* (Göttingen, 1997), pp. 168–171.

75 Hans R. Guggisberg, 'Tolerance and Intolerance in Sixteenth-Century Basle', in Ole Peter Grell and Bob Scribner (eds), *Tolerance and Intolerance in the European Reformation* (Cambridge, 1996), p. 162.

7
Church-building

Much of the opposition from the Anabaptists and the radicals grew from an intense disappointment with the Reformed churches which emerged after 1525. In the eyes of their critics, the new Reformed churches were as obsessed with authority and structure as the medieval church they had supplanted. It was the gulf between ideological purity and pragmatism. The Swiss Reformed churches were born in compromise; in order to take root they had had to embrace established political, social, and economic structures. The radical theological agenda which spawned them was tempered by this accommodation, a settlement made all the more urgent by the fear engendered by the unrest of 1524–25. Nevertheless, from the late 1520s new churches began to emerge which gave expression to the fundamental aspirations of the Swiss reformers. In this chapter we shall explore the key aspects of these churches. Central to the vision was an educated, professional ministry which was able to exposit and expound scripture to the laity; that naturally leads us to an examination of printed Bibles. True religion for Zwingli was, primarily, the pure worship of God, free of idolatry, and the forms of Reformed services will be examined. Finally, the godly society required godly conduct, and the vexatious issue of church discipline, a subject on which the Swiss reformers disagreed, requires attention.

The godly society and pastoral care

At the heart of Zwingli's theology was the idea of the covenantal relationship between God and humanity.[1] In Christ is the new covenant, a relationship which is the fulfilment of the promises made by God to the Israelites; men and women are saved through faith in

Christ. Yet, just as the Lord had told the Israelites that he would be their God if they obeyed his commandments, for Zwingli, the same rules still applied. The power of the Word of God in the world was transformative, when communities respond in obedience to God's will they are made holy. A distinguishing aspect of the Swiss Reformation was its emphasis on the ordering of the world according to God's will. The Bible was treated as a law book, full of guidelines for Christian conduct and the powers of the state. It was a vision which emerged from a mixture of Swiss communalism, Luther's reading of St Paul, Erasmian humanism, and Zwingli's own experiences of the horrors of war and the mercenary service. One frequently encounters in Zwingli's writings the terms *integritas*, *sanctimonia*, and *Reinigkeit*, all terms for purity, which Zwingli linked to holiness. This emphasis on the holiness of God was taken by the Swiss reformers from Leviticus 19:2 ('Be holy because I, the Lord your God, am holy'). The condition of God's covenantal relationship was that Christian communities had to purify themselves of all defilement and keep themselves holy. For Zwingli, this connection between holiness and purity found expression in the Christian's first duty, to worship God, and again he took this from the same passage from Leviticus: 'Do not turn to idols or make gods of cast metal for yourselves. I am the Lord your God' (Lev. 19:4).[2] This was the motivation for iconoclasm. Human freedom and true service to God lay in the removal of all forms of idolatry, a rejection of the material understandings of God, and in submission to the spirit. This was Zwingli's most enduring legacy, the idea which continued to inspire long after he was gone. But, as we have seen, it was not an idea which easily leant itself to the institutional life of society.

Purity of worship and the holiness of the community chimed well with the early themes of the urban preachers, but over the course of the Reformation there was a distinct shift in emphasis. The defeat at Kappel, the failure of the Reformation to make any further progress into Catholic regions, and the realities of parish life moved the second-generation reformers to a different perspective, one shaped more clearly by their belief in predestination. The second-generation reformers were much less sanguine about the possibility of creating a godly society. They knew that the elect were few and that the ordinances of the church and state were essentially designed to keep human conduct in check; to restrain people from drinking too much, dancing, wearing inappropriate clothing, or beating their wives and children. The work of churchmen like Bullinger, Myconius, and Grynaeus was consumed in attempts to apply the theological principles of the Reformed church to the social and political realities of their time. The chasm between the ideal and reality was bridged by pastoral care, a flexible approach to religious teachings which endeavoured to meet the spiritual needs of the people.

The reformers stripped the church of most of its intercessory powers and rites; the saints and Mary, so beloved by the Swiss, were withdrawn. Yet the Reformed ministers still had to explain the world and how God was present in it. The theological and humanist discourses which created the intellectual world of the Reformed churches meant nothing to the people in the parish churches. The reformers had to speak to the artisans and farmers in a different language; they had to bring comfort and consolation in a world where people could no longer turn to the familiar figures of the saints. The reformers did not do this as critical outsiders, for they too suffered the vicissitudes of sixteenth-century life: they, their wives, and children died of the plague, they went hungry when crops failed (which occurred often in the second half of the century), and, most importantly, they believed that human actions brought the direct intervention of God in the world, whether to reward or punish. The reformers may have banished many of the old rites, but they did not dispense with the belief that humans still negotiated their relationship with God in the world. In both the pastoral care of the Reformed ministers and the daily lives of men and women in the parishes a residual belief in the efficacy of the power of good works and in intercession was clearly evident. That this flexible attitude towards God, the world, and human nature, did not easily square with some central points of Reformed theology was evident, yet it was not especially troublesome for men like Heinrich Bullinger, who understood that in his different capacities he had to emphasise different aspects of the faith.[3] Bullinger saw himself as a bishop in the tradition of John Chrysostom, responsible for the provision of pastoral care as well as the training and supervision of the ministers.

Education and the ministry

The Reformation drew upon the growing literacy of the laity by emphasising the responsibility of each Christian to enter into an active relationship with God through obedience to his Word as found in the Bible. For the reformers, the primacy of faith depended upon access to the Bible, and Luther had made his name by proclaiming *sola scriptura* and *sola fide* in the same breath. Zwingli's preaching, as we have seen, attacked the perceived materialism of late medieval religion and emphasised Christian freedom. God is spirit, Zwingli frequently quoted from the Gospel of John, and must be worshipped in spirit. There was in his early preaching an explicit criticism of the hierarchical church and a strong hint of anticlericalism; the critique was grounded in the unflattering comparison of the institution and practices of the church with the commands of Christ as found in scripture.

But who was to interpret scripture? What made one reading of a passage more authoritative than another? The quick rise of the radicals in Zurich and their spread across the Confederation brought that question into relief. In a society where literacy rates were low – in the rural areas virtually non-existent – what could *sola scriptura* mean? Few could read the Bible, and even fewer could make sense of it. The records of the Swiss churches are full of accounts of men and women who, often disastrously, emulated actions of biblical characters in the belief that this constituted obedience to God's Word. The Swiss Reformation of the sixteenth century was marked by the multivalency of religious beliefs; the contradictions and incompatibilities were legion as men and women struggled to understand what the Bible was saying to them. Like life, their religion was profoundly inconsistent, and, as Luther and Zwingli had dramatically demonstrated, there was more than one way to interpret a simple sentence of the Bible.

The early years of the Reformation had been marked by sanguine hopes that the unfettered Gospel would carry all before it. Luther's quarrels in Wittenberg, the rise of radicalism in Zurich, and the Peasants' War, were dark omens that the Reformation would fall at the first hurdle unless some form of authority was established. For Luther and Zwingli this authority was derived from their belief that they were called to prophetic offices in the tradition of the Old and New Testaments. If the Reformation was to survive, however, this prophetic authority had to be translated from a few charismatic individuals to some sort of institutional basis. Central to this process was the establishment of an educated ministry capable of instructing and guiding the faithful.[4] Ministers, using Zwingli's favoured biblical image of the 'Good Shepherd', were intended to instruct, for the Christian faith was held to be something eminently teachable, and it was the duty of each Christian to understand the basics.[5] The influence of Erasmus was profound. Like many of the Dutch humanist's students, Zwingli believed that educational reform was integral to religious renewal, for only Christian learning could banish superstition and idolatry. The way had been opened in Zurich with the reform of the Grossmünster chapter in 1524. The secularisation of religious houses across the Confederation led to the founding of schools, and during the sixteenth century, drawing upon changes begun in the fifteenth, there was a transformation of education at all levels. This, however, did not proceed effortlessly. Shortages of money, the constant threat of war, and persistent economic hardships in the rural areas required magistrates to deploy their financial resources prudently, and frequently this meant emptying the pockets of the church. Bullinger faced the bitter disappointment of losing resources intended for the schools to the more worldly interests of the Zurich council. This experience was to repeat itself across the Protestant lands of the Confederation, but times were very hard.

The *Prophezei* in Zurich

On 19 June 1525 the *Prophezei* opened in the Grossmünster, thus commencing the first chapter of Reformed higher education. The name, which was subsequently given to the meetings, was derived from the Greek word for 'prophecy', following Zwingli's interpretation of 1 Corinthians 14: 26–33, where Paul says 'it is for prophets to control prophetic inspiration, for the God who inspires them is not a God of disorder but of peace.'[6] The foundation of the institution was drawn from Zwingli's circle of friends, or sodality, which had been meeting regularly to interpret scripture. The intention for the *Prophezei* was, following Paul's instructions to the Corinthians, quite simple: the learning of those who were trained scholars of the Bible was to be put to the service of the church. Instruction was closely linked to worship, as the fruits of prophetic wisdom were communicated to the faithful in the daily sermon. This, for Zwingli was the bridge between the spirit and the institutional form of the church.

The *Prophezei* was only for the interpretation of the Old Testament. Among its first goals was the production of a German translation of the prophetic books of the Bible, and this was achieved in 1529. Its first teacher was a native son, Jakob Ceporin, from Dinhard (Zurich territory), a talented linguist who had studied in Cologne and possessed an impressive and, for Zurich, a unique knowledge of Greek, Latin, and Hebrew. Scholars of Greek and especially Hebrew were thin on the ground. Ceporin had been Zwingli's Hebrew instructor and fully supported the reformer's educational goals. His duties were twofold: daily in the *Prophezei* he was to explicate the Hebrew text, whilst on alternate days in the theological school he was to teach Greek and Hebrew.

The opening of the *Prophezei* in Zurich was delayed on account of the radical challenge in the city during 1524–25; one key issue between the parties was the vexed question of whether or not laymen were to preach. This point divided the Zurich church, and eventually Felix Mantz and Konrad Grebel founded their own, alternative '*prophezei*'. For Zwingli and his circle, the goals of the *Prophezei* in the Grossmünster could be identified as the reading of the text in the original language, the exegesis of the text using humanist principles, and the translation of the exegesis into the vernacular. Zwingli had determined, in his reply to the question of lay preaching, that a trained ministry was essential, and that the mark of a such a ministry was knowledge of biblical languages. Given that the vast majority of the ministers of the newly formed church in Zurich had previously been parish priests, this remained a distant goal. However, as Karin Maag has shown, the goal proved reachable with the education of subsequent generations of ministers.[7]

The *Prophezei* met in the choir of the Grossmünster each weekday at 8 a.m., with the exception of Fridays and market days. For the members of the Grossmünster chapter, the city clergy and students of both Latin schools attendance was obligatory; laymen and laywomen could attend at no cost. As the sessions were in Latin, the number of people who could derive any benefit from the meetings was severely limited. The form of the sessions was simple: an opening prayer in Latin was followed by a reading of the text from the Vulgate. Ceporin then read the Hebrew text and translated it into Greek and Latin, giving a full explanation of its philological import. Zwingli then read the text from the Septuagint (Greek) and translated it into Latin, giving a theological explication. Finally Leo Jud gathered the fruits of the morning's learning in a sermon which he would deliver in German to the wider community. Jud was the public face of the *Prophezei*.

Across the Limmat in the Fraumünster, the New Testament was being treated in a similar manner by Oswald Myconius, friend and colleague of Zwingli and Jud. One year before the foundation of the *Prophezei* Myconius had begun his *lectiones publicae* in the Latin school attached to the Fraumünster. These were held in German, and following the abolition of the mass in the city, the lectures were moved to the choir of the church. Myconius taught in the afternoon in order to avoid conflicting with the *Prophezei*, and it was a measure of Zwingli's public engagements that he took an active role in these afternoon sessions, as his annotations to the New Testament, later printed in 1539, indicate.

The development of education and biblical exegesis in Zurich was complicated. Insufficient funds to finance the reform of education along the lines envisaged, the persistence of opposition within the city to the Reformation, and the swelling dispute with Luther all served to deflect Zwingli from his pedagogical work. There were also terrible setbacks: just before Christmas 1525 Ceporin collapsed from overwork and died, depriving Zurich of its most gifted Hebraist. It was several months before a replacement could be found, but in Konrad Pellikan Zwingli procured a highly talented scholar.[8] The torrential pace of change in the 1520s, set against the background of constant theological controversy and political instability, meant that the educational reforms emerged piecemeal. Basically, we can identify three streams: the *lectiones publicae* (*Prophezei*), principally taught by Zwingli and Pellikan; the Arts faculty, where Collin and Ammann taught Latin, dialectic, and rhetoric; and the Fraumünster lectures of Myconius and Zwingli. Historians have debated exactly how these institutions were related to one another, but in the period before Bullinger it seems that no strict distinctions were made.

What is clear is the extent to which the whole edifice was held together by Zwingli. He was the principal theologian and biblical scholar: Pellikan's work was largely philological, while Leo Jud and Kaspar Megander worked closely with Zwingli, but mostly as editorial assistants. It is difficult for us to know exactly what Zwingli did, as little of the public lectures have survived. During the years 1525–31 Zwingli preached and wrote commentaries on Genesis, Exodus, Psalms, Isaiah, Jeremiah, and several of the minor prophets, but only the notes from Isaiah and Jeremiah exist in his hand, the others were edited by Megander and Jud. A debate among scholars lingers as to how much is authentic Zwingli, though given the manner in which Leo Jud worked it is likely that he faithfully reproduced Zwingli's words.

The relationship between the *lectiones* in the *Prophezei* and Zwingli's preaching seems to have been that Zwingli held sermons on the Old Testament books some months after he lectured on them in the Grossmünster. He was also working on translations of these books for the Zurich Bible. Zwingli would listen to Jud preach at the end of the session of the *Prophezei*, for the sermon would be the synopsis of what Zwingli and Pellikan had squeezed from their texts.[9] These *Prophezei* sermons would then serve as notes for Zwingli's own sermons and translations of the text. Thus the *Prophezei* served two purposes: it was to educate the clergy and laity, and, secondly, it was a workshop for the production of biblical commentaries and translations.

The disaster at Kappel in October 1531 threatened to undo the achievement of the 1520s. Zwingli and his followers were roundly blamed for having led Zurich into a disastrous campaign of civil war, and following the reformer's death many of his followers went into hiding as the defeated army returned home eager to lynch the clerics. The *Prophezei* looked as though it would fall victim to the designs of the Zurich magistrates, who needed the money of the Grossmünster chapter to pay war reparations as part of the Second Peace of Kappel.[10] Bullinger, who had taught at the monastery of Kappel, made education a primary concern when he was chosen to succeed Zwingli in 1532. He reformed the structure of the Latin schools and developed the provision for formal theological education through the founding of the *Lectorium*. After four or five years at the Latin schools young men of age seventeen or eighteen would enter the *Lectorium*, where they would study Greek and Latin texts, rhetoric, dialectic, the biblical languages, and scriptural exegesis.[11]

Bullinger's interest in education was primarily directed towards preparing young men to serve as ministers in the rural parishes, but as the *Lectorium* began to take shape during the 1530s it was also seen as the breeding-ground for future professors. In comparison with the Genevan Academy the achievements of the Zurich *Lectorium* were modest. Karin Maag has estimated that in the period between 1560–1620 (there are no matriculation records before 1559) approximately 800 students studied at the *Lectorium*. Just under half of those students were from Zurich itself whilst most of the others came from other parts of the Swiss Confederation, or lands linked to the Confederation. Interestingly, the greatest number of non-Zurich students came from the Graubünden in the east, an area where the Zurich Reformed church had exercised considerable influence.[12] Essentially, the influence of the *Lectorium* was regional, training local boys to be ministers, but it marked an important step in the evolution of Reformed theological education. As Maag has shown, there was considerable co-operation between Zurich and Geneva under the leadership of Bullinger and Beza: student exchanges took place offering young men the chance to learn French and German. The Academy in Geneva was more intellectually high-powered, yet during the sixteenth century students from the Reformed churches started to tour higher education centres in Europe. Geneva was one stop, but the universities in Heidelberg and Basle enjoyed greater status. The Zurich council actively supported these foreign tours of theological faculties and thus played its part in the formation of international Protestant networks.

The *Lectorium* in Zurich was not tightly regulated. Degrees were not granted and attendance was open. The typical student was between sixteen and twenty, and he studied for three to four years, but the audience for the lectures was mixed: next to young students sat ministers from the parishes, visitors from across Europe – whether religious refugees or merchants – and distinguished reformers. The lectures were public and without charge. There were four professors: Konrad Pellikan and Theodor Bibliander, who were *Professores theologici* (Old Testament); Rudolf Collin (Greek) and Johann Jakob Ammann (rhetoric and dialectic). In 1540 a fifth chair for natural philosophy and natural history was added with the appointment of Konrad Gesner. The professors would lecture each day for an hour and were paid by benefices from the Grossmünster. Remuneration was a mixture of money and goods, usually grain and wine. The level of payment is not easy to determine in modern terms, but we do know that Konrad Pellikan, on the basis of his income, was able to purchase his own house in 1542 and then ten years later purchased a second for his son.[13]

With the arrival of the Reformation in Berne in 1528 there was a similar need to make provision for the training and education of ministers. Kaspar Megander, who had been sent by Zwingli to Berne with the brief of modelling the nascent church after the example of Zurich, undertook this task with speed. Megander had only played a subordinate role in the Zurich *Prophezei*, but his humanist credentials were sound, and he knew his biblical languages. Alongside Megander were Sebastian Hofmeister (Hebrew) and the schoolmaster Johann Müller von Rellikon (Rhellikan). Rhellikan had studied in Wittenberg and taught dialectic and rhetoric.[14] In May 1528 the three began their *lectiones publicae*, the foundation of theological education in the city. The format followed the Zurich *Prophezei*: on Tuesdays and Thursdays in the choir of the Münster an Old Testament passage was read in Latin, Greek (Septuagint), and Hebrew before being subjected to critical interpretation. As in Zurich, the fruits of the exegesis were translated into German in the form of a sermon designed for lay ears.

All, however, was not well. Berchtold Haller, the church leader in Berne, wrote to Bullinger in 1532 that only Megander and Rhellikan were really able to understand the texts in Latin, Greek, and Hebrew. The situation in Berne was not aided by the departure of Hofmeister, whose quavering voice proved insufficient in the cavernous Münster. He went to Zofingen to defend the Reformed church against Catholics, only to die in 1533 from a sudden stroke whilst in the pulpit, leaving Megander and Rhellikan to labour on.

In 1535 the *lectiones* shifted to the Franciscan house, which became the leading school in Berne – a position it would retain until the nineteenth century. To prepare students for *das Kloster*, as the school became known, there were Latin schools in the city and rural areas. Many of these schools were crafted from the secularisation of religious houses in Thun, Zofingen, Brugg, and Burgdorf. Although during the sixteenth century the development of education was to pass into the hands of the magistrates, it was a long time before uniformity of practice was achieved. In the early years the curricula remained somewhat haphazard; Bullinger sent his text on study to Berchtold Haller in 1532 and two years later Simon Sulzer was engaged by the council to draw up a programme of study.[15] Essentially, until the middle of the century education remained in private hands; it was not until the school ordinance of 1548 that changes were effected, and it was not until 1575 that a separate authority with responsibility for schools was founded. As in Zurich, the *Prophezei* was really only the beginning point: soon academic study was separated from the edification of the laity. What remained of the *Prophezei*s in Zurich and Berne for common men and women was a morning sermon; the linguistic exercises were removed to the schools, which emphasised the humanist tools of dialectic, rhetoric and exegesis. In both cities care was taken to make provision for impecunious students; in Berne digs were provided in the Franciscan house, eventually providing places for twenty students. From 1539 students were provided with money in order to promote their zeal for learning.

The intellectual culture in Berne was greatly enhanced by the founding of a library in 1540 for the professors and students. This was aided by the arrival of printing: Matthias Apiarius came to the city in 1537 to found a print shop, to be followed two years later by Sebastian Franck. Printing in Berne remained modest, but by the middle of the century impressive editions of Franck's *Chronica* and Leo Jud's *Proverbia Salomonis* had appeared.

Following the Bernese conquest of the Pays de Vaud in 1536 there was a concern to establish the Reformed religion among the French-speaking laity, and this required a trained ministry. In the wake of the Disputation of Lausanne the *Schola Lausannensis* was founded in January 1537. It had a Latin school and *schola divina* to instruct men in theology. The two parts were known collectively as the Lausanne Academy, and it remained until the founding of the Genevan Academy in 1559 the only Protestant school for French-speaking students. Following the models in Zurich and Berne, the Academy was to provide students with instruction in biblical languages and theology. The first head of the Academy was Pierre Viret, a native of the Pays de Vaud, who was supported by the Zurich humanist, Konrad Gesner. Berne and Strasbourg served as models for the developing Academy in Lausanne, and in 1547 the number of professorial chairs was increased to four (philosophy, Hebrew, Greek, theology). With the arrival of Theodor Beza in 1549 the Academy really began to acquire an international reputation, bringing students from France, Poland, England, and Scandinavia.[16] Among the prominent theologians of the sixteenth century who passed through Lausanne as students we can count Kaspar Olevian and Zacharias Ursinus, authors of the *Heidelberg Catechism* and Guy de Brès, author of the *Belgic Confession* of 1561.

It was a matter of church doctrine which brought about the fall of the Lausanne Academy; a growing Calvinist party among the teachers rejected the Zwinglianism of the Bernese church and demanded a separate ecclesiastical discipline. The matter came to a head in 1558 when Beza left Lausanne for Geneva and Viret was dismissed and left for France. Many of the French students followed

Viret. The dispute greatly weakened the academy, and in the wake of the founding of another academy in Geneva, Lausanne struggled. It was only the desire of the Bernese magistrates to maintain an institution for the education of ministers in the Pays de Vaud – and Berne's hostility to Calvin's Geneva – which ensured its survival.

The situation in Basle was radically different on account of its university. Basle alone among the Swiss Protestant cities had an institution which could grant academic degrees, and we have seen how many of the Swiss reformers had spent some of their student years in the city on the Rhine. The university, under the influence of Oecolampadius reopened after the Reformation in 1529, and in the autumn of 1532 it began to receive students.[17] By 1539, after a bitter dispute between the clergy and magistrates, all of the ministers of the city and rural areas were required to enter the theological faculty. Unlike Zurich and Berne, which had to found educational bodies to train ministers, Basle had an established theological faculty, and already in the 1530s it obtained the services of some very distinguished scholars. Some of the first professors in Basle following the Reformation included Andreas Bodenstein von Karlstadt, Simon Grynaeus, and Sebastian Münster. Although Erasmus formally had nothing to do with the university, he was close to many of the professors and his presence in the city was a principal enticement in attracting men of high quality. One of Erasmus's legacies to the city was an endowment to support poor students of the university.[18]

The sixteenth and early seventeenth centuries were a brilliant age for the university in Basle, a period lasting from the early 1530s until the outbreak of the Thirty Years' War. The work of Grynaeus and Münster will be discussed below, but there are many others worthy of mention. Sebastian Castellio, proponent of religious toleration and opponent of Calvin, was professor of Greek, while Johannes Oporinus was a printer, a Greek scholar, and professor of rhetoric. It was his press which produced the first edition of Calvin's *Institutes of the Christian Religion* (1536), and in 1543 Oporinus was to cause a Europe-wide sensation by printing Theodor Bibliander's translation of the Koran.[19] Other works of international importance from Oporinus included Vesal's *Anatomy* of 1543. Oporinus also had close links with the Italian refugees in Basle and his workshop became an important centre for the production of books intended to be sent back into Italy.

During this period academic dynasties emerged: the Amerbachs in jurisprudence; the Bernoulli and Eulers, who made Basle one of the most important places in Europe for the study of physics and mathematics; and the Buxtorfs, who held the chair of Hebrew from 1550 until 1732. The medical faculty reached its zenith towards the end of the century with men such as Felix Platter, Theodor Zwinger, and Caspar Bauhin. In theology men such as Johann Jacob Grynaeus, Sebastian Beck, and Samuel Werenfels led the way towards the formation of Protestant orthodoxy. The richness of cultural life in Basle found expression in the collections amassed by scholars which were to become the basis for museums in the city. The university had its museum, whilst the museums of natural history, art, and history in the city owe much of their material to the sixteenth-century collectors in Basle.

In contrast to Zurich, Berne, and Geneva, Basle's university was an international institution, drawing students from England, Germany, France, Holland, Poland, Scandinavia, and Italy. The intellectual life in the city owed much to a happy conjunction of factors: Basle's prominent place on the Rhine, its printing industry, the medieval university and the presence of many leading scholars. The arrival of religious refugees, principally from Italy and France, greatly enhanced the variegated nature of the intellectual culture. This is to be observed in men such as Secundo Curione and Sebastian Castellio. Sixteenth-century Basle was not, however, the haven of toleration it has been portrayed in later scholarship. The regent of the university, among his many duties, was responsible for book censorship in the city, and this was carried out with zeal, as Castellio found during his quarrel with Calvin in the 1550s. From the period of Erasmus through to the death of Simon Sulzer Basle retained a reputation for irenicism, but with the advent of the orthodoxy the city not only shifted towards the theological views of Beza's Geneva, but it became a centre of Reformed scholasticism.

The Bible

From his arrival in Zurich the study of the Bible was central to the life and work of Huldrych Zwingli: his 1518 edition of the Greek New Testament, published in Venice by Aldus Manutius, was his daily companion. He met with friends and colleagues in family homes, a circle known as the *Sodalitium Literarium Tigurinense*, to discuss biblical passages and their importance for the reform of the church. During these early years Zwingli concentrated on the Hebrew scriptures, improving his grasp of the ancient language, but his mind was turned to making the Bible more available to the laity, and in 1522 he addressed the clergy of Zurich on the importance of learning scripture.[20]

In terms of printing and intellectual culture, Zurich was a backwater. Basle, as we know, was home to Erasmus during the 1520s and through the efforts of Adam Petri it had become one of the most important centres for the printing of both Luther's early works and his Bible.[21] Erasmus's Greek and Latin edition of the New Testament had appeared from the press of his good friend Johannes Froben in Basle in 1516; this more than any other work shaped the character of the Swiss Reformation. At the same time between 1517 and 1527 there was a torrent of works by Luther printed in the city, made possible by enthusiastic supporters of the Wittenberg professor among the printing trade, men such as Froben, Pamphilus Gengenbach, Valentin Curio, and Andreas Cratander.[22] Four months after the first printing of Luther's New Testament in Wittenberg in September 1522 an edition was produced in Basle, and Petri would reprint it at least a dozen times before 1527.[23] The enthusiasm of these printers for Luther and the evangelical cause is arresting, but it must not be forgotten that Luther was something of a cash cow, and businessmen like Froben were well aware of the enormous market for pamphlets written by the German reformer. It has recently been argued that it was Wolfgang Capito who played a crucial role in working with Froben to produce these works of Luther and that Capito anonymously wrote prefaces to some of the works.[24] In the period before the adoption of the Reformation in Basle the Luther controversy, following on the heels of Erasmus, had been an enormous boon for the printing industry in the city. Ironically, this came to an end when Basle embraced the Reformation, by which point the atmosphere between Wittenberg and Zurich had become so poisoned that Basle had no choice but to stand by Zwingli.

In Zurich, Zwingli from 1523 had been contemplating a German edition of the Bible, and the Grossmünster reforms of 1523, which led to the founding of the *Prophezei*, seemed a good starting point. Through Leo Jud, who had translated Erasmus's paraphrases of the Pauline Epistles, Zwingli made contact with the printer Christoph Froschauer.[25] Little is known about Froschauer – even the date of his arrival in Zurich is uncertain – but he was probably born in Oberbayern around 1490, an illegitimate son raised by an uncle in Augsburg. Froschauer came to Zurich some time between 1513 and 1516 and by 1519 had joined the guild *Zur Saffran*, becoming a citizen in the same year. His first printed work appeared in 1521 and it was in his house that the breaking of the Lenten fast took place in 1522; it has been assumed that he was won to the evangelical cause by Jud and Zwingli. Froschauer was one of the most important figures of the early Swiss Reformation not only for his printing, but for his international contacts. He travelled every year to the Frankfurt book fair, which until the 1550s remained the most important part of his sales, carrying letters, gathering news, and exchanging contracts with printers in the empire. Froschauer was crucial in making the work of Zwingli known in Germany.

The first New Testament to appear in Zurich came in 1524 and was likely the work of Zwingli, Jud, and Konrad Pellikan, who had worked on the Basle edition of Luther's Bible.[26] The 1524 Zurich Bible was an adapted version of the Basle edition; the Saxon language of Luther's Bible was not appropriate for Swiss ears and the Zurich reformers set about rendering High German into Alemanic vernacular. The alterations went beyond linguistic accommodations and extended to theology. In changing many of Luther's key terms Zwingli signalled a different interpretation of many texts. One well-known example is how Luther's *gerechtickeyt* (justificiation) became, in Zwingli's edition *fromkeit* in the translation of the Pauline Epistles. The differences between the two bibles were underscored in the gloss prepared by the Zurichers. The glosses were printed marginal notes for the reader, providing clear guidance on how the passage was to be interpreted, and it is here that we find early expression of Zwingli's teaching on the Lord's Supper. A recent study of Zwingli's biblical work has concluded that the 1524 Bible marked the reformer's central interests as justification and ethics, thus placing him between Luther and Erasmus.[27] This is an overstatement. We have argued in chapter 2 that Zwingli's understanding of justification did not differ significantly from Luther's, it was rather more a case of emphasis.[28] The principal difference between the two was over how God's grace is conveyed to humanity; where Luther looked to the word preached or said over the bread and wine to bring faith, Zwingli sought to keep the divine and human as far apart as possible, attributing everything to God. It was two very different theological structures and they were not compatible.

Froschauer's octavo edition of the Bible in 1524 was hugely popular and must be seen alongside the developing theological positions in Zurich. The most important of these, as we have seen, was the idea of prophecy. The provenance of Zwingli's thought of prophecy as biblical interpretation was likely in the works of Ambrose and Erasmus. The word 'prophecy' is evident in the 1524 Bible, the rendering of Luther's *Weissagen* and the Greek προρητάζω. The frequency of the glosses suggest that the Old Testament prophets were of central interest to Zwingli in the years 1523–25. The key text in the development of prophecy in Zurich was 1 Corinthians 14:5: 'Now I would like all of you to speak in tongues, but even more to prophesy. One who prophesies is greater than one who speaks in tongues, unless someone interprets, so that the church is built up.' Zwingli's gloss on this text in the 1524 Bible is the first evidence for the word *Prophezeien* to be used in terms of exegesis.[29] It was during the summer of 1524 that Zwingli was developing his idea of the twofold nature of the prophetic office and of his own self-understanding as a prophet.

The 1525 folio edition of the Old Testament produced in Zurich continued to follow Luther's translation, but here we see for the first time the impressive woodcuts which were to distinguish later Zurich editions. The iconoclasm and debates over images from 1523 in Zurich seem to have had no influence on the place of pictures in the early Bibles printed in this period. The intention of the woodcuts which accompanied Holy Writ was pedagogical; they were to make the text as comprehensible as possible, though they were intentionally smaller than those found in Wittenberg and Basle editions, making the point that the images were not to distract from essentials. Further, the 1525 Old Testament came with a map that was to aid readers in placing events in their historical and geographical contexts. Like the New Testament of 1524 there were numerous linguistic changes from Luther's translation, though in the case of the Old Testament the Zurichers often had recourse to the Hebrew original in preference to Luther's use of the Septuagint and the Vulgate. It is now thought that the work on the Hebrew text was undertaken by Zwingli, who was a better linguist than Jud. From September 1527 until January 1529 the *Prophezei* in Zurich was engaged in the study of the prophets, and in March 1529 the *Prophetenbibel* appeared from Froschauer's press with an anonymous preface by Zwingli. The title page of the volume indicated that this translation was the work of the 'preachers of Zurich', though few doubted the seminal role played by Zwingli. In Lutheran polemic Zwingli was frequently branded a 'mere philosopher' who had an insufficient grasp of scripture. There was a certain irony in this pejorative tag, for in his student days Zwingli was called the 'Philosopher' on account of his fondness for Aristotle. His careful scholarship in the preparation of the 1531 Bible revealed that not only was his theology not simply drawn from philosophical texts, but that Zwingli was among the most skilled biblical exegetes of his generation.

The major achievement in biblical translation during Zwingli's time was the 1531 Zurich Bible. This work was an amalgam of the revised version of Luther's translation of the historical books of the Old Testament, his New Testament, and the Zurich translations of the prophets and the Apocrypha. The poetic books of the Old Testament, which the *Prophezei* had studied between February 1529 and February 1530, were the latest texts to be added. The technical achievements of this edition were impressive: Zwingli wrote chapter summaries for the whole Bible, and a massive concordance consisting of 14,775 parallel texts alongside 1,800 marginal notes was appended. The Bible also had two appendices: a general one as well as one for selected theological themes. The sheer beauty of the text is stunning: Froschauer, in his choice of type, sought to bring an elegance to the Bible which reflected its status. The technical and artistic quality of the Bible were the visible expression of the humanist scholarship now residing in Zurich. The 1531 Bible is a feast for the eyes. Of the 190 woodcuts 140 were first-time prints by Hans Holbein the younger. This work reflected the amazing speed with which humanist biblical scholarship had taken root in Zurich, yet as one admires its handsome pages with their cross-references, notes, and woodcuts it becomes very apparent that the Word of God is being presented with a particular interpretation. Within ten years, the Zurich Reformation had produced a Bible which told men and women how it was to be understood, and those who sanctioned the interpretations were a small band of theologians in the city. The principles of 'scripture alone' or the 'pure scripture' had been considerably modified in light of the Peasants' War, Anabaptism, the attacks of Johannes Eck and the Catholic theologians, and disputes with the Lutherans.

The theological underpinnings of the Zurich Bible are evident in its structure. Unlike the Luther Bible, where the Apocrypha was placed at the end, in the Zurich Bible it was found after the historical books. This was intended to enable the smooth transition from the prophetic books to the New Testament, giving expression to Zwingli's understanding of the prophetic link between the Old Testament and Christ. In this arrangement we find Zurich's rejection of Luther's law/Gospel dialectic, on the one hand, and the radical reformers' repudiation of the Old Testament on the other.[30] The Zurich Bible expressed the polity of the Old Testament kings which Zwingli had appropriated for the magistrates as well as the covenantal theology which would receive mature expression during the time of Heinrich Bullinger.

During the sixteenth century about 120 editions of the Bible, either in parts or the whole, were printed in Zurich. Following the death of Zwingli in 1531 the work was carried on by men of considerable international reputation: Leo Jud, Konrad Pellikan, and Theodor Bibliander. Jud, Zwingli's closest friend and confidant, had willingly lived in the reformer's shadow during the 1520s, but in the decade remaining to him following the battle of Kappel he showed himself capable of sophisticated textual work. The Zurich Bible of 1534, prepared under his guidance, not only corrected errors of 1531 but contained new chapter summaries and more parallel texts. Jud, who had begun his career as a reformer in translating the biblical paraphrases of Erasmus, also added new translations of the historical, poetic, prophetic, and apocryphal books. These would appear in the octavo Bible of 1542 and the richly illustrated Bible of 1546, both of which are monuments to his now rather forgotten scholarship.

There were at least forty editions of the Bible in German produced in Zurich in the sixteenth century. Latin Bibles were also produced: Konrad Pellikan and Rudolf Gwalther had prepared revised versions of the Vulgate, but there was a desire to produce a new Latin translation in accordance with humanist scholarship. The first of these to be produced in Zurich was Konrad Pellikan's version of 1539, a reworking of the Basle Latin Bible of Erasmus and Sebastian Münster, which had been printed in 1535. The first entirely 'Reformed' Latin Bible, however, was the final labour of Leo Jud, who had worked on it through the 1530s until illness brought the curtain down. His colleagues Bibliander, Gwalther, Pellikan, Michael Adam, and Peter Collin stepped in and the *Biblia Sacrosancta* appeared in 1543, a year after Jud's death. The work was well received in the scholarly world and was reprinted in Spain, France, and Germany.

In the second half of the sixteenth century the pace of Bible translation and production slackened. Bibles continued to be produced, but Zurich was no longer the centre of intellectual development. From Geneva came the Bible of Robert Estienne in 1557 and Theodor Beza produced his Latin New Testament in 1557. The Swiss Reformed Bibles after 1550 reflected the changing theological dynamic; themes such as predestination, Christology and the sacraments were very much at the heart of the prefaces and dogmatic summaries, and the emphasis was upon a more Calvinist understanding of these topics.

Basle and Zurich very much dominated the production of Bibles in the Swiss Confederation. Berne produced none of its own during the sixteenth century, waiting until the Piscator Bible of 1640 for its own edition. In the Graubünden the most important figure was Jachiam Bifrun (1506–72), who wrote his *Fuorma*, a catechism in Rhaetish, published in 1552 by the printer Landolf in Poschiavo. Bifrun was deeply influenced by Pietro Paulo Vergerio, former bishop of Capo d'Istria, who was printing large amounts of material in the Graubünden for circulation in Italy.

Worship

The Reformed churches abolished most of the important dates of the Catholic Christian year. In Zurich the mandate of 1526 left only Christmas, Candlemas, the Annunciation, the Assumption, the feasts of John the Baptist, Mary Magdalene, All Saints, and the patronal feast of Felix and Regula. In 1530 this was further reduced to only those pertaining to Christ. In Berne the Annunciation remained until the nineteenth century. Otherwise the Christian year consisted only of Christmas, Easter, and Pentecost. There were, however, some variations within the Reformed churches: in Basle the Ascension of Christ was marked, while Appenzell kept Good Friday. In other churches, the Circumcision of Christ and Maundy Thursday remained. Basle was unique in retaining saints' days, and on these days the people went to church to remember the martyrs of the Christian church from its earliest days.

The normal expectation after the Reformation was that people should attend services on Sundays and during the week. There was considerable diversity within the Swiss Reformed churches in the appearance and order of worship and local variations and traditions soon found expression. In Zurich the Sunday services in the city took place between 7 a.m. and 8 a.m. and then from three until four in the afternoon. In Basle the timing was similar with the minor difference that the afternoon service was at noon and the evening service at 4 p.m. By 1540 there were services for children in most of the urban churches of the Reformed states, generally on Sunday afternoons, but in the rural areas these remained *desiderata*, often too much for seriously overworked ministers. These services were built around the catechisms which began to appear in the Swiss churches from the 1530s. The most influential catechisms were the two prepared by Leo Jud in 1534 and 1541.

Services were held most days of the week except, for some reason, Tuesdays. Attendance was compulsory, as the mandates of the Reformed states unequivocally declared. For the rural areas the evidence is patchy, but it is clear that most services were held early in the morning, though in response to complaints from farmers who did not wish to interrupt their work, particularly in spring and autumn, a degree of flexibility was permitted. During the hours of worship merchants were not to sell their wares and the taverns were to close their doors. However, even a cursory glance at the records of the morals courts in any of the Reformed states indicates the degree to which these strictures were honoured in the breech.

We have little documentary evidence of what the Swiss Reformed services looked like during the sixteenth century, and for the most part we have to rely upon printed liturgies. In 1559, Ludwig Lavater, minister in Zurich, wrote a small book in Latin entitled *De Ritibus et Institutis Ecclesiae Tigurinae* in which he offered the first systematic description of the practices of the Reformed church.[31] The book was, in some respects, an apology for the Bullinger church in light of the *Consensus Tigurinus*, but it is invaluable as a source for our understanding of the practices of the sixteenth-century Zurich church. Lavater's work shared the didactic quality found in most of the writings from the Bullinger circle; *De Ritibus* was prescriptive rather than descriptive. However Lavater's book, along with letters, diaries, and some pastoral works of other writers offer a glimpse of the reality behind the ordinances. The churches were crowded, with most people standing – particularly in rural churches. Ministers often complained that they had to compete with crying babies, barking dogs, children running around, and people gossiping with their neighbours. In return a frequent complaint against ministers was that they could not make themselves heard, that their voices were too weak, or (for those who were from elsewhere) that their accents were incomprehensible. Fighting in churches was not uncommon, particularly as it was the one place where members of the community were legally bound to come in contact with each other.

The centre of the service, naturally, was the sermon, and it was affirmed that this should be accompanied by a prayer. In his church order of 1535 Bullinger provided a structure which we can take as broadly representative of services from the period.

1. Greeting
2. Prayer (Lord's Prayer, Ave Maria)
3. Bible reading
4. Sermon
5. Confession of sin
6. Petition for forgiveness followed by Lord's Prayer and Ave Maria again
7. Ten Commandments and Creed
8. Remembrance of those who have died in the week
9. Prayer for the poor
10. Petitions and intercessions
11. Dismissal and blessing

The theology behind the liturgy was straightforward. The proclamation of the Word was to lead the people to repentance and knowledge of God's forgiveness. This was followed by a statement of faith and intercessory prayers for the world.

Singing was not part of the church worship in Zurich, but in this respect Bullinger's city was the exception.[32] In Basle a spontaneous outbreak of psalm-singing had been part of the Reformation in 1526, and the city was greatly influenced by practices in Strasbourg. In 1551 a psalm book was printed for services in Basle, but before that it is likely that the people simply sang psalms and hymns from memory or from printed sheets. St Gall had a hymn book as early as 1532 or 1534 and in Schaffhausen one was printed in 1559. For most of the sixteenth century Berne followed the example of Zurich, but in 1558 a school choir began to sing psalms in the city and by 1574 hymn-singing was introduced in the parishes.

Singing in churches was a somewhat uncomfortable subject for the Swiss reformers. Bullinger did not really take a firm position in line with Zwingli's exclusion of hymns from the churches.[33] In the *Second Helvetic Confession* he rather obliquely defended those who did not wish to sing, but he certainly did not condemn those who did. Despite its official position on singing, Zurich remained a centre for the printing of hymn books in the Confederation. Most important was the 1540 hymnal from Ambrosius Blarer. The development of psalm-singing in Geneva, however, must have also influenced the Swiss churches. Ludwig Lavater, in his 1559 work on liturgy and worship in Zurich, remarked that singing in the home was common.

Baptism was a simple ceremony in the Reformed churches. It is interesting to see that in the Reformed liturgies of the sixteenth century reference is made to the role of the godparents, not the parents. Godparenting remained a crucial religious and social element of life in the Reformed states, and the natural parents seem not to have been particularly important for the sacrament. From shreds of evidence left to us it is known that many people, particularly in Basle, continued to present their child wrapped in a white cloth or robe. Instead of renouncing the devil, as they previously did, the godparents were simply admonished to bring up the child in the faith. In the earliest liturgies they were expected to recite the Apostles' Creed, but this seems to have disappeared by the middle of the century. In Berne the godparents were to recite the Ave Maria and kneel during the baptism, while in most other areas they seemed to have remained standing through the ceremony. Baptismal names, such a source of conflict in Calvin's Geneva, remained traditional in the Swiss lands. For the most part the saints' names remained most common, such as Felix and Regula in Zurich, or Beat in Berne.

For the first celebration of the Reformed service of the Lord's Supper Zwingli had prepared a liturgy in which important aspects of the mass were retained but with an entirely new emphasis on the covenantal relationship with God.[34] Oecolampadius in Basle developed a liturgy in 1526 which differed in a few aspects. Zwingli was much more determined not to use the names and terms associated with the mass, while Oecolampadius was comfortable retaining the terms 'altar' and 'absolution'. In the case of both Zurich and Basle the liturgies for the Lord's Supper were revised ten years later by the second generation of leaders, Bullinger and Myconius. The principal changes lay in the simplification of the service. The 1537 Basle liturgy gives us an idea of the basic form in the Swiss Confederation:

1. Admonishment to self-examination
2. Creed
3. Ban
4. Confession of sin
5. Absolution
6. Bidding prayer
7. Prayer

8. Reading from the Passion or Philippians 2
9. Admonition
10. Communion prayer
11. Gospel reading
12. Lord's Prayer
13. Admonition
14. Communion (during which psalms were sung – though not in Zurich or Berne)
15. Dismissal and blessing.

There were numerous variations on this form in the Swiss lands but the Basle liturgy represents the essential structure of Reformed worship.

If one looks at church records of the sixteenth century from the Swiss Reformed states one finds a mantra-like repetition of the command to attend the Lord's Supper. Clearly some people were staying away from the celebration of the sacrament. Why? It is hard to generalise, but for the church leaders and magistrates attendance at the Lord's Supper was a barometer of public opinion. Where large numbers were staying away it was often, especially in rural areas, an indication of Anabaptist or Catholic sympathies. What most irritated ministers and officials was when parishioners would cross over into Catholic territory to attend mass or to have their children baptised according to the Catholic rite. The borders between the Confederates were largely notional and it was not uncommon for priests and monks to be apprehended in Reformed areas. This seems to have continued throughout the sixteenth century, despite the threats issued by Reformed councils. When questioned on this issue, some simply responded that they had done so because of family connections or because they did not like their local minister. Without doubt there remained genuine Catholic sentiments among the populations of the Reformed states, especially in border communities, but very few people actually moved on account of their religion. What they did do, to the consternation of the Reformed ministers and officials, was to adopt a highly syncretistic view of religion. Clearly Catholic sacraments such as the last rites held a strong pastoral attraction and people risked punishment in seeking priests to administer them.

More frequently people stayed away from the Lord's Supper because they were quarrelling with their neighbours or with the minister. The Reformed clergy did not enjoy the status conferred on Catholic priests through the seven sacraments, most especially as celebrators of the mass. The Reformed minister was above all a preacher and pastor who was to raise a family in the parish. He was at once to be integrated into the community whilst standing apart as the person charged with bringing the Word of God. The minister was caught between two worlds, the ruling authorities and church and the village. The personality of the minister played a far greater role in determining his place in the community. What he said from the pulpit and did in the village was crucial, for he had no essential sacramental powers which he could dispense or withhold from the laity. Relations between the minister and the parishioners had a powerful effect on matters such as attendance; many took exception to what was preached and expressed their resistance by staying away from the sacraments. Likewise, the Reformed emphasis on examination of conscience before partaking in the sacrament seems to have troubled those who were in dispute with their neighbours. While there was friction in the community, many felt reluctant to eat the bread and drink the wine with their opponents.

Research over the past few years has shown that these issues were widespread in both the Protestant and Catholic Reformations in Europe. It took a long time for the Reformed practices in Swiss lands to win over the people. As new generations of children were brought up in the Reformed faith, knowing nothing of Catholicism, attitudes began to change, but this depended on the availability of ministers of sufficient quality, learning, and pastoral dexterity.

Morals courts

For the most part, the moral and ecclesiastical legislation brought in by the Reformations in the Swiss Confederation was drawn from late medieval sources. Already in the fifteenth century we find guild documents in Berne which use the word 'reformation' to mean moral improvement. The reformers had also been taught by their mentors that true reformation lay in the conversion of people; Zwingli's teacher and mentor in Basle, Hans Ulrich Surgant, had instilled in his pupils a strong sense of pastoral care and moral rectitude.[35] Through men such as Surgant Zwingli had access to the tradition of church reform which extended back to the Council of Basle, whose legislation on clerical and lay conduct became normative in the second half of the fifteenth century. The subsequent synods of the diocese of Constance reprinted the legislation, calling, for example, for the abolition of concubinage, the establishment of proper worship, and the enforcement of regular church attendance.[36]

After the reform of worship in Zurich at Easter 1525, when the mass was replaced with an evangelical Lord's Supper, the next stage was the introduction of means to regulate the lives of the clergy and laity. The beginning point was the founding of a marriage court in Zurich. From the early 1520s there is evidence that the Zurich council had taken it upon itself to resolve some marriage cases, but the bishop of Constance had continued to assert his jurisdiction. On 10 May 1525 the Zurich council issued a mandate, written by Zwingli, declaring that on account of the exorbitant cost and dislocation of taking cases to Constance a court consisting of four men was to be founded.[37] This institution, known as the *Ehegericht*, became the model (with minor variations) for similar tribunals among the emerging Swiss states of the late 1520s. In Zurich two representatives of the greater and smaller councils sat alongside two ministers from the city, but, as Pamela Biel has shown, the records of the court reflect the decisive role played by the clerical members, who generally pronounced the court's final decision.[38]

The document of May 1525 also provided the first Reformed statement on the nature of marriage and how it should be performed. First, no one was to marry without at least two witnesses, and children could not marry without the permission of their parents or that of the local bailiff (*Vogt*). Until the age of nineteen young people could have their marriage prohibited by their parents, although at the same time parents were forbidden from coercing their children into marriages against their will. In both cases the guilty parties were to be punished. Zwingli believed that the laws of the Old Testament were relevant to the Christian church; with the exceptions of the ceremonial and dietary laws, the moral commands given to the Israelites still formed the basis for Christian conduct, and Leviticus 18 was the authority for the sexual norms and the acceptable degree of relation. No other text from the Bible so succinctly expressed the contractual nature of the Christian community, and at its centre the family, which lay at the heart of the thought of Zwingli and Bullinger:

> The Lord spoke to Moses and said, speak to the Israelites in these words: I am the Lord your God. You shall not do as they do in Egypt where you once dwelt, nor shall you do as they do in the land of Canaan to which I am bringing you; you shall not conform to their institutions. You must keep my laws and conform to my institutions without fail: I am the Lord your God. You shall observe my institutions and my laws: the man who keeps them shall have life through them. I am the Lord.[39]

The process of marriage was strictly determined. When two people made their promise to each another, and there was no impediment, they were to be regarded as married. The girl had to be at least fourteen and the boy sixteen. Pre-marital sex was forbidden and those known to have slept together before marriage were fined. The marriage was to be a public affair in the local church; the reformers were anxious that marriages take place before the whole community in order to avoid secret weddings between two people of different confessions, which were forbidden.

The marriage mandate of 1525 also set out the conditions for divorce.[40] Zwingli and the other reformers regarded the Catholic prohibition of divorce as a major cause of sexual sin, driving honest and Christian men and women, the innocent victims of a bad marriage, into illicit relationships that burdened their consciences with guilt and shame. Divorce was not considered desirable, but rather a necessary last step taken only when a marriage breakdown resisted all efforts at reconciliation. It was not legal separation but the dissolution of the marriage which carried with it the expectation that the innocent party would soon remarry. The principal grounds on which the Swiss reformers were prepared to allow divorce was adultery, but there were others: impotence, lunacy, desertion, and incurable disease.

The *Ehegericht* was given considerable latitude in dealing with marital problems. Formulaic resolutions were avoided, as the judges were to consider each case on its own and attempt to find the solution which best suited the problem at hand. In making their judgements the members of the court were guided by various authorities: the biblical statements on marriage, custom, and canon law. Heinrich Uttinger, who was a jurist, played a crucial role in Zurich in drawing up the judgements of the *Ehegericht*, and its success owed much to the depth and subtlety of his legal knowledge.

In April 1528 the council passed a mandate creating the synod, the principal means by which the clergy were regulated, through fraternal correction and admonition, by the leaders of the church. The synod was the partner institution of the *Ehegericht*; this model of two bodies responsible for the clergy and laity was adopted by the other Swiss churches. Zwingli laid the foundations for the synod in 1528, but it was not until Bullinger took over in 1532 that the institution acquired its real character. After the defeat at Kappel the synod was a crucial part of Bullinger's relationship with the magistrates of Zurich, who were deeply suspicious of clerical power. It was a Faustian bargain, for in order to retain its authority to preach the Gospel as the spirit dictated the church had to promise to cooperate with the state, or, as some would say, do the state's bidding by tailoring its message to suit the political needs of the magistrates. In any case, Bullinger's responsibility was to keep all clerical issues to the closed sessions of the synod, away from the public eye.

The ordinances of the restored synod in Zurich were written by Heinrich Bullinger and Leo Jud and issued by the council on 22 October 1532 at the first meeting of the Zurich synod after Kappel.[41] It was a seminal document of the Swiss Reformation, a full account of the Reformed polity in light of the theological and political turmoil of the previous ten years.[42] For the first time the working of the Reformed church was described in detail, surpassing the adumbrative texts of the 1520s. Bullinger and Jud's work was divided into three parts: the election of ministers; the life and learning of ministers; and, finally, the constitution of the synod.[43] When a minister was chosen by the Zurich council to serve in a particular parish he was to be jointly introduced to the community by the dean of the local chapter and the bailiff. These two officials represented the church and council in each of the parishes. If no objections arose from the community, the ordination took place the following Sunday during the regular hour of worship. The dean would preach at the ordination on the duties of the minister whilst the bailiff would remind the community of its obligations to the state. The new minister would then take the oath of office at the next session of the synod in Zurich.

The second part of the ordinances give us a clear idea of the duties of the Reformed minister: learning, the extirpation of false belief in the parish, the reading of the council's mandates from the pulpit, care of the poor, guarding against blasphemy, the upholding of the oath in the community, regular worship, the teaching of the catechism, the education of children, visiting the sick, burial of the dead, and the maintenance of a proper household. This litany not only defined the brief of the minister but indicated the matters for which he was to be held to account before the synod. The Reformed minister had three separate, though related duties: lead the people in worship; supervise the morality of the parish; work with the bailiff as the representative of the state in the community.

The synod was presided over by the head of the Zurich church (Bullinger until 1575) and the Bürgermeister.[44] Essentially, however, Heinrich Bullinger was in complete control, acting as the *de facto* bishop of Zurich. The surviving records of the Zurich synod are in Bullinger's handwriting; he not only passed judgement on miscreant ministers, he recommended the forms of punishment to be meted out. Some fragments of his notes have shown that he played a pivotal role in deciding which cases should be heard before the synod – some matters were resolved quietly and discretely, never emerging into the public. Bullinger's pragmatic view of church discipline was a mixture of ideology and realism. He disliked the medieval practice of excommunication because it could be so easily abused; he also rejected the view, held by Calvin and others, which tied discipline to the sacraments – Bullinger often remarked that Christ did not exclude Judas from the Last Supper. For Bullinger, discipline was about reconciliation and the resolution of conflict; he sought practical solutions to often intractable problems. However, his hands were bound by the shortage of clergy which bedevilled the Zurich church until the 1550s. Bullinger took the view, not shared by many other reformers, that a deficient minister was better than none. As a result, Bullinger had to micro-manage the parishes of Zurich to ensure that at least a basic level of pastoral services was provided. His sermons were printed for the parochial ministers to read from their pulpits, and he used the synod to instruct the clergy in the rudiments of Reformed theology. The situation improved as a new generation of ministers educated in the schools and academies became available, but this was not for some decades. Ministers were suspended, fined and even put in prison for short periods of time, but they were almost never banished. One of Bullinger's principal means of resolving a conflict between a minister and his parish was to move the minister to another community.

The synod and *Ehegericht* stood at the top of two parallel ladders of social discipline in Zurich. These two bodies dealt with those matters which arose out of local tribunals in the villages scattered across the countryside. The disciplinary structures of the Reformed churches, for the most part, were erected from existing institutions and ordinances. The Reformed churches of Zurich, Basle, Berne, and Schaffhausen retained intact the parochial structures with their systems of tithes, benefices, and patronage. At the centre of each parish was a minister who resided in the parish house with his family and was supported by living off the benefice. The ideal for each parish was to be self-sufficient, but the sad reality remained that many communities lacked houses for the clergy, did not have sufficient income to support a clerical family, or could not maintain the material fabric of the church buildings. The church leaders had enormous problems with the gross disparities of income between parishes. During the financial crises and bad weather which afflicted the Swiss during the second half of the sixteenth century it proved impossible both to provide incomes for ministers with families and to sustain the upkeep of the church buildings.

In each parish there were several important figures alongside the minister responsible for the running of the community. The churchwarden (*Kirchenpfleger*) kept the accounts. The magistrates required the churchwardens to keep detailed records of the money, land, and other forms of income belonging to the parish church so that they could keep a weather eye on the expenditures of each community. The bailiff was responsible for the preservation of law and order in the community. He reported directly to the council in the city and was in charge of the local police. The bailiff administered the oath of allegiance taken by members of the community, and he was a crucial witness in disciplinary cases heard either in the *Ehegericht* or the synod. The bailiff was chosen from among the elders of the community and there is ample evidence in the records that this position was not actively sought on account of the resentment it created in the villages.

In each village there was a local morals tribunal which generally met in the parish church. This court, which had various names in different parts of the Confederation, was known in Zurich as the *Stillstand*, and it was presided over by the minister and by the *Ehegaumer*. The *Ehegaumer* were chosen from among the elders of the community and were originally responsible for ensuring compliance with the marriage ordinances of 1526, though their brief was then extended to cover the morals mandates. In many parishes the positions of *Ehegaumer* and churchwarden were held by the same person. Together the *Ehegaumer* and minister could attempt to resolve a conflict in the community, but their authority was limited to admonition. If the case was serious enough then they had to summon the bailiff or pass the matter on to the *Ehegericht* (or *Chorgericht*) in the city.

The parishes of the rural areas were organised into chapters, retaining their medieval structures, and a rural dean was responsible for each of the chapters. The deans were chosen from the senior ministers in the area and their chief responsibility was to watch over the life and preaching of the ministers in their chapter. Like the local morals courts, the intention was to deal with disciplinary matters before they reached the city. The rural deans would hold meetings of their chapters and offer fraternal corrections when necessary, but they were not permitted to discipline. The deans would then come to the city to meet with the head of the church before the general synods. At the synod sessions each of the deans would offer a report on events in his area; thus the magistrates and church leaders were constantly kept informed.

Finally, the synod itself was run by an executive known in Zurich as the *Examinatorenkonvent*. In Zurich the committee consisted of the three principal ministers of the city, two members of the council, two professors of theology and three archdeacons of the Grossmünster. In 1564 this was expanded by the addition of two more members of the council. This committee set the agenda of the synod sessions, it considered all the evidence and information which had come from the rural parishes, and it made decisions on the courses of action to be taken. As suggested above, in Zurich the committee was dominated by Heinrich Bullinger. The committee was also responsible for recommending candidates to the council when a parish became vacant.

The confluence of secular and ecclesiastical authority in the Swiss Reformed churches is evident when one looks at the institutional structures which took shape during the sixteenth century. From the village to the city, each church official had a corresponding secular official with whom he was expected to cooperate in the maintenance of true religion, peace, and order. The disciplinary bodies, the *Ehegericht* and synod, were run by a mixture of church and political leaders, all under the rule of the council, which alone wielded the sword.

In Basle a different system arose, for although a synod was created for the preservation of clerical discipline, it was hardly used during the sixteenth century.[45] The reason for this was quite simple: unlike Zurich, Basle's clergy were divided by serious disputes over doctrinal matters, and the church leaders believed that a gathering of the whole clergy would only increase the conflict between the warring parties. The Basle magistrates continued to remind their clergy that ultimate authority over the church resided with them, and not the ministers, and that they preferred a different manner of administering discipline, through visitations and the use of rural deans. The deans were given control over the clergy in their chapters and each dean was directly responsible to the head of the Basle church (*Antistes*) and the *Kirchenrat*. Synods were only occasionally held and were not, for the most part, an important part of the supervision of the clergy.[46] Thus in Basle we see a different resolution to the same problem. The relationship between the church and the state was worked out by the direct control of ecclesiastical matters by the magistrates, who sought to quash debates over doctrine and the conduct of the clergy by avoiding any public discussion. This would also be the favoured route in Berne, bringing home the point that Zurich was the exception among the Swiss Reformed churches. The greater critical distance of the church from the magistrates in Zurich was the work of Heinrich Bullinger. Without his pastoral and administrative genius, his international status, and his political acumen, the church in Zurich would have resembled those in Berne, Basle, and Schaffhausen, where the magistrates called the shots.

In Berne the council issued a mandate in September 1528 enacting marriage laws and a marriage court similar to that created in Zurich two years earlier.[47] Such similarities are hardly surprising as one of the authors of the Bernese mandate was Kaspar Megander, Zwingli's friend and colleague who had been sent to Berne to lead the implementation of the Reformation. In one respect the Bernese *Chorgericht* (the name used for the court) differed from the Zurich *Ehegericht*; the city council was more strongly represented on the court in the former. In each of the rural parishes of Berne a local morals court, known as the *Ehrbarkeit*, was set up on October 1529. These courts consisted of the parish minister and at least two elders from the community, chosen by the bailiff. The *Ehrbarkeit* could not excommunicate, nor could it use torture; its competence was limited to admonition, fines, imprisonment to a maximum of three days, and the pillory. When necessary the case could be sent to the *Chorgericht* in the city. In communities where there was no pillory those found guilty of some moral offence were made to stand next to the church door during the Sunday service. Most galling of all was when the court required men or women to come before their neighbours in church to seek their forgiveness.

The morals mandates issued by all the Swiss Reformed churches directly after the adoption of the Reformation were frequently reprinted throughout the century.[48] The Bernese mandate of 30 March 1529 was typical. It contained measures against such proscribed activities as games, swearing, blasphemy, inappropriate clothing, drinking, licentiousness, marital conflict, impiety, unbelief, magic, superstition. Later, the condemnation of dancing, child abuse, gambling, and jewellery, amongst other transgressions, augmented the list. Every member of the community was expected to attend church regularly, to bring their children forward for baptism in the parish church, and to partake in the Reformed celebration of the Lord's Supper. During hours of worship it was forbidden to wander about the streets, to conduct business, to remain in the tavern or in one's bed.[49] A particular concern for the communities was the behaviour of the youth; little wonder that the mercenary service, with its possibilities for travel and money, was so attractive when the alternative was discipline for drinking, fighting, and swearing.[50] The disciplinary records of the sixteenth century offer us a window on the problems faced by the Reformed church at the local level. Heinrich Richard Schmidt has produced an exhaustive study of the *Chorgerichte* in the Bernese rural territory during the early modern period, and he has written of the nature of cases heard by these local tribunals:

> Very often the disputes erupted over the theft of provisions or other goods that belonged to the household, also over the children of the parties involved. The infringement of borders or rights of use of water or agricultural land weighed heavily on the disputants, as all of these were important for the disputants' existence. The moving of boundary posts, ploughing across field borders, and the diversion of water constituted theft of the most important means of production in agricultural society, the land. Self-defence, or defence of the family, also frequently led to accusations of maledictory magic ...[51]

The implementation of discipline was highly problematic for the Reformed churches of the sixteenth century.[52] The maintenance of order was understood to be essential to the preservation of the community; God had commanded that his laws be obeyed. Yet this required ministers to involve themselves in the lives of their parishioners, and this bred a resentment which threatened the pedagogical mission of the church. Ministers frequently found themselves entangled in local conflicts, with the result that the worship and work of the church in the parish collapsed on account of breakdown in relations. At the same time, the minister was a servant of the state, required to assist in the enforcement of the laws of the land. This meant, in most communities, that the minister was regarded as an agent of the city, and co-operation with the minister might vary according to the people's views of the urban magistrates. Nevertheless the disciplinary bodies were not merely seen as oppressive tools of a centralising state; the vast number of cases brought forward by the people argue for the importance which the communities placed on the morals courts. They were the primary forums for arbitration. The minister and the local officials were expected to decide on cases, but the resolutions which they reached could be highly divisive.

Notes

1 The crucial work on the Zurich understanding of the covenant is J. Wayne Baker, *Heinrich Bullinger and the Covenant: The Other Reformed Tradition* (Athens, OH, 1980).

2 For a fuller discussion of this see Bruce Gordon, 'Transcendence and Community in Zwinglian Worship: The Liturgy of 1525 in Zurich', in R.N. Swanson (ed.), *Continuity and Change in Christian Worship*, Studies in Church History, 35 (Woodbridge, 1999), pp. 128–150.

3 On Bullinger's flexible attitude towards questions of belief, see my 'Incubus and Succubus in Zurich: Heinrich Bullinger on the Power of the Devil', in Kathryn Edwards (ed.), *Demons, Vampires and Werewolves. The Revenant in European Culture* (Sixteenth Century Essays and Studies, Kirksville, MI, forthcoming).

4 On the late medieval roots of education in the Confederation, see Urs Martin Zahnd, 'Chordienst und Schule in eidgenössichen Städten des Spätmittelalters', *Zwingliana*, 22 (1995), pp. 5–35.

5 On Zwingli's understanding of the 'Good Shepherd', see Lee Palmer Wandel, *Always Among Us: Images of the Poor in Zwingli's Zurich* (Cambridge, 1990), pp. 42–44.

6 Martin Brecht has argued for the influence of Wittenberg on the Zurich Prophezei, pointing to the shared use of 1 Cor. 14; see his 'Die Reform des Wittenberger Horengottesdientes und die Entstehung der Zürcher Prophezei', *Zwingliana*, 19 (1992), pp. 49–62.

7 Karin Maag, *Seminary or University. The Genevan Academy and Reformed Higher Education 1560–1620* (Aldershot, 1995), pp. 129–153.

8 Martin Rose, 'Konrad Pellikans Wirken in Zürich 1526–1556', *Zwingliana*, 14 (1977), pp. 380–386. Rose placed Pellikan in the Erasmian–Bucer tradition of theology.

9 On Pellikan's exegetical work, see Christoph Zürcher, *Konrad Pellikans Wirken in Zürich, 1526–1556* (Berne, 1975), pp. 85–154.

10 Maag, *Seminary or University*, pp. 132–133.

11 Ibid., p. 134.

12 Conradin Bonorand, *Die Entwicklung des reformierten Bildungswesens in Graubünden zur Zeit der Reformation und Gegenreformation* (Thusis, 1949); also, his 'Bündner Studierende an höhern Schulen der Schweiz und des Auslandes im Zeitalter der Reformation und Gegenreformation', *JHGG* (1949), 91–174.

13 Michael Baumann and Rainer Henrich, 'Das Lektorium, sein Lehrkörper, seine Studenten', in Hans Ulrich Bächtold (ed.), *Schola Tigurina. Die Zürcher Hohe Schule und ihre Gelehrten um 1550* (Zurich and Freiburg-im-Breisgau, 1999), p. 25.

14 *Biographisch-Bibliographisches Kirchenlexicon (1996–)*, VIII, esp. pp. 136–137.

15 Guggisberg, *Bernische Kirchengeschichte*, pp. 170–171.

16 Louis Junod and Henri Meylan, *L'Académie de Lausanne au XVIe siècle* (Lausanne, 1947), pp. 87ff.

17 Hans Guggisberg, *Basel in the Sixteenth Century* (St Louis, 1982), pp. 40–41.

18 Edgar Bonjour, *Die Universität Basel von den Anfängen bis zur Gegenwart, 1460–1960* (Basle, 1971), pp. 127ff.

19 Harry Clark, 'The Publication of the Koran in Latin, A Reformation Diliemma', *SCJ*, 15 (1984), pp. 3–12; also, Martin Steinmann, *Johannes Oporinus: Ein Basler Buchdrucker um die Mitte des 16. Jahrhunderts* (Basle, 1967).

20 *Z*, 1, pp. 562–563.

21 On Basle printing, see Peter Bietenholz 'Printing and the Basle Reformation 1517–1565' in Jean-François Gilmont (ed.), *The Reformation and the Book*, transl. Karin Maag (Aldershot, 1998), pp. 235–263.

22 Josef Benzing, *Die Buchdrucker des 16. Und 17. Jahrhunderts im deutschen Sprachgebiet*, 2nd edn (Wiesbaden, 1982).

23 Hans Guggisberg, 'Die Bibel an einem Kreuzweg Europas: Basel in 16. Jahrhundert', in Urs Joerg and David Marc Hoffmann (eds), *Die Bibel in der Schweiz. Ursprung und Geschichte* (Basle, 1997), pp. 147–149.

24 Thomas Kaufmann, 'Capito als heimlicher Propagandist der frühen Wittenberger Theologie', *Zeitschrift für Kirchengeschichte*, 103 (1992), pp. 81–86.

25 See Iren L. Snavely Jr, 'Zwingli, Froshauer, and the Word of God in Print', *Journal of Religious and Theological Information*, 3 (2000), pp. 65–87.

26 Traudel Himmighöfer, *Die Zürcher Bibel bis zum Tode Zwinglis* (1531) (Mainz, 1995), p. 140.

27 Ibid., p. 149.

28 A useful discussion is found in W.P. Stephens, *The Theology of Huldrych Zwingli* (Oxford, 1986), pp. 177–179.

29 Himmighöfer, *Die Zürcher Bibel*, p. 184.

30 Hans Rudolf Lavater, 'Die Zürcher Bibel von 1524 bis Heute', in *Die Bibel in der Schweiz. Ursprung und Geschichte* (Basle, 1997), p. 205.

31 Ludwig Lavater, *Die Gebräuche und Einrichtungen der Zürcher Kirche*, ed. and transl. Gottfried Albert Keller (Zurich, 1987).

32 Markus Jenny, 'Reformierte Kirchenmusik? Zwingli, Bullinger und die Folgen', *Zwingliana*, 19 (1992), pp. 187–205.

33 John Kmetz, *The Sixteenth-Century Basel Songbooks. Origins, Contents, and Contexts* (Berne, 1995).

34 Gordon, 'Transcendence and Community in Zwinglian Worship', pp. 128–150.

35 On Surgant's role, see above pp. 28–29.

36 K. Maier, 'Die Konstanzer Diözesansynoden im Mittelalter und in der Neuzeit', *Rottenburger Jahrbuch für Kirchengeschichte*, 5 (1986), pp. 53–70.

37 Emil Egli (ed.), *Aktensammlung zur Geschichte der Zürcher Reformation* (Zurich, 1879), 711, pp. 326–329.

38 Pamela Biel, *Doorkeepers at the House of Righteousness* (Berne, 1991), p. 161.

39 Leviticus 18:1–5.

40 Egli, *Aktensammlung*, 712, p. 329.

41 Bruce Gordon, *Clerical Discipline and the Rural Reformation* (Berne, 1982), pp. 78–83.

42 J. Wayne Baker, 'Church, State, and Dissent: The Crisis of the Swiss Reformation 1531–1536', *Church History*, 57 (1988), pp. 135–152.

43 Egli, *Aktensammlung*, 1899, pp. 825–837.

44 See Gordon, *Clerical Discipline*, pp. 90–95.

45 Amy Nelson Burnett, 'Controlling the Clergy. The Oversight of Basel's Rural Pastors in the Sixteenth Century', *Zwingliana*, 25 (1998), 129–142.

46 The situation was different in the Graubünden, where synods were regularly held. See Jakob Rudolf Truog, 'Aus der Geschichte der evangelischen Gemeinden in den bündnerischen Untertanenlanden: Ein Beitrag zur bündnerischen Synodalgeschichte', *BM* (1935), pp. 236–248, 257–285, 311–318.

47 Hans Guggisberg, *Bernische Kirchengeschichte* (Berne, 1958), p. 178.

48 The case of Schaffhausen has been studied by Roland Hofer in his *"üppiges, unzüchtiges Lebwesen'. Schaffhauser Ehegerichtsbarkeit von der Reformation bis zum Ende des Ancien Régime (1529–1789)* (Berne, 1993).

49 Heinrich Richard Schmidt, *Dorf und Religion. Reformierte Sittenzucht in Berner Landgemeinden der Frühen Neuzeit* (Stuttgart, Jena, and New York, 1995), pp. 354–358.

50 S. Burghartz, 'Jugendfräulichkeit oder Reinheit? Zur Änderung von Argumentationsmustern vor dem Baler Ehegericht im 16. und 17. Jahrhundert', in R. van Dülmen (ed.), *Dynamik der Tradition* (Frankfurt-am-Main, 1992), pp. 13–38.

51 Heinrich Richard Schmidt, 'Morals Courts in Rural Berne during the Early Modern Period', in Karin Maag (ed.), *The Reformation in Eastern and Central Europe* (Aldershot, 1997), p. 176.

52 On the Graubünden, see Randolf C. Head, 'Rhaetian Ministers, from Shepherds to Citizens: Calvinism and Democracy in the Republic of the Three Leagues 1550–1620', in Fred Graham (ed.), *Later Calvinism: International Perspectives* (Kirksville, MO, 1994); Ulrich Pfister, 'Reformierte

Sittenzucht zwischen kommunaler und territorialer Organisation: Graubünden, 16.–18. Jahrhundert', *ARG*, 87 (1996), pp. 287–333; and Jakob Rudolf Truog, *Die Pfarrer der evangelischen Gemeinden in Graubünden und seinen ehemaligen Untertanenlanden* (Chur, 1935).

8

Church and society

The social and economic situation

The lands of the Swiss Confederation suffered terribly during the sixteenth century. It is difficult to speak in terms of figures, but the economic historian Wilhelm Bickel has suggested that the population of the Confederation stood at between 800,000 and 850,000 in 1500 and a million in 1600.[1] This meant a yearly growth rate of between 1.6 and 2.2 per cent, which placed the Swiss considerably behind their neighbours. Within the Confederation there were variations, with the cities generally growing quickly while the Alpine regions lost large numbers of inhabitants. Plagues certainly played their part, as did cholera and the pox, all of which meant that during the late fifteenth century the Swiss lands sank to their lowest population levels. The cities of the Confederation were small: Basle was the largest with between nine and ten thousand inhabitants.

The rhythms of life for the Swiss reflected the norms of daily existence across Europe for an agrarian society. The frequency of marriages often reflected the price of the crops; in Geneva, for example, it has been demonstrated that the number of marriages directly reflected the health of the corn crop in that year.[2] Every epidemic resulted in a huge increase in the number of weddings as lost husbands and wives were replaced. It was not uncommon in the sixteenth century for people to marry three or four times. Summer was the time of plague and few marriages took place, while most children were conceived during the winter months when the demands of work on the land were diminished. Martin Körner, in his work on population history in the early modern Swiss Confederation, has found that during economic crises the birth rates declined up to 40 per cent as families could not feed themselves and sought to avoid the arrival of more mouths to feed.[3] Plagues, however, had the opposite effect. More children were born as people struggled to cope with the huge loss of life among adults and children.[4]

Clothing

The morals mandates which accompanied the Reformations in the Swiss Confederation reflected the concern of both the councils and churches that men and women dress in a seemly manner. Most of the regulations dated back to the early part of the century and they were simply reissued as part of the new religious order. In St Gall the chronicler Johannes Kessler remarked that the women wore such clothing on festival days that their breasts were highly visible, a fashion which he compared to the manner in which altar screens in Catholic churches were opened up so that the people might revere the image inside.[5] The length of a woman's skirt had been the subject of a mandate in St Gall in 1508 in which the magistrates declared that neither short skirts nor failure to wear a skirt at all would go without punishment.[6]

In Swiss lands male fashion changed towards the end of the fifteenth century, as it did across Europe. Men began to wear brighter colours. Konrad Pellikan wrote in his *Chronicle* that until 1489 no one had ever seen such colours as the men were now accustomed to wearing. It has been suggested that the Swiss triumphs over the Burgundians opened up the Confederates to new types of materials, new colours, and different styles of clothes. It is certainly the case that Swiss involvement in the Italian wars at the end of the century resulted in the arrival of many strange customs and material articles. Weapons, precious goods, pictures, relics, and a variety of other precious and expensive goods became common in the Confederation. When the Swiss attempted to wear these clothes they often found them too small, so they cut slits in the arms and legs, so that their undergarments were revealed. Later these slits were filled with other material, developing a style which was to be seen not only on the wealthy and the soldiers, but also on the peasants. The tearing of the clothes seriously damaged the material and limited its usefulness, so that the torn trousers and shirts worn by the soldiers and others were seen as signs of extravagance and consequently banned. In Berne the clothing mandate of 1530 contained many of the same proscriptions. Men were not to tear their clothes in the manner adopted by the soldiers.

It also became common for men in the Confederation to wear a type of trousers which were so tight that nothing was left to the imagination. This especially brought the opprobrium of the magistrates, who objected to both the obscene manner in which the protrusions were embellished as well as to the bawdy humour which they incited. Soon these pouches were filled to such an extent that they no longer merely served as an expression of virility but as a rather handy place to carry money, handkerchiefs and other goods. There was a close connection between these displays of male potency and military power; the drawings of Urs Graf (1485–1529) show Swiss soldiers with their full manhood. Jürg Stockar, in his history of fashion in Zurich, has remarked 'it is typical for the Swiss that the one style of clothing they created was not developed in a salon but on the battlefield'.[7] However, the outlandish dress of the mercenaries, as well as of German *Landsknechte*, was to make a very serious point; that these groups considered themselves exempted from normal social conventions and they openly flaunted the regulations of the magistrates and churchmen.

Marriage and divorce

There was a tradition in Zurich that whoever accompanied the bride and groom to the church, remained through the service, and then accompanied them home, was entitled to attend the marriage supper. This tradition was known as an 'open wedding' and for many it was a free meal and the chance to celebrate. Weddings could be large and expensive and during the troubled economic times of the sixteenth century they often meant financial ruin for the parents. Many prudent couples sought to keep their wedding as secret as possible to avoid the cost of feeding the entire community. The council and churches were extremely concerned about the disastrous effects that wedding costs had upon the community. They were also alarmed by the amount of drinking and dancing that went on at such occasions. The mandates from the Bernese council were typical: wedding festivities were limited to one day and each invited guest was to pay for his or her meal. Dancing was limited to three seemly dances at which the men were not to remove their shirts, regardless of how warm it was.[8]

Marriage was no longer a sacrament of the church, although the Reformed theologians declared that the union of man and woman was sacred and part of God's creative purpose.[9] The marriage courts developed by the Reformed churches were extremely reluctant to recommend a divorce until every attempt at reconciliation had been exhausted.[10] Broken families brought poverty, crime, and drunkenness as well as a range of other problems which taxed the resources of the state. For the church, as we shall see, the family was the crucial building-block of society.[11] Thus the most extraordinary efforts were given to save relationships which had clearly broken beyond repair. A well-known case from Berne involved a man and women being put in prison with one bowl and one spoon on the assumption that if they could come to some sort of arrangement for eating they could manage the rest of their affairs. A shared meal, the marriage court noted, was an essential part of married life.[12] Other cases involved a variation on this theme: some couples were locked in a room with only one bed. All of this was done in the hope of preserving the marriage, not on any sentimental grounds of love or happiness, but rather because the state and church regarded marriage as the proper form of relationship which would serve the stability of the community. Single people, especially single woman, often required social assistance and were expensive; the council saw marriage, family, and a stable household as the best defence against the economic vicissitudes of the period.

Women

The Swiss Reformation was very much a male affair. In contrast to the work of Katharina Zell in Strasbourg or Argula vom Grumbach, Luther's fervent supporter, we have virtually no theological writings from Swiss women of the sixteenth century. The most notable exception was Marie Dentière, a former abbess who supported the Reformation cause in Geneva. For the most part, we are left with what the reformers thought about women and what ministers, officials, and scribes chose to say about those women who appeared before local tribunals. The reformers, most prominently Heinrich Bullinger, who wrote extensively about marriage and the family, believed that motherhood was the principal expression of female piety.[13] Zwingli wrote of Mary, the Mother of Christ, venerating her not as an intercessor, but as the model of humility and obedience. This was the role to be emulated.

The issues of marriage and family were very much at the heart of early evangelical preaching as many clergy rebelled against the requirement to be celibate. Zwingli's own marriage was a crucial statement of his rejection of the Catholic understanding of the priesthood. For women, evangelical freedom meant that they were to marry, obey their husbands, and raise children, thus creating and sustaining the family, that most crucial of building-blocks for the Christian society. On this subject there was little dissent among the main reformers. While men and women were regarded as spiritually equal, the ordinances of the Swiss Reformed states clearly delineated male and female roles: there was no place for women in the Reformed church outside motherhood.

For many women, evangelical preaching had offered encouragement to leave religious houses, where many had been placed against their will, and the call was enthusiastically heard. Anna von Zwingen, for example, in the religious house of Steinen in Basle, had spent sixty unhappy years as a nun. The slogans of the 'priesthood of all believers' and 'Christian liberty' were attractive, and numerous literate women embarked on epistolary contact with Zwingli, Oecolampadius, Capito, and Bucer.[14] The Reformation attack on monasticism was accompanied by sermons and letters encouraging religious women to return to the world. To ease the transition these women were offered pensions or work by the new Reformed civic councils. Many women left the religious houses on account of their desire to marry. Margaretha von Wattenwyl, the daughter of a prominent politician in Berne and nun in the religious house of Königsfelden, had corresponded with Zwingli, indicating her great pleasure at the spread of the evangelical faith and how she saw no further purpose in the monastic life.[15] She had become engaged to a young man and asked Zwingli to intervene on her behalf. He was happy to oblige and permission was granted from the Bernese council in August 1525 for the two to marry. But we must not exaggerate evangelical support among the female religious, because for many the dissolution of the religious houses was an unwelcome and disorientating experience. The nuns of St Leonhard in St Gall faced the wrath of the Bürgermeister when they petitioned to be allowed back into their house, where, they argued, their work had been of great value to the community.[16]

The world which awaited those who exited their houses, whether willingly or not, was hostile. The financial situation confronting them was confusing and burdensome. Many women married former priests or monks, and some of these marriages were neither happy nor prosperous, as couples were rarely able to survive on their living. The Reformed councils provided former religious women with some financial support, but this was soon reclaimed in tax, with the consequence that many former nuns found themselves living in poverty in the cities.

Their backgrounds in the convents had ill prepared them for life in the world, and they had no idea of what to do with either themselves or the money which they had been given. One example was Engel Schwytzer in Zurich, a former nun in Oetenbach, who was destitute and threw herself on the mercy of the magistrates.[17] The council decided to grant her a yearly allowance, but paid it to her mother, as the daughter was incapable of looking after her own affairs. Those who found the world too hostile, or their marriages too dreadful, were frequently permitted to return to their former institutions on the condition that they returned the pensions. Although no longer religious, these houses continued to accommodate a large number of former monks and nuns. By no means did all marry; many returned to live with their families, lived in the secularised religious houses, or went to religious houses in Catholic areas. No longer part of an order or the religious life of the community, they lived in exile from the world. Before the Reformation women who were heads of religious houses had some authority in the communities; they knew how to deal with their political and ecclesiastical masters. With the Reformation there were no more women in positions of authority.

The reality of life for women was harsh. Women were frequently pregnant and childbirth was extremely dangerous. The single life for women in the Reformation was no replacement for the religious house. Bullinger, in his influential work *On Christian Marriage*, simply reiterated the established view that women's role was in keeping the household, giving birth and raising children. All of this was placed under the authority of the father.

> A man must remain with his wife, and the wife with her husband. They must delight in one another's company so that they do not desire another. Thus they are bound to love one another in all godliness and honesty. Likewise they have the duty to raise their children and to provide that they do not fall into Satan's snare or into any uncleanness, but that they come purely and honestly to marriage, when the time requires.[18]

Before the Reformation it was common for women to live as the concubines of priests, to raise their children and conduct themselves for all intents and purposes as wives. The Reformation demand that the clergy should marry certainly improved their lot in certain respects. For one thing the women and their children now lived in a legal relationship. Zwingli had raised the status of marriage to one of the most revered aspects of the Christian faith, but there is no doubt that the Reformation closed off to women all careers other than the household. The Reformation emphasis upon the family as a discrete unit within the social hierarchy meant that the wife and mother was confined to the world of her husband and children.

The position of women in the Swiss cities mirrored the changes taking place in Germany, where the emphasis on the household as the basic unit of social control led to a restriction of the legal rights of women. Women, however, did work and make an important contribution to the economic life of the communities. In the rural areas they were heavily involved in working the land, selling goods at markets, and in carrying out duties on behalf of their husbands, such as the collection of debts. In the cities, as Merry Wiesner has shown, their work depended on their familial and marital status.[19] Women were involved in the guilds – in Basle women had their own guild – often running the guild shop. Most women who worked in the guilds were either the wives, daughters, or maids of guildsmen, and they worked alongside the journeymen and apprentices. The most important figure was the wife of the master. The daughters of guild masters were highly prized for their knowledge of the trade and craft. The place of women in the guilds, however, was severely challenged by the economic decline of the mid sixteenth century; at this point the younger men saw themselves pitted against women for jobs, and the guilds introduced new restrictions to limit women working. Faced with new hardships, the councils sought to encourage women to take up spinning, a useful activity which required little training and could be carried out in the home alongside other domestic activities. Spinning was seen as a particularly appropriate skill, and it became a means for women to earn money, but for the most part it provided them only with low-paid, low-status jobs. Widows, who had previously enjoyed a degree of social and economic status in the cities found by the end of the sixteenth century that their ability to run businesses and own property had been severely curtailed. The Reformation emphasis on social order and discipline, combined with male-orientated structures of power, served to confine the place of women in Swiss society. This pressure was equally evident in Reformed and Catholic regions.

This did not mean, however, that there were not women who became significant religious figures during the sixteenth century. One such woman was Margaretha Hottingerin in St Gall, a mystic who spoke of her love for God in ways which troubled the Reformed ministers and magistrates. Her spiritual enthusiasm and charismatic personality attracted a considerable following, making the St Gall council uneasy. Margaretha claimed to be a prophet and in her prophecies she was highly critical of the established Reformed order, which, according to her, sought to chain the spirit of God with ordinances and institutions. She spoke of spiritual freedom and of a rapturous response to the presence of God in her soul. This language was highly threatening to the Reformed churches on many grounds: Margaretha was a women claiming spiritual authority, and she had appropriated the language of prophecy so central to Swiss Protestantism. Further, she had drawn the distinction between the spiritual and institutional church so damaging to the Reformed churches. The magistrates in St Gall had her imprisoned.

Women were prominent among the Anabaptists and were amongst the first to be executed.[20] The accusations against these and other women were not dissimilar to the charges of witchcraft which were rife in the sixteenth century. They were accused of sexual promiscuity and of appearing naked during their ecstatic pronouncements. Many of these belonged to the circle of Anabaptists in St Gall.

Their effect upon the people was recorded by chroniclers like Kessler.[21] Kessler's view of women is captured in a remark concerning the execution of a female martyr for the evangelical cause: 'God be honoured and praised for having effected such strength in so feeble a vessel, to his honour and to our salvation.'[22]

The burning of witches was common in certain parts of the Swiss Confederation and recent work on late medieval witchcraft cases in the Confederation has stressed the role of the community in the process. The accusations generally reflected internal tensions and the charges themselves almost always arose out of the community.[23] In this account of Verena Kerez taken from the *Wickiana* of the sixteenth century we find that the situation had not changed much. Kerez's case throws light on prevailing attitudes towards women and sexuality.

> On 10 September 1571 Verena Kerez, the wife of Rudolf Müller in Meilen [on Lake Zurich], was burnt on account of her denial of God the Almighty and her surrender to the devil. Also, according to some of her neighbours in Meilen, she had killed or lamed some of their cattle out of envy and hate. Verena Kerez, who is now here in Zurich, stated the following: she had for some time suffered great poverty, hunger, and deprivation, and about three years ago an evil spirit, the devil, came to her with the appearance of a rich man. He had seen her wretched state, and he promised her that she would no longer suffer in poverty or be a burden to anyone else if she gave herself to him and did what he wished. He persuaded her with his eloquence that she should turn away from God her creator and surrender herself to the evil spirit. Then he embraced her and bit her on the right arm, introduced himself as Herr Hämmerli and suggested that they sleep together, to which she consented. Then when she was full of hate towards her neighbour Hans Erb in Meilen she was incited by the malevolent spirit to strike his cow with a rod, which the devil had pointed out to her, and for a long time the cow no longer provided any milk. Indeed the cow has since died.

The account describes a series of cow murders before continuing:

> On account of her godless, shameless, unchristian life, during which she not only with the help of the devil wounded and killed cattle and people, but also because she had turned away from God Almighty and given herself to the evil one, she deserved a harsh death. However, on account of her remorse and conversion mercy was shown to her in the judgement. She was handed over to the executioner, who tied her hands together and led her to the Sihl river along the gravel path. He placed her on a huge pile and tied her to a pole, so that she might be burnt. Thus were her flesh and bones reduced to ash and she repented before the law. If anyone

> should object to her execution or seek to avenge the death then he or they are guilty of the same crime and should receive the same treatment that Kerez did.[24]

Throughout the Reformation period women continued to be tried and executed for witchcraft; the power of the devil was seen to be everywhere, and women were his agents.[25] In 1554 in the Bernese territory of Nidau the local bailiff was required to ask of some imprisoned women whether they were responsible for setting alight several houses in the locality and whether the cause of these actions was money promised to them by the devil. In the village of Ins four women were executed one after another on 28 August 1568, while in 1582 in Thun, Margeret Wyss, at the age of 102, was put in the flames for causing bad weather.[26]

The Swiss Confederation was one of the flash-points of witch-hunting during the sixteenth and seventeenth centuries. As Brian Levack has argued, the religious and cultural diversity within the Confederation resulted in varying patterns of witch-hunts. In the Pays de Vaud over 90 per cent of those tried for witchcraft were executed (about 2,000 victims), while in other areas of the Confederation the numbers were entirely different.[27] The jurisdictional particularism of the Confederation meant that intense witch-hunts could take place with impunity. Levack has advanced the theory that the uneven geographical distribution of witchcraft prosecutions in Europe had some connection to the religious conflicts of the Reformation. The persecutions in the Swiss Confederation were most ferocious in those areas, such as Berne and the Pays de Vaud, which had a history of trials running back into the fifteenth century. This legacy of executions was stirred by the confessional debates of the sixteenth century, and it is in the confessionally mixed areas of the Confederation that we see the most savage trials.[28] This observation fits well with recent research which has demonstrated the prominence of witch-hunts in border lands. Numbers are difficult to establish, but it is clear that in the Swiss Confederation the picture was varied. Basle and Zurich did not, on the whole, execute many witches, but in Berne and the Pays de Vaud the situation was very different. In Bernese lands alone it has been estimated that between 1591 and 1595 there were approximately eleven women a year burnt for witchcraft, but this number grew to 150 between 1596 and 1600. Between 1601 and 1610 approximately 420 died.[29] The reason for this in the Swiss lands are complex, but one important aspect was the influence of the Reformed culture of the Bible on the people. An increasingly biblically literate society was well informed about the denunciations of witchcraft in scripture. The local clergy, encouraged by the authorities, preached against the devil and his minions, explaining to the people how Satan's agents were active in the world. Finally, as we have previously mentioned, there was a growing corpus of vernacular works by the reformers which addressed such issues as the devil, witches, and ghosts, and the argument of these works was that Christians were locked in a battle against these enemies of God.[30] In addition to these aspects of Reformed religious culture there was the reality of severe economic and climatic difficulties. In both the urban and rural areas this not only brought destitution but bred resentment of outsiders and those perceived as the possible causes of the trouble. The persecution of witches fits well into this worldview.

Disease and fire: fear in the community

We can hardly imagine the brutality of early modern life. In the Swiss Confederation about one-quarter of babies died in the first year. Another third would die before they reached their tenth birthday. Plague generally spared the very young, but it was merciless in its treatment of those between the ages of ten and nineteen. The numbers of plagues in the Confederation cannot be counted for certain, but it is thought that between 1500 and 1640 there were, for example, at least fourteen in St Gall and thirteen in Geneva. The greatest killer of the children was smallpox, which between 1580 and 1599 killed over 90 per cent of the children under five who died during that period. Children over five were generally immune from the disease.

The struggle against plague was never ending. Streets and passage ways were blocked off, while merchants who came from plague-infected areas were quarantined. The results of plague in a region were normally a dramatic rise in the price of food, a doubling of the death rate, and a serious decline in the birth rate. Death rates from plague were always at their highest in August and September and their lowest during the winter months. As Körner has remarked, life had a fairly simple routine: one married in winter, procreated in the new year and died in the summer.[31] We can see from the modest rise in the population level that procreation did little more than sustain the numbers. It took three to four births to produce someone who would live into adulthood. This meant that for the parents to replace themselves six to seven children had to be born. Infant mortality was between 30 and 40 per cent. The cities grew largely because of immigration from rural areas, but it was also the urban areas which were most heavily affected by plague.

Care of the sick and the mentally ill was a major concern in all the cities. In Zurich the medieval hospital was augmented by the former Dominican house in which those who could pay could live out the rest of their days on a regular diet of meat and wine. In the lower part of the building, which was the former convent of St Verena, the sick of the city were tended to. In addition to the hospital (*Spital*), there was a house specifically for care of the poor, where every morning soup, stewed fruit or bread was distributed. Here too the poor, pilgrims, and foreigners on their way through Zurich could find a place to sleep for the night.

By the second half of the sixteenth century the social and economic problems were so great that these buildings no longer sufficed to handle the throngs of poor and sick who made their way to the city from the countryside. A new building was erected, called the 'Neue Sammlung', which was to serve as a hospital for all the sick, and following the starvation of the 1570s another house was built to feed the hungry. For the mentally ill there was a hospital just outside the walls of the city, though the 'Neue Sammlung' had a room in which men or women could be locked up. Mental illness was a serious matter in the sixteenth century but in most Reformed states it was hidden behind language. Most commonly in the records one finds terms like *arbeitselig*, a word which could have a variety of meanings ranging from physical infirmity to lunacy. For most of the sixteenth century madness and depression were interpreted by the preachers as signs of the devil at work. Suicide was hardly ever mentioned, remaining for the Reformed the terrible sin it was for Catholics. Bullinger in his *Berichts der Kranken* denied that melancholy was an explanation for suicide; that people chose to end their lives, he wrote, was a sign of weakness in the face of the onslaught of the devil. Bullinger described how these people acted out of *toubsucht*, by which he meant they were out of control, violent, and abusive. His colleague Ludwig Lavater had a slightly different perspective as he described in his book on ghosts how these people were prone to seeing apparitions.[32] The terrible economic conditions of the second half of the century did, however, lead to widespread despair, and suicides were not uncommon. Although the Reformed churches were disinclined to talk about suicide, the parish ministers in their reports to the synods often spoke of those unfortunate persons who had been moved to end their lives. The pastoral situation in this period was extremely difficult.

Most frightening of all was the threat of fire, particularly in the cities. In 1560 most of the town of Appenzell was burnt to the ground by a fire which destroyed not only the town church, but over a hundred houses. Bakers' ovens were a particular risk, but every household with its cooking fire posed a danger and in Zurich no one was allowed to dispose of their dishwater until the kitchen fires had been extinguished. Every city employed men to fight fires and incentives were offered to people who built homes made of stone rather than wood. Once a fire broke out in the closely packed neighbourhoods, however, there was virtually nothing that could be done; burning buildings were torn down to prevent the fire from spreading, but the only means of extinguishing the flames was with water passed from hand to hand in buckets. Faced with a raging fire which easily jumped over streets and narrow passages, this method was virtually useless.

More hardships: prices and weather

The Swiss Reformation took place during a period of profound economic change: prices for goods such as wine, grain, and meat increased dramatically, while those of vegetables, cheese, and butter seem to have risen more slowly, with some regional variations. The increase in prices in the Swiss Confederation generally matched those in the empire, though they were not as bad as, for example, France. The reasons for this are far more complicated than can be related here, but essentially wages did not keep up with the cost of living in sixteenth-century Swiss lands. By 1600 the basic wages had doubled from their 1500 level, but grain prices, for instance, had increased at least two and a half times. There is evidence from Geneva that the situation was worst for women. Washerwomen, for example, had their pay increased at a slower rate than men.[33] The amount of poverty in both the cities and rural areas rose dramatically. This was augmented by a steep rise in the price of land. In Zurich land prices remained at their late fifteenth-century level until about 1540, after that they increased first fivefold and then by the end of the century tenfold. The misery which this brought to the people formed a daily part of Bullinger's life as head of the church. He was constantly in negotiations with the council about poor relief and what to do with the large number of people who left the land and headed for the city, where they often ended up on the streets begging. The synodal records in Zurich are full of accounts from ministers of the dreadful circumstances in which their parishioners found themselves. The people could not pay the tithes, nor could they afford to look after their children. The result was, as the ministers reported, large numbers of children running through the villages, abandoned by their parents.

In the rural areas the situation was especially grim as most men laboured as day workers (*Taglöhner*), meaning there was little security. In the rural areas land was increasingly fenced, diminishing public access and leading to the development of local farmers becoming large landowners at the cost of the smaller farmers. In these regions there was a huge underclass of workers who are virtually invisible in the records. They survived by hand-to-mouth living. The better-off might have owned a few cows, but most found themselves looking for a day's work. It is from this class of people that the mercenary recruiters found plenty of men looking for something better.

The weather during this period was extremely changeable. In the period 1530–60 the Swiss Confederation endured a heat wave which was not matched until the twentieth century. In this period there were only two seriously cold winters, in 1527 and 1542, otherwise the winters were so mild and the summers so hot (especially during the 1550s) that the wine was ready very early in the autumn.[34] In 1565 the climate took a turn for the worse. All of the seasons were much colder and it rained heavily. Numerous chroniclers have left accounts of how Lake Zurich froze and that houses, men, and animals were buried under the snow. The heavy snowfalls and the frequent rain brought severe flooding. In the summer of 1588, for example, the Lucerne writer Renward Cysat recorded seventy-seven days of rain in three months. Likewise, hail, which totally destroyed the crops, was frequently mentioned. Weather was understood in providential terms, it was not simply a matter of bad luck but rather it reflected God's disposition towards the people. Freezing cold, like plague, was a punishment for the sins of the community, and the difficult conditions of the second half of the sixteenth century led many, including Bullinger, to believe that there was a great deal wrong with the Christian communities which had emerged from the Reformation.[35]

Death

Zwingli's rejection of the Catholic doctrine of purgatory radically transformed the geography of the afterlife for the Reformed church. Without a third place where souls could be purged before entering eternal bliss, from the moment of death there were only two possibilities for each individual, heaven or hell. Purgatory, Zwingli argued, had no warrant in scripture, and he spoke of 'the figment of purgatorial fire [which] is as much an affront to the redemption of Christ freely granted to us as it has been a lucrative business to its authors'. His position on purgatory was adopted without alteration by virtually all of the Swiss Reformed theologians, for whom any notion of a transitory state implied a rejection of the sufficiency of Christ's sacrifice on the cross for the sins of humanity. The implications of this argument were enormous. If souls are either in heaven or hell they are beyond the reach of human intercession, their fates are sealed, and the whole medieval Catholic liturgy of death had become hollow ceremonies. This was the theological position. What the reformers soon discovered, however, was that the old rites offered a great deal of pastoral comfort and simply to abolish them left a terrible void.

In place of the last rites of the Catholic church the Swiss reformers concentrated on comforting the dying and their families. In this respect there were some differences among the Swiss churches. In Basle, for example, the dying could receive the eucharist on their deathbeds from the minister, while in Zurich this was rejected.[36] For those who objected there were two problems: to carry the bread from the celebration of the Lord's Supper in the church to the bedside resembled the Catholic practice of the reserved sacrament, while a celebration of the Lord's Supper at the bedside denied its essentially communal nature. The minister was required to be with the dying in their last hours, encouraging them in the faith and defending them through prayer from the final onslaughts of the devil and his minions. The basic framework of the Reformed death retained key elements of medieval death culture. In a person's last hour the demonic forces in the world would intensify their attempts to snatch the soul, and family and friends were to gather around in prayer, hoping to be edified by a good death in the faith. The minister still played a key role, but more as comforter and leader in prayer than through the administration of any rites. Some Reformed writers, such as Ambrosius Blarer, reworked the medieval texts known as the *ars moriendi*, so that a distinctive Reformed art of dying was fashioned.[37]

According to Ludwig Lavater's account of practices in the Zurich church, after death the body was wrapped in a sheet and laid out in the house, and the head of the appropriate guild was informed.[38] A clear sign of continuity with medieval practice was found in the custom of the women from the neighbourhood gathering to remain with the body in the home. This practice seems to have continued through the Reformation period. In his diary Heinrich Bullinger noted that it was the custom to bury the body on the next day.[39] Many aspects of late medieval burial practices were to be found in the Reformed rituals: the family gathered outside the house as the body was brought out; wooden planks were laid on the ground along the way to the grave – a practice surviving from the days before the streets were cobbled. The procession was also strictly ordered. First in line were the sons of the dead person, followed by family and friends, and then the others in the community according to rank. As in the Middle Ages, the poor were also included in the procession. If the person was a guild member the body was borne by several colleagues.

A clear break with medieval practice was to be seen when the procession passed the church. The bells would not be rung. In rural areas, however, bells continued to be rung to announce the burial, summoning the people either to the grave or to prayer. Although the

Reformed churches in Zurich and Berne expressed their displeasure, there is evidence that men and women continued to be buried to the sound of ringing bells until well into the seventeenth century. Once the procession reached the open grave the minister would say a few words, but unlike in Lutheran lands a funeral sermon or oration was not permitted. Mostly the minister or local official would thank the people on behalf of the family for their support and presence. After the burial the mourners would gather in the parish church for prayer; the only time that the church building played any role in the service.[40]

The morals mandates of the Reformed states were very clear that post-burial festivities of any sort were proscribed. The dead were not to be remembered through drinking or dancing – the same applied to births, baptisms, and marriages – and people were to return to their houses after the church service. The disciplinary records and the laments of the clergy, however, paint a very different picture. The dead were remembered by the living with wakes that lasted several days. It is impossible to know exactly how widespread such occasions were, but the frequency with which they were denounced and forbidden provides us with at least an indication of how the formal church service was accompanied by local rites and traditions by which the people took leave of their dead. It was common for the men of the community to gather after the funeral in the local tavern, deaf to the threats from the council that drinking in such circumstances would bring a heavy fine.

Funerals, like most sacred moments in the life of a community, were complex affairs with competing expectations. The church wanted both to ensure that the rite was performed according to its understanding of death and to comfort and instruct the living. The families and communities had to come to terms with the human reality of loss, and they needed to express their grief in traditional ways. The civil rulers, finally, wanted to preserve public order and discipline. The council and church were concerned about the level of drinking and the resultant violence, but perhaps more acutely about the heavy costs to be borne by those who felt obligated to hold receptions.

Once the Reformed church had done away with the intercessory nature of Catholic death culture it remained a question of whether any form of remembrance should be permitted. In Zurich the headstones and epitaphs for the wealthy were attacked by those who resented their wealth and prestige. Zwingli himself was opposed to any form of marking for the grave, but naturally the older families saw this as part of their prestige in the city. Already in 1524, under Zwingli's influence, the council in Zurich forbade the marking of a person's death on the seventh and thirtieth days and on the one-year anniversary. Remembrance in Zwingli's Zurich was limited to the final act of the Sunday worship, when the names of those who had died in the previous week were read from the pulpit. In Basle this was also done, but instead of just once on Sunday the names were read during the weekday services.

As Martin Illi has noted, not all Reformed dead were equal. Despite the rubric that no form of remembrance was acceptable, for prominent reformers and politicians new ways of honouring their memories began to appear, such as poems, funeral orations, biographies, portraits, and books dedicated to the memory of the departed learned man. In most of the Reformed cities the headstones were removed, but exceptions were made, such as when Erasmus was buried in Basle. At the funeral of the Basle reformer Oswald Myconius the new head of the church, Simon Sulzer, gave a long funeral sermon, indicative of the extent of Lutheran influence in the city.

During the Reformation period many aspects of death and burial were more carefully regulated. By the early sixteenth century it was customary for every city to have gravediggers in its employment. As a result of plague and the growth in urban populations there was increased concern about hygiene and a plethora of regulations were introduced dictating, for example, the required depth of graves.[41] A grave was to be at least 1.8 metres deep and when it had to remain open for a prolonged period then chalk was to be distributed on the bodies to prevent infection. Other regulations were also applied. The Zurich council, in order to economise on space, declared that no one was to be buried in a coffin except pregnant women, women who died in childbirth, and new-born children. The reason for this was the common belief that contact with the bodies of such persons would lead to the spread of misbirths.[42] Further, all deaths were to be recorded by the local officials and burials at night were explicitly proscribed. The gravediggers and ministers were to vouch for the identity of the dead person.

The situation in the Swiss cities was similar to that across the empire. In times of plague the council would employ men to remove bodies from the city. These men had to live apart from the community during epidemics in order to prevent the spread of the disease. It was generally the case that when the cities required men to undertake these highly unpleasant and perilous duties they looked to those from the lower classes or those who lived on the periphery of the community. Poor people were often required to take up these jobs.

In all of the Reformed states there was disagreement over what to do with the cemeteries. Many, including Zwingli, wanted the break between the church and the cemetery to be expressed by the removal of the dead outside the city walls. Others, however, were less persuaded. A commission was formed in Zurich and both sides of the argument were heard. In 1528 the council decided that certain of the cemeteries in the city were to be closed, while others, such as those attached to the Grossmünster, Fraumünster, and St Peter's were to remain. In Zurich, however, the cemeteries became a source of controversy. Many people did not wish to be buried in new cemeteries outside the walls; they wished to be buried in the old cemeteries where their ancestors lay. The connection between church and cemetery, severed in Reformed theology, was very strong in the minds of most Zurichers in the sixteenth century. Bullinger had wanted one cemetery to be set aside for all outside the walls of the city, but public resistance prevented this and a new cemetery in the precincts of the old Dominican church in Zurich was created, thus restoring the link between church building and the dead.[43] The story was similar in all the other Reformed Swiss states. Despite plans to move the dead outside the walls of the city, public outcry prevented this from taking place. Secularised monastic lands in the city were employed to bury the dead, who for most of the sixteenth century remained an integral part of the community.

The cemeteries remained contested spaces during the sixteenth century as the churches sought to limit traditional uses of the place where the dead lay. It was the medieval custom to remove bones from the mass graves after the flesh had decayed away and place them in charnel houses where they could be venerated and serve as a *memento mori*. Throughout the sixteenth century the Reformed churches sought to have these charnel houses torn down and they insisted that the bones should be buried so as to prevent them from becoming objects of worship. The resistance to this demand was so great, especially in rural areas, that little headway was made in their removal. Charnel houses, with their collection of bones, did represent an anonymous and corporate form of commemoration, but the Reformed were severely allergic to any material form of devotion. The charnel houses, however, belonged to a deep-rooted culture of commemoration, both religious and familial, with which the Reformed faith simply had to come to terms. Similarly, there were repeated attempts to remove living people from the cemeteries. It was common in the Middle Ages that cemeteries were not only for the dead but for the living, who took up residence there, played, met, and even sold their wares. Cemeteries were places for wisewomen and charlatans, and the efforts of the Reformed churches to make them seemly locations for the dead required a profound change in mentality, and a great deal of time.

The rituals of death not only provided the people with pastoral comfort in the face of loss but also a variety of means by which they could protect themselves from both the dead and demonic forces in the world. The Reformed churches introduced a radically different understanding of eternity, but its dissemination in the parishes was a complex process of negotiation between doctrine and spiritual needs.

World of wonders: Johann Jakob Wick (1522–28)

The middle and second half of the sixteenth century saw a burst of literary activity as the writers of the Swiss Reformation moved beyond pure theology to engage with a growing body of subjects. In the next chapter we shall look at history-writing and texts on natural science, but alongside these learned works appeared a rich corpus of collective texts, reflections, medical books for the laity, biographies, and diaries which offer us insights on the daily life and mentalities of the period. Heinrich Bullinger's diary is but one example, his colleague and friend Johannes Haller in Berne wrote a wonderfully descriptive and laconic description of events in his day, but it is the journals and travel accounts of the Platter family which are perhaps best known.[44] Ludwig Lavater in Zurich collected ghost stories from around Europe, while in Basle Konrad Lykosthenes produced in 1557 a collection of wondrous stories and prognostications complete with beautiful woodcuts. In Catholic Lucerne the politician and medical doctor Renward Cysat brought together a huge collection of material gathered from letters and chronicles from across Europe. Cysat wanted to use the information for a history of Lucerne and the Swiss Confederation, but what interested him greatly were stories about the daily lives of men and women. The collecting of information which revealed the beliefs and anxieties of the people, the struggle between God and the devil in the world, and the curiosities of nature, was part of a pan-fascination. One of its greatest exponents, however, was Johann Jakob Wick in Zurich. His great work, known as the *Wickiana*, was a twenty-four-volume collection of stories richly illustrated with 1,028 pictures.

Most of the texts are chronologically arranged, but that is the extent of the organisation, and for the most part the volumes are filled with stories and pictures which Wick made no attempt to present systematically. Heinrich Bullinger, himself a learned historian, took great delight in Wick's collection of stories and documents and he made his enormous correspondence available to the young man as a source. For example there is a great deal of information about Geneva and the tribulations of the Huguenots in France taken from Calvin's letters to Bullinger.[45] Wick was well known in the city, and not only did his close connections with the leading churchmen in Zurich avail him of material for his work, but we know that ordinary people would knock on his door and relay stories to him that they had heard.

The pages of the *Wickiana* are full of stories of murders, executions, the works of witches, and fantastic events, but Wick's underlying purpose was not simply to relate the sensational.[46] The deeper intention was to provide men and women with an idea of how the forces of good and evil are at work in the world and how one should strive in this battle to live better. As with most collections the final goal was moral instruction, but it was to be achieved through entertainment. Wick had no difficulty believing that these stories he was recording were true. For Bullinger, Lavater, Wick, and the other Reformed writers of the sixteenth century, demons, angels, wonders, and providences were signs of divine or demonic activity and, therefore, simply belonged to the natural order. They drew a sharp distinction between these events and 'miracles', which were not natural occurrences, and according to the reformers had ceased during the early days of the church.

Strange occurrences in the heavens, monstrous children, and abnormal plants and animals were a particular interest of Wick. All of these were given a theological and moral interpretation, and Wick does not hesitate to use his stories in religious polemic against Catholics and Lutherans. Above all, however, Wick loved interesting stories, such as this account from 1570:

> As I have described above, strange birds have been seen in Flaachtal, where they were captured, as well as in large groups on Lake Zurich and in and around the city of Zurich, so that there are many of the birds, dead and alive, at the market. People have wondered what these birds, which no one has seen before, might mean.
>
> The late Dr Gesner [Konrad Gesner] mentions them in his bird book and calls them Bohemer. Among other things he says that they are certainly harbingers of bad luck. One hears that they were seen before the terrible plague of 1519 as well as before the Council of Constance. The chronicler Johannes Stumpf writes on fol. 440 of the second volume that these birds were also seen in 1488, mostly near the Thur and in Flaachtal, flying about in great numbers. They spent the night in the woods where on 6 April 1489 Hans Waldmann was beheaded. In 1552 these birds were seen in the city and bishopric of Mainz.[47]

For scholar, merchant, and peasant these birds were mysterious portents, somehow revealing something of God's will and telling the people of their history. Whether speaking of devils, witches, ghosts, monstrous births, or strange birds there were few sceptics; these aspects of God's creation were accepted by the whole society, and those who wrote about them did not do so as objective outsiders. The world was dangerous and wondrous, full of curses and blessings, and we must remember that it was in this world that the theology, ordinances, worship, and life of the Swiss Reformation existed.

Notes

1 Wilhelm Bickel, *Bevölkerungsgeschichte und Bevölkerungspolitik der Schweiz seit dem Ausgang des Mittelalters* (Zurich, 1947), p. 254.

2 Martin Körner, 'Glaubensspaltung und Wirtschaftssolidarität (1515–1648), in *Geschichte der Schweiz und der Schweizer* (Basle and Frankfurt-am-Main, 1983), II, p. 13.

3 Ibid.

4 Ibid., p. 14.

5 Johannes Kessler, *Sabbata: Mit kleineren Schriften und Briefen*, ed. Emil Egli (St. Gall, 1902), p. 233.

6 Ernst Ziegler, *Sitte und Moral in früheren Zeiten* (Sigmaringen, 1991), p. 34.

7 Jürg Stockar, *Zürich. Mode durch Jahrhunderte* (Zurich, 1974), p. 52.

8 Theodor de Quervain, *Kirchliche und soziale Zustände in Bern unmittelbar nach der Einführung der Reformation (1528–1536)* (Berne, 1906), p. 117.

9 See Thomas Max Safley, 'Canon Law and Swiss Reform: Legal Theory and Practice in the Marital Courts of Zurich, Bern, Basel and St Gall', in R.E. Helmholz (ed.), *Canon Law in Protestant Lands* (Berlin, 1992), pp. 187–201.

10 The most important work on this subject is Thomas Max Safley, *Let No Man Put Asunder. The Control of Marriage in the German Southwest: A Comparative Study, 1550–1600* (Kirksville, MO, 1984). See also his helpful article, 'To Preserve the Marital State: The Basler Ehegericht, 1550–1592', *Journal of Family History*, 7 (1982), pp. 162–179.

11 Auke Jelsma, '"What Men and Women Are Made For": On Marriage and Family at the Time of the Reformation', *Frontiers of the Reformation* (Aldershot, 1998), pp. 133–143.

12 The story is told in Frida Bünzli and Martin Illi, *Hirsebarden und Heldenbrei* (Berne, 1995), p. 38.

13 Charles William Pfeiffer, 'Heinrich Bullinger and Marriage' (dissertation, St Louis University, 1982).

14 Edward J. Furcha (ed.), 'Women in Zwingli's World', in Heiko Oberman, Ernst Saxer, Alfred Schindler, and Heinzpeter Stucki (eds), *Reformiertes Erbe. Festschrift für Gottfried W. Locher* (Zurich, 1992), pp. 131–142.

15 Z, VIII, pp. 49ff, n. 289.

16 Alice Zimmerli-Witschi, 'Vom Kloster zur Küche –Frauen in der Reformationszeit', in Sophia Bietenhard, Rudolf Dellsperger, Hermann Kocher and Brigitta Stoll (eds), *Zwischen Macht und Dienst. Beiträge zur Geschichte und Gegenwart von Frauen im kirchlichen Leben der Schweiz* (Berne, 1991), pp. 56–57.

17 Ibid., p. 64.

18 Heinrich Bullinger, *Der Christlich Eestand* (Zurich, Froschauer, 1540), sigs. E7[v]–E8[r].

19 Merry E. Wiesner, *Gender, Church and State in Early Modern Germany* (Harlow, 1998), pp. 14–162.

20 Auke Jelsma, 'A "Messiah for Women": Religious Commotion in North-East Switzerland, 1525–1526', in his *Frontiers of the Reformation* (Aldershot, 1998), pp. 40–51.

21 Zimmerli-Witschi, 'Vom Kloster', p. 78.

22 Kessler, *Sabbata*, II, p. 141.

23 Andreas Blauert, 'Hexenverfolgung in einer spätmittelalterlichen Gemeinde: Das Beispiel Kriens/Luzern um 1500', *Geschichte und Gesellschaft*, 16 (1990), pp. 8–25. On the diocese of Geneva, Louis Binz, 'Les Débuts de la chasse aux sorcières dans le Diocese de Gèneve', *Bibliothèque d'Humanisme et Renaissance*, 59 (1997), pp. 561–581.

24 Matthias Senn, *Die Wickiana. Johann Jakob Wicks Nachrichtensammlung aus dem 16. Jahrhundert* (Zurich 1975), p. 208.

25 Jelsma, 'The Devil and Protestantism', *Frontiers of the Reformation*, pp. 25–39.

26 Hans Guggisberg, *Bernische Kirchengeschichte* (Berne, 1958), p. 286.

27 Brian P. Levack, *The Witch-Hunt in Early Modern Europe* (London and New York, 1987), p. 179.

28 See E. William Monter, 'Patterns of Witchcraft in the Jura', *Journal of Social History*, 5 (1971), pp. 1–25.

29 Guggisberg, *Bernische Kirchengeschichte*, p. 355.

30 See Bruce Gordon, 'Incubus and Succubus in Zurich: Heinrich Bullinger on the Power of the Devil', in Kathryn Edwards (ed.), *Demons, Vampires and Werewolves. The Revenant in European Culture*, Sixteenth Century Essays and Studies (Kirksville, MI, forthcoming).

31 Körner, 'Glaubensspaltung', p. 15.

32 Markus Schär, *Seelenöte der Untertanen. Selbsmord, Melancholie und Religion im Alten Zürich 1500–1800* (Zurich, 1985), pp. 91–92.

33 Ibid., p. 32.

34 Christian Pfister, *Klimageschichte der Schweiz 1525–1860*, 2 vols (Berne and Stuttgart, 1984), II, pp. 118–121.

35 Hans Ulrich Bächtold, 'Gegen den Hunger beten. Heinrich Bullinger, Zürich und die Einführung des Gemeinen Gebetes im Jahre 1571', in Hans Ulrich Bächtold, Rainer Henrich, and Kurt Jakob Rüetschi (eds), *Vom Beten, vom Verketzern, vom Predigen. Beiträge zum Zeitalter Heinrich Bullingers und Rudolf Gwalthers* (Zug, 1999), pp. 9–44.

36 Martin Illi, *Wohin die Toten gingen. Begräbnis und Kirchof in der vorindustriellen Stadt* (Zurich, 1992), p. 112.

37 Gordon, 'Malevolent Ghosts and Ministering Angels', in Bruce Gorden and Peter Marshall (eds), *The Place of the Dead* (Cambridge, 2000), pp. 87–109.

38 Lavater, *Die Gebräuche*, pp. 114–115.

39 Illi, *Wohin die Toten*, p. 113.

40 Ibid., pp. 113–114.

41 Ibid., pp. 122–123.

42 Ibid., p. 123.

43 Ibid., p. 129.

44 On the Platter family, see Emmanuel Le Roy Ladurie, *The Beggar and the Professor. A Sixteenth-Century Family Saga*, transl. Arthur Goldhammer (Chicago, 1997).

45 Matthias Senn, *Die Wickiana. Johann Jakob Wicks Nachrichtensammlung aus dem 16. Jahrhundert* (Zurich 1975), p. 15.

46 Bruno Weber, *Wunderzeichen und Winkeldrucker 1543–1586. Einblattdrucke aus der Sammlung Wickiana in der Zentralbibliothek Zürich* (Dietikon and Zurich, 1972).

47 Ibid., p. 197.

9

International Zwinglianism: the Swiss Churches and Europe

Following the defeat at Kappel in 1531 the only significant expansion of the Swiss Reformed churches was in the Pays de Vaud from 1536. Beyond the boundaries of the Confederation, however, Swiss influence made its way across Europe and played a significant role in the development of Reformations from England to Transylvania. It is far beyond the scope of this overview to chart this dissemination of ideas in any detail, but some attention should be given to those areas where Zurich, Basle, and to a lesser extent Berne, left their mark. The Swiss political and military influence outside the Confederation was negligible, so we must look to personal contacts and printing as the means by which their theology and ecclesiology was translated to other lands. Of greatest importance was southern Germany, where Zwingli had placed such hope in a confessional alliance. Swiss evangelical thought spread like wildfire through the southern German cities, appealing to artisans and craftsmen; Zwingli's work was often read in preference to Luther's, largely on account of its emphasis on the communal nature of the church and the lucidity of the Zurich reformer's position on the sacraments. The southern German cities formed a dense web of connections to which the Swiss cities belonged, and the linguistic and cultural affinities were key to the reception of Zwingli's ideas. We must, however, insert a cautionary note; the theology which developed in south-western Germany, although heavily influenced by the Swiss, had its own character. The southern German and Alsatian reformers had to tread carefully between Zurich and Wittenberg and ultimately, following the Diet of Augsburg in 1530, they drifted towards Lutheranism.

With England, Eastern Europe, France, and the Netherlands we see the enduring importance of personal contacts. Students travelled to

Basle and Zurich to study and returned home carrying the printed works of the Swiss reformers. The location of the Confederation at the heart of Europe, with access to both the Rhine and the transalpine passes, meant that not only students, but merchants came in contact with the Swiss churches, and took back ideas and information, both printed and oral. Zwingli's works were admired for many reasons, but perhaps above all they were esteemed for their putative biblicism and humanist learning. We know from the accounts of learned men such as Celio Secundo Curione that it was Zwingli's attack on the mass, as well as his rejection of the mediating role of the church, that made his writings attractive. It is easy to oversimplify, but we can argue that the attraction of Zwingli's writings was, in large part, due to his unambiguous recognition that the church was corrupt and his forceful resolve that the situation, as a necessity, had to be remedied. The cure was not by improvements to the offices of the church, but in a radical reorientation of the church back to its biblical, and especially, Pauline basis. What drove Zwingli and made him such a powerful speaker and writer was his profound sense of dualism, as we have discussed earlier.[1] He used a variety of images, such as flesh and spirit, to make the point that the world witnesses the battle between God and the forces of darkness. Although Zwingli would not allow that it is a battle of equals, and he was clear that God's will prevails, he asserted nevertheless that there is potent force in God's created order which resists his will. The daringly antithetical terms in which Zwingli spoke, as well as the radical solutions he proposed, made his work highly attractive to those who felt a deep spiritual need for reform.

After Zwingli's death his legacy was complicated. The manner of his death, the effectiveness of Catholic and Lutheran polemic in vilifying his teaching on the sacraments, and the lingering suspicion that his ideas were pregnant with radical implications, made Zwingli a dangerous association. It was through the work of Simon Grynaeus, Vadianus, and above all Heinrich Bullinger that the intellectual achievements of the Swiss Reformation began to receive attention throughout Europe. Bullinger was the great communicator of the European Reformation: during his life he published about 124 works, most of which were translated into the major languages of Europe. His correspondence, which runs to about 12,000 letters, is one of the great repositories of information from the sixteenth century; Bullinger corresponded with over 1,000 men and women across Europe, from kings to schoolteachers. Not only did he counsel nascent reform movements, but was a pivotal link in the well-established lines of communication which developed between the Reformed communities in which letters full of news and rumours were circulated.

Alongside his letter-writing, which must have occupied a good portion of his day, Bullinger and his family resided in a large house next to the Grossmünster in Zurich in which hundreds of students, reformers, and refugees were given hospitality and accommodation over four decades. Bullinger recorded in his diary how they would share the evening meal at which news was exchanged and theology discussed. Bullinger, like Zwingli, did not work alone, he was at the centre of a sodality of churchmen, scholars, and politicians, committed to the Reformed cause in Europe. He depended on these men, learned from them, and trusted them, but in the end it was Bullinger's name which was esteemed above all others.

Southern Germany

Zwingli's preaching quickly spread beyond the boundaries of the Swiss Confederation to the imperial cities of Strasbourg, Constance, and Nuremberg, where it influenced men and women who had been stirred by the Luther controversy. Just after Zurich had adopted the Reformation in 1525 the city had begun to form alliances with Strasbourg and Constance. We have discussed these developments earlier in chapter 2.[2] By 1529, just as Lutheran opposition to Zwingli was reaching its zenith, Zurich was looking to create an alliance of cities which would serve both as a defence against the Catholic Habsburgs and provide the weight to crush the Five Inner States. Zwingli's evangelical message and the model of the urban Reformation provided by Zurich appealed to powerful elements in the cities of Nuremberg, Ulm, Augsburg, and Constance. As Thomas A. Brady has noted,

> Evangelical clergymen began to clothe the evangelical message in the language of revitalised civic and communal ideals, the language of the sacral corporation. The message of the evangelical urban reformers interacted powerfully with the burghers' communal values, so that 'the victory of the "Reformed" Reformation in Upper German imperial cities is finally explained by the encounter of the peculiarly "urban" theology of Zwingli and Bucer with the particularly communal spirit in Upper Germany.[3]

Heinrich Richard Schmidt has further argued that Zwinglian theology was highly attractive to the magistrates of the southern German cities on account of its emphasis on the sovereignty of God; this formulation of divine authority allowed the Zwinglian cities to adapt more readily to the political realities of the 1530s which required new alliances with their erstwhile bitter enemies, the territorial princes.[4] The shift which the cities had to make away from the Catholic emperor, their traditional ally, towards the princes was more accommodated in Zwingli's theology, according to Schmidt.

One of the most interesting cases is of the imperial city of Rottweil which lies on the Neckar at the eastern edge of the Black Forest.[5] Although it was a middling city, Rottweil was of considerable importance as it was the seat of an imperial court (*Hofgericht*). What further distinguished Rottweil was its 1519 alliance with the Swiss by which the city became an associated territory of the Confederation. Rottweil and Mülhausen were the only German cities to have sought this status. Although the *Hofgericht* meant that Rottweil had a direct and close relationship with the Holy Roman Emperor, the city had sought from the middle of the fifteenth century to draw closer to the Swiss Confederation. Schaffhausen acted as mediator in the negotiations. During the period between 1500 and 1520, when many of the cities in south-western Germany were drawn towards the Swiss, Rottweil was the only one to make concrete political relations. The reasons for this were clear. Economically Rottweil was closely connected to the Swiss Confederation through the linen trade.[6] The market at Zurzach (north-west of Zurich) was extremely important for Rottweil merchants. The Swiss lands imported meat and fruit from the rich lands of southern Germany and the Alsace. With the death of Maximilian I in 1519 the Rottweil magistrates seized the opportunity of strengthening the formal relationship with the Swiss begun in 1463. This proved a fateful decision as it placed Rottweil in between the emperor and the Swiss during the Reformation.

Unlike most of the other southern German cities, there was virtually no Reformation movement in Rottweil. In fact, there was no sign of any evangelical sentiments until after the Peasants' War, when Valerius Anshelm arrived in Rottweil from Berne, where he had been expelled on account of Zwinglian sympathies. The other important person was Konrad Stücklin, who when he was appointed civic priest by the council evinced no obvious attachment to evangelical teachings. From 1526 Anshelm and Stücklin began spreading the new ideas and secret conventicles were formed.[7] When the council attempted to suppress the movement by imprisoning the evangelicals, it appeared that there was broader support for the movement in the guilds, especially among the weavers and smiths – those who had closest contact with the Swiss. The council, however, remained firmly in the hands of the Catholics, who were assured of the support of Rottweil's rural inhabitants, who were unmoved by the evangelical preaching. The pro-Reformation party in Rottweil was a small, urban group drawn from the guilds, and while they received fair words of support from Zurich and Basle, they were beyond the reach of Zwingli's supporting hand.

In 1528 the emperor threatened to withdraw the *Hofgericht* should Rottweil adopt the Reformation. In December of the same year a delegation from Rottweil arrived at the Swiss diet in Baden and asked Zurich and Berne to send emissaries to their city in support of the Reformation. A Swiss delegation arrived in Rottweil on Christmas eve and proposed to the assembled guildsmen and magistrates that the 'free preaching of the Gospel' be permitted in the city. A vote by the assembly went against the Swiss. This was the one occasion where a vote of a southern German city went against the evangelicals. The Catholic Swiss states had played a role in this rejection by writing to Rottweil urging the city to remain with the old faith, and shortly after the vote against the Reformation a delegation from the seven Catholic states arrived.

During 1529 the council relentlessly rooted out the evangelicals in Rottweil. The preachers were expelled and the council rejected a supplication that at least some provision be made for the evangelicals. This rejection led to an armed confrontation between some evangelicals and the council, but the magistrates held all the cards. With an armed force at the ready and the complete support of the rural communities the council could quash the movement without difficulty. The city was not prepared to risk losing the *Hofgericht*, which made Rottweil important beyond its size, and the evangelical preaching had simply failed to ignite the crowds. When the council finally decreed that those with evangelical sympathies would have to leave the city, 400–450 men and women, a considerable number, passed out through the city gate.

The other imperial free city closely connected with the Swiss Confederation was Mülhausen, a city of four thousand inhabitants in Alsace. Already in the fifteenth century Mülhausen had made alliances with Berne and Solothurn and had fought alongside the Confederates against the Burgundians. In 1515, through the mediation of Basle, Mülhausen entered into a formal alliance with thirteen Swiss Confederates, occupying a position similar to that of St Gall. The city retained its Swiss connection until it was finally handed over to France in 1798. Already in 1518 there were important figures in Mülhausen who were attracted to Luther's cause, and in 1523 the German imperial knight Ulrich von Hutten took up residence in the city, from where he launched one of his bitter attacks against Erasmus. A key early figure was the Augustinian prior Nikolaus Prugner, who was the civic preacher in the church of St Stephen. In July 1523 the Mülhausen council issued a preaching mandate similar to those of Zurich and Basle whereby the clergy were bound to preach only from scripture. Prugner was a native of Colmar and had come to Mülhausen in 1519; by 1522 he was already preaching evangelical ideas and two years later he married. He had close contacts with both Froben and the Amerbach family in Basle and during his time in

Mülhausen he came to know both Ulrich von Hutten and Balthasar Hubmaier. He also became close to Zwingli, who dedicated a work to him in 1523. As a preacher, however, Prugner was suspected of harbouring sympathies for the rebellious peasants during the years 1524–25 and he was dismissed from his post in 1526. Undaunted by his misfortune, Prugner went on to serve in a number of Alsatian churches before travelling north to Cologne, where he worked under Archbishop Hermann von Wied. Quite remarkably, he ended his days a professor of astronomy in Tübingen university, where he died in 1557.[8]

Following Prugner's departure Wolfgang Capito recommended Otto Binder, a native of Baden who had studied in Basle and imbibed Erasmian humanism. When he returned to Baden he was converted to the evangelical faith by Otto Brunfels and he preached, with varying levels of success, in a series of towns throughout Baden before going to Strasbourg, where he came into contact with Capito, who took him on as an assistant. From 1526 until his death in 1555 he served as the preacher in Mülhausen, much admired for his learning and pastoral sensitivities.

The religious situation in Mülhausen was extremely murky. Support for the Reformation was strongest among the guilds, who were closely connected to Basle. While Prugner was fairly clearly a Zwinglian, the influence of Strasbourg was also pronounced; both Otto Binder and the native son Augustin Gschmus, who became city preacher in 1527, were much closer to Martin Bucer in their theology. Gschmus had attended the Baden Disputation of 1526 and opposed Oecolampadius, and then at the Berne Disputation of 1528 he refused to accept the article on the eucharist, thus revealing his Lutheran views.

Although Mülhausen was heavily influenced by Basle the council anticipated events in the Swiss city by removing images from the churches in April 1528. By the end of 1528 an evangelical Lord's Supper had been designed by Binder and Gschmus. The mass was abolished on 15 February 1529 at the same time as in Basle. A marriage court (*Ehegericht*) was introduced according to the Zurich model. The greatest threat to Mülhausen was the Austrian lands in southern Germany, and for protection the city joined the Christian Federation in the summer of 1528. Mülhausen sent troops to the Confederation in both of the Kappel Wars, losing eleven out of seventy men in 1531, and according to the terms of the Second Kappel Peace the city had to quit the Christian Federation. But Mülhausen remained part of the community of Swiss Reformed churches, participating in meetings of church leaders and was consulted by Bullinger and others when matters of great importance arose. Theologically it remained under the influence of Basle and Strasbourg; the

1534 *Basle Confession* became the theological standard of the Mülhausen church, though the city declared itself in favour of Bucer's ill-fated 1536 *Wittenberg Accord*. The 1534 confession formed the basis of the *Mülhausen Confession* of 1537, which was used until 1566, when in contrast to Basle Mülhausen accepted the *Second Helvetic Confession*. In almost every other respect Mülhausen adopted practices usual in Basle: Oecolampadius's catechism, subsequently revised by Myconius, was the standard for religious education until the *Heidelberg Catechism* of 1564. In worship and church organisation the Basle pattern was adopted, including the 1540 hymn book and the Lobwasser Psalter.

With a population of about twenty thousand, sixteenth-century Strasbourg was much larger than any of the Swiss cities.[9] It was about twice the size of Basle, the city with which it had the closest economic and cultural relations. During the early 1520s the evangelical message made rapid progress in the city. The first evangelical preaching was by Matthias Zell, and he was soon reinforced by the arrival of Wolfgang Capito and Martin Bucer in 1523. That same year the first preaching mandate was issued by the Strasbourg council. The campaign against the mass had begun during the Peasants' War. In the ensuing split between Zwingli and Luther over the sacrament of the Lord's Supper the preachers in Strasbourg lined up behind Zurich. Jakob Sturm, member of the Senate and the large council, was deeply influenced by Zwinglian theology. Finally in 1529, in the face of vociferous agitation from clergy and laity, the mass was abolished in the city. Strasbourg followed the example of Zurich. The two cities were closely connected by the Swabian–Alemanic language, a common social situation and a 'dense network of correspondence and acquaintance among the evangelical clergymen'.[10] A year later Strasbourg entered the Christian Federation with Zurich, Basle, and Berne.

The alliance with the Swiss cities badly split the clergy in Strasbourg, who divided along Zwinglian and Lutheran lines. The principal issue remained the eucharistic dispute, but the main thrust of the Lutheran offensive was that by allowing Zwinglian ideas of a 'spiritualised' faith in the empire the door was being opened for another peasants' war. A direct connection was drawn between Zwinglianism and subversion. For those in Strasbourg the decision was extremely difficult; there was the cultural attraction of the Swiss Reformed cities, but the response of the Lutherans, alongside a general belief that Charles V would move into southern Germany to restore Catholicism, made the Swiss connection problematic.

At the 1530 Diet of Augsburg the Strasbourg delegation was received with hostility by the Lutherans, who accused them of Zwinglian errors. In reply Jakob Sturm secretly brought Martin Bucer and Wolfgang Capito to Augsburg where they penned the *Tetrapolitan Confession*. It was to be signed only by Strasbourg, Constance, Lindau, and Memmingen, and it was treated with total contempt by the theologians surrounding Charles V. Sturm remained undaunted and he played a key role in the negotiations which led to the formation of the Schmalkaldic League in December 1530. Sturm had wanted the Swiss cities to be part of this wider alliance, but he knew that the doctrinal split between Zurich and Wittenberg was too deep to permit this. If Strasbourg was to be part of imperial religious politics the city would have to find some form of accommodation with the Lutherans, even if this meant abandoning the Swiss, who, according to the Christian Federation, were co-citizens. The Swiss were of crucial regional importance to Strasbourg, the city's best defence against attack, but after Augsburg in 1530 their influence in the empire was negligible. Although there remained in Strasbourg considerable support for Zwingli's theology, the formation of the Schmalkaldic League spelled the end of Reformed Swiss influence in southern Germany. By February 1531 the cities of Ulm, Constance, Memmingen, Isny, and Biberach had likewise joined the league. The southern German cities did nothing to support Zwingli and Zurich in the Second Kappel War. Zwinglianism would remain an important theological force in the empire, but even before the death of the reformer its days as the ideological basis for a political alliance were over.

Although the Schmalkaldic League had been founded in 1531, it acquired its theological profile with the *Wittenberg Accord* of May 1536, when Martin Bucer and Philip Melanchthon, along with a few others, cobbled together an agreement on the eucharist which would allow the southern German cities to join in alliance with the Lutheran states. Although as Bullinger stressed, it made little sense theologically, and did nothing to resolve the real differences between Zwingli and Luther on the issue of real presence in the eucharist, the agreement removed the major obstacle to a political alliance.[11] The German cities needed the support of the Lutheran princes, for although the Swiss may have inspired much of their theology, they could offer no military or political support. Although Augsburg and Constance rejected the document, the *Wittenberg Accord* prepared the way for the ultimate triumph of Lutheranism in southern Germany. Johannes Marbach, one of Bucer's students, was sent to study under Luther in Wittenberg, and he would later play a central role in shifting Strasbourg towards Lutheranism.

The defeat of the Schmalkaldic League in 1547 brought no more painful loss to the Swiss than that Constance, which was occupied by Austrian troops in 1548. Of all the southern German cities, Constance was the most Swiss, and as we have noted earlier, if it had not been for the opposition of the inner rural states Constance might well have followed Basle and Schaffhausen into the Confederation at the beginning of the sixteenth century.

There was a group of humanist churchmen in Constance, mostly canons of the cathedral, who welcomed Luther's attack on the abuses of the church, and from 1520 voices were raised in the city in favour of Gospel-preaching. Johannes Wanner, who was part of Bishop Hugo von Hohenlandenburg's delegation to Zurich to investigate the breaking of the Lenten fast, had been impressed by Zwingli when the two men met. When Wanner was subsequently dismissed from his post for his evangelical sympathies the Constance council, which had supported the advocates of scriptural preaching, appointed him to the church of St Stephen. On 9 February 1524 the preaching mandate was issued in Constance. Unlike the preaching mandates in Zurich, Strasbourg, and Basle, the Constance edict mentioned neither disputations to discuss the religious situation nor any punishments for those clergy who refused to accept the new order. Constance had to keep a weather eye on the emperor. Nevertheless, support for the evangelical cause was strong in the guilds, and already at a meeting of the southern German cities in December 1524 Constance took the lead in advocating the introduction of the evangelical faith.

The Reformation in Constance was led by a group of preachers who were very close to Zwingli and Oecolampadius. The Blarer brothers, Thomas and Ambrosius, were natives of Constance. Thomas studied theology in Wittenberg under Luther and Melanchthon from 1520 and had accompanied Luther to Worms in 1521. He returned to Constance to serve as a jurist and then, between 1537 and 1547, he held the office of Bürgermeister several times. Thomas converted to Lutheranism his brother Ambrosius, who had entered the Benedictine house at Alpirsbach, and in 1525 Ambrosius was ordained as civic preacher in Constance. From 1522 Ambrosius had been in epistolary contact with Zwingli and Oecolampadius. The other key preacher was Johannes Zwick, who was made a civic preacher in 1526, and had attended the 1523 Zurich Disputation.

In contrast to most of the German and Swiss cities where the evangelical faith took hold, the movement in Constance faced fierce and effective Catholic opposition. Most influential were Zwingli's rival Johannes Fabri, vicar-general of the diocese of Constance, and the provincial of the Dominican order, Antonius Pyrata. The evangelicals were supported by key members of the council, and in 1526 the bishop and most of the Catholic officials withdrew from Constance to take up residence in Meersburg. With the flight of the bishop Catholic resistance collapsed and church ordinances modelled on those in Basle were introduced. The mass was abolished in early 1528 at the same time as Constance entered the Christian Federation with Zurich and Berne.

As in Basle, the issue of religious images was particularly vexed in Constance. The debate raged over whether the magistrates possessed overriding authority in the external matters of religion. Within Constance there were conflicting perspectives; the Zwinglian clergy represented only one faction as strong Lutheran and Anabaptist groups rejected the Zurich position on the authority of secular rulers. Both Zwingli and Oecolampadius wrote to Constance with advice on the orderly removal of images from the churches.[12] During the winter of 1528–29 the churches in Constance were stripped of religious art and their walls were whitewashed.

Despite the close relations with Zurich and Basle the Constance Reformation had its own theological character. At the Diet of Augsburg in 1530, Constance was one of the four cities to sign Bucer's *Tetrapolitan Confession* and Johannes Zwick participated in the negotiations leading to the *Wittenberg Accord* in 1536, though he refused to sign the document. In two aspects the Constance church distinguished itself from Zurich and Basle: from 1531, with the introduction of the morals mandate and the *Zuchtherren*, a much stricter form of church discipline was enforced in the city; and in 1533–34 the Constance hymn book was introduced, giving music and singing a much more prominent place in Reformed worship than was to be found in the Swiss churches. Nevertheless, under Ambrosius Blarer Constance remained the most Zwinglian of the southern German cities.[13]

Ambrosius Blarer was the most significant reformer of the Swabian cities. He had been closely connected to the Swiss reformers, as well as to Bucer and Capito, and his theology, which he refused to articulate in detail, lay somewhere between Zurich and Strasbourg. Blarer was no theologian, he spent his entire career avoiding doctrinal formulations, but he was an indefatigable reformer who devoted himself to preaching, liturgy, music, and pastoral care. Between 1528 and 1540 he concentrated his energies on preaching and organising reform movements in the towns and cities in the eastern part of the Swiss Confederation and Swabia. His work was crucial to the development of the Reformation in the Swabian imperial cities of Memmingen, Isny, Esslingen, Ulm, and Lindau. Between 1534 and 1538 Blarer, alongside Erhard Schnepf, was responsible for the development of the Reformation in Württemberg, which had been returned to the Protestant Duke Ulrich in 1534. As the leading voice of Zwinglian thought in the southern German cities, Blarer faced considerable opposition from Lutherans, but he won the respect of many for his energy and commitment to spiritual renewal.

Along with Bucer and Capito Blarer created the unique theological climate of the southern German cities in which greater emphasis was placed on reform of the church and community and pastoral care than doctrinal precision. Caught between Luther and Zwingli, and drawing on the strong communal traditions of the southern cities, these reformers stressed unity and corporate spiritual welfare. Their vagueness on central doctrinal matters left men like Luther and Bullinger baffled and exasperated. In many respects their great contribution to the Reformation lay in their church-building: Ambrosius Blarer, from 1540, stayed in Constance to cultivate the nascent Reformed churches. Blarer worked to develop the disciplinary body in Constance, to establish provision for the education of the clergy, and to provide new tools for Reformed worship and devotion. He wrote liturgies and devotional works for the laity, and many of his sermons were printed. Above all, however, Blarer was a poet and hymn-writer. His Constance hymn book was printed in 1533, 1536/37, and 1540 in Zurich and it set the standard for Reformed church music. The liturgy for the Lord's Supper in Constance, for example, reflected Blarer's emphasis on ethics and communal singing.[14] His hymns, with their beautiful language and phrasing, expressed the profound inner spirituality which was so distinctive of Blarer and other Swabian and Alsatian writers. With the fall of Constance in 1548 Blarer, like Johannes Haller and Wolfgang Musculus from Augsburg, fled to the Swiss Confederation. From 1551 until 1559 Blarer served as a minister in Biel, preaching and tending to a congregation, and he refused the many offers of more lucrative and prestigious posts in the Confederation and Germany. His heart was broken by the recatholisisation of Constance, and most of his later hymns and sermons are on the theme of death and the afterlife.

In Augsburg, like all the German cities, the magistrates had to balance public agitation for religious reform against the political and economic interests of the city. Augsburg was particularly vulnerable to external pressures as many of its merchants had heavily invested in the metal trade in Habsburg territories. Nevertheless from 1524 there was iconoclasm in the city and evangelical ideas were being preached to large numbers of men and women, many of whom came from the labouring classes.[15] Officially, the magistrates declared themselves neutral, a position they found increasingly untenable in the face of popular pressure. The evangelical preachers and the populace were so strong by the end of the 1520s that the city was not able to sign the *Reichstagsabschied* of 1530 when the emperor sought to force the city to return to Catholicism. Following the Diet of Augsburg in 1530 famine and pestilence fell upon the land, making the population restive, and the evangelical preachers alighted upon the discontent to press for more radical religious reforms.

Zwinglianism had made deep inroads in Augsburg in the 1520s and by the early 1530s most of the clergy in the city were in sympathy with the theology of Zurich. These sympathies extended to important lay officials, such as the court secretary Franz Kötzler and Hans Hagk, a lawyer employed by the council.[16] The magistrates in the city seemed uncertain and nervous of how to proceed, while among the evangelicals the usual dispute about the sacraments broke out between the Zwinglians and the Lutherans. As in Strasbourg, the principal attack by both Catholics and Lutherans against the Zwinglians was that with their emphasis on communal reform and scripture as law they were peddlers of social unrest, seeking to pull down the established hierarchy of power. There was also a strong sentiment that in their preaching the Zwinglian clergy had shown a distinct lack of respect for the authorities. For those who adhered to the Swiss Reformed teachings, however, it was imperative that the authority of the Bible be established (which meant the abolition of the mass and the removal of images from the churches) and that the council act as God's representative and take the lead in bringing about reform. Hagk, a Zwinglian who became a civic clerk in 1535, declared that the emperor had no authority to act against the commandments of the Bible.

The Augsburg council remained concerned with the legal implications of reform and the economic and political consequences of breaking with the Catholic church. Although the city was split between conservative and reforming parties, public agitation, as well as evangelical preaching, forced the council's hand and reform was introduced in July 1534. As Philip Broadhead has remarked, this happened 'not because their council was dedicated to the Protestant cause, nor yet because they believed religious reform would best serve the long-term interests of Augsburg. They went ahead solely to maintain their authority as a council and prevent the popular rebellion of their own citizenry.'[17]

With the Reformation mandate of 22 July 1534 the mass was limited to eight churches in the city. This proved only a temporary measure, for on 17 January 1537 these eight churches were handed over to the Protestants, who stripped them of all images and introduced a new form of worship. The church order of 1537 marked the official adoption of Zwinglianism in Augsburg.

The leading churchman in Augsburg was Wolfgang Musculus (1497–1563), a man who never studied at a university yet was to become one of the leading theologians of the Swiss Reformed churches.[18] At the time of his arrival in Augsburg in 1531 Musculus was a convinced Zwinglian, though during the 1530s he shifted towards the mediating ideas of Martin Bucer, under whom he had studied in Strasbourg during the late 1520s. Musculus signed the *Wittenberg Accord* of 1536, which was largely written by Melanchthon, but quickly retreated when he realised that Bullinger and the other Swiss theologians would not accept Bucer's prolix expansion of Melanchthon's work. Musculus was a powerful voice for reform in Augsburg, urging the magistrates to move beyond accommodation with the Catholics and complete the changes begun in 1534. He held the first evangelical service in Augsburg's cathedral in 1537. With the victory of Charles V at Mühlberg in 1547 Augsburg's fate was sealed; the emperor rode into the city as a triumphant victor and the Reformation was vanquished, though not eradicated, in Constance.[19] But for just over a dozen years the powerful city of Augsburg had been a centre of Zwinglianism in southern Germany, much to the chagrin of Luther and the emperor. Its Reformation bore witness to the powerful popular appeal of Zwingli's ideas.

Ulm, with a population of between 17,000 and 21,000, was the largest city state after Nuremberg to emerge in southern Germany during the fourteenth and fifteenth centuries.[20] Unlike nearby Augsburg, however, Ulm did not develop into a centre of commerce. The city and its territory was ruled by seventeen guild masters and fourteen patricians. Also unlike the other southern German cities the guilds did not dominate political life in Ulm.

In the early years of the Reformation Ulm showed little interest in the new movement. There were few humanists in the city and the magistrates published the Edict of Worms against Luther. Although the Ulm council was not actively hostile towards the evangelical movement, it soon emerged that it was deeply divided on the issue. The Bürgermeisters Ulrich Neithart and Matthäus Krafft were solidly loyal to the old religion, while Bernhard Besserer (1514–38) and the city clerk, Conrad Aitinger (1520–40), provided key support for the evangelicals. Besserer had represented Ulm's affairs abroad and was well aware of the developing situation in Germany. From 1523 his support for the Reformation was effected through a careful policy of calling clergy to the city who were evangelicals. At the same time under Besserer the Ulm council followed a cautious policy of giving no offence to the emperor by not making any legal or ecclesiastical changes in the city. Thus for most of the 1520s the council remained undecided. It faced the dilemma confronting the German cities; they had to balance popular support (as well as among the magistrates) for religious changes with a realistic assessment of the dangers posed by breaking with the emperor. Ulm, like many of the other cities, looked to see what would come of the negotiations for a Protestant civic alliance with the Swiss. In the period 1529–30 Ulm under Besserer looked at a variety of alternatives, ranging from an alliance with the

Swiss, to closer relations with the emperor, and even isolation. The pressure from the guilds for religious change, however, was beginning to lift the lid off the pot. And shortly after a vote of the guildsmen in favour the Reformation, Ulm joined the Schmalkaldic League.

The city looked to Martin Bucer, Ambrosius Blarer, and Johannes Oecolampadius to write evangelical church ordinances. On 6 August 1531 a Reformation mandate crafted from Lutheran and Zwinglian ideas was declared. Two months earlier Martin Bucer had prepared an outline of evangelical teachings in eighteen theses which were put to the clergy. All but two of the priests had rejected the new teachings, but the council gave a clear indication of what it thought of their their views by immediately abolishing the mass on 16 June. Three days later the council permitted families to remove from the churches the art which they had commissioned. The churches were then stripped bare and over fifty altars were destroyed.

By the autumn the religious orders had been expelled from the city and their houses appropriated, and over the next five years other convents and religious institutions were suppressed. Attempts by Catholics to seek compensation through the imperial chamber court went unheeded in Ulm. Under Konrad Sam, who served as preacher in Ulm from 1524 until his death in 1533, there was a strong Zwinglian influence in the city, and close connections had been kept with Oecolampadius in Basle. The form of the Reformation in 1531 closely followed the Zurich–Basle model. But with Sam's death in 1533 the leadership of the evangelical church passed to Martin Frecht, a close friend of Johannes Brenz, who was much closer to Wittenberg and ensured, for example, that Ulm accepted the *Wittenberg Accord* of 1536. Swiss influence remained strong in the city, especially until Besserer's death in 1538. Ulm remained confessionally mixed until 1555: alongside the Zwinglian and Lutheran circles a small, but influential, group of Catholics remained on the council, and radical groups began to appear.

France

The close connection between Geneva and France during the sixteenth century is a familiar story, but it should not blind us to the significant role played by the Swiss churches in supporting their co-religionists. The Swiss states had for a long time enjoyed a special relationship with the French crown. Basle printers had well-established connections in France and through the 1520s they provided a range of religious literature into the kingdom that raised the ire of Catholic authorities. Through the printing houses of Wattenschnee, Vaugris, and Resch, Basle was at the forefront of the growing religious debate in France; not only were the works of Erasmus exported, but also the New Testament of Lefèvre as well as numerous Lutheran pamphlets. Francis I, recently freed from prison in Spain after the battle of Pavia, allowed the Vaugris family to continue selling books in Paris as long as they removed the suspect titles and took them back to Basle.[21] Even during the 1530s, following the Placards affair in 1534, Basle book merchants confidently sold their wares in France. Basle was a curious place in the 1530s: the evangelical Farel had been expelled for his views while Erasmus was allowed to retain an Olympian distance from the Reformed church. The book industry was no different. It was a business and Basle booksellers were used to dealing with clients on both sides of the religious divide. Some printers had strong ideological commitments, but others, such as Conrad Resch, were more flexible.

The Swiss were, however, willing to involve themselves more directly in French religious affairs. In 1537 a delegation from the Reformed states appeared before Francis I to petition on behalf of those evangelicals suffering persecution on account of their faith. In particular the delegation had in mind their co-religionists in Nîmes, though the intervention of the Swiss made little difference. A year later another petition was sent to Paris on behalf of Philippe Oudriez, who had been sentenced to death for his beliefs. The appeal fell on deaf ears and Oudriez was duly executed. This pattern continued for several years, with Basle taking the lead in attempting to stir the other Reformed states into supporting the evangelicals in France.

1552 brought a fresh crisis when five young Frenchmen who had studied at the Lausanne Academy were arrested in Lyons. The young men had engaged in religious discussions and had been invited to the house of man who, it turned out, worked for the Inquisition. The evangelicals were arrested and examined before the vicar-general of the cardinal François de Tournon, where they were found guilty of treason against the king on account of their heresy. The Swiss Reformed states actively campaigned for their release. Zurich, Basle, and Schaffhausen sent a delegation to King Henry II, while Berne wrote on behalf of the imprisoned men. Bürgermeister Johannes Haab of Zurich led the delegation, which met the king at Tours, but the discussions proved fruitless. The king declared that all evangelicals in France were seditious and that there could be no mercy for those arrested in Lyons. The prisoners maintained correspondence, particularly with Calvin in Geneva and with the Zurich ministers. All efforts to save them failed and on 16 May 1553 they died in the flames kindled in the Place de Terreaux in Lyons.

With the outbreak of the French Wars of Religion the Swiss found themselves increasingly drawn into events on their western frontier.

Swiss soldiers fought and died on both sides, with approximately 10 per cent of the French crown's military budget allocated for the payment of pensions to the Swiss states. In 1567 Charles IX's ambassador to the Swiss Confederation, Pomponne de Bellièvre, recruited six thousand troops to defend the northern French frontier. The Huguenots, however, believed that these troops were to be used as part of a Franco-Spanish alliance to annihilate them.[22] At the same time the Huguenots also sought to hire Swiss mercenaries, and in 1559 Jean du Barry, seigneur de la Renaudie, travelled through the Confederation seeking troops and support.

The importance of the Swiss in the dissemination of evangelical ideas in France is hard to measure. A crucial early contact was Guillaume Farel, who was introduced to Zwingli's thought by Oecolampadius, and who remained until at least 1536 Zwinglian in his theology. Zwingli was keenly interested in developments in France, dedicating a series of works to Francis I, including his 1531 *Exposition of the Faith*. The text of Zwingli's *Exposition* was taken to the court of Francis I by Rudolf Collin, but the work was not printed until 1536, when Bullinger, who especially valued this late writing of Zwingli, produced an edition.

The extent of Zwingli's influence in France was at least sufficient to force Martin Luther to complain to Philip Melanchthon about the views of French evangelicals. Absolute connections, however, are virtually impossible to find; some scholars have detected Zwinglian influences in a variety of early French evangelical texts, but as we have found elsewhere, theological eclecticism prevailed. Between 1542 and 1556 the Sorbonne placed Zwingli's works on the Index of forbidden literature six times.

On Bullinger's influence in France we know something more, thanks to the seminal, yet often overlooked, work of André Bouvier. In February 1572 François Hotman wrote to Bullinger

> I congratulate the church of Zurich and her sisters in France and Germany, for they are your daughters and charges. You can see here in France the results of your labours. Do not believe that your learned works are valued more highly in your own land than in ours. The old adage is correct: A prophet is without honour in his land. But your commentary on Revelation has freed more Frenchmen from the tyranny of Antichrist than have been diverted from the light of the Gospel by the books of the Sorbonnists. For my family and me at least, as we fled to Sancerre during the recent chaos, we have found in the chronology which you have provided in your commentary on Daniel such great comfort that we cannot do without that book. Our church considers you to be its father and pastor; they pray for you, and for the most part they attribute their welfare to you.[23]

The first French-language editions of Bullinger's *Decades* appeared from presses in Geneva in 1559 and 1560. Although it was not as widely read as Calvin's works in France, the work enjoyed great esteem in France.

England

The key figure in the early development of contacts between England and the Reformed Swiss churches was Simon Grynaeus, who travelled to England in 1531 to see what capital could be made for the Reformation out of Henry VIII's marital dispute. The Swiss reformers, in opposition to the German Lutherans, were clearly of the opinion that the king should be permitted to divorce. During his time in England Grynaeus became acquainted with numerous high-ranking members of the English court and church, including Thomas Cranmer, with whom he became close friends.[24] Grynaeus had arrived in England with a letter of introduction from Erasmus, but he soon irritated the Dutchman with his involvement in English religious politics. Grynaeus was to remain until his death in 1541 in close contact with Cranmer, and he became the leading figure in developing relations between the English church and the Zwinglian churches in south-western Germany and the Swiss Confederation.

The first signs of such contact, however, were as early as 1526, when an unnamed work by Zwingli against the Anabaptists was listed by the archbishop of Canterbury as a forbidden work. We know from Catholic sources that Swiss evangelical works made their way to England at an early date. Under lists of proscribed 'Lutheran' books the names Zwingli and Oecolampadius stood alongside the Wittenberg reformer. In fact, Oecolampadius was specifically condemned in the Pontefract Articles of the Pilgrimage of Grace in December 1536. The first writing by Zwingli to appear in English was a translation of his *Fidei Ratio*, which he had prepared for the Diet of Augsburg in 1530. The work was reprinted in 1548 and then a new translation appeared in 1555. In each case the place of publication given was Geneva, but it is more likely that the books were printed in Emden. In 1550 Zwingli's *A short pathwaye to the ryghte and true understanding of the holye sacred scriptures* was translated by John Veron and printed in Worcester by J. Oswen.

The 1531 Zurich Bible translation had a profound influence on English translations through the work of Miles Coverdale, whose 1535 Bible was translated from Latin and German. There is strong evidence that the German text which Coverdale used was not that of Luther, but the 1531 Zurich Bible. The parallels are striking: Coverdale translated the psalms directly from the Zurich Bible and the order, style, and presentation of his work directly follows the Zwinglian work. Coverdale even used woodcuts from the Zurich Bible.

During 1536, as the Swiss began to speak again with one theological voice with the *First Helvetic Confession*, Bullinger looked to cultivate links with Thomas Cranmer. He encouraged others, such as Vadianus in St Gall, to write to the archbishop of Canterbury. Bullinger's interests in establishing contact with the English church had many angles; relations with the German Lutherans had taken a serious turn for the worse in 1536 due to the *Wittenberg Accord*. The situation in Germany was uncertain, while in France it was hardly much better. England was the great hope for the Zurich reformer, who was as concerned about the advance of the Reformation across Europe as he was about his own church.

Cranmer, although polite and interested, was uncomfortable with the Swiss teaching on the Lord's Supper and did not hesitate to communicate his disapproval. It was not until the 1540s that he began to move towards Bullinger's teaching on the eucharist. Nevertheless, there were positive signs that Cranmer wished to draw closer to the Swiss Reformed churches. In August 1536 three young men, John Butler, William Udroph, and Nicholas Partridge arrived in Zurich on their way to Italy. They were followed a few years later by Nicholas Eliot and Bartholomew Traheron. There is no doubt that all these men were connected to Cranmer, and that they were in Zurich with his approval. Bullinger took great interest in this circle of Englishmen, meeting with them to discuss the book of Isaiah. When Partridge returned to England in 1537 he was accompanied by Rudolf Gwalther, through whom Bullinger hoped to deepen his contact with Cranmer. Gwalther wrote an account of his travels to England, detailing whom he met and where. Many of these youthful acquaintances became lifelong friends, men such as John Parkhurst, Richard Turner, and Richard Master. Their hospitality was reciprocated when they were forced to leave England during Mary's reign; Parkhurst lived in Gwalther's house from 1554 until 1558.[25]

It was during the short reign of Edward VI that Swiss influence in England reached its zenith.[26] The 1549 Book of Common Prayer prepared by Cranmer drew on a range of continental sources, amongst which was Zwingli's liturgical work. Although one should not overstate the case, there are traces of Zwingli's liturgical work in the prayer book, including the wording and placement of prayers for the eucharist and the so-called 'Comfortable Words' ('Come unto me all ye who labour …') of assurance of Christ's sacrifice for the faithful.[27] These echoes of Zwingli may well have been mediated through the work of John à Lasco, Martin Bucer, and Peter Martyr Vermigli. In attempting to distil Swiss influences in England, or in any area of the

Reformation, one must exercise a good deal of caution, for in the flow of oral and written information nothing existed either in isolation from other ideas or in a pure, unadulterated form. The evangelical world in England was eclectic, and among the continental Reformed writers whose works were read a general theological consensus on most issues sat uneasily alongside serious disagreement on others.

A central figure in the connection between the Swiss churches and England under Edward was John Hooper, who had married in Basle before moving to Zurich, where he remained from March 1547 until 1549. Hooper became a close friend of Heinrich Bullinger, and when his daughter was baptised in the Grossmünster on 29 March 1548, the head of the Zurich church stood as godfather. During his two years in Zurich Hooper observed the practices of the Reformed church and imbibed the theology of Bullinger, who at that point was in the midst of the negotiations with John Calvin over the eucharist which would lead to the *Consensus Tigurinus* of 1549. When Hooper returned to England it was as an outspoken proponent of Bullinger's theology, emphasising the purity of religion and the rejection of all external forms not sanctioned by scripture.

Although Archbishop Cranmer did not disagree with most of Hooper's theology, the latter's impatience for a full Reformation of the English church put a tremendous strain on relations. In 1550 Hooper's consecration as bishop of Gloucester became mired in a debate over the wearing of vestments as required by the Ordinal. Hooper's position left no latitude either to the church or the magistrates in matters on which the Bible is silent. He insisted that everything had to possess scriptural warrant – certainly not a position ever taken by either Zwingli or Bullinger – and, therefore, he could not accept the vestments of office. For Cranmer and others this was an intolerable act of disobedience to legitimate authority.[28] Crucially, Bullinger did not support Hooper, but wrote that vestments were a matter of indifference, and that as such could be tolerated for the sake of order until the time was propitious for their removal. Ultimately Hooper had to submit to Cranmer. This has been represented as a blow for Swiss influence in England, but in fact the vestment controversy in England might be better viewed as mirroring the enduring tensions of the Zwinglian inheritance. Hooper had failed to grasp that for Bullinger theology could not be separated from its application. In 1525 with the outbreak of Anabaptism and in 1531 with Zwingli's death the Swiss had learned the bitter lesson of compromise. The Zwinglian legacy was the unresolved question of the relationship between the demand for pure religion and fidelity to scripture with the need for ordered change mediated through established political authorities. The vestment episode in England was for Bullinger yet another manifestation of this tension, and we can hardly be surprised that he backed Cranmer against his friend Hooper. Zwingli's radical prophetic voice had been silenced, replaced by Bullinger's reverence for ordered government.

There were others in England at this time who likewise pushed for further reforms to bring the English church in line with the Swiss Reformed. An important figure in this respect was the Polish reformer John à Lasco, who had begun building the stranger churches in London in 1550.[29] Lasco supported Hooper in the vestment controversy and had opposed the eucharistic teaching of Martin Bucer, also now in England. Lasco's views on the Lord's Supper were much closer to Zwingli's, and in writing the church order for the London stranger churches he viewed Zurich as the model to be emulated.[30] The leading figures of the London community, Lasco, Martin Micron, and Jan Utenhove, had all spent time in Zurich and corresponded with Bullinger. Their theological sympathies lay with Zurich and this was reflected in their church order, sacramental beliefs, and in their reservations about Calvin's doctrine of double predestination.[31]

With the accession of Mary in 1553 large numbers of Protestants fled to take refuge on the Continent. The vast majority went to Emden, Wesel, and Frankfurt. A small number travelled further south to Zurich, where Heinrich Bullinger recorded in his diary in March and April 1554 that a number of English refugees had arrived in Zurich, including ten students.[32] These students formed a community in Froschauer's house. Among the Marian exiles in Zurich were Richard Chambers, Robert Horne, James Pilkington, Michael Reniger, Thomas Spencer, Thomas Bentham, William Cole, and John Parkhurst. When the Lutherans expelled twenty-five families from Wesel Bullinger arranged for them to settle in Aarau. Among those in this community were Thomas Lever, future archdeacon of Coventry, and Miles Coverdale, who had translated several of Bullinger's writings into English. Other individuals made their way to Geneva, Berne, and Lausanne. Although the number was relatively small, many of the Marian exiles in the Swiss Confederation would return under Elizabeth to senior positions: Robert Horne became bishop of Winchester, John Parkhurst bishop of Norwich, Thomas Bentham became bishop of Coventry, and John Jewel became bishop of Salisbury. Their gratitude for the hospitality shown by the Swiss was reflected in the enduring epistolary relationships they maintained after their return to England.

In Basle, John Foxe, who had originally fled to Frankfurt, worked in the book trade, where he had access to the major printing houses of Froben and Oporinus. During his time in Basle he worked on his martyrology, fed by a rich stream of material through colleagues and friends in Strasbourg. In 1559 Nicholas Brilinger and Johannes Oporinus printed Foxe's *Rerum in Ecclesia Gestarum*, a history of martyrs up to the reign of Queen Mary, which was to develop into his famous *Acts and Monuments of these Latter and Perilous Days*, one of the most influential works of the English Reformation. Basle, as a centre of humanist scholarship, printing, and international Protestantism, afforded Foxe the opportunity to work in peace, even if he lived in penury.

Many of these men, particularly John Jewel, remembered with the greatest affection the Swiss churches which had given them refuge. William Cole wrote to Rudolf Gwalther in 1573 that 'the kindness, most honoured sir, which I experienced from you beyond all others at Zurich, can never escape from my memory; wherefore I wish you to believe that, although I am far removed from you in person, in mind and inclination, I shall always be a Zuricher.'[33] The former exiles did have the opportunity to reciprocate some of the hospitality of their Swiss hosts when in 1573 a group of students, among whom was Gwalther's son, arrived in Oxford from the Confederation. A second group of Swiss students, including the son of Wolfgang Musculus, arrived in 1577. These personal contacts, combined with the dense correspondence which passed back and forth, kept the Swiss churches closely in touch with England.[34]

Although news of the accession of Elizabeth was greeted with joy in the Swiss Reformed cities, there was the worry that she might prefer either German Lutheranism or opt for a composite form of the faith which would leave the English church half-reformed. From Zurich Bullinger and Peter Martyr Vermigli wrote extensively to England sharing news and offering advice. Among the important correspondents was Edmund Grindal, the future archbishop of Canterbury, who in a 1567 letter to Bullinger credited the Zurich reformer's *De Origine Erroris* with his conversion to the Swiss view on the eucharist.[35] Grindal, along with many of the Elizabethan bishops, wrote to Bullinger not only to apprise him of developments, but to seek support in crucial matters. For example, when the vestarian controversy arose again in the 1560s, Bullinger once more backed those who advocated obedience to the magistrates over the radicals impatient to remove all unsanctioned externals of the church. Bullinger was the voice of magisterial reformation, and his moderate tones were welcomed by Elizabeth, whom Bullinger defended in his 1571 refutation of the papal bull issued against the queen.

Apart from Bullinger's correspondence, from 1556 the Zurich church had a very strong connection with England in the person of Peter Martyr Vermigli, who was in England from 1548 until the death of Edward VI. Vermigli first went to Strasbourg after his flight from

Mary, and in the cathedral school he held lectures on the Old Testament book of Judges and Aristotle's *Ethics* to an audience which included such Englishmen as Jewel, Sandys, and Christopher Goodman. Jewel and Sandys then followed him to Zurich. Vermigli remained a great authority for the English exiles, and when Mary died there was talk of bringing him back to England to oversee the completion of the reformation of the English church. After his death, his work acquired new importance in England when Antony Marten assembled the voluminous *Common Places*, a collection of Martyr's theological writings and correspondence thematically arranged. The work was published in 1583 and stood alongside Bullinger's *Decades* as one of the most important theological and pastoral works in England during the last decades of the sixteenth century.

During the Elizabethan period the Swiss writers were widely read in England. The first work by Bullinger to be circulated in English was his sermons on the book of Revelation, which was published in a translation by John Parkhurst in 1561. Parkhurst was Bullinger's voice in English; he was responsible for a large number of works, including the English version of the *Second Helvetic Confession*. Parts of Bullinger's *Decades* were translated into English and circulated, but it was not until 1577 that the complete work appeared, and it soon became a bestseller. This large work was reprinted in 1584 and 1587, and was recommended by numerous bishops as essential reading, in either Latin or English, for their clergy. Bishop Thomas Cooper of Lincoln wrote in 1577 that

> Every parson and vicar under the degree of a Master of Art, or a preacher allowed by the hand and seal of the bishop, and also every curate serving in a benefice where a preacher is not resident shall, before the first of September next coming, buy the *Decades* of Bullinger in either Latin or English (being now for that purpose translated), and every week to read over one sermon in such sort that he be able to make a reasonable account of it ...[36]

As Patrick Collinson and others have demonstrated, the Elizabethan and Jacobean church often looked to Geneva for theological rectitude, and something like a 'Calvinist consensus' emerged. Nevertheless, the deep respect in which the Swiss reformers, particularly Bullinger, were held, and the influence their works exercised deserve to be more widely recognised.

Eastern Europe

In Eastern Europe the spread of Swiss Reformation thought had a distinct ethnic dimension as many Slavs were attracted to Reformed ideas because their German neighbours were inclined to adopt

Lutheranism. Already in the 1520s there were connections between Bohemia and the Swiss Reformation.[37] In 1525, Johann Zeising and Johann Mönch, attacked the official teaching of the Bohemian Brethren on the eucharist, and in so doing they made use of some of Zwingli's writings. Zeising continued to propagate Zwingli's writings in Bohemia during the 1520s, ensuring that the Zurich reformer became an important figure in the enduring debates over the sacraments which raged between branches of the Hussite movement. The arrival of Balthasar Hubmaier in Moravia brought Anabaptism, but he was removed and burnt as a heretic on 14 April 1528.

The most important figure was the poet, hymn-writer, and preacher of Landskron, Michael Weiß, whose 1531 hymnal for the Bohemian Brethren contains strong traces of Zwinglianism. Likewise his reforms of the Brethren liturgy contained elements taken from the Zurich liturgy of the 1520s. The connection between the Brethren and Zurich, however, made the latter uncomfortable. The 1532 *Justification of Faith*, edited and translated into German by Weiß, was printed by Froschauer in Zurich. Leo Jud, Zwingli's old friend, was deeply drawn to the ideas of the Bohemian Brethren in this period and he was involved in the preparation of the text. Certain points, such as the rejection of the authority of the magistrates over the church, had been taken up by Jud in his disillusionment with the Zurich council in the aftermath of Zwingli's death. Bullinger saw the influence of the Bohemian Brethren as akin to that of Schwenckfeld, and he sought to draw Jud away from this association.[38]

The works of Zwingli, Oecolampadius, Bucer, and the other southern German writers were being read in the east, along with texts by Luther and Erasmus. It is difficult to separate out clear lines of influence as texts were exchanged and read as part of the unique religious situation in the east, where the Brethren and Utraquists sought to find some sort of unity. The situation was made even murkier with the arrival of radical sects, against which King Ferdinand of Bohemia took a hard line. In men such as Johannes Dubcansky in Habrovany we find someone who was clearly attached to the work of Zwingli. He led a circle of well-educated men committed to reform who saw that there was to be no reconciliation between the Brethren and the Utraquists, and thus believed that the work of the Swiss reformers offered new possibilities. He fell victim to Ferdinand's persecutions of the radicals, and after a period of imprisonment from 1535 to 1538 he was a broken man. His *Apologia*, printed in 1536, bears an unmistakable resemblance to Zwingli's *Fidei Ratio*, which the Zurich reformer had prepared for the Diet of Augsburg in 1530.[39]

In Hungary there was a direct connection between the Swiss and the nascent evangelical movement. Simon Grynaeus, who was to emerge as the leading intellectual light in Basle after Erasmus's departure, was rector of the Academy in Buda during the years 1523 and 1524. His personal connections and reputation would bring many students from Hungary and Transylvania to Basle to study theology at the university. Zwingli's name was already being invoked in 1525 in debates in Hungary over the Lord's Supper; it is thought that pilgrims to Einsiedeln in 1523 were responsible for bringing back to Hungary the works of Zwingli and Leo Jud. The diffusion of their works must have moved apace as in 1527 the new king of Hungary, Ferdinand I, issued a mandate against the heresies of Zwingli and Oecolampadius.

Matthias Biro Dévai (1500–45) from Transylvania was a student of Grynaeus in Buda before travelling to Wittenberg in 1529 to study under Luther. Fleeing persecution, he arrived in Basle in 1542, one year after the death of his erstwhile teacher, and by 1544 he was named by Luther as a sacramentarian, a pejorative tag for supporters of the Swiss position on the Lord's Supper. In fact, insofar as one can dissect Dévai's theology it seems to have been a miscellany of ideas drawn from Swiss, south German, and Wittenberg writers (in particular Melanchthon). This was typical of most reformers in the east until the 1540s; there was considerable theological eclecticism, and it would be foolhardy to pinpoint one place as authoritative. The fluid situation in the east with the Turkish wars raised practical matters of the church over the theological as communities fought for survival.

The leading reformer in Transylvania was Johannes Honterus, who was in Basle in the 1530s, where he worked with some of the printers and became familiar with the work of Oecolampadius. When he returned to Brasov he attempted to implement reforms along the lines of the Basle Reformation. On 10 May 1543 Sebastian Münster wrote to his friend Konrad Pellikan in Zurich that Honterus had studied in Basle and was now carrying out reform of educational and ecclesiastical institutions in accordance with the vision of Oecolampadius.[40] Honterus remained in close contact with several of the Swiss reformers, including Vadianus, with whom he had a regular correspondence, and Oswald Myconius. Basle played an important role for many students from the east, and men like Grynaeus, Myconius, and Münster served as mentors, often housing the students in their homes. The Swiss reformers kept each other informed about the movements of these students, and they exchanged letters of introduction and recommendation. It was not at all uncommon for students from Hungary and Transylvania to make their way to study in Wittenberg and then Basle, and none of the Swiss reformers objected to this mixed theological education. How could they have? Bullinger and Myconius were sending their own students to Wittenberg and other Lutheran universities to study.[41] The movement of students was an important means for the exchange of books, letters, and other gifts. In many ways they formed the lifeline of the Swiss churches for the other developing Reformations of Europe.

Heinrich Bullinger was deeply interested in events in Hungary, Poland, and Transylvania.[42] He wrote frequently to contacts in these lands and his influence should not be underestimated. In 1551 Bullinger sent a letter to persecuted communities in Hungary; it was a tract on pastoral care, full of practical advice for the situations in which the faithful found themselves. Many other of Bullinger's works circulated through Eastern Europe. In 1557 the printer Gál Huszár sought Bullinger's assistance in dealing with the liturgical differences in the Hungarian church, and in reply he received a copy of Ludwig Lavater's 1559 description of church practices in Zurich, a book which had considerable influence on the forms of Hungarian worship.

Swiss influence in the Hungarian church reached its peak in 1567, when at the Synod of Debrecen Bullinger's *Second Helvetic Confession* was adopted as the official statement of faith for the Hungarian Reformed church. The man largely responsible for this development was Petrus Melius, who had close contacts with both Zurich and Geneva, and was encouraged to accept the Helvetic Creed by Theodor Beza, who had himself accepted it. Thus the line of Swiss influence which emerged in the 1520s continued through to the period of confessionalisation in Hungary, when the Reformed and Lutheran churches divided along dogmatic lines.

The Swiss had close connections with Poland that predated the Reformation. Vadianus had visited his nephew, who worked for the family business in Cracow, in 1519. There were long-established trade links between the Confederation and Poland, but equally important were the connections made by Swiss mercenaries and humanist scholars, who had been at the Polish court and academies. Polish humanists had their work printed in Basle, and two of them, Modrevius and Orzechowski, made contact with Zwingli.

While most of Poland was firmly Lutheran, many of the magnates corresponded with Bullinger and Calvin. Among the important correspondents with Bullinger were Bishop Georg Israel and Prince Nikolaus Radziwill, who in 1553 converted to the Reformed faith. His son Nikolaus Christoph visited Bullinger in Zurich in 1566, although he was later to reconvert to Catholicism under Jesuit influence. Although Calvin had misgivings about the Polish church, especially because of the protection afforded to heretics like Biandrata and other antitrinitarians, Bullinger kept a busy correspondence with a wide range of figures in Poland, hoping to combat both radicalism and Lutheran influence.

The complicating factor was the influence of the radicals in Poland. From 1551, following his first visit, the antitrinitarian views of Lelio Sozzini took root in Poland and by the mid 1570s there was a well-organised antitrinitarian movement known as the Polish Brethren. Lelio's nephew Fausto, came to Poland to live permanently in 1580. The radical church, known as the Minor Church, was protected by the powerful magnate Micha Sieniecki (1521–82) and had its centre in Raków, where they composed their catechism.

Nevertheless, Bullinger's work bore fruit. In 1570 the synod of the Polish Reformed church more or less adopted the *Second Helvetic Confession*, which was reformulated by Christoph Thretius as the *Confessio Sendomiriensis*. It was hoped that this confession would form the basis of a reconciliation of the Reformed with the Lutherans and Bohemian Brethren, but this was not to be. Instead, at a meeting of the three confessions in April 1570 there was broad agreement on a more fluid doctrinal basis, which did give centre stage to the *Confessio Sendomiriensis*, but alongside Lutheran and Bohemian statements of faith.

Italy and Spain

Zwingli's works were read in Italy from an early date.[43] In the preface to his *Concerning True and False Religion* (1525), Zwingli wrote that he had been petitioned by evangelical brethren in Italy and France to pen a summary of Christian doctrine. Many of the Italian evangelicals who made their way north following pressure from the Inquisition cited Zwingli's works as their principal inspiration. Zwingli's humanism and biblicism were clearly highly attractive among Italian evangelicals. The fateful year 1542 brought numerous refugees to the Swiss Confederation from Italy who would figure prominently in theological disputes among the Reformed churches: Jerome Bolsec, Celio Secundo Curione, Peter Martyr Vermigli, Bernardino Ochino, Lelio Sozzini, and the former bishop of Capo d'Istria, Pietro Paulo Vergerio.[44] We have already discussed many of these figures in a previous chapter.[45]

In Spain we find evidence from the Inquisition that works by Zwingli, Bullinger, Gesner, and Pellikan were circulated and read, along with the writings of Erasmus, Luther, and other northern European authors.[46] These Swiss books were naturally proscribed and burnt as heretical tracts, but they do seem to have had some influence. The colourful and controversial Antonio del Corro (1527–91), a former Observant Hieronymite from Seville and nephew of an inquisitor, had introduced evangelical literature into Spain before being forced to flee to Geneva. He was given a scholarship by the magistrates of Berne to study in Lausanne under Theodor Beza. He was a prolific writer, espousing a moderate Reformed theology and stressing toleration. He arrived in London in 1567, where his learning was much admired, and he found powerful patrons in William Cecil and Robert Dudley. In 1574 he sent a letter to Zurich through Rudolf Gwalther the younger, who had been studying in Oxford, in which he informed Bullinger that he had read his works whilst still in Spain, and that these writings had been central to his religious development.[47]

Another itinerant Spaniard was Francisco de Enzinas (Dryander) who was born in Burgos in 1520, who seems to have come in contact with evangelical ideas while studying at the university of Paris. He went to Wittenberg to further his studies in 1541 before making his way to Zurich in 1546, where he met with Heinrich Bullinger. He also visited Vadianus in St Gall and Ambrosius Blarer in Constance before furthering his studies in Basle, where he wrote and had printed an attack on the Council of Trent. After a brief period in England he returned to Basle to continue his scholarly work; he made contact with Calvin and had close relations with the church in Strasbourg, where he died of the plague in December 1552.

Alongside these scholars is the story of Doña Isabel Briceño from Naples who was greatly influenced by the circle of religious figures gathered around Juan de Valdés. Isabel was closely connected to Giulia Gonzaga, the patroness of Valdés who appears in his *Christian Alphabet*. Isabel was clearly regarded as harbouring heretical ideas and numerous prominent Catholic figures, including Ignatius Loyola, were summoned to return her to the fold. Although they appeared to have successfully disabused Isabel of her evangelical sentiments, some time between 1555 and 1557 she fled Italy with her son and arrived in Tübingen, where her friend Pietro Paulo Vergerio was residing. It has been suggested that she wanted to go to Vienna where she would find a place at the irenic court of Emperor Maximilian II. She was invited to Zurich and arrived in the city in 1558, where she met her old friend Bernardino Ochino, who dedicated to her his work on the eucharist. Bullinger treated her most courteously and she departed from the city to Chiavenna with a letter of recommendation from the Zurich church leader. Although ill, she was reunited with her sons in Chiavenna, though they were unable to persuade her to return to Catholicism. She died in 1567 in Chiavenna, true to her evangelical faith in defiance of her family. She was greatly honoured by the Reformed Swiss church leaders.

The Netherlands

There is evidence that Zwingli's writings were read in the Low Countries from an early date; both Bucer and Capito wrote to Zwingli declaring that his views on the Lord's Supper were widely supported, particularly in the provinces of West Friesland and Geldern. And in 1529 an edict from Emperor Charles V forbade the possession or distribution of books by the Zurich reformer. Beyond this, however, the trail goes cold. No editions of the works of either Zwingli or Oecolampadius were printed in the Low Countries, though men such as Martin Micron and Jan Utenhove, who played an important role in the London stranger church during the reign of Edward, were familiar with Swiss theology.

It was the work of Bullinger which proved of greater importance in the development of the Reformation in the Low Countries. In 1563 his *Decades* were translated into Netherlandish and it soon became one of the most widely read books. Already in the 1540s Froschauer had written to Bullinger that 'I sell more of your books, and those of other Zurich authors, in the Netherlands than anywhere else, and I am certain that you will experience the great changes which are taking place there and how your teaching will bear fruit.'[48] The centre of this printing activity was Emden. The great concern of the Emden church leaders to provide the Dutch churches with sermons, pastoral literature, and theological texts led to an explosion of printing, of which the works of Bullinger formed a considerable part. Bullinger's *Decades* were frequently reprinted, along with a broad selection of his other works.

Inevitably for one so eagerly read in the Low Countries Bullinger was to be posthumously drawn into bitter debate between the Remonstrants and Counter-Remonstrants which tore apart the Dutch church in the early seventeenth century. Aware that Bullinger and Calvin had never entirely agreed on the question of predestination, the Remonstrants made numerous attempts to claim the theological heritage of Bullinger in their attack on the doctrine of double predestination. This claim embarrassed Zurich and the other Swiss Reformed churches, which by the early seventeenth century were entirely in the orthodox camp. A Swiss delegation was sent to the Synod of Dordrecht, headed by Johann Jakob Breitinger, head of the Zurich church and minister in the Grossmünster. Breitinger addressed the synod, and in a long and carefully constructed account of Bullinger's theology he rejected the Remonstrant claim that Zwingli's successor would have supported their views.[49] It was a bitter blow for the Remonstrants, as well as a strong indication of the changes which had come over the Swiss Reformed churches in the late sixteenth and early seventeenth century. Bullinger's theology had given way to the work of Beza and the orthodox interpreters of Calvin. Zurich and Basle no longer spoke with a distinctive voice. The theological period of the Swiss Reformation was well and truly over.

Refugees

It is tempting to romanticise the role of the Swiss Reformed states in providing refuge for religious exiles during the sixteenth century, especially when one reads the correspondence of men like John Jewel, who wrote of his undying gratitude to the Swiss and of Zurich as his 'second home'. The experiences of leading churchmen and scholars, who often lived in the homes of Heinrich Bullinger, Simon Grynaeus, or Sebastian Münster, were very different from those of men and women who arrived in Zurich, Berne, and Basle as displaced artisans and merchants.[50] Even among the learned there was considerable variation: both John Foxe and Sebastian Castellio in Basle knew nothing but impecuniosity, while another English exile wrote of eating mice in Zurich.

In truth the religious refugees were never greatly welcomed in the Swiss cities. Bullinger had to tread carefully in negotiating terms for their arrival and maintenance. Most came from France, Italy, and the Netherlands, with the greatest number arriving between 1567 and 1577.[51] The refugees were often resented by the locals, who saw them as foreigners who deprived them of much-needed resources and who brought unwelcome competition for jobs and business. A good example of this was the rough treatment given the refugees from Locarno following their arrival in Zurich in 1555.[52] The Locarnese were suspected by the Zurich guildsmen of using their status as religious refugees to gain business advantages and there were numerous complaints to the council about their conduct. This played an important role in the eventual move by many in the community to Basle.

In Basle, however, the situation was equally difficult. In February 1546 the magistrates issued a decree (*Welschenerlass*) which stated that every Frenchman or Italian applying for residence should be rejected unless he be 'a rich or skilful man'.[53] As Hans Guggisberg has pointed out, the only good thing about this decree was that it was never enforced, but it reflected the prevalent mood. Like other cities across Europe, Zurich and Basle took a very pragmatic approach to refugees; they were not encouraged to remain permanently unless they brought obvious economic benefit. In Basle without doubt it was the printing industry which drew most foreigners.

The Swiss were nervous about allowing refugee communities to have their own churches and worship in their own language. In Zurich the Italian community was allowed to have its own congregation and minister, which met in the church of St Peter. Bernardino Ochino was appointed to serve the community, but as his theology fell under suspicion there was growing concern about what was being preached and taught in the community. Vernacular linguistic divides were absolute, so few had any idea of what was going on in the refugee communities. Bullinger's plan was that the Italian community should only have its own church during the transitional phase of integration into the wider Zurich community. The Ochino controversy, as we mentioned in chapter 6, hastened the demise of a separate Italian church. In Basle the Italian, Dutch, and English communities never formed their own churches. Permission was reluctantly given to the French to hold their own services after the Massacre of St Bartholomew's Day in 1572.

In defence of the cities, however, we should note that it was extremely difficult to regulate the arrivals and departures of foreigners. As the Joris case illustrated, it was quite possible to arrive and live with a fabricated identity. Most refugees, such as the English, had no intention of remaining in Basle or Zurich; they awaited the time when they might return home and they regarded their Swiss addresses as temporary havens in a storm. Most foreigners did not wish to become citizens, nor could they have afforded it. They did not become integrated into the communities. Sebastian Castellio, long-time resident in Basle, claimed, perhaps disingenuously, that he had never learnt German.

The presence of large numbers of foreigners in the Swiss cities, above all Basle, did have a profound influence on both local culture and the status of the Swiss churches abroad. Hans Guggisberg has drawn our attention to the role played by the university of Basle in attracting foreigners to the Confederation. He has calculated from the university matriculation records for the period 1532 to 1600 that while the vast majority of students came from south-western Germany, over 500 students came from France, 250 from the Netherlands, 150 from Poland and Lithuania, 100 from England, 70 from Italy and 60 from Scandinavia.[54] Many of these people were not students but tradesmen or travellers who matriculated in order to enjoy the academic privileges in the city.

Historians have drawn our attention to the importance of international Calvinism as a movement in the sixteenth and seventeenth centuries, but during Calvin's life, with the exception of France, the more important influence came from the Swiss Reformed churches. Gradually the two streams would merge, but for fifty years after the start of their Reformation the Swiss had a profound and distinctive influence on reform movements throughout Europe.

Notes

1 See chapter 2, pp. 80–81.

2 See above, pp. 114–115.

3 Thomas A. Brady Jr, *Turning Swiss. Cities and Empire 1450–1550* (Cambridge, 1985), p. 203. See also his, 'Göttliche Republiken: Die Domestizierung der Religion in der deutschen Stadtreformation', in Peter Blickle, Andreas Lindt, and Alfred Schindler (eds), *Zwingli und Europa* (Zurich, 1985), pp. 109–136.

4 Heinrich Richard Schmidt, *Reichstädte, Reich und Reformation. Korporative Religionspolitik 1521–1529/30* (Stuttgart, 1986), pp. 324–326.

5 See Jason K. Nye, 'Catholic Reform and Society: Rottweil, 1525–1618' (dissertation, University of St Andrews, 2000).

6 Winfred Hecht, 'Rottweil und die Städte am oberen Neckar', in F. Quarthal (ed.), *Zwischen Schwarzwald und Schwäbischer Alb. Das Land am oberen Neckar* (Stuttgart, 1984), pp. 483–500.

7 Nye, 'Catholic Reform and Society', pp. 19–53.

8 Johann Adam, *Evangelische Kirchengeschichte der elsässischen Territorien bis zur französischen Revolution* (Strasbourg, 1928), p. 563.

9 On the Reformation in Strasbourg, see Lorna Jane Abray, *The People's Reformation. Magistrates, Clergy, and Commons in Strasbourg 1500–1598* (Toronto, 1985), esp. pp. 21–43, and Thomas A. Brady Jr, *Ruling Class, Regime and Reformation at Strasbourg, 1520–1555* (Leiden, 1978). Miriam Usher Chrisman, *Conflicting Visions of Reform. German Lay Propaganda Pamplets 1519–1530* (Atlantic Highlands, NJ, 1996), puts the lay views in Strasbourg into the broader German context.

10 Thomas A. Brady, *Protestant Politics: Jacob Sturm (1489–1553) and the German Reformation* (Atlantic Highlands, NJ, 1995), p. 65.

11 Martin Friedrich, 'Heinrich Bullinger und die Wittenberger Konkordie: Ein Ökumerniker im Streit um das Abendmahl', *Zwingliana*, 24 (1997), pp. 59–79.

12 Zwingli's text is found in Z, IX, pp. 451–467.

13 This is explored in Hans Rudolf Lavater, 'Regnum Christi etiam externum – Huldrych Zwinglis Brief vom 4. Mai 1528 an Ambrosius Blarer in Konstanz', *Zwingliana*, 15 (1981), pp. 338–381.

14 Wilfried Bührer, 'Der Abendmahlgottesdienst der Stadt Konstanz im Reformationszeitalter', *Zwingliana*, 15 (1979), pp. 93–123.

15 See Peter Rummel, 'Kirchliches Leben in der Reichstadt Augsburg vom Ausgehenden Mittelalter bis 1537', *Historisches Jahrbuch*, 108 (1988), pp. 359–378.

16 Philip Broadhead, 'Politics and Expediency in the Augsburg

Reformation', in Peter Newman Brooks (ed.), *Reformation Principle and Practice. Essays in Honour of Arthur Geoffrey Dickens* (London, 1980), p. 57; also his 'Guildsmen, Religious Reform and the Search for the Common Good: The Role of the Guilds in the Early Reformation in Augsburg', *Historical Journal*, 39 (1996), pp. 577–597

17 Broadhead, 'Politics and Expediency', p. 70.

18 On Musculus's career in Augsburg, see James Thomas Ford, 'Unter dem Schein der Concordien und Confession: Wolfgang Musculus and the Confessional Identity of Augsburg 1531–1548' in Rudolf Dellsperger, Rudolf Freudenberger, and Wolfgang Weber (eds), *Wolfgang Musculus (1497–1563) und die oberdeutsche Reformation* (Berlin, 1997), pp. 111–129; also his recent dissertation, James Thomas Ford, 'Wolfgang Musculus and the Struggle for Confessional Hegemony in Reformation Augsburg, 1531–1548' (dissertation, University of Wisconsin, Madison, 2000).

19 For a study of the religious culture in Augsburg, see Michele Cathleen Zelinsky, 'Religion as a Civic Virtue: Religious Identity and Communal Relations in Augsburg, 1517–1555' (dissertation, University of Pennsylvania, 2000).

20 On Ulm, see G.N. Locher, *Die Zwinglische Reformation* (Göttingen, 1979), pp. 469–471.

21 Peter G. Bietenholz, *Basle and France in the Sixteenth Century* (Geneva, 1971), p. 35.

22 Robert J. Knecht, *The French Civil Wars* (London, 2000), p. 134.

23 Quoted from André Bouvier, *Henri Bullinger* (Paris, 1940), p. 367.

24 Diarmaid MacCulloch, *Thomas Cranmer. A Life* (New Haven, 1996), p. 174.

25 Helmet Kressner, *Schweizer Ursprünge des anglikanischen Staatkirchentums* (Gütersloh, 1953), pp. 73–98.

26 The most important work on this subject is Diarmaid MacCulloch, *Tudor Church Militant. Edward VI and the Protestant Reformation* (Harmondsworth, 1999). See esp. pp. 170–172.

27 Walter J. Hollenweger, 'Zwinglis Einfluß in England', in Heiko A. Oberman, Ernst Saxer, Alfred Schindler, and Heinzpeter Stucki (eds), *Reformiertes Erbe. Festschrift für Gottfried W. Locher*, 2 vols (Zurich, 1992), pp. 182–183.

28 MacCulloch, *Thomas Cranmer*, p. 483.

29 Diarmaid MacCulloch, 'The Importance of Jan Laski in the English Reformation', in Christoph Strohm (ed.), *Johannes a Lasco (1499–1560). Polnischer Baron, Humanist und europäischer Reformator* (Tübingen, 2000), pp. 325–345.

30 Andrew Pettegree, *Foreign Protestant Communities in Sixteenth-Century London* (Oxford, 1996), p. 70.

31 Cornel A. Zwierlein, 'Der reformierte Erasmianer a Lasco und die Herausbildung seiner Abendmahlslehre 1544–1552', in Strohm, *Johannes a Lasco*, pp. 35–99. Zwierlein points to the influence of Oecolampadius on Lasco as well as the seminal importance of Bullinger's *Decades*.

32 *Heinrich Bullinger Diarium (Annales Vitae)*, ed. Emil Egli (rpt. Zurich, 1985), p. 46.

33 *The Zurich Letters, Second Series, 1558–1602*, ed. Hastings Robinson (Cambridge, Parker Society, 1845), p. 222. Quoted in C.M. Dent, *Protestant Reformers in Elizabethan Oxford* (Oxford, 1983), p. 75.

34 See Dent, *Protestant Reformers*, pp. 74–78.

35 Patrick Collinson, *Archbishop Grindal 1519–1583. The Struggle for a Reformed Church* (London, 1979), p. 44.

36 Quoted in David J. Keep, 'Zur Verbreitung von Bullingers Dekaden in England zur Zeit Elisabeths I.', *Zwingliana*, 14, p. 333.

37 The best outlines of the Reformations in Bohemia, Moravia, Hungary, and Transylvania are by Winfried Eberhard and David P. Daniel in Andrew Pettegree (ed.), *The Early Reformation in Europe* (Cambridge, 1992), pp. 23–48, 49–69.

38 For discussion of Jud, Schwenckfeld, and the situation after Kappel, see chapter 4 pp. 215–216.

39 Locher, *Die zwinglische Reformation*, p. 656.

40 L. Binder, 'Johannes Honterus und die Reformation im süden Siebenbürgens mit besonderer Berucksichtigung der Schweizer und Wittenberger Einflüsse', *Zwingliana*, 13 (1973), p. 557.

41 On education see chapter 8.

42 On Bullinger's correspondence with Hungarian reformers, see Endre Zsindely, 'Bullinger und Ungarn', in Ulrich Gäbler and Erland Herkenrath (eds), *Heinrich Bullinger 1504–1575. Gesammelte Aufsätze zum 400. Todestag*, 2 vols (Zurich, 1975), II, pp. 361–382.

43 Walther Köhler, 'Zwingli und Italien', Theological Faculty of the University of Basle (ed.), in *Festschrift zum 60. Geburtstag von Paul Wernle: Aus fünf Jahrhunderten schweizerischer Kirchengeschichte* (Basle, 1932), pp. 22–38.

44 Peter G. Bietenholz, *Der italienischer Humanismus und die Blützeit des Buchdrucks in Basel: Die Baler Drucke italienischer Autoren von 1530 bis zum Ende des 16. Jahrhunderts* (Basle, 1959).

45 See chapter 6, pp. 217–221.

46 The seminal work on this subject is Carlos Gilly, *Spanien und der Basler Buchdruck bis 1600: Ein Querschnitt durch die spanische Geistesgeschichte aus der Sicht einer europäischen Buchdruckerstadt* (Basle and Frankfurt, 1985).

47 Pfister, *Kirchengeschichte*, p. 292.

48 StAZ, EII, 377, 2425. Quoted from Walter Hollweg, *Heinrich Bullingers Hausbuch* (Neukirchen, 1956), p. 84.

49 Max Geiger, *Die Basler Kirche und Theologie im Zeitalter der Hochorthodoxie* (Zollikon and Zurich, 1952), p. 182.

50 The pioneering work, still of great value, is J.C. Mörikofer, *Geschichte der evangelischen Flüchtlinge in der Schweiz* (Leipzig, 1876).

51 Hans Guggisberg, *Basel in the Sixteenth Century* (St Louis, 1982), p. 39.

52 Rudolf Pfister, *Um des Glaubens Willen: Die evangelischen Flüchtlinge von Locarno und ihre Aufnahme zu Zürich im Jahre 1555* (Zollikon and Zurich, 1955).

53 Guggisberg, *Basel in the Sixteenth Century*, p. 39.

54 Ibid., p. 41.

10

The culture of the Swiss Reformation

This book has been occupied with an examination of the people, events, structures, and ideas of the Swiss Reformation. The uniqueness of the Swiss historical identity, the Confederation's propitious geographical position, and the intellectual and spiritual provenance of Swiss evangelical thought created a movement both distinct in character and intricately connected to the broader European Reformation. Whilst recognising that the term 'Swiss Reformation' is something of an artificial construct, suggesting a homogeneity which did not exist, it might be helpful to conclude with a broad brush in hand and ask whether this movement produced anything of enduring significance. Outside of libraries, archives, and museums, little of that world remains visible. The ecclesiastical and political structures of the Swiss Reformation vanished with the *Ancien Régime*, while most Reformed churches of today have little sympathy for the central theological ideas of the sixteenth-century reformers. The legacy of the Swiss Reformation, I would suggest, does not reside in the structures, ordinances, and liturgies of the Swiss Reformed churches, but rather in the intellectual and cultural developments made possible by the potent mixture of Erasmian humanism, evangelical biblicism, and vernacular culture that shaped that Reformation.

The Swiss Reformation was driven forward by men and women who believed in the possibility that God's will could be realised on earth, that the godly community was not only possible, but imperative. The fissures which erupted were not so much disagreements over the end, but over the means to that end. This goal was in many ways Erasmus's vision of the harmony of the divine and the human, and indeed the intellectual culture which I shall discuss shortly was imbued with the humanist search for the underlying unity in things. The godly community would reconcile within itself all human endeavour by subordinating it to and directing it towards the fulfilment of God's will. Erasmus, however, was only one parent. The rural communes and urban republics of the Confederation, defined by oath-taking, spoke a language of liberty, freedom, and unity. Zwingli's language of communal reform had a strong Swiss accent, his writings are replete with images and phrases taken from the communal discourse of the Confederates.

The link between religion and corporate identity was very strong; the process of communalisation described by Peter Blickle and others has pointed to the centrality of religion to the communal ideal. At the same time the discourses of fifteenth-century Swiss humanist historians created the idea of the Confederates as a chosen people, the new Israelites, bound by covenant to God and directed by his providence. The reformers sought to elide this Swiss historical identity with biblical narratives, though they quickly learned how problematic this could be.[1] Indeed, as we have seen, Zwingli's biblical theology did not rest easily alongside his humanist impulses; it was an unresolved, yet extremely creative tension. This potent yet unstable fusion of humanism, vernacular communalism, and evangelical thought formed the spiritual core of the Reformation and it manifested itself in innumerable ways throughout the Confederation. Zwingli was most interested in the life of the regenerated Christian and in ethics, the implications for the Christian of life in the world, and thus the intellectual thrust of the Swiss Reformation was towards the relationship between religion and the world. Thus it should not surprise us that the Swiss contribution to Renaissance culture was in areas such as history, drama, and natural science, and I have chosen these to illustrate the creative energy which flowed through the Swiss Reformed cities in the sixteenth century.

There is no easy explanation as to why the half-century after the beginning of the Reformation should have witnessed such robust intellectual and artistic accomplishments; the answer lies somewhere in an unfathomable combination of favourable circumstances and remarkable personalities. The historical development of the Swiss Confederation placed it in a unique, if perilous, position in the sixteenth century. Technically within the Holy Roman Empire, the Swiss had effectively removed themselves from imperial religious politics by the time of Zwingli's death in 1531. Marginalised, but not isolated, the Swiss Reformed cities formed a small oasis of calm and stability surrounded by religious wars.

The debt to Erasmus was enormous, even if he had repudiated the movement. One can hardly find a figure of the Swiss Reformation who did not credit the Dutch humanist as his inspiration for religious reform and intellectual endeavour. Naturally there were differing and even contradictory interpretations of his ideas, but familiar themes appear again and again in different measures: inward spiritual renewal, outward moral conduct, scholarly fidelity to the sources, and intellectual enquiry in all its forms. The spiritual and intellectual ethos of the Swiss Reformation was created by the powerful mixture of Erasmian humanism, vernacular cultures, and the senses of alienation, difference and providence brought by those who came to Confederation from other lands. This conjunction of forces, mixed with the creative potential of humanity, produced a range of cultural achievements which belong to the story of the Swiss Confederation as much as confessions and catechisms.

In the fifteenth and early sixteenth centuries, the Confederation, with the exception of Basle, was an intellectual backwater, possessing neither the university nor court cultures of Germany, England, France, and Italy. The Reformation, with its emphasis on education and humanist scholarship, brought a profound change to the intellectual culture of the Swiss Confederation. The relative stability and tranquillity of the Swiss states enabled a Reformed culture to take root as schools, academies, printing houses, and libraries were built and occupied by men of great learning. Further, within the relatively small world of the Swiss Reformed churches sodalities arose as the leading figures, men such as Bullinger and Oswald Myconius, sought to gather scholars committed to the intellectual agenda of Reformed humanism. In the decades following the Second Kappel War the Swiss Reformed churches bubbled with intellectual activity grounded in principles of biblical exegesis pioneered by Zwingli and others but which stretched into such fields as mathematics, geography, history, language, bibliography, and natural science. The religious controversies which in so many ways paralysed the Confederation also proved the forging fires of cultural achievement, for these men both broadened the horizons of Reformed thought as well as challenged many of its basic tenets.

Historical thought

The most significant cultural events of the fifteenth century for the Swiss were the two great councils of the church at Constance (1414–18) and Basle (1431–49). This brought humanism into the Confederation as learned men came through the St Gotthard Pass from Italy bearing the new ideas of the Renaissance. One of the most remarkable results was the flowering of Swiss historical writing over the next century and a half. The fifteenth century saw the rise of great chronicle-writers, especially in Berne, who were fascinated with the origins of the Confederation. The development of this robust chronicle tradition gave Swiss humanism a distinct flavour; it was consumed with the question of how classical culture meshed with patriotic fervour. On one level the humanists were talking about the Swiss Confederation and its virtues, while on the other in every city chroniclers were busy detailing the unique achievements of their own communities. This zeal for history meant that almost all of the Swiss reformers also wrote historical works, and the link between history and theology became characteristic of the movement. We can turn to some of the most prominent examples.

The most distinguished historian and scholar of our period was Vadianus, and we shall discuss him separately below.[2] He was the model for the other historians, with unsurpassed knowledge of Roman and canon law, scholastic theology, and humanist techniques. He was resolute in his dedication to the sources and his belief that history was primarily intended to instruct the community. He applied rigorous, if not always correct, methods for determining which documents were older. In his writing he espoused no grand theories but rather sought to detail events and demonstrate the connections between them. He was fascinated by the rhythms of life and by cultural peculiarities, in particular language and customs. His writings are also remarkable for his understanding of periodisation and his historical judgements.[3] He sought to assess people and events in terms relative to their period and not simply in light of posterity; he was fascinated by evolution and he sought to chart change. Vadianus had a very high regard for Erasmus, and his historical writings were largely free of polemic, though curiously he was not a great Swiss patriot and chose to praise the House of Austria.

Vadianus's knowledge was so prodigious and his standards of historical research so demanding that he brought intellectual rigour to the evangelical cause in areas outside Zwingli's range. His influence on the development of historical writing in the Reformed states was immense. He was a towering figure in scholarship, much greater than Bullinger, and he became the measure for work carried out by other writers. As so little of Vadianus's work was printed in the sixteenth century, many of the things which he discovered and discussed remained unknown until they were discovered again in the nineteenth century.[4] Although he was the greatest Swiss historian of his day, Vadianus was nervous about writing on contemporary events. In 1544 he wrote to Bullinger about the possibility of a Zwingli biography, but although he was a friend and follower of the reformer he thought the subject too controversial and advised against it.[5]

Vadianus's near contemporary was Valerius Anshelm (1475–1547), whose great work was his *Chronik*, an enormous vernacular work divided into four parts. The first was an extensive introduction, part 2 covered 1030–1298, part 3 was on the Burgundian wars 1474–77, and the final part was a contemporary history from 1477 to 1530. Like Vadianus his historical accounts were panoramic, but he lacked the sophistication of the great master. Whereas Vadianus was sceptical in his historical judgements, Anshelm was rigorously faithful to his fixed interpretation.[6] What was remarkable about Anshelm, however, was that the Bernese magistrates provided him with a post as paid historian. He was able to spend his whole time preparing his *Chronik*; an advantage which tells us much about the importance of history to the political masters of the Reformation.

Anshelm is an important representative of historical tradition which took shape in the Swiss Confederation. His work attempted to portray the diversity of human experience, yet underlying this was the search for cultural unity. This unity was to be found in God's providence and in moral rectitude. His writing has a strong moral tone and there were very particular lessons which he wanted his readers to draw: most prominently, that France, with its money for mercenaries, was the source of moral corruption in the Confederation. Alongside his Reformed morality, however, lay a remarkable vision of world history. Anshelm made an important contribution to Swiss thought by attempting to integrate the Confederation into the wider spectrum of European affairs. He also wrote a great deal about prominent Swiss figures of the Middle Ages and thereby taught the Swiss a good deal about their own history. His *Chronik* is a marvellous text, worthy of greater attention, as it reflects the hybrid intellectual and spiritual world of Reformed writers in the sixteenth century. His intention was to produce a work congenial to the Reformation, which he saw as God's work, but the language and images he employed allows us to see how far the reformers thought and spoke in medieval terms.

It is remarkable how many of these key Swiss historians, like Valerius Anshelm, were not born in the Confederation. Another example is Johannes Stumpf, whose account of Zwingli's death we referred to earlier.[7] In fact, Stumpf is our most important biographical source for Zwingli. His greatest works, however, were his *Schweizerchronik* and his encyclopaedic *Gemeiner loblicher Eydgnosschaft Stetten Landen und Völkeren Chronikwirdiger thaaten beschrybung* (1548). His position was very clear: he wanted to demonstrate the essential unity of the Confederation in every respect – historically, culturally, and geographically. That desire runs across every page. He sought to demonstrate to the rest of Europe that the Swiss were not peasant rebels, but a distinguished race with a glorious past.[8] His arguments were fairly conventional and he was a commitment Protestant, but his work was important for other reasons. He was an excellent writer with a flair for story-telling and his language and style were greatly admired. The quality of his German was such that his *Gemeiner loblycher*, his topographical and historical account of the Confederation, was widely read in Europe, thus reaching a far greater audience than the subject might otherwise have done. Also, the work was an important cultural and printing achievement as it was distinguished by extremely high-quality maps. Again, these were so highly thought of throughout Europe that the book was eagerly sought.

Stumpf's colleague and fellow historian in Zurich was Heinrich Bullinger, who throughout his life tirelessly gathered material for his histories. His range was extraordinary: he wrote histories of the religious houses of Einsiedeln and Kappel, a history of the Habsburgs, and one of the bishops of Constance. He also wrote a history of the Confederation, but his greatest work arguably was his history of Zurich, which contains his history of the Reformation. Like Stumpf, Bullinger could tell a story well, but his purpose was rather different. Above all else he was an apologist for the Reformation; he wrote an extensive account of the Zwingli years, though for political reasons it was never printed. His historical methodology was deeply influenced by Vadianus, and Bullinger was a meticulous critic of his sources. Despite his confessional position, his scholarship was humane and expansive. When one reads his history of the Reformation, which is a history of the Reformation in Zurich, Bullinger's bitterness towards Luther is arresting. The work was written late in life, at a time when all efforts at reconciliation had fallen to the ground exhausted. Bullinger's historical works reflect his strengths and weaknesses: beautifully written and lucid, they are scholarly and pedagogical. Bullinger's ethical rigour is always apparent. They are, however, confined by their ideological standpoint; Bullinger tends to make the same points repeatedly in order to teach. His work lacks Vadianus's subtlety and self-awareness of the relativity of historical analysis and writing. History, as we have noted, was a fundamental component of his theology, and he saw historical research and writing as serving theology and religious instruction.

No survey, however brief, of sixteenth-century Swiss historians could omit Thomas Platter, a remarkable figure who does not fit into any category and certainly was not a historian of the ilk discussed above. His considerable contribution to the cultural legacy of the Swiss Reformation, however, was through his autobiography. Felix Platter (1500–82) was from Wallis and had spent some of his youth in Zurich, where he was very taken with Zwingli. He experienced the terrible events in the city after the Second Kappel War and describes fearing for his life as the reformer's supporters were sought out. He was a restless soul, moving from city to city, and among his many accomplishments was his involvement in the printing of Calvin's *Institutes* in 1536. In 1572 he wrote his memoirs in two weeks, providing a bracing account of his youth which became a landmark in sixteenth-century writing.[9] As Alfred Kohler has argued, one of the striking aspects of Platter's autobiography is his emphasis on his own achievements as a means of social mobility.[10] He did not attempt to downplay God's hand in his life, but his personality and actions in all their humanity are explored, often with great humour. Although Platter was an individual, his work retains a strong Zwinglian tone in its emphasis on moral conduct and the Christian life, but it also reflected the broadminded, inquisitive humanism characteristic in the Confederation in the middle decades of the century, eager to explore the world in all its diversity. It was part of a new literature in Europe, exploring the self in relationship to God, asking new questions and in its account of the self-made man, opening new possibilities.

The historical tradition of the Swiss Confederation was integral to the Reformation movement, and that movement gave new impetus to the field. Fascinating questions remain to be explored about the relationship between history and identity in the development of the Reformation, but in this evolution the Swiss made important contributions.

Drama

The Swiss had a strong dramatic tradition which blossomed during the sixteenth century. Scholars of medieval and early modern drama have noted that the primary transition in German theatre between the fifteenth and sixteenth centuries was from devotional Passion plays to the performance of biblical plays.[11] Between the thirteenth and fourteenth centuries dramas performed at Shrovetide (Shrove Tuesday and the two days proceeding) were popular in Basle, Zurich, and Lucerne. The influence of both humanism and the Luther affair had an important effect upon dramatists in the Swiss cities, and this is evident in the work of Pamphilus Gengenbach, who wrote most of his works in Basle between 1513 and 1523. Like many of his contemporaries Gengenbach was emboldened by Luther's protest, and the plays from this period, *Die Zehn Alter* (1515), *Die Gouchmatt* (1516), *Der Nollhart* (1517), and *Die Totenfresser* (1521) are redolent of the optimistic humanist agenda for reform of the church.

Gengenbach was overshadowed by a more significant Renaissance figure: Niklaus Manuel Deutsch. Manuel was a mercenary, artist and, later, politician, who seems to embody the Renaissance spirit.[12] Where Gengenbach had spoken in muted tones, Manuel unleashed a torrid assault upon the papacy and Roman clerics. His works *Vom Papst und seiner Priesterschaft* and *Von Papst und Christi Gegensatz*, both from 1523, and his *Ablasskrämer* of 1525 demonstrate Manuel's understanding of the power of the spoken word to move people. Essentially, these are sermons in dramatic form. *Der Ablasskrämer* tells the story of an indulgence-seller who is strung up by a crowd which suspects him of deception. At first he lies in order to be set free; when the crowd realise his mendacity they hoist him up again and give him a good hiding. The cleric then confesses the conceit of his peddling of indulgences, their immorality, and venality. His money is taken from him and divided amongst the crowd. The peasants take no more money than is their due; they have not strung up the indulgence preacher of their own gain. As Glenn Ehrstine has argued, Manuel's portrayal of the peasants was an idealised picture, it was not a mirror of real events.[13]

Manuel's robust dramas extolling the virtuous peasant and vilifying money-grabbing clerics belonged to the torrid period of the 1520s.[14] As the Reformation took hold in Berne Manuel became increasingly involved in government, and soon the peasants came to be seen not so much as guileless souls but as recalcitrant opponents of the new urban-centred Reformed order. Nevertheless, drama remained one of the most important media for the propagation of religious teaching. In Zurich the radical Konrad Grebel had adapted *Dives and Lazarus* in 1524, a story of the divide between faith and unbelief. Biblical stories were mixed with classical myths and set in contexts such as the home, the church, or the morals court, all of which were familiar to the viewers. The dramatic productions accommodated biblical truths to the domestic reality of the laity, and thus they formed an integral part in the formation of a vernacular religious culture. The young Heinrich Bullinger, whilst still at Kappel, penned in 1526 the classical drama *Lucretia*. The work spoke to many of the issues of the day: the power of guilds, the mercenary service, the threat of religious radicalism, and the danger of tyranny.

It was in the 1530s, after the defeat at Kappel, that the biblical dramas began to appear. Johann Kolross, schoolmaster in Basle and cousin of Oswald Myconius conceived the most successful of the Swiss biblical dramas, the *Tragedi wider die Abgötterey* in 1535. The play is a version of the story of Daniel in the lions' den. He had already written the *Spil von fünfferley betrachtnussen* in 1532, a play with an *ars moriendi* theme depicting a young man who is killed by Death after refusing to repent; after a fight with the devil, in which he repents, an angel comes and takes him directly to heaven. The morality of the play strikes the modern reader as heavy-handed in the extreme, but in all his work Kolross infused considerable humour, the import of which is often lost on us. It has been said that while the Swiss dramatic tradition was lively, it remained ritualistic and allegorical.[15] The biblical dramas, both those in Latin and German, were intended not only to edify but also entertain, yet the question of fidelity to scripture was problematic. Simply extracting passages from the Bible and putting them on stage would have been insufferably dull; yet, one might ask, how much liberty can one take with a biblical text in a society whose church was based on the principle of *sola scriptura*?

The resolution was somewhat surprising. Even in the 1530s, when the religious situation in the Confederation was still fragile, the dramatists were relatively free in their use of the Bible. Sixt Birck in Basle wrote his *Joseph* between 1532 and 1534, but the story departs significantly from the account in Genesis. To make his plays more than characters simply speaking at one another, Birck infused drama and colour into the story by making drastic alterations. The dialogue was embellished, enabling Joseph to speak to his brothers in a language more redolent of the family. In Zurich we find something similar: the biblical plays of Jakob Ruoff were comic and satirical without a great concern for fidelity to the biblical original. Ruoff was a convinced Zwinglian, and key elements of Zurich theology found expression in his plays, but he, like many others of the period, was also a dramatist. He knew how to draw real characters who could express truths which would resonate with the audience. Liberty was taken in order to animate the story and allegory remained at the heart of Swiss biblical dramas, Latin and vernacular. This adaptation of the Bible in order to make the play both entertaining and instructive closely paralleled the dialogue between preachers and the laity in the churches. The biblical message had to be made accessible in ways which would make a lasting impact, and this required a degree of creativity.

The Reformed Swiss dramatic tradition differed from the Lutheran in various respects, perhaps most notably in the matter of *Osterspiele*. Luther hated the Easter plays and forbade them, but in south Germany and Swiss lands the sixteenth century saw a continuing place for these passion plays among the Reformed. In Basle, Berne, and Zurich men like Hans von Rüte, Jos Murer, Jacob Funckelin, Valentin Boltz, and Matthias Holtzwart created a vibrant theatrical culture in which the theology and beliefs of the period found expression on the stage. Perhaps the best known of all these dramatists was Rudolf Gwalther, son-in-law of Zwingli and Bullinger's successor as chief minister in Zurich. His biblical drama *Nabal*, taken from the story of David, is a morality tale, but with no particular confession or political colour. Indeed, Gwalther wrote in the preface to the work that the individual Christian is shaped not only in the church, but in the marketplace and theatre (*foro et theatris*).[16]

Some portraits

To give a sense of the diversity and strength of intellectual and cultural achievement in the Swiss Confederation during the Reformation, I have prepared a series of 'snapshots' of some of the most influential figures. This is by no means a complete list, and for the most part, with the exception of Vadianus, I have chosen individuals who have not to this point appeared prominently in the narrative.

Joachim von Watt (Vadianus) 1484–1551

We have spoken of Vadianus as the leading Swiss humanist scholar of the early sixteenth century, having received the laurel wreath from Maximilian I before returning to his native land. Joachim von Watt (better known as Vadianus) was born 1484 in St Gall, in the eastern part of the Confederation. He was the most prominent scholar to join the Reformation; his reputation far surpassed Zwingli's, being crowned *Poeta laureatus* by Emperor Maximilian I. Like Zwingli, Vadianus studied at the university of Vienna, where he embraced the humanist studies of natural science, astronomy and geography.[17] By 1526 he held the chair of Greek and had embarked on the editing of classical texts, including Sallust, Ovid, the natural history of Pliny, and the great geographical work of Pomponius Mela. Vadianus would produce his own work of geography in 1534, *Epitome Trium Terrae Partium, Asiae, Africae et Europae*. The breadth and depth of Vadianus's learning was arresting, and by 1517, at the age of only thirty-one, he was made rector of the university in Vienna. Nevertheless, he had other ambitions, and after having taken a doctorate in medicine, he returned to his native St Gall to work as the city doctor. By 1526 he was Bürgermeister and had brought about the introduction of the Reformation.[18]

It was during his time as a politician and doctor that Vadianus began his most important and influential scholarly work. The Reformation in St Gall was a struggle between the town and the great monastery; Vadianus's original intention was to pen a refutation of monasticism, after the fashion of Luther, but, in the end, he used the marvellous library available to him to write the *Great Chronicle of the Abbey* (1529–31), an enormous historical work in German recounting the story from 1199 to 1490.[19] The chronicle was indeed a justification of the Reformation, but it was more than that. It was a magisterial history of the Holy Roman Empire and of the Swiss Confederation. The scope of Vadianus's work is breathtaking, and his surviving notes permit us a glimpse of the care with which he used primary sources.

There followed a series of historical works: a geographical survey of the Thurgau, a history of monasticism; a history of St Gall; a history of the Roman emperors from Caesar to Caligula; and a survey of the constitutional history of St Gall.[20] Nevertheless, Vadianus was virtually alone in St Gall; apart from his friend Kessler, there were neither any other scholars in this town of artisans nor any printers. Vadianus's works remained mostly unpublished until this century.

As a scholar Vadianus felt akin to Erasmus, and his own religious views, though he did not regard himself as a theologian, were moderate. As a historian his work marked an important stage in humanist history writing. Vadianus worked closely with archival material in crafting his histories and was highly sceptical of the legends with which fifteenth-century historians had woven the story of the Confederation's founding. For Vadianus, these legends had to be tested, and if their veracity was in doubt, they were to be discarded as mere fables. There was more than a taste of polemic in his work (particularly against Austria and the papacy), but what distinguished Vadianus was the enormous amount of information he discovered, both about the antique world and his own time. The fact that his work has remained unpublished has meant that he has never really received credit for these discoveries. History-writing became an integral part of the Swiss Reformed church; men like Heinrich Bullinger, Ludwig Lavater, and others wrote chronicles. Indeed we know that history plays an important part in Reformed theology, with its emphasis upon the link between Israel and the church. Vadianus was the founder of this enduring tradition of historical writing, and his work was deeply influential in shaping the Swiss Protestant mind.

Bonifacius Amerbach 1495–1562

It is in the figure of Bonifacius Amerbach that we have the best encounter with that other view of Reformed Protestantism which took root in Basle.[21] Amerbach came from a distinguished Basle family which greatly valued education and had embraced humanism with zeal.[22] The young Bonifacius was educated in Greek and Latin at schools in the Alsace before returning to his native city, where he met Erasmus in 1516. Amerbach was to be Erasmus's closest friend and colleague in Basle; he served as executor of the Dutchman's will. It was not to the church but the law that Bonifacius was attracted, and he studied in the legal faculties in Freiburg and Avignon, where he became a proponent of the *mos gallica* tradition. He returned to Basle in the early 1520s, where there was a flourishing tradition of humanist legal studies under Claudius Cantiuncula, who held the chair at the university. When Cantiuncula retired in 1524 he wanted Bonifacius to succeed him, but Amerbach refused, deciding instead to take his doctorate in Avignon. From 1530 until 1536, however, Amerbach did hold the chair of Roman law in Basle, and until his death in 1562 he was employed as legal counsellor to the city.

Amerbach was the greatest legal mind in the Swiss Confederation, and one of his major contributions was in steering Basle university through the stormy waters of the Reformation. It was under Amerbach's leadership that the university emerged in the 1530s as one of the leading centres of learning in the Protestant world.[23] He was not himself a fervent supporter of the Reformation; in 1529 he had opposed the introduction of the Reformation and his relationship with Oecolampadius was fraught. Unlike Erasmus, Amerbach did not leave Basle in 1529 as his roots in the city were too deep, although he received plenty of offers of employment from Catholic universities. From 1529 until 1531 he refused to participate in Reformed worship and he would not attend the sacrament of the Lord's Supper despite increasing pressure from the council to conform. What seems to have most appalled Amerbach was the way in which the Basle Reformation had degenerated into a popular movement. He claimed that he was exempted from the Reformation ordinances on the grounds of academic liberties, but he clearly was trying the patience of Oecolampadius and the magistrates, who three times summoned him to a disciplinary hearing. Following the death of Oecolampadius Amerbach underwent a conversion to a moderate form of evangelical religion, most likely akin to the ideas of Martin Bucer. Like his friend Simon Grynaeus, he was in sympathy with the attempts by Bucer and Capito to find a middle way between Zurich and Wittenberg. He held these views until his death thirty years later.

During those thirty years Amerbach distinguished himself through his legal pronouncements, his authority as a moderate, and as a patron to religious refugees. Amerbach published nothing, and what we know of his thought comes from his papers, his extensive correspondence, and his legal judgements. He was a thorough-going humanist who believed in the moral foundation of the law; indeed, he worked to establish a chair of moral philosophy in Basle. The principal influences on Amerbach were the Christian philosophy of Erasmus and the legal thought of Aristotle. With Simon Grynaeus Amerbach played a central role in bringing Aristotle into the nascent Reformed world, and it is not surprising that he had good relations with Philip Melanchthon.

From 1530 until his death Amerbach was closely associated with the university of Basle, serving five times as rector. He played a crucial role in mediating in the dispute which erupted between the magistrates and the clergy shortly after the reopening of the university in 1532. The magistrates wanted the professors to hold higher degrees (doctorates) because they believed that these would increase the prestige of the university. Many of the leading churchmen and scholars, including Oswald Myconius and Simon Grynaeus objected on the grounds that such degrees were symbols of the medieval university system, with its emphasis on scholastic theology. The debate was part of wider struggle in Basle between the church and the magistrates over control of the clergy. Although Amerbach favoured the position of the magistrates, he recognised that the clergy were struggling to assert their freedom as preachers of the Gospel, and his wise guidance prevented the dispute from destroying the Basle church.

As Erasmus's heir, Amerbach was charged with the distribution of monies left for the care of the poor and students. Amerbach used the money to help students from across Europe to study in Basle, and it was through his influence that Basle university became a meeting point for students of evangelical sentiments from Ireland to the Balkans. He was liberal in his support of scholars who sought refuge in Basle and he was a patron of men such as Curione and Ochino. Whether he entirely shared their views is another thing, but he certainly had sympathy for a broad range of intellectual enquiry. He evidently had no interest in doctrinal exactitude as a measure of the Christian church. Basle's reputation for tolerance in the sixteenth century owed a great deal to the influence of Bonifacius Amerbach, who in many ways was Erasmus's heir in the Swiss Confederation.

Simon Grynaeus 1494–1541

Simon Grynaeus was the leading intellectual figure of the early Swiss Reformation. A Swabian by birth, he held the chair of Greek at Heidelberg from 1524 until Oecolampadius and Jakob Meyer, the Bürgermeister, persuaded him to come to Basle in 1529 as professor of Greek. During his time in Heidelberg Grynaeus had gradually eased towards Zwingli's theology. The presence of Erasmus in Basle, although he was to depart with the introduction of the Reformation, was without question the irresistible carrot. From Basle's point of view, Grynaeus was highly attractive not only as a leading scholar, but as a man who had a reputation for finding rare books and manuscripts. His arrival in Basle was a relief for those who feared that Erasmus's flight would diminish the city's reputation as a centre of learning. Grynaeus was also a close friend of Melanchthon, who was not only a fellow Greek scholar but an advocate of moderate theological views which Grynaeus found sympathetic. Erasmus, for his part, highly esteemed the Swabian on account of his learning and affable nature, though Grynaeus's tendency towards Zwinglian thought ultimately strained the relationship. Again the printing culture in Basle was crucial: before coming to the city Grynaeus had made a name for himself by discovering five missing books of the Roman historian Livy in a Benedictine abbey at Lorch, and by 1531 he was able to publish a new critical edition.

Grynaeus's contribution to the development of a Protestant intellectual culture was primarily through his editions of classical philosophy, most notably Aristotle and Plato. In this endeavour he shifted the emphasis of Basle printing away from Erasmus's concern with the Fathers towards philosophical and scientific texts. The years 1531–32 were particularly fecund as Grynaeus produced a Greek edition of Aristotle (Johann Bebel) and revised Ficino's Latin translations of Plato.[24] The point of editing these works of classical philosophy lay in Grynaeus's belief that natural science was an essential component of sacred studies. In his 1533 edition of Euclid Grynaeus argued that mathematics was crucial on account of the exactitude of its arguments and proofs.[25] The clarity of mathematics made it a basis for other disciplines, for it 'frees the human mind to appreciate the wondrous spectacles of God's works'.[26] As Charlotte Methuen has argued, Grynaeus saw in mathematics a means to transcend the ambiguity of words, supplying lucid principles with which to analyse knowledge brought by the senses. Thus, following Aristotle, he understood mathematics as a secure foundation for knowledge of God and for human ethics. These views proved highly influential in the development of sixteenth-century theology and scientific thought. Grynaeus's lectures on Aristotle and the Greek language made him the leading scholar in the Swiss Confederation. Through his teaching and writing he brought Aristotle into the Reformed tradition and laid the foundations for the integration of theological, philosophical, and scientific thought which would blossom under such men as Konrad Gesner.

In matters of religion Grynaeus, following his friend Oecolampadius, was attracted to Zwingli's theology, though his spirit was drawn to concord and unity, Erasmian principles. In the difficult years following 1531 Grynaeus, though not formally head of the Basle church, was undoubtedly its best mind, and he employed his talents to restore order and avoid conflict. When the magistrates of Basle reopened the university in 1532 following the tumult of the Reformation, Grynaeus was probably their greatest adornment. Against his friend Bonifacius Amerbach Grynaeus supported the clergy in the struggle against the magistrates over the matter of academic degrees in the university. Shortly before his death, however, he served as rector of the university, and with Amerbach he played a key role in the development of Reformed higher education.

Sebastian Münster 1488–1552

Sebastian Münster came from peasant stock, joining the Franciscans at the age of seventeen, where he learnt Hebrew, and became a priest in 1512. When he arrived at the Franciscan house in Basle in 1518 it was to teach philosophy, though clearly his knowledge of Hebrew was impressive. It was at this time that Basle was at the centre of the Luther controversy, and Münster made his contribution by translating into German the Wittenberg reformer's work on the Ten Commandments. During the 1520s Münster moved between Basle and Heidelberg before abandoning the Franciscans in 1529 and taking a chair at Basle university. Although a committed supporter of the evangelical cause, Münster regarded himself as more of a philologist than a theologian, and he was distinctly uncomfortable in the chair of Old Testament, which he held from 1542 until 1544. Finally, he served as rector of the university from 1547 until his death from the plague of 1552.[27]

Münster's intellectual achievements were primarily in two areas: Hebrew and geography. Linguistically, his most important work was the Hebrew edition of the Old Testament with a translation into Latin of 1534–35. Münster was a diffident man, an unlikely source of controversy, but his translations outraged many, including Luther and Melanchthon, who attacked him for his fidelity to the Hebrew language. This might appear curious, but Münster's method in preparing his text was to make extensive use of rabbinical commentaries in both the correction of the text and in his commentary. Münster's openness to Jewish religious culture touched a very raw wound – the memory of the Reuchlin affair. Between 1529 and 1538 he composed a number of tracts designed to convert the Jews to Christianity.[28]

Münster's other remarkable achievement was his *Cosmographia* (first printed in German in 1544 and then in Latin in 1550), a description of all the known lands of the world.[29] This became one of the most popular works of the century, quickly being translated into most European languages (though not English). It went through eight printings in his lifetime and by 1628 there had been thirty-five editions. Münster's *Cosmographia* ran to 1,162 folio pages. The book is an elegant compendium of learning, full of maps, drawings and historical and cultural reflections.[30] Münster's correspondence gives us a sense of the time expended in the accumulation of this material; he wrote to people in every corner of Europe requesting detailed information about their communities, physical and cultural. In his introduction to the work Münster gave his understanding of what he sought to achieve:

> The art of cosmography concerns itself not only with the countries, habitations, and lives of the various peoples of the earth, but also with many other things, such as strange animals, trees, metals, and so on, things both useful and useless, to be found on the land and in the sea; [also] the habits, customs, laws, governments of men, the origins of countries, regions, cities and towns, how nature has endowed them and what human inventiveness has produced in them, [also] what notable things have happened elsewhere.[31]

Münster intended the work to provide both entertainment and edification. He wanted to glorify the lands of his contributors, but also to glorify God by demonstrating the diversity of creation which stands under God's providence.[32] The rise and fall of societies is charted in terms of their moral worth, reflecting Münster's indebtedness to Erasmian Christian morality. Like Gesner, Münster also saw himself working for posterity, preserving knowledge for the future should calamity (the Turks) befall his time. He wrote to Stanislaus Laski:

> What if Carthage in Africa, Athens in Greece, Alexia in Burgundy or many other cities which have succumbed to fate were to have been preserved in pictures? Surely they would present a gratefully received spectacle for study today. Therefore, we undertake this study for our posterity, so that after three or four hundred years have passed, those who come after us will be able to see from our books what appearance the regions and cities of our time had, as if we should have sent them letters with pictures.[33]

The work belongs to the encyclopaedic learning of the age and was a milestone in the development of Renaissance geography and ethnography. Although he owed a great debt to the classical works of Pliny and Ptolemy, Münster's creation was highly original, made possible by a vast array of willing accomplices across Europe who believed in his humanist endeavour. Although Bullinger declared that Münster's style was 'atrocious', the *Cosmographia* became one of the great works of learning to emerge from the Swiss Confederation during the sixteenth century, and its fantastic success might even have made the virtuous head of the Zurich church just a little jealous.

Konrad Gesner

Among the leading lights of sixteenth-century Swiss intellectual culture was Konrad Gesner, a native Zuricher who studied in Bourges and Paris, who was appointed to teach natural science and ethics in *Lectorium* in 1541, before being elevated to a chair in 1558.[34] Theologically Gesner was deeply influenced by Heinrich Bullinger, whose sermons he heard daily, and it was through Zwingli and Bullinger that he was educated in the thought of Erasmus. Gesner was the pre-eminent product of the Zurich school system, being introduced to natural science by Zwingli himself, who taught the young student that theology and natural science were not separate but interwoven disciplines which revealed the nature of God. Although Bullinger was more hostile to the concept of natural theology than Zwingli, he did not disabuse Gesner of the link between the two. Gesner graduated in medicine from Basle in 1541 and he worked as a medical doctor in Zurich, supplementing his income from teaching. Medicine was not a distinct discipline but formed an organic part of his thought-world which focused on the revelation of God in the created order. Between 2 and 3 p.m. on Mondays, Tuesdays, Wednesdays, and Fridays Gesner lectured to students on the foundations of natural science, using as his texts Aristotle and the Paduan philosopher Hermolaus Barbarus, whose work Gesner edited in 1548.[35] Gesner argued for the place of philosophy in the study of theology, though its role could only be a supporting one. Under the name philosophy he understood all profane studies, of which physics, which he was employed to teach, was a branch. He rejected any notion of a separate authority for philosophy; its truths were only valid in light of the higher science of theology, which it served.[36] Gesner outlined four ways in which philosophy served the Christian: it enabled men and women to discern God's gifts to them in the natural world and to use them for their benefit; consideration of nature propels individuals to great devotion to God; knowledge of nature leads in steps towards knowledge of God; and in contemplation of nature the mind is given greater pleasure.[37] The key theme which ran through his work was that the study of nature was useful; it was a good work.

Gesner was fascinated by the New World and its plants, animals and drugs. He was the first Swiss to grow tomatoes and raise guinea-pigs, both brought from America, and he was the first to write a survey of native American languages.[38] He also wrote a work on fish.[39]

Gesner's most influential works were his *Historia Animalium*, the *Historia Plantarum* and the *Bibliotheca Universalis*. These three appeared from the press of Froschauer between 1545 and 1549. He had an enormous respect for classical learning but his method was to combine the learning of ancient writers with empirical knowledge. The *Bibliotheca Universalis* was an enormous undertaking in which Gesner attempted to list the works, printed or in manuscript, of all the authors who had ever written in Hebrew, Greek, and Latin. In 1,262 pages he enumerated 15,000 books by 2,700 writers. The work was revised several times, with the assistance of Josias Simler, and by 1574 there were 8,000 authors, with vernacular works included. It was a monumental step in the development of bibliography, and Gesner articulated in his volume his reasons for undertaking such a task. The threat of the Turks from the east was such that the civilised world might soon be robbed of its intellectual heritage. By listing all the books ever written he might ensure that knowledge of their existence might be preserved even if they were lost.[40] The destruction of the great library of Alexandria and, more recently, the loss of the library of Matthias Corvinus of Hungary at the hands of the Ottoman were sufficient proof for Gesner of the danger in which Europe stood. What Gesner put together was not simply a list of books, but a comprehensive study of Western culture; for each of the authors he wrote a description of their life and work, denoting their importance to the development of Christian culture. The *Bibliotheca* is perhaps our most important witness to the sixteenth-century Reformed tradition's understanding of its intellectual heritage.

Two printers: Froschauer and Oporinus

The importance of printing to the Reformation has long been recognised, and we have seen that Zwingli's association with Froschauer in Zurich was a decisive moment. We have also discussed the importance of Basle as an intellectual and commercial centre. Printing in sixteenth-century Europe was a heady mixture of commerce and scholarship, for not only did the printers have to make sober business decisions, they also often had profound sympathies with what they produced. The situation in the Swiss cities is a good example of this. The printing houses of Basle and Zurich not only played a crucial role in the dissemination of ideas, but the printers were themselves committed to the ideas. Unlike painters like Dürer and Cranach, they were deeply involved in the struggle over beliefs, and as men of the world they often served as conduits between learned and lay cultures. One of the most remarkable figures of the early Swiss Reformation was Hieronymus Froben, who ran the family printing business from 1528 until his death in 1563. He was a learned man who had been taught Hebrew by Pellikan and then served Erasmus and later the papal legate Antonio Pucci as an assistant. During more than thirty years of business Froben developed a Europe-wide network of booksellers.[41]

Christoph Froschauer was an illegitimate son, born in Bavaria, educated in Augsburg, who worked in Zurich from around 1513 with the printer Rüegger.[42] When Rüegger died Froschauer married his widow and inherited the business, and in 1519 he received citizenship in Zurich. Alongside printing, Froschauer was also involved in the paper business and he ran several bookshops in the city. The timing of Froschauer's conversion to the evangelical cause is not known, but we do know that shortly after 1520 he anonymously printed works by Luther. Famously, it was at his house during Lent 1522 that the breaking of the fast took place. Between 1521 and 1564 he printed the works of Zwingli, Jud, Bullinger, and Gwalther.[43] He was a regular visitor to the Frankfurt book fair and he had extensive contacts in Germany for the distribution of his works. During his life he oversaw the printing of more than 100 full or partial editions of the Bible and approximately 900 other titles.

Froschauer was a deeply religious man and he took the greatest care in choosing the typefaces and decorative borders for his bibles. For the 1531 Bible Froschauer employed artists to produce the woodcuts, and throughout his career he continued to produce wonderfully illustrated editions of the scriptures. With the publication of the 1531 Bible Froschauer was at the height of his printing powers and he had four presses working in the city. With the terrible defeat at Kappel in 1531 and Zwingli's death there was a sharp falling off of his activities. He ceased production of religious works in the fraught atmosphere of the period and turned to other subjects, such as geographical works by Vadianus. With an ever-expanding list of books Froschauer remained committed to the integration of word and picture in his volumes. This was not straightforward as there was no woodcutter in Zurich (the person who transformed the picture into a woodcut). All the drawings had to be sent to either Basle or Strasbourg. Froschauer sought to remedy the situation by bringing Heinrich Vogtherr to Zurich in 1544 where he remained for two years training local craftsmen in the art of woodcutting. Before they left, however, Vogtherr and his assistants played a crucial role in the production of one of the most ambitious books of the century, the *Schweizer Chronik* of Johannes Stumpf in 1547. This great work of history, ethnology, and geography was accompanied by dozens of maps and thousands of woodcuts. Vogtherr began work on the text but by the time he left Zurich there were many local craftsmen employed in turning the pictures of artists like Hans Asper and Jos Murer into woodcuts of the highest quality. Stumpf's work was seen as a rival to Münster's *Cosmographia*, as it contained beautiful cityscapes and detailed descriptions of mountains, valleys, and lowlands. The difference was that Stumpf limited his work to the Swiss Confederation.

When Froschauer died in 1564 he was an extremely wealthy man. He had put his financial resources to the service of the Reformation. As early as the late 1520s he had himself written prefaces to religious works outlining his understanding of the faith as a layman. He played a key role in the dissemination of evangelical literature and he was the main printer for the Zurich reformers until his death. In his love of the visual image and devotion to printing works of the highest quality he made a significant contribution to the establishment of the relationship between art and religion in the Reformed world.

Johannes Oporinus was the Greek form of Hans Herbster, the learned printer and business man in Basle from 1540 until 1567. He was born in Strasbourg and then served as an apprentice under Froben in Basle. He worked as a teacher in a Latin school and he studied medicine and worked with Paracelsus, who was the city physician. Oporinus's medical interests became evident when he published in 1543 *De Humani Corporis Fabrica* by the renowned anatomist Andreas Vesalius. Among his many projects he undertook the printing of an edition of the Koran by Theodor Bibliander in Zurich.[44] This caused a

Europe-wide sensation as all the leading reformers, including Luther, voiced their opinions on whether this was acceptable. Throughout his career Oporinus suffered many financial setbacks but he became one of the most respected printers in Europe on account of the high quality of the editions of classical and patristic texts.[45] Through his work Oporinus became well acquainted with humanist circles in the empire, Italy, Poland, France, and Holland. He produced more than 750 books, but not all in Basle; he contracted some of the work to smaller printers in Berne, Strasbourg, and Basle.[46]

The educated and refined Oporinus was much more of an artist than a business man. He was married five times, always to widows, and was not especially good with money, as he had to be rescued from debt by his last two wives. He corresponded with many of the great figures of the day and his letters throw light on the world of sixteenth-century printing and book-selling. In 1549 Oporinus wrote to the archbishop of Mainz relating how a shipment of his books had been lost when the boat sank in the Rhine, and asked if he might be compensated for the financial burden.

The printers played an essential role in the development of the Swiss Reformation, not only because they made the works of the reformers and humanist scholars available, but because they opened up networks of communications through their contacts. The printers Froben, Froschauer, and Oporinus had friendships and business relations which stretched across confessional boundaries. As the Swiss theologians became increasingly isolated these men kept open important lines of communication. They also served as conduits for the reception of artistic and intellectual currents in the Swiss Confederation.

Hans Holbein

The development of printing in Basle has already been noted, but one important by-product of this industry was the evolution of an advanced culture of book illustration. Already by the early years of the sixteenth century notable works of book illustration were being produced in Basle by men such as Urs Graf from Solothurn and Hans Herbster from Strasbourg. The art of book illustration had been imported from Italy and was already practised in Basle from the 1470s, and Albrecht Dürer, during a short stay in the city, had done some fine work. Hans Holbein and his brother Ambrosius, having been taught by their father in his large workshop in Augsburg, emerged as leaders in producing illustrations remarkable for their elegance and intricacy. Augsburg and Basle were cities closely connected through trade, and it was natural that the Holbein brothers should make their way to the Swiss city, where they arrived at the end of 1515. Their connection in Basle was the goldsmith Jörg Schweiger, who knew their father in Augsburg, and their first work was an illustration in 1515 for Erasmus's *Praise of Folly*. Hans's first contract for a portrait came in 1516 when he was commissioned to paint pictures of the Bürgermeister Jakob Meyer and his wife, Dorothea.

From 1516 Hans and Ambrosius worked for the Basle printers Johann Froben and Adam Petri. Between 1517 and 1519 Hans then travelled to Lucerne where he worked on murals for a series of houses while his father painted the interiors.[47] He also worked on an altar for the Augustinian church in the city. It is unclear whether during this time Hans travelled to Italy – the evidence is slender – but he certainly became well acquainted with Lombard and Venetian styles, which he translated to northern European culture. In 1519 Hans returned to Basle, where he became a member of the *Zum Himmel* guild, and in July 1520 he became a citizen of Basle. Although he had now made Basle his home, and married a woman from a local family, his real fame in the city did not come until 1521, when he received the contract to paint the council chamber of the Rathaus with scenes from antiquity.[48] The period between 1520 and 1523 was particularly fecund as Hans prepared altars, the Solothurn Madonna, and a variety of series of woodcuts. His reputation grew so quickly that he travelled to France in 1524 in the hope of becoming a court painter for Francis I. During this time Holbein also painted a series of portraits of Erasmus, who was to emerge as an important patron. In 1526 Holbein travelled to London with a letter of recommendation from Erasmus. He stayed in the house of Thomas More, whom he painted along with a portrait of the More family. When Holbein returned to Basle in 1528 he found himself amidst the growing storm of the Reformation, and the place of images in the church was the most hotly disputed issue. Nevertheless, Holbein continued to paint religious work, including the south wall of the Basle Münster, which he worked on until mid 1531. In 1532 he left Basle to return to England, returning only for a brief visit to his adopted city.[49]

Holbein's work as a portrait painter is most familiar to us, but his enormous talents contributed to the flourishing of the printing industry in Basle during the crucial years of the 1520s. He greatly advanced the techniques of woodcutting and engraving and his work set a new standard for book illustration. In providing woodcuts for the Bibles and Old Testaments of 1522, 1524, and 1526 he gave pictorial representation to evangelical ideas.[50] For the Swiss Reformation this would be most influential in his woodcuts for the 1531 Zurich Bible. It is often argued that Zwinglians were allergic to the visual arts; such a statement cannot stand in the face of the contribution of Hans Holbein to the connection of word and image so central to the transmission of Reformed Christianity in the sixteenth century.

Paracelsus

One of the most remarkable figures to emerge out of the Swiss Confederation during the sixteenth century was Theophrast Bombast von Hohenheim, better known as Paracelsus. His father was a medical doctor who looked after the pilgrims who made their way to the Benedictine abbey at Einsiedeln. After the early death of his mother he moved with his father to Austria, where he began to train in medicine. He studied at the universities of Vienna, Montpellier, Oxford, and Ferrara before making his way to Strasbourg in 1525. The Basle humanists, including Erasmus, arranged for Paracelsus to be appointed city doctor and professor of medicine. The reason for his great reputation in Basle was the manner in which he had healed Froben. When Paracelsus arrived in the Rhenish city to take up his chair of medicine in 1526 he caused an uproar by promoting a series of lectures in which he proposed to overturn the traditional world of medicine dating back to Hippocrates and Galen.

Paracelsus's reception by the Basle medical faculty was extremely hostile and he was branded a charlatan. He was driven from the city and after several years of wandering around Germany he arrived in St Gall in 1531. For two years he worked as a doctor in St Gall and Appenzell before once again being forced to leave. He returned to Austria, remaining in Salzburg until his death in 1541.

What was the cause of the uproar? During the 1520s and 1530s Paracelsus was in contact with various Anabaptist circles and without doubt he sympathised with certain of their beliefs. He was deeply critical of the established church, and he attacked the academic community for its pretentiousness, self-consciously fashioning himself after the peasant hero Karsthans with his simple dress. Paracelsus lived among the country folk and learned their natural remedies, which he argued were of far greater use than Galen and all the academic books on medicine. He linked medicine with faith by asserting that only those who followed the example of apostolic life could be true medical doctors. Only those who followed God and led a life of abstinence and moral rectitude would be provided the 'light of nature'. He sought to understand nature, which he held to be a visible reflection of the invisible work of God.[51] This was to be done empirically. One had to abandon the fleshpots of university life and head out into the world to discern the truth in nature. Paracelsus sought to uncover the relationship between God and humanity which was made possible by God's presence in humanity and nature. Men and women were the apex of God's creation and they had, on account of their divine power and free will, enormous potential. This potential should not, according to Paracelsus, be fettered by abstract social or political structures.[52] It has recently been argued that Paracelsus's medical system can only be understood in light of his biblical interpretations.[53]

One reason why Paraselsus was so utterly detested by the Reformed theologians was his seeming limitless medical empiricism. In *About Curing Supernatural Illnesses*, he wrote:

> It is necessary for all physicians who wish to be perfect to know how to give assistance by what logic and with what methods in those illnesses which have been inflicted by the magic art. On such cures neither Avicenna nor Galen wrote or knew anything. For not all skills are discussed in academies. Therefore it is necessary for the physician sometimes to go to old women, witches, zigneros [gypsies with magical powers], rustic people, and marginals, *die Zaubrecher* [curse-breakers], and to learn that skill from those people who know more about these things than all the professors of the academy; although the professors of the academy may laugh, you use these things in strong imagination, and you will experience the results.[54]

Paracelsus says that if someone is stricken down with a supernatural disease or pain, then no natural remedy will work, but one must use a magical remedy to remove the disease, like the one with which it was inflicted in the first place.

Paracelsus's thought must have sent the Reformed theologians into spasms of rage, but there can be little doubt that the provenance of his thought was in the intellectual world of the early Swiss Reformation; he belonged to that generation of figures who were deeply influenced by the mixture of humanist learning, evangelical ideas, and social unrest. Although few of his works were published during his life, he radically reworked the relationship between religion and medicine by identifying healing with the major religious ideas of the day. His assertion of free will, although contrary to the dogmatic formulations of the Swiss churches, found considerable sympathy among leading figures, and his exploration of the relationship of humanity and nature as an expression of God's purpose for creation was directly at the heart of the evolving intellectual culture of the Swiss Reformation. Paracelsus was a unique figure, and a brilliant one, but the fecund interplay of religion, science, and social comment in his life and work was a stunning expression of the genius of the Swiss Reformation.

Although Paracelus might seem a curious place to end a discussion of the intellectual culture of the Swiss Reformation, his desire to topple the existing medical order, his profound mysticism, and his scholarly acumen embody what was most exciting about the Swiss Reformation. Zwingli, far more than Luther, had opposed the medieval church and espoused a radical vision of how society might look. This vigorous exploration of the world and the interplay between ideas and their implementation reflected the Swiss concern with practical knowledge. Paracelsus also reminds us that although he was not a Zwinglian by any stretch of the imagination the intellectual boldness of Zwingli's revolt inspired a range of individuals to wildly different positions. There were numerous creative tensions in Swiss evangelical thought, such as the essential but uneasy relationship with humanism, or with Swiss patriotism, and these pushed scholars and artists in new directions. These men were cosmopolitan figures who, for the most part, rose above the polemical barracking and sought the underlying unity in God's creation. They sought to integrate knowledge and action, antiquity and modernity, religion and the world. The Confederation was never a cultural capital but the intellectual energy of its Reformation brought it, for a time, into the front rank of Renaissance Europe.

Notes

1 Hans Ulrich Bächtold, 'History, Ideology, and Propaganda in the Reformation: The early writing "Anklag und ernstliches ermanen Gottes" (1525) of Heinrich Bullinger', in Bruce Gordon (ed.), *Protestant History and Identity in Sixteenth-Century Europe*, 2 vols. (Aldershot, 1996), I, pp. 46–59.

2 Most recently, Hans Conrad Peyer. 'Der St. Galler Reformator Vadian als Geschichtsschreiber: Pragmatische und mystische Geschichtsauffassung in der Schweiz des 16. Jahrhunderts', *Schweizer Monatshefte*, 65 (1985), pp. 315–328.

3 Peter Schaeffer, 'The Emergence of the Concept 'Medieval' in Central European humanism', *Sixteenth Century Journal*, 7 (1976), pp. 21–30. Schaeffer discusses critically Vadianus's understanding of the Middle Ages.

4 Richard Feller and Edgar Bonjour, *Geschichtsschreibung der Schweiz vom Spätmittelalter zur Neuzeit*, 2 vols (Basle and Stuttgart, 1962), I, p. 237.

5 Ernst Gerhard Rüsch, 'Vadians Gutachten für eine Zwingli-Vita, 1544', *Zwingliana*, 15 (1979), pp. 40–49.

6 Feller and Bonjour, *Geschichtsschreibung der Schweiz*, p. 204.

7 See above, pp. 133–134.

8 Feller and Bonjour, *Gechichtsschreibung der Schweiz*, p. 183.

9 This is explored in Ralph Frenken, 'The History of German Childhood through Autobiographies', *Journal of Psychohistory*, 24 (1997), pp. 390–402.

10 Alfred Kohler, '"Jögli, nun buck dich, du must in den offen!" Beobachtungen zum Erscheinungsbild protestantischer Identität in der frühneuzeitlichen Autobiographie', *Wiener Beiträge zur Geschichte der Neuzeit*, 22 (1997), pp. 55–66.

11 Derek van Abbé, *Drama in Renaissance Germany and Switzerland* (Melbourne, 1961), p. 26.

12 On Manuel's role in Berne at the time of the First Kappel War, see chapter 4, pp. 124–126.

13 Glenn Ellis Ehrstine, 'Of Peasants, Women, and Bears: Political

Agency and the Demise of Carnival Transgression in Bernese Reformation Drama', *SCJ*, 16 (2000), p. 683.

14 Glenn Ellis Ehrstine, 'From Iconoclasm to Iconography: Reformation Drama in Sixteenth-Century Bern' (dissertation, University of Texas, Austin, 1996).

15 Abbé, *Drama*, p. 56.

16 Wolfgang F. Michael, *Das deutsche Drama der Reformationszeit* (Berne, 1984), p. 232.

17 On his education and humanist work in Vienna, Frans Graf-Stuhlhofer, 'Vadian als Lehrer am Wiener Poetenkolleg', *Zwingliana*, 26 (1999), pp. 93–98.

18 On Vadianus, see Werner Näf, *Vadian und seine Stadt St. Gallen*, 2 vols (St Gall, 1944, 1957).

19 Feller and Bonjour, *Geschichtsschreibung der Schweiz*, p. 232.

20 Ibid., pp. 233–234.

21 The best work on Amerbach is the introductions to the ten volumes of the printed Amerbach correspondence, *Die Amerbachkorrespondenz* (Basle, 1942–1991).

22 Myron P. Gilmore, 'Boniface Amerbach', in his *Humanists and Jurists: Six Studies in the Renaissance* (Cambridge, MA, 1963), pp. 146–177.

23 Hans-Rudolf Hagemann, 'Rechtsunterricht im 16. Jahrhundert: Die Juristischen Vorlesgungen im Basler Amerbachnachlass', *Zeitschrift für Neuere Rechtsgeschichte*, 14 (1992), pp. 162–190.

24 John Monfasani, 'For the History of Marsilio Ficino's Translation of Plato: The Revision Mistakenly Attributed to Ambrogio Flandino, Simon Grynaeus' Revision of 1532, and the Anonymous Revision of 1532, and the Anonymous Revision of 1556/1557', *Rinascimento* (1987), pp. 293–299.

25 Charlotte Methuen, *Kepler's Tübingen. Stimulus to a Theological Mathematics* (Aldershot, 1998), p. 166.

26 Ibid., p. 167.

27 Karl Heinz Burmeister, *Sebastian Münster. Versuch eines biographischen Gesamtbildes* (Basle and Stuttgart, 1969).

28 Jerome Friedman, 'Sebastian Münster, The Jewish Mission, and Protestant Antisemitism', *ARG*, 70, (1979), pp. 238–259; also his *Most Ancient Testimony: Sixteenth-Century Christian Hebraica in the Age of Renaissance Nostalgia* (Athens, GA, 1983).

29 Jean Lebeau, 'Novus Orbis. Les Cosmographes allemands du XVIe Siècle et les grandes découvertes', *Revue d'Allemagne*, 13 (1981), pp. 197–215.

30 On the remarkable achievement of the illustrations in the *Cosmographia*, see Hans Jakob Meier, 'Das Bildnis in der Reproduktionsgraphik des 16. Jahrhunderts: Ein Beitrag zu den Anfängen serieller Produktion', *Zeitschrift für Kunstgeschichte*, 58 (1995), pp. 449–477.

31 Sebastian Münster, *Cosmographia* (Basle, 1578), fo. iii[r].

32 On the relationship between Münster's religious ideas and the development of geography, see M. Büttner, 'The Significance of the Reformation for the Reorientation of Geography in Lutheran Germany', *History of Science*, 17 (1979), pp. 151–169.

33 Karl Heinz Burmeister, *Briefe Sebastian Münsters. Lateinisch und Deutsch* (1964), letter 33, April 1548.

34 The most extensive work in English is Hans Wellisch, 'Conrad Gessner: A Bio-Biography', *Journal of the Society for the Bibliography of Natural History*, 7 (1975), pp. 151–247.

35 Urs B. Leu, *Conrad Gesner als Theologe. Ein Beitrag zur Zürcher Geistesgeschichte des 16. Jahrhunderts* (Berne, 1990), p. 53.

36 Bernhard Milt, 'Conrad Gesners theologische Enzyklopädie', *Zwingliana*, 8 (1948), pp. 571–587.

37 Leu, *Conrad Gesner*, p. 58.

38 Urs B. Leu, 'Konrad Gessner und die neue Welt', *Gesnerus*, 49 (1992), pp. 279–309; also, C. Gmelig Meyling-Nyboer, 'Conrad Gesner (1516–1565) Considered as a Modern Naturalist', *Janus*, 60 (1973), pp. 41–51.

39 Änne Bäumer, 'De Piscibus et aquatilibus libelli III novi (Zurich 1556): Ein bisher unbeachtetes zoologisches Werk von Conrad Gesner', *Berichte zur Wissenschaftsgeschichte*, 13 (1990), pp. 177–181.

40 Leu, *Conrad Gesner*, p. 106.

41 Bertold Hack and Bernhard Wendt (eds), *Archiv für Geschichte des Buchwesens*, vol. VII (Frankfurt-am-Main, 1966), p. 1378.

42 Paul Leemann-van Elck, *Die Offizin Froschauer, Zürichs berühmte Druckerei im 16. Jahrhundert: Ein Beitrag zur Geschichte der Buchdruckerkunst anläßlich der Halbjahrtausendfeier ihrer Erfindung* (Zurich, 1940).

43 Iren L. Snavely, 'Zwingli, Froschauer, and the Word of God in Print', *Journal of Religious & Theological Information*, 3 (2000), pp. 65–87.

44 Harry Clark, 'The Publication of the Koran in Latin, A Reformation Diliemma', *Sixteenth Century Journal*, 15 (1984), pp. 3–12.

45 Anja Wolkenhauer, 'Humanistische Bildung und neues Selbstverständnis in Druckerzeichen des 16. Jahrhunderts', *Gutenberg-Jahrbuch*, 73 (1998), pp. 165–179. The author has examined Oporinus's printer marks as reflections of his learning.

46 Leemann-van Elck, *Die Offizin*, p. 1401.

47 On Holbein's life, see Derek Wilson, *Hans Holbein: Portrait of an Unknown Man* (London, 1997).

48 Christian Müller, *Die Druckgraphik im Kupferstichkabinett Basel* (Basle, 1997), p. 10.

49 On Holbein in England, see Andrew Pettegree, 'Art', in his *The Reformation World* (London, 2000), esp. pp. 477–482.

50 Max Engammare, 'Les Figures de la Bible: Le Destin oublié d'un genre littéraire en image (XVIe-XVIIe S.)', *Mélanges de l'Ecole Française de Rome. Italie et Méditerranée*, 106 (1994), pp. 549–591.

51 Goodrick-Clarke, *Paracelsus. Essential Readings*, p. 28.

52 Ibid., p. 320.

53 Mitchell Hammond, 'The Religious Roots of Paracelsus's Medical Theory', *ARG* 89 (1998), pp. 7–21.

54 *De occulta philosophia*, quoted from Paracelsus, *Opera omnia* (Geneva, 1658), II, p. 487.

Conclusion

The Swiss Reformation occurred because of Huldrych Zwingli. He brought about a theological revolution by creating a distinctive understanding of God, the church, and humanity which contrasted sharply with late medieval Catholicism. Zwingli's intellectual and spiritual debts were legion: Ulrich Surgant, Erasmus, Luther, the Church Fathers, and the medieval scholastics. But Zwingli's book-laden desk was not remote from his own traumatic experiences as either a chaplain with the Swiss armies in Italy or as a victim of the plague expecting to die as a young man. Zwingli's intense study of scripture and the Church Fathers was realised in his daily activities as a preacher; almost all of his central ideas evolved out of the endless conflicts in which he became entangled. He was a charismatic figure who could lead, and who attracted followers, but most of his time between 1519 and 1531 was spent fighting the fires kindled by his own words.

If Luther's life gave the Wittenberg reformer a profound understanding of the torments of the spirit, and Calvin the Frenchman in Geneva knew what it meant to be a refugee, Zwingli was driven by a visceral hatred of human corruption and impurity. He was repelled by what he saw in the world: bribes, prostitution, poverty, and injustice. Most offensive, for Zwingli, was the grotesque manner in which the church seemed to connive in this despoiling of God's creation. In the mass, above all, Zwingli believed that once more a golden calf had been erected; a cheap, material image of the invisible God – an idol to beguile the people. He detested every aspect of this false religion, and as a preacher he used the pulpit to attack the established religion by linking his vision of reform with issues which stirred deep resentment in the community: the tithe, political corruption, mercenary service, and the indolence of the clergy. Zwingli hammered away at the contrast between the harsh and sordid reality of daily life and the promises of scripture. He used contrasting images to make his point, speaking in polarities to rouse the people. In so doing, Zwingli not only spiritualised dissent, but held out the promise that society could be made better; the justice of God could be realised in this world. In contrast to Luther, Zwingli created a positive language of religious reform that was clearly defined against Catholicism, or at least his portrayal of Catholicism.

His message fell on fertile ground in a society that was changing. In the cities the guilds were winning their struggle to supplant the patrician families, while in the rural areas the restive peasants in the Confederation had contributed to the collapse of feudal structures. Zwingli's message of a better society was readily taken up by large numbers of people for whom it was a screen on to which they could project hopes, aspirations, and frustrations. It would be wrong to suggest that these people did not really grasp the full import of Zwingli's message, for that message emerged piecemeal from the disputations, pamphlets, sermons, and the work of the '*Prophezei*' in the Grossmünster. There was nothing inevitable about what happened in Zurich in the 1520s. Opposition to the reformer remained strong and it was only through a few close friendships, such as with the Röist family, that Zwingli was able to sustain his position. Zwingli's theology must be understood in terms of the events which shaped it: the iconoclasm, the revolt of the peasants, the break with the radicals, the split with Luther, the failure to meet the Catholics at Baden, the triumph at Berne in 1528, the failed negotiations with Philip of Hesse, etc. These are the events which dictated that infant baptism, the eucharist, and the nature of the church should become hallmarks of Zwinglian theology. From the comfort of a study in Basle Zwingli might well have chosen a different agenda.

Zwingli's ultimate success in Zurich made the Reformation in the rest of the Swiss Confederation possible. Although it would be unsustainable to argue that Zwingli was personally responsible for events in St Gall, Berne, and Basle, we can assert without injury to local circumstances and figures that none of these cities would have turned to the Reformation without the bastion of Zurich behind them. We have attempted in this survey to convey something of the unique characteristics of these states and to examine how their reformations took shape, but for better or worse they all fell under the shadow of Zurich.

This book has attempted to map the development and dissemination of evangelical ideas against the historical context of the Swiss Confederation. We can underscore a few points. By 1520 the Swiss Confederation had largely taken shape after the tumultuous events of the previous century and a half. The addition of Appenzell as a full member in 1513 brought a period of remarkable territorial growth to an end. One of the key lessons which had been learnt from the Old Zurich War of the 1450s was that the Confederation was not simply a loose alliance of trade pacts and defensive alliances; it was a closely spun web of relationships which could no longer be easily pulled apart. It was not a nation state, but the notion of confederacy (*Eidgenossenschaft*) did mean a great deal. Zurich had pushed the Confederation to the brink, as it would do again, but nobody wished to leave. Yet within this collection there were important differences. The original three Confederates saw themselves as the guardians of the very idea of the Swiss Confederation, and the eight 'older' Confederates certainly ranked themselves above the five latecomers.

This meant that when the Reformation began it was not simply a case of Reformed versus Catholic, but rather it was a division which must be understood in terms of the older, and rural, Confederates against their long-standing rivals, Zurich and Berne. The other states of Appenzell, Glarus, Fribourg, and Solothurn fell between these two camps. Schaffhausen and Basle, on account of their geography and late entry into the Confederation, remained somewhat marginal figures with close connections to Alsace and Swabia. With Zwingli leading from Zurich there was no chance of the movement making any headway in Uri, Schwyz, Unterwalden, Zug, and Lucerne. Bad memories of Zurich's earlier hegemonic aspirations quickly reappeared. That is why the principal battlegrounds of the Swiss Reformation were not in any of the Confederates, which quickly fell into one camp or the other, but in the Mandated Territories which they jointly administered.

The immediate confrontation of the evangelical movement with a well-organised Catholic resistance backed by the rulers of the Five Inner States meant that the differences between the two parties were established early and unequivocally. This was in contrast to the empire, where religious developments occurred at a different pace with the Confession of Augsburg and the religious colloquies. In the Swiss Confederation Catholics and Reformed found a *modus vivendi* in 1531, a way in which they could live alongside each other and preserve the Confederation, but they did not attempt to reconcile their differences. There were no colloquies aimed at reconciling the two theological positions; the divide was absolute and final unless, of course, one side proved strong enough to conquer the other. But the political arrangement of the Confederation made this impossible.

The Second Kappel Peace essentially froze the growth of the Confederation. Although Berne extended its authority to the west with the conquest of the Pays de Vaud in 1536, the Catholic states did officially acknowledge these French-speaking lands as part of the Confederation, and they accepted no responsibility for the defence of this territory. But at the same time the Catholics built their own position in the west by securing Fribourg, Solothurn, and Greyerz for the old faith. An alliance was also made with the bishopric of Basle. Every move by one side after 1531 was balanced by an acquisition by the other, thereby sustaining a form of equilibrium in the Confederation. Geneva and Constance, two natural members of the Confederation, were denied entry by the Catholic states on the grounds that this carefully wrought balance would be upset.

After the Peace of Kappel the Reformed and Catholic states remained deeply suspicious of one another, but there was little violence. Even the events in Glarus, which might have brought about a confessional war, were defused by the co-operation of Catholic and Reformed states in putting pressure on the local hotheads. Zwingli's death at Kappel removed the most divisive figure from the Swiss Reformation. The Catholics had no desire to wreak havoc on Reformed states but they wanted the head of Zwingli, whom they loathed. Once he was dead the Catholics were satisfied with rolling back the Reformation in the Mandated Territories and to receive money. They made no effort to undo the Reformation in the other Confederates.

The story of the Swiss Reformation was not written in the blood of martyrs, nor was it to be told by exiles in foreign lands. There were plenty of disputes, but little violence. Although Zwingli had appealed to a broad spectrum of people in the early 1520s the Reformation was never a popular movement. Zwingli's peasant background was without doubt important in restraining rural rebellion during 1524–25, and the positive responses of the Confederate rulers to the demands of the peasants obviated the carnage which took place in the empire. Nevertheless, the rural communities had no place in Zwingli's reforming agenda. The connection between the reform movement and rural objections to the tithe was quickly dropped and the rural areas were regarded with suspicion once the Anabaptists had been driven from Zurich. Zwingli's ignoring of the rural communities during the 1520s, an attitude replicated in Berne and Basle, was repaid with the hostility expressed by these communities after his death. Demands were presented to ensure that what Zwingli had done in acting without consultation would never be repeated, but a change of religion was not demanded. There were no calls for the restoration of Catholicism. To argue that this was because the Reformation had quickly taken hold would be incorrect.

The people in the rural communities wanted churches that functioned with a resident minister who carried out his duties. They also wished to be left alone by their urban masters. The church found itself in a difficult position between the locality and its place in the hierarchy of authority presided over by the magistrates. That is why from 1532 Heinrich Bullinger in Zurich and Oswald Myconius in Basle devoted themselves to the cultivation of educated ministers in well-ordered churches. The church was part of the centralising interests of the state, a process which had been evident from the late Middle Ages, but it had to adapt to life in the localities if the Reformation was to survive. The battle was not against a recalcitrant Catholic rural population, but rather to establish Reformed beliefs and practices in a society that was syncretistic in its religious views. The people were highly practical in their approach to religion, they chose what worked in providing comfort and protection. The Reformed church had to make its beliefs and practices relevant to the needs of these people. There was resistance, some out of loyalty to Catholicism, but mostly for reasons found throughout Europe in Lutheran and Catholic areas: resentment of intrusion by local officials or clergy, strong attachment to traditional medicine and rituals, drinking, violence, adultery, dancing, etc. These should not be confused with a rejection of the Reformation. There were neither revolts against the Reformed orders in the Confederation nor mass migrations of the faithful. There were always individuals or small groups which acted on their convictions, but the vast majority of the population in the Confederation simply accepted their lot. As new generations were born they knew nothing of Catholicism and were content to accept their religion. It slowly became part of who they were. Religion, kinship, language, and one's ancestors formed a powerful bond to the land. It was not to be abandoned lightly.

The people did not migrate, but this did not make them either pliant or willing disciples of the new Reformed churches. The most fascinating aspect of the Swiss Reformation from the 1530s onwards was not dramatic events, of which there were few, but the development of religious cultures as the Reformed religion encountered the realities of daily life. In the application of the new theology ministers of the church realised that they had to reclaim important aspects of the medieval religion they had turned against. In order to give the people the pastoral care they demanded in the face of the vicissitudes of sixteenth-century life the Reformed ministers had to talk about God's intercession in the world. A relationship between the Reformed faith and people's lives and needs had to be negotiated in such a way that Zwingli's ferocious denial of materialistic religion could be somewhat modified. People needed visible signs of God's love. The Reformed churches learned to speak the language of pastoral care, which was much more flexible than the language of theological discourse. Bullinger would never allow that the devil had any independent authority in the world, for he was part of God's creation. But in his sermons he, and other reformers, portrayed the world in dualistic terms, a struggle between good and evil, in which the actions and beliefs of individuals were crucial.

The Swiss Reformation did not operate by mass movement or through political alliance. Its success was first and foremost due to a network of churchmen, scholars, and laity who passionately shared their evangelical ideas. These networks were always a minority in their communities, but through the sharing of information, talents, and writings they emerged as a formidable force for change. Throughout the book we have noticed how personal contacts were key to the development of local reformations. At the centre of these networks was Basle and its university, where most of these men had studied. The basis of the Zurich reformation was the sodality around Zwingli, which, in turn, was modelled on Erasmus's circle in Basle. Heinrich Bullinger raised the art of networking to a new level. The head of the Zurich church was at the centre of a Europe-wide communications system. He, more than anyone else, was responsible for the dissemination of the Swiss Reformation in foreign lands. Bullinger had saved the Reformation in 1531–32 by integrating the essential core of Zwingli's reforming vision into the political realities of the post-Kappel Confederation. Bullinger's success, however, depended on his ability to negotiate between the needs of the church and magistrates. This exposed the central weakness of the Swiss Reformation, its dependence on personalities. It was Bullinger's personal authority and status which enabled the Zurich church to retain its prophetic character. Had Bullinger not taken over in 1532 the Zurich church would have been reduced to the role of supplicant, similar to the churches in Basle and Berne. Bullinger had to work behind the scenes to preserve this polity; the institutional life of the church depended on decisions made in private. That was the only way they would be tolerated. Bullinger was both the centre of the Swiss Reformation and an anomaly. He alone commanded great authority in Zurich and the other Reformed states, and no one replaced him.

This survey has concluded with the *Second Helvetic Confession* of 1566, which was the fullest expression of Swiss Reformed theology. By the time of Bullinger's death Calvinism was ascendant and the Swiss churches were members of a broad Reformed Protestant culture in Europe which they did not lead. The Peace of Kappel, which had preserved the Reformation in its darkest hour, had led to stasis. The Swiss Confederation slipped back into obscurity as the most important religious developments took place elsewhere. But for just over fifty years the Confederation stood at the centre of change in Europe and made a crucial contribution.

Selected further reading

I have emphasised here the literature available in English. For a fuller record of the work which I have consulted see the notes at the end of each chapter.

It should be noted that a bibliography of recent work on the Swiss Reformation appears each year in *Zwingliana*. This remains the most important source for new literature in the field.

General studies

There are virtually no general studies of the Swiss Reformation in English. The best in German are now fairly old: Leonhard von Muralt, 'Renaissance und Reformation', in *Handbuch der Schweizer Geschichte*, vol. 1 (2nd edn, Zurich, 1980), pp. 389–570; Rudolf Pfister, *Kirchengeschichte der Schweiz*, vol. 2, *Von der Reformation bis zum Zweiten Villmerger Krieg* (Zurich, 1974). The monumental work of Gottfried W. Locher, *Die Zwinglische Reformation im Rahmen der europäischen Kirchengeschichte* (Göttingen, 1979) is an enormously useful repository of information. A very useful overview is to be found in *Geschichte der Schweiz und der Schweizer*, vol. 2 (Basle and Frankfurt-am-Main, 1983). A still useful history of Switzerland is E. Bonjour, H.S. Offler, and G.R. Potter, *A Short History of Switzerland* (Oxford, 1952). More recently there have been a series of short overviews: Bruce Gordon, 'Switzerland', in Andrew Pettegree (ed.), *The Early Reformation in Europe* (Cambridge, 1992), pp. 70–93; Kaspar von Greyerz, 'Switzerland', in Bob Scribner, Roy Porter, and Mikulás Teich (eds), *The Reformation in National Context* (Cambridge, 1994), pp. 30–46; and Mark Taplin, 'Switzerland', in Andrew Pettegree (ed.), *The Reformation World* (London, 2000), pp. 169–189.

There are important histories of individual Confederates which remain essential as reference works: *Geschichte des Kantons Zürich*, 3 vols. (Zurich, 1995–99); Karl Dändliker, *Geschichte der Stadt und des Kantons*

Zürich, 2 vols (Zurich, 1908–10); Richard Feller, *Geschichte Berns*, 3 vols (Berne, 1946); R. Wackernagel, *Geschichte der Stadt Basel*, 2 vols (Basle, 1916); Hans Guggisberg, *Basel in the Sixteenth Century* (St Louis, 1982).

Chapter 1

The literature in English on the Confederation in the late Middle Ages is extremely limited. The most recent survey is to be found in the *New Cambridge History of the Middle Ages* (1997).

On church life: the excellent article by Carl Pfaff, 'Pfarrei und Pfarreileben. Ein Beitrag zur spätmittelalterlichen Kirchengeschichte', in Hansjakob Achermann, Josef Brülisauer, and Peter Hoppe (eds), *Innerschweiz und frühe Eidgenossenschaft*, 2 vols (Lucerne, 1991). Also highly recommended is Magdalen Bless-Grabher, 'Veränderungen im kirchlichen Bereich 1350–1520', in Niklaus Flüeler and Marianne Flüeler-Grauwiler (eds), *Geschichte des Kantons Zürich. Frühzeit bis Spätmittelalter* (Zurich, 1995). Also Peter Jezler, 'Spätmittelalterliche Frömmigkeit und reformatorischer Bildersturm', in Bernhard Schneider (ed.) *Alltag in der Schweiz seit 1300* (Zurich, 1991). Kurt Guggisberg, *Bernische Kirchengeschichte* (Berne, 1958) is a rich source of information on the late medieval church. For some stunning visual material see Peter Jezler (ed.), *Himmel – Hölle – Fegefeuer. Das Jenseits im Mittelalter, Katalog zur Ausstellung im Schweizerischen Landesmuseum* (Zurich, 1994). An important older work is Oskar Vasella, *Reform und Reformation in der Schweiz: Zur Würdigung der Anfänge der Glaubenskrise* (Münster, 1958), which concentrates largely on concubinage and clerical problems.

Some more specialised studies include: Walter Baumann, *Zürichs Kirchen, Klöster und Kapellen bis zur Reformation* (Zurich, 1994); Peter Felder, 'Memento Mori. Art and the Cult of the Dead in Central Switzerland', in Heinz Horat (ed.), *1000 Years of Swiss Art* (New York, 1992); Kathrin Temp-Utz, 'Gottesdienst, Ablasswesen und Predigt am Vinzenzstift in Bern (1484/85–1528) *ZKG*, 80 (1986), pp. 31–98.

On the political development, see Wilhelm Baum, *Reichs- und Territorialgewalt (1273–1437): Königtum, Haus Österreich und Schweizer Eidgenossen im späten Mittelalter* (Vienna, 1994). On the role of mercenary service in the Confederation there is some good work in English: John McCormack, *One Million Mercenaries. Swiss Soldiers in the Armies of the World* (London, 1993), and Douglas Miller, *The Swiss at War 1300–1500* (London, 1979).

On late medieval society and daily life there are some fine books, many well illustrated: Hans-Jörg Gilomen, 'Sozial- und Wirtschaftsgeschichte der Schweiz im Spätmittelalter', *ZSKG*, 41 (1991), pp. 467–492; Albert Hauser, *Was für ein Leben. Schweizer Alltag vom 15. bis 18. Jahrhundert* (Zurich, 1988); Werner Meyer, *Hirsebrei und Hellebarde. Auf den Spuren des mittelalterlichen Lebens in der Schweiz* (Olten, 1985); Matthias Weishaupt, *Bauern, Hirten, und 'frume edle puren'. Bauern- und Bauernstaatsideologie in der spätmittelalterlichen Eidgenossenschaft und der nationalen Geschichtsschreibung der Schweiz* (Basle and Frankfurt, 1992).

Chapter 2

The standard biography of Zwingli in English remains G.R. Potter, *Zwingli* (Cambridge, 1976) which is excellent in many respects but desperately needs updating. Also useful is W.P. Stephens's short *Zwingli: An introduction to his Thought* (Oxford, 1992). In German, highly recommended are Martin Haas, *Ulrich Zwingli und seine Zeit: Leben und Werk des Zürcher Reformators* (Zurich, 1969), and Oskar Farner, *Ulrich Zwingli*, 3 vols (Zurich, 1943). Another fine introduction is Ulrich Gäbler, *Ulrich Zwingli: His Life and Work* (Edinburgh, 1987). Zwingli's youth is well covered in James M. Stayer, 'Zwingli before Zürich: Humanist Reformer and Papal Partisan', *ARG*, 72 (1981), pp. 55–68. On Zwingli's theology the most comprehensive work in English W.P. Stephens, *The Theology of Ulrich Zwingli* (Oxford, 1986). The work of the leading Swiss scholar on Zwingli is available in English in Gottfried W. Locher, *Zwingli's Thought. New Perspectives* (Leiden, 1981). Some of best work on Zwingli's thought is by the German scholar Berndt Hamm. Particularly noteworthy is his *Zwinglis Reformation der Freiheit* (Neukirchen-Vluyn, 1988), and 'Laientheologie zwischen Luther und Zwingli', in Josef Nolte, Hella Tompert, and Christof Windhorst (eds), *Kontinuität und Umbruch. Theologie und Frömmigkeit in Flugschriften und Kleinliteratur an der Wende vom 15. zum 16. Jahrhundert* (Stuttgart, 1978), pp. 222–295. Available in English is his 'What Was the Reformation Doctrine of Justification?', in C. Scott Dixon (ed.), *The German Reformation* (Oxford, 1999), pp. 53–90.

On the Reformation in Zurich see the work of Lee Palmer Wandel: *Always Among Us: Images of the Poor in Zwingli's Zurich* (Cambridge, 1990) and her *Voracious Idols and Violent Hands* (New Haven and London, 1995). Robert C. Walton, *Zwingli's Theocracy* (Toronto, 1967) is still useful, as is his 'The Institutionalisation of the Reformation at Zurich', *Zwingliana*, 13 (1972), pp. 497–515. On the reform of the clergy under Zwingli, see Bruce Gordon, 'Preaching and the Reform of the Clergy in the Swiss Reformation', in Andrew Pettegree (ed.), *The Reformation of the Parishes* (Manchester, 1993), pp. 63–84, and his 'Die Entwicklung der Kirchenzucht in Zürich am Beginn der Reformation', in Heinz Schilling (ed.), *Kirchenzucht und Sozialdisziplinierung im frühneuzeitlichen Europa* (Berlin, 1994), pp. 65–90. On Zwingli's preaching, see Arnold Snyder, 'Word and Power in Reformation Zurich', *ARG*, 81 (1990), pp. 263–285. Also important in this respect is Hans-Jürgen Goertz, *Pfaffenhass und gross Geschrei* (Munich, 1987), esp. pp. 134–147.

The following works in German are extremely important: Christian Dietrich, *Die Stadt Zürich und ihre Landgemeinden während der Bauernunruhen von 1489 bis 1525* (Frankfurt-am-Main and Bern, 1985); Walter Jacob, *Politische Führungsschichte und Reformation* (Zurich, 1970); Peter Kamber, 'Die Reformation auf der Zürcher Landschaft am Beispiel des Dorfes Marthalen. Fallstudie zur Struktur bäuerlicher Reformation', in Peter Blickle (ed.), *Zugänge zur bäuerlicher Reformation* (Zurich, 1987), pp. 85–125; Hans Morf, *Zunftverfassung und Obrigkeit in Zürich von Waldmann bis Zwingli* (Zurich, 1969).

Chapter 3

Once one moves away from Zurich it is extremely difficult to find literature in English. For Basle there is the fine overview by Hans Guggisberg in his *Basel in the Sixteenth Century. Aspects of the City Republic before, during, and after the Reformation* (St Louis, 1982). On Oecolampadius, there is Gordon Rupp, 'Johannes Oecolampadius. The Reformer as Scholar', in his *Patterns of Reformation* (London, 1969), pp. 3–48. Palmer Wandel, in her book *Voracious Idols*, has a chapter on Basle. Also important is Peter Blickle, *Communal Reformation: The quest for salvation in Sixteenth-Century Germany* (Atlantic Highlands, 1992). The principal works on the Basle reformation remain Ernst Staehelin, *Das theologische Lebenswerk Johannes Oekolampads* (Leipzig, 1939), and Paul Roth, *Durchbruch und Festsetzung der Reformation in Basel* (Basle, 1942). Julia Gauss, 'Basels politisches Dilemma in der Reformationszeit', *Zwingliana*, 15 (1982), pp. 509–548; Hans Füglister, *Handwerksregiment: Untersuchungen und Matrialen zur sozialen und politischen Struktur der Stadt Basel in ersten Hälfte des 16. Jh.* (Basle, 1981).

For the eastern part of the Confederation there are some very useful articles: John P. Maarbjerg, 'Iconoclasm in the Thurgau: Two Related Incidents in the Summer of 1524', *SCJ*, 24 (1993), pp. 577–593; Randolph C. Head, 'Shared Lordship, Authority, and Administration: The Exercise of Dominion in the Gemeine Herrschaften of the Swiss Confederation, 1417–1600', *Central European History*, 30 (1997), pp. 489–512; C. Arnold Snyder, 'Communication and the People: The case of the Reformation in St Gall', *Mennonite Quarterly Review*, 67 (1993), pp. 152–173.

The principal work remains Kurt Guggisberg, *Bernische Kirchengeschichte* (Berne, 1958). On the introduction of the Reformation in Berne, Hans Rudolf Lavater, 'Zwingli und Bern', in *450 Jahre Berner Reformation* (Berne, 1980), pp. 60–103. On the urban reformation in Berne, Heinrich Richard Schmidt, 'Stadtreformation in Bern und Nürnberg – ein Vergleich', in Rudolf Endres (ed.), *Nürnberg und Bern. Zwei Reichsstädte und ihre Landgebiete* (Erlangen, 1990). Leonhard von Muralt, 'Berns westliche Politik zur Zeit der Reformation' in his *Der Historiker und die Geschichte* (Zurich, 1960), pp. 88–96. An important work on the Berne Disputation of 1528 is Irene Backus, 'The Disputations of Baden, 1526 and Berne, 1528: Neutralising the Early Church', *Studies in Reformed Religion*, 1 (1993). Also, Dan L. Hendricks, *The Berne Reformation of 1528: The Preacher's Vision, The People's Work, an Occasion of State* (Ann Arbor, MI, 1981), and Gottfried Locher, 'Die Berner Disputation 1528: Charakter, Verlauf, Bedeutung und theologischer Gehalt', *Zwingliana*, 14 (1978), pp. 542–564.

On Niklaus Manuel and the Bernese reformation, see Bruce Gordon, 'Toleration in the Early Swiss Reformation: the Art and Politics of Niklaus Manuel of Berne', in Ole Peter Grell and Bob Scribner (eds), *Tolerance and Intolerance in the European Reformation* (Cambridge, 1996), pp. 128–144. Also, J.P. Tardent, *Niklaus Manuel als Staatsmann* (Berne, 1979), and Derek van Abbé, 'Niklaus Manuel of Berne and his Interest in the Reformation', *Journal of Modern History*, 24 (1952), pp. 287–300. On the festival culture of Berne, the essential work is Peter Pfrunder, *Pfaffen Ketzer Totenfresser.*

Fastnachtskultur der Reformationszeit – Die Berner Spiele von Niklaus Manuel (Zurich, 1989), and Glenn Ehrstine, 'Of Peasants, Women, and Bears: Political Agency and the Demise of Carnival Tradition in Bernese Reformation Drama', *Sixteenth Century Journal*, 30 (2000), pp. 675–697.

The literature available on the Basle Reformation is fairly dated. The best study is Hans R. Guggisberg, *Basel in the Sixteenth Century: Aspects of the City Republic before, during, and after the Reformation* (St Louis, 1982). See also Lee Palmer Wandel, *Violent Hands* (Cambridge, 1995). On Oecolampadius, see Gordon Rupp, 'Johannes Oecolampadius. The Reformer as Scholar', in his *Patterns of Reformation* (London, 1969), pp. 3–46; Thomas A. Fudge, 'Icarus of Basel. Oecolampadius and the Early Swiss Reformation', *Journal of Religious History*, 21 (1997), pp. 268–284; and Karl Hammer, 'Der Reformator Oekolampad, 1482–1531', in Heiko Oberman et al. (eds) *Reformiertes Erbe*, 2 vols (Zurich, 1992), I, pp. 157–160. The most detailed treatment of the Reformation in Basle remains Paul Roth, *Die Reformation in Basel. Die Vorbereitungsjahre, 1525–1528* (Basle, 1936). See also Ernst Gerhard Rüsch, Die Schaffhauser Reformationsordnung von 1529', in *Schaffhauser Beiträge zur Geschichte*, 56 (1979); Jakob Wipf, *Reformations Geschichte der Stadt und Landschaft Schaffhausen* (Zurich, 1929). On the Reformation in the eastern part of the Confederation, see Ursula Kägi, *Die Aufnahme der Reformation in den ostschweizerischen Untertanengebieten – der Weg Zürichs zu einem obrigkeitlichen Kirchenregiment bis zum Frühjahr 1529* (Zurich, 1972). Also, Alfred L. Knittel, *Die Reformation im Thurgau* (Frauenfeld, 1929). See also the articles in Peter Blickle (ed.), *Zugänge zur bäuerlichen Reformation* (Zurich, 1987); and Huldreich Gustav Sulzberger, *Geschichte der Reformation im Kanton Appenzell* (Appenzell, 1866). More recently, Franz Stark, 'Die Reformation', in R. Fischer, W. Schläpfer and F. Stark (eds), *Appenzeller Geschichte* (Appenzell and Herisau, 1964), pp. 303–400. Jakob Winteler, *Geschichte des Landes Glarus*, 2 vols (Glaraus, 1957).

Chapter 4

The most useful article is Hans R. Guggisberg, 'The Problem of "Failure" in the Swiss Reformation: Some Preliminary Reflections', in E.I. Kouri and Tom Scott (eds), *Politics and Society in Reformation Society. Essays for Sir Geoffrey Elton on his Sixty-Fifth Birthday* (London, 1987). The recent book by André Zünd, *Gescheiterte Stadt- und Landreformationen des 16. und 17. Jahrhunderts in der Schweiz* (Basle, 1999) adds detail but does not advance much beyond Guggisberg's conclusions. Also important is Peter Blickle, 'Warum blieb die Innerschweiz katholisch?', *Mitteilungen des Historischen Vereins des Kantons Schwyz*, 86 (1994), pp. 29–38.

The standard work on the Kappel Wars is Helmut Meyer, *Der Zweite Kappeler Krieg. Die Krise der Schweizerischen Reformation* (Zurich, 1976). Other key works are Hans Ulrich Bächtold, 'Bullinger und die Krise der Zücher Reformation im Jahre 1532', in U. Gäbler and E. Herkenrath (eds), *Heinrich Bullinger 1504–1575. Gesammelte Aufsätze zum 400. Todestag*, 2 vols (Zurich, 1975), I, pp. 269–289.

There are, however, some useful studies in English. See Wayne J. Baker, 'Church, State and Dissent: The Crisis of the Swiss Reformation, 1531–1536', *Church History*, 57 (1988), pp. 135–152. On Bullinger's appointment and early years, see Pamela Biel, *Doorkeepers at the House of Righteousness. Heinrich Bullinger and the Zurich Clergy 1535–1575* (Berne, 1991). For an overview of Bullinger's life, Robert Walton, 'Heinrich Bullinger', in Jill Rait (ed.), *Shapers of Religious Traditions in Germany, Switzerland, and Poland 1560–1600* (New Haven, 1981), pp. 69–88.

On the troubles in Berne and the Berne Synod of 1532, see Bruce Gordon, 'Preaching and the Reform of the Clergy in the Swiss Reformation', in Andrew Pettegree (ed.), *The Reformation of the Parishes. The Ministry and the Reformation in Town and Country* (Manchester, 1993), pp. 63–84. The acts of the Berne Synod of 1532 have been edited along with a collection of scholarly essays in Gottfried W. Locher (ed.), *Der Berner Synodus von 1532*, 2 vols (Neukirchen-Vluyn, 1984).

Chapter 5

On the development of Swiss theology from 1534 to 1564 see Bruce Gordon, 'Calvin and the Swiss Reformed Churches', in A.D.M. Pettegree, A. Duke, and G. Lewis (eds), *Calvinism in Europe 1540–1620* (Cambridge, 1994), pp. 82–111. Also, his 'Wary Allies: Melanchthon and the Swiss Reformers', in Karin Maag (ed.), *Melanchthon in Europe. His Work and Influence beyond Wittenberg* (Grand Rapids, MI, 1999), pp. 45–67. In the same volume edited by Maag, see Amy Nelson Burnett, 'Melanchthon's Reception in Basle', pp. 69–85. On Simon Sulzer, Amy Nelson Burnett, 'Simon Sulzer and the Consequences of the 1563 Strasbourg Consensus in Switzerland', *ARG*, 83 (1992).

On Bullinger there is a growing body of work in English. Bruce Gordon, 'Heinrich Bullinger', in Carter Lindberg (ed.), *Blackwell's Encyclopedia of Reformation Theologians* (Oxford, 2002). Edward A. Dowey, 'Heinrich Bullinger's Theology: Thematic, Comprehensive, Schematic', in John H. Leith (ed.), *Calvin Studies V* (Davidson, NC, 1990), pp. 41–60. The most comprehensive monograph study remains Wayne J. Baker, *Heinrich Bullinger and the Covenant. The Other Reformed Tradition* (Athens, Ohio, 1980). Also, Charles McCoy and J. Wayne Baker, *Fountainhead of Federalism: Heinrich Bullinger and the Covenantal Tradition; With a Translation of De testamento seu foedere Dei unico et aeterno 1534 and a Bibliography on Federal Theology and Political Philosophy* (Louisville, KY, 1991). Joel E. Kok, 'Heinrich Bullinger's Exegetical Method: The Model for Calvin?', in Richard A. Muller and John L. Thompson (eds), *Biblical Interpretation in the Era of the Reformation* (Grand Rapids, MI, 1996). On the eucharistic developments, see Paul Rorem, Calvin and Bullinger on the Lord's Supper (Bramcote, 1989); Timothy George, 'John Calvin and the Agreement of Zurich (1549)', in Timothy George (ed.), *John Calvin and the Church: A Prism of Reform* (Louisville, KY, 1990), pp. 42–58; Mark S. Burrows, '"Christus intra nos Vivens" The Peculiar Genius of Bullinger's Doctrine of Sanctification', *Zeitschrift für Kirchengeschichte*, 98 (1987), pp. 47–69;

Cornelis P. Venema, 'Heinrich Bullinger's Correspondence on Calvin's Doctrine of Predestination, 1551–1553', *SCJ*, 17 (1986); Aurelio A. Garcia Archilla, *The Theology of History and Apologetic Historiography in Heinrich Bullinger. Truth in History* (San Francisco, 1992). On the theological development, Richard Muller, *Christ and the Decree. Christology and Predestination in Reformed Theology from Calvin to Perkins* (Grand Rapids, MI, 1988).

Other useful works on the theological developments are: Mark Edwards, *Luther and the False Brethren* (Stanford, CA, 1975); Craig Farmer, 'Eucharistic Exhibition and Sacramental Presence in the New Testament Commentaries of Wolfgang Musculus', in Rudolf Dellsperger, Rudolf Freudenberger, and Wolfgang Weber (eds), *Wolfgang Musculus (1497–1563) und die oberdeutsche Reformation* (Berlin, 1997), 299–310; Hans Berner, *'Die gute Correspondenz'. Die Politik der Stadt Basel gegenüber dem Fürstbistum Basel in den Jahren 1525–1585* (Basle, 1989); Rudolf Pfister, 'Ambrosius Blarer in der Schweiz 1548–1564', in Bernd Moeller (ed.), *Ambrosius Blarer 1492–1564. Gedenkschrift zu seinem 400. Todestag* (Constance and Stuttgart, 1964), pp. 205–220.

On the Reformation in the Pays de Vaud, the standard work remains Henri Vuilleumier, *Histoire de l'église réformée du Pays de Vaud sous le régime bernois*, 4 vols (Lausanne, 1927–33). On the conquest, Charles Gilliard, *La Conquête du Pays de Vaud par les Bernois* (Lausanne, 1985). On Farel, see Heiko A. Oberman, 'Calvin and Farel: The Dynamics of Legitimation in Early Calvinism', *Journal of Early Modern History*, 2 (1998), pp. 32–60. On the theological disputes in Geneva, Philip C. Holtrop, *The Bolsec Controversy on Predestination from 1551–1555: The Statements of Jerome Bolsec, and the Responses of John Calvin, Theodore Beza, and Other Reformed Theologians* (Lewiston, NY, 1993). On Viret, see Robert D. Linder, *The Political Ideas of Pierre Viret* (Geneva, 1964).

Chapter 6

The literature on Anabaptism is extensive. The following consists only of some relevant suggestions. It is important to consult Hans J. Hillerbrand (ed.), *Anabaptist Bibliography 1520–1630* (St Louis, 1991). A seminal study is James M. Stayer, *Anabaptists and the Sword* (2nd edn (Lawrence, KA, 1976); also, Hans Jürgen Goertz, *The Anabaptists* (London, 1996); C. Arnold Snyder, *Anabaptist History and Theology. An Introduction* (Scottdale, PA, 1995); W. Packull, 'The Origins of Swiss Anabaptism in the Context of the Reformation of the Common Man', *Journal of Mennonite Studies*, 3 (1985), pp. 35–59. Also, James M. Sayer, Werner O. Packull, and Klaus Depperman, 'From Monogenesis to Polygenesis: The Historical Discussion of Anabaptist Origins', *Mennonite Quarterly Review*, 49 (1975), pp. 83–121; James M. Stayer, 'Reublin and Brötli: The Revolutionary Beginnings of Swiss Anabaptism', in Marc Lienhard (ed.), *The Origins and Characteristics of Anabaptism* (The Hague, 1977), pp. 83–102; James M. Stayer, *The German Peasants' War and Anabaptist Community of Goods* (Montreal and Kingston, 1991), pp. 95–96; C. Arnold Snyder, *The Life and Thought of Michael Sattler*

(Scottdale, PA, 1984). On Sattler and the *Schleitheim Articles*, see Sean F. Winter, 'Michael Sattler and the Schleitheim Articles: A Study in the Background of the First Anabaptist Confession of Faith', *Baptist Quarterly*, 34 (1991), pp. 52–66; C. Arnold Snyder, 'Orality, Literacy, and the Study of Anabaptism', *Mennonite Quarterly Review*, 65 (1991), pp. 371–392. On Hubmaier, Eddie Mabry, *Balthasar Hubmaier's Doctrine of the Church* (Lanham, MD, 1994).

On the radical thinkers the best point of departure is George H. Williams, *The Radical Reformation*, 2nd edn (Kirkesvilee, MO, 1992). On Schwenckfeld, R. Emmet McLaughlin, *Caspar Schwenckfeld. Reluctant Radical. His Life to 1540* (New Haven and London, 1986). On Servetus, Marian Hillar, *The Case of Michael Servetus (1511–1553) – The Turning Point in the Struggle for Freedom of Conscience.* Texts and Studies in Religion, 74 (Lewiston, NY, 1997). Also, Jerome Friedman, *Michael Servetus: A Case Study in Total Heresy* (Geneva, 1978). David Joris, particularly his Basle period, is well treated in Gary K. Waite, *David Joris and Dutch Anabaptism 1524–1543* (Waterloo, Ont., 1990). Hans Guggisberg's work on Castellio is his extensive. See biography *Sebastian Castellio Defender of Religious Freedom* (Aldershot, 2002). On Basle and its circle of humanists, see Hans R. Guggisberg, 'Tolerance and Intolerance in Sixteenth-Century Basle', in Ole Peter Grell and Bob Scribner (eds), *Tolerance and Intolerance in the European Reformation* (Cambridge, 1996), pp. 145–163.

Chapter 7

On the development of worship in Zurich, Bruce Gordon, 'Transcendence and Community in Zwinglian Worship: The Liturgy of 1525 in Zurich', in R.N. Swanson (ed.), *Continuity and Change in Christian Worship*, Studies in Church History, 35 (Woodbridge, 1999), pp. 128–150. On the development of education, Karin Maag, *Seminary or University. The Genevan Academy and Reformed Higher Education 1560–1620* (Aldershot, 1995). The best account of Basle printing is Peter Bietenholz 'Printing and the Basle Reformation 1517–1565', in Jean-François Gilmont (ed.), *The Reformation and the Book,* transl. Karin Maag (Aldershot, 1998). On the Zurich Bible the authoritative work is Traudel Himmighöfer, *Die Zürcher Bibel bis zum Tode Zwinglis (1531)* (Mainz, 1995). For Zurich, Iren L. Snavely Jr, 'Zwingli, Froshauer, and the Word of God in Print', *Journal of Religious & Theological Information*, 3 (2000), pp. 65–87. Also very helpful, H.O. Old, *The Patristic Roots of Reformed Worship* (Zurich, 1975), and John Kmetz, *The Sixteenth-Century Basel Songbooks. Origins, Contents, and Contexts* (Berne, 1995).

On the clergy in Zurich, see Bruce Gordon, *Clerical Discipline and the Rural Reformation. The Synod in Zurich 1532–1580* (Berne, 1992). Also essential, Amy Nelson Burnett, 'Controlling the Clergy. The Oversight of Basel's Rural pastors in the Sixteenth Century', *Zwingliana*, 25 (1998), pp. 129–142; Heinrich Richard Schmidt, *Dorf und Religion. Reformierte Sittenzucht in Berner Landgemeinden der Frühen Neuzeit* (Stuttgart, Jena, and New York, 1995); Heinrich Richard Schmidt, 'Morals Courts in Rural Berne during the Early Modern Period', in Karin Maag (ed.), *The Reformation in Eastern and*

Central Europe (Aldershot, 1997), pp. 155–181; and Randolf C. Head, 'Rhaetian Ministers, from Shepherds to Citizens: Calvinism and Democracy in the Republic of the Three Leagues 1550–1620', in Fred Graham (ed.), *Later Calvinism: International Perspectives* (Kirksville, MO, 1994).

Chapter 8

On the reform of marriage laws and courts, see Thomas Max Safley, 'Canon Law and Swiss Reform: Legal Theory and Practice in the Marital Courts of Zurich, Bern, Basel and St Gall', in R.E. Helmholz (ed.), *Canon Law in Protestant Lands* (Berlin, 1992), pp. 187–201, and Thomas Max Safley, *Let No Man Put Asunder. The Control of Marriage in the German Southwest: A Comparative Study, 1550–1600* (Kirksville, MO, 1984). See also his helpful article, 'To Preserve the Marital State: The Basler Ehegericht, 1550–1592', *Journal of Family History*, 7 (1982), pp. 162–179. On women in the Confederation, the literature is thin, but there are some helpful pieces. See Auke Jelsma, '"What Men and Women Are Made For": On Marriage and Family at the Time of the Reformation', in *Frontiers of the Reformation* (Aldershot, 1998), pp. 133–143; Merry E. Wiesner, *Gender, Church and State in Early Modern Germany* (Harlow, 1998), and the classic study of the impact of the Reformation on women, Lyndal Roper, *The Holy Household. Women and Morals in Reformation Augsburg* (Oxford, 1989). On witchcraft, Brian P. Levack, *The Witch-Hunt in Early Modern Europe* (London and New York, 1987), and E. William Monter, 'Patterns of Witchcraft in the Jura', *Journal of Social History*, 5 (1971), pp. 1–25. On Bullinger's attitude towards popular belief, Bruce Gordon, 'Incubus and Succubus in Zurich: Heinrich Bullinger on the Power of the Devil', in Kathryn Edwards (ed.), *Demons, Vampires and Werewolves. The Revenant in European Culture* (Sixteenth Century Essays and Studies, Kirksville, MI, forthcoming).

Chapter 9

On Swiss influence in southern Germany the standard work is Thomas A. Brady, *Turning Swiss. Cities and Empire 1450–1550* (Cambridge, 1985). Also his *Protestant Politics: Jacob Sturm (1489–1553) and the German Reformation* (Atlantic Highlands, NJ, 1995). On Strasbourg, Lorna Jane Abray, *The People's Reformation. Magistrates, Clergy, and Commons in Strasbourg 1500–1598* (Toronto, 1985); Thomas A. Brady Jr, *Ruling Class, Regime and Reformation at Strasbourg, 1520–1555* (Leiden, 1978). For Augsburg, Philip Broadhead, 'Politics and Expediency in the Augsburg Reformation', in Peter Newman Brooks (ed.), *Reformation Principle and Practice. Essays in Honour of Arthur Geoffrey Dickens* (London, 1980), and his 'Guildsmen, Religious Reform and the Search for the Common Good: The Role of the Guilds in the Early Reformation in Augsburg', *Historical Journal*, 39 (1996), pp. 577–597.

The literature on England and the Confederation is now extensive. See epecially Diarmaid MacCulloch, *Thomas Cranmer. A Life* (New Haven, 1996); Andrew Pettegree, *Foreign Protestant Communities in Sixteenth-Century London* (Oxford, 1996); Diarmaid MacCulloch, *Tudor Church*

Militant. Edward VI and the Protestant Reformation (Harmondsworth, 1999); C.M. Dent, *Protestant Reformers in Elizabethan Oxford* (Oxford, 1983); Patrick Collinson, *Archbishop Grindal 1519–1583. The Struggle for a Reformed Church* (London, 1979); and Carl R. Trueman, *Luther's Legacy. Salvation and English Reformers 1525–1556* (Oxford, 1994).

There is virtually no literature in English on the relations between the Swiss and the other parts of Europe. There are, however, some notable exceptions, such as Peter G. Bietenholz, *Basle and France in the Sixteenth Century* (Geneva, 1971).

Chapter 10

The essential work on Swiss history-writing is Richard Feller and Edgar Bonjour, *Geschichtsschreibung der Schweiz*, 2 vols (Basle and Stuttgart, 1962). There is little in English on the subject. On religious drama, see Derek van Abbé, *Drama in Renaissance Germany and Switzerland* (Melbourne, 1961); Glenn Ellis Ehrstine, 'Of Peasants, Women, and Bears: Political Agency and the Demise of Carnival Transgression in Bernese Reformation Drama', *Sixteenth Century Journal*, 16 (2000), pp. 675–697; Eckehard Simon, 'Shrovetide Plays in Late-Medieval Switzerland: An Appraisal', *Modern Language Notes*, 85 (1970), pp. 323–331; Bruce Gordon, 'Toleration in the Early Swiss Reformation: The Art and Politics of Niklaus Manuel of Berne', in Ole Peter Grell and Bob Scribner (eds), *Tolerance and Intolerance in the European Reformation* (Cambridge, 1996), pp. 128–144.

On Vadianus there is little in English. A very useful biography is provided by Gordon Rupp in his *Patterns of Reformation* (London, 1969), pp. 357–379. On Amerbach, Myron P. Gilmore, 'Boniface Amerbach', in his *Humanists and Jurists: Six Studies in the Renaissance* (Cambridge, MA, 1963), pp. 146–177. On Simon Grynaeus and scientific culture, Charlotte Methuen, *Kepler's Tübingen. Stimulus to a Theological Mathematics* (Aldershot, 1998). On Sebastian Münster, see Jerome Friedman, 'Sebastian Münster, The Jewish Mission, and Protestant Antisemitism', *ARG*, 70 (1979), pp. 238–259; and his *Most Ancient Testimony: Sixteenth-Century Christian Hebraica in the Age of Renaissance Nostalgia* (Athens, GA, 1983). On Gesner, Hans Wellisch, 'Conrad Gessner: A Bio-Biography', *Journal of the Society for the Bibliography of Natural History*, 7 (1975), pp. 151–247.

The essential work on Zurich printing is Paul Leemann-van Elck, *Die Offizin Froschauer, Zürichs berühmte Druckerei im 16. Jahrhundert: Ein Beitrag zur Geschichte der Buchdruckerkunst anläßlich der Halbjahrtausendfeier ihrer Erfindung* (Zurich, 1940). Also good is Iren L. Snavely, 'Zwingli, Froschauer, and the Word of God in Print', *Journal of Religious & Theological Information*, 3 (2000), pp. 65–87. On Holbein, the literature is extensive, but useful is Derek Wilson, *Hans Holbein: Portrait of an Unknown Man* (London, 1997). See also Andrew Pettegree, 'Art', in his *The Reformation World* (London, 2000), pp. 461–489. Likewise, the literature on Paracelsus is vast: helpful for our purposes are Mitchell Hammond, 'The Religious Roots of Paracelsus's Medical Theory', *ARG*, 89 (1998), pp. 7–21, and Charles Webster, *From Paracelsus to Newton: Magic and the Making of Modern Science* (Cambridge, 1982).

Index